TECHNOLOGY
AND THE FUTURE

TECHNOLOGY AND THE FUTURE

EIGHTH EDITION

ALBERT H. TEICH

EDITOR

American Association
for the Advancement of Science

BEDFORD/ST. MARTIN'S

Boston • New York

For Bedford/St. Martin's

Political Science Editor: James R. Headley
Senior Editor, Publishing Services: Douglas Bell
Production Supervisor: Cheryl Mamaril
Project Management: Stratford Publishing Services, Inc.
Cover Design: Paul Lacy
Composition: Stratford Publishing Services, Inc.
Printing and Binding: Haddon Craftsmen, an R.R. Donnelley & Sons Company

President: Charles H. Christensen
Editorial Director: Joan E. Feinberg
Director of Editing, Design, and Production: Marcia Cohen
Manager, Publishing Services: Emily Berleth

Library of Congress Catalog Card Number: 99-62369

Manufactured in the United States of America.

5 4 3 2 1 0
f e d c b a

For information, write: Bedford/St. Martin's, 75 Arlington Street, Boston, MA 02116 (617-426-7440)

ISBN: 0-312-20858-8

Acknowledgments

Acknowledgments and copyrights are continued at the back of the book on page 341, which constitutes an extension of the copyright page.

It is a violation of the law to reproduce these selections by any means whatsoever without the written permission of the copyright holder.

Leo Marx. "Does Improved Technology Mean Progress?" From *Technology Review* (January 1987): pp. 33–41, 71. Copyright © 1987. Reprinted with permission from *Technology Review.*
Neil Postman, "Technology: The Broken Defenses." From *Technopoly* by Neil Postman. Copyright © 1992 by Neil Postman. Reprinted by permission of Alfred A. Knopf, Inc.
Thomas P. Hughes. "Technological Momentum," in Smith, Merritt Roe & Leo Marx, eds., *Does Technology Drive History?* (Cambridge, MA: MIT Press, 1994), pp. 101–113. Copyright © 1994 Massachusetts Institute of Technology.
Alvin M. Weinberg, "Can Technology Replace Social Engineering?" From *University of Chicago Magazine,* 59 (October 1966): pp. 6–10. Reprinted by permission of the author.

To Jill, Samantha, Mitch, and Ken

Preface

"We need to remember that the measure of a civilization is not the tools it owns but the use it makes of them." So cautioned an editorial entitled "The Limits of Technology" that appeared in the *New York Times* in early January 1999.[1] A more appropriate note on which to open this book is hard to imagine.

The unpredictable consequences of technological change have long been a source of worry to society. Today, however, new technologies and their antici-pated benefits are increasingly welcomed, while the possible negative impacts of these technologies are often given little more than lip service. For example, Alan Greenspan, chairman of the U.S. Federal Reserve Board and an individual with unique influence in global economic affairs, credits rapid technological change for the "sparkling performance" of the U.S. economy in the late 1990s.[2] The utopian prospects of accelerating technological change — epitomized by the transformation of the Internet from a tool for researchers into an entirely new global medium of communication in the space of less than a decade — are touted by technologists, entrepreneurs, political leaders, and the mass media. Undoubt-edly, we are seeing great technological progress. But is it human progress?

I must confess that I am thoroughly addicted to much of contemporary tech-nology. I drafted this preface on my laptop Pentium while flying back to Washing-ton, D.C., from a meeting in southern California in a new Boeing 777. I am editing the draft at home on my desktop while listening, on the Internet, to music from Joy FM, a radio station in Accra, Ghana. When I am done, I will e-mail the text to my editor. Nevertheless, I am troubled by how little we understand about where the technologies we see arising on all sides are taking us.

My reflections on technology and the future cannot help but be influenced by the fact that the calendar of the Western world is soon to flip over to a new mil-lennium. Round numbers carry a near-mystical significance in our culture, and through the latter part of the twentieth century, the advent of the year 2000 has provoked an accelerating torrent of reflection, speculation, and soul-searching — not to mention religious prophecy, crackpot rantings and supersti-tion. That much of this torrent related to technology is no surprise. We are living in an era characterized in a fundamental way by an explosion of technological innovation. Indeed, in the words of the *Times* editorial, technological change "seems like the most salient feature of human culture during the last 200 years."

Our understanding of technology and its role in society and our attitudes toward technological change have changed substantially over the years. I first

---

[1] "The Limits of Technology," *New York Times*, January 3, 1999, p. 8.

[2] Testimony of Chairman Alan Greenspan, "State of the Economy," Committee on Ways and Means, U.S. House of Representatives, January 20, 1999. Available at <http://www.bog.frb.fed.us/boarddocs/testimony/current/19990120.htm>.

conceived of *Technology and the Future*[3] in an era when many Americans looked upon technology with fear rather than excitement. In the atmosphere of social turmoil that gripped the United States in the late 1960s and early 1970s, a large segment of society (at least in the academic world, of which I was part) saw technology either as a force that was careening out of control or a tool by which those in positions of power maintained their hold over the rest of the populace.

Technologists, who had been lionized for their accomplishments during World War II and the years that followed, were now put on the defensive, and discussions of technology often degenerated into sterile "pro" and "con" debates. I developed this book in the hope that it might contribute to reasoned discussion of the relations between technology and society. I wanted to give students an opportunity to examine the subtleties in these relations and the tools with which to examine the thoughts of some of the most significant writers on the subject and to form their own opinions.

Today, although the problems created by human uses of technology are very much with us, technology itself is no longer demonized as it was in the early 1970s. Indeed, technologies are increasingly woven into the fabric of our everyday lives. Moreover, for large segments of society, concerns about the negative impacts of technology (or technologies), with a few exceptions, are apparently taking a back seat to a broad-based enthusiasm for these technologies and a desire to share in their benefits.

Current predictions of a digital future and a genetic revolution may turn out to be no more realistic than some of the wilder forecasts of forty or fifty years ago — nuclear-powered cars, daily commuting by personal helicopter, lunar colonies, and human control over the weather, for example — which seem hopelessly naïve in retrospect. On the other hand, they may be much too conservative.

The possibilities for technological change are being created by the huge engine of research, development, and innovation that involves governments, universities, and private sector firms and organizations in an increasingly globalized network of knowledge generation. However, whether these possibilities will be exploited and, if so, who will gain and who will lose depends on the structures of human society. Moreover, as the *Times* editorial observes, the sometimes startling rate of technological change may well cause us to overlook the fundamental stability of human nature. There is a tension here that revolves around the need for societies to employ the tools of technology to promote change, not for the sake of change itself, but as a means of advancing civilization according to moral and ethical principles that cannot come from science and technology alone.

This edition of *Technology and the Future* represents the most substantial revision and reorganization of the book since the early 1980s. The literature of technology and society has matured. The concerns of scholars, teachers, and students have changed. While many of the issues that the early editions of this book sought to cover remain important, the context in which they are viewed today is different. I have attempted to preserve the best elements of previous editions

---

[3] Instructors who have used this book over the years may recall that it was originally called *Technology and Man's Future*, a title that was retained through the first three editions but that seems almost impossibly inappropriate today.

while making room for more recent contributions to the literature. To accommo-date this blend of old and new, I have organized the book's twenty-seven chapters into eight sections instead of four, as in the past several editions.

Part I, "Thinking about Technology," is the least changed section of the book. The authors in this part raise the big questions: Is technology good, bad, or neutral? Is it synonymous with progress? How does it influence society? Wendell Berry's essay, "Why I Am Not Going to Buy a Computer," which was dropped from the seventh edition, returns to this edition, and "Technological Momentum," by Thomas Hughes, replaces a different piece by the same author.

The dated, but still very relevant, debate over the role of technology in society between the late Emmanuel Mesthene and John McDermott, a feature of the book since the first edition, has been placed in a separate section, Part II, entitled, "Debating Technology: 1960s Style." Both the substance and the rhetoric of the Mesthene–McDermott debate present a sharp contrast to Part VII, "Debating Technology: Turn-of-the-Millennium Style," in which Nicholas Negroponte and Donald Norman, two of the leading innovators and thinkers of the information age, argue over the human–machine interface in the technology of today (and tomorrow).

Part III brings together six authors who challenge the status quo. Their essays discuss alternatives to contemporary mainstream technology or view mainstream technology from unorthodox perspectives. Langdon Winner's provocative chapter, "Do Artifacts Have Politics?" is new to this edition and replaces a different essay by Winner, while a new piece by Timothy Jenkins adds an up-to-date African American perspective to the mix, complementing a number of articles retained from the seventh edition. In Part IV, "Envisioning the Future through Technology," two excerpts from systematic studies of the future, one from 1967 and the other from 1998, bookend two other articles that suggest some of the reasons why technologically based predictions are so often wrong.

Some of the ethical, social, and human dimensions of two areas of technology that are likely to play a particularly important role in our future — genetics and information technology — are explored in Parts V and VI. Included here are discussions of the exquisitely difficult dilemmas posed by our growing knowledge of molecular genetics and biotechnology — discussion of the prospects for human cloning, the meaning of family in light of new reproductive technologies, and the possibilities for choosing traits in our offspring. Also included are the impact of computers on the organization and character of work, issues of electronic privacy, and a broad-based survey of the ethical issues raised by computers and information technology. Finally, Douglas Coupland's funny, but also serious and thought-provoking, article, "Packing Tips for Your Trip (to the Year 2195)," constitutes Part VIII, the coda to *Technology and the Future*.

As in previous editions, my selections are a mixed bag. Not all students or all instructors will like all twenty-seven readings. Most readers will probably love some and hate others; find some fascinating, others tedious. The individual essays do not represent my own views, and I do not necessarily endorse their perspectives. As a whole, however, the book reflects my sense of the important issues in the field of technology and society, a sense that I hope will be useful to others who are interested in these topics.

Technology and the Future has been a part of my life throughout most of my professional career. It is gratifying to have watched the growing interest in the study of science, technology, and society in American colleges and universities over the past three decades and to feel that the book may have made a modest contribution to this important intellectual development.

Throughout the life of this book, I have benefited from the interest, suggestions, and helpful feedback from the book's users. This feedback increased significantly with the establishment, in 1996, of the *Technology and the Future* Web site, which includes an e-mail link to make it easier to reach me. I am particularly grateful to the many students who provided their perspectives on the book and asked questions about it, and to the following faculty members who responded to an on-line questionnaire about the seventh edition posted on the Web site: Don Beaver, Williams College; David D. Bradney, Wheeling Jesuit University; Stephen H. Cutcliffe, Lehigh University; Ray J. Davis, North Carolina AT&T State University; William H. Dutton, University of Southern California; Thomas A. Easton, Thomas College; Patrick W. Hamlett, North Carolina State University; Florence Mason, University of North Texas; Brian K. McAlister, University of Wisconsin–Stout; Philip M. Ogden, Roberts Wesleyan College; George A. Randall, Gloucester County College; Douglas Taylor, DePaul University; and Anthony Tovar, Murray State University. Many of these individuals will recognize their suggestions incorporated in this edition.

My thanks go also to the staff of the college division of Bedford/St. Martin's, the latest incarnation of the St. Martin's Press College Division, who had the foresight to publish the first edition of this book in 1972 and who, through a generation of staff changes, mergers, acquisitions, and restructurings, have remained helpful, interested, and unfailingly supportive. I have been fortunate in having a series of editors over the years with whom it has always been a pleasure to work. Most recently, my editor has been James R. Headley. I appreciate his feedback and encouragement as well as the assistance of his staff members, Brian Nobile and Scott Hitchcock.

Finally, a very special note of appreciation goes to my family, to whom I have dedicated this edition: my wife, Jill; my daughter, Samantha; and my grown sons, Mitch and Ken; for the meaning they have given to my life and for the strength I draw from our relationships.

In the hope that readers continue to find this book useful and that there will be future editions, I once again invite readers — both faculty and students — to contact me with comments and suggestions. I can be reached most readily by e-mail either directly, at <ateich@aaas.org> or through the links on the new *Technology and the Future* Web site <http://www.ateich.com>. The Web site also contains a variety of supplementary resources related to the book, including links to more information about the authors of the various articles, tables of contents of earlier editions, the full text of several hard-to-find articles from earlier editions, and my personal home page.

Albert H. Teich

Contents

Topical Contents

TECHNOLOGY AND SOCIAL PROBLEMS

About the Editor

Albert H. Teich has served as Director of Science and Policy Programs at the American Association for the Advancement of Science (AAAS), since 1990. In this position, he is responsible for the association's activities in science and technology policy and serves as its chief spokesperson on science policy issues.

AAAS, founded in 1848, is the world's largest federation of scientific and engineering societies as well as a professional organization with over 140,000 members and the publisher of *Science* magazine. The Directorate for Science and Policy Programs, which includes activities in ethics, law, science and religion, human rights, and science policy, has a staff of thirty-five and a yearly budget of over $4 million.

Dr. Teich received a B.S. degree in physics and a Ph.D. in political science, both from the Massachusetts Institute of Technology. Prior to joining the AAAS staff in 1980, he held positions at George Washington University, the State University of New York, and Syracuse University.

Dr. Teich is quoted frequently in the press and has made many appearances on radio and television. He is well known as a speaker on science and technology policy and is the author of numerous articles, reports, and book chapters. Recent books include *The Genetic Frontier: Ethics, Law and Policy* (AAAS, 1994, co-edited with Mark S. Frankel) and *Science Evaluation and Its Management* (IOS Press, 1999, co-edited with Vaclav Pačes and Ladislav Pivec). He is a Fellow of AAAS and a member of the editorial advisory boards to the journals *Science Communication; Science, Technology, and Human Values;* and *Prometheus;* as well as a consultant to government agencies, national laboratories, industrial firms, and international organizations. He chaired the advisory committee to the National Science Foundation's Division of Science Resources Studies from 1987 through 1990 and is currently a member of the advisory boards of the School of Public Policy at Georgia Tech, the School of Management and Technology at the University of Maryland, and the Loka Institute, as well as the Policy Council of the Association of Public Policy Analysis and Management. His home page may be found at <http://www.ateich.com>.

TECHNOLOGY AND THE FUTURE

PART I
THINKING ABOUT TECHNOLOGY

Technology is more than just machines. It is a pervasive, complex system whose cultural, social, political, and intellectual elements are manifest in virtually every aspect of our lives. Small wonder, then, that it has attracted the attention of such a large and diverse group of writers and commentators. A small sampling of the range of writings on the social dimensions of technology is contained in this first section of *Technology and the Future*. All of the writers represented here are attempting to understand — from one perspective or another — these social dimensions of technology. Little else ties them together. Their points of view are vastly different. Their common goal is not so much to prescribe particular courses of action as it is to explore the conceptual, metaphysical issues underlying technology–society interactions.

In the opening selection, historian Leo Marx explores the development of the American notion of progress and looks at its connections with technological advance. Humanist and media critic Neil Postman, following in the tradition of Paul Goodman (see his chapter in Part III) and French scholar Jacques Ellul, sees modern society as a "technopoly" in which technology is the supreme force and supreme authority — a situation he finds extremely troublesome. A very different way of looking at technology's role in society is presented by Thomas Hughes in "Technological Momentum." Drawing on many years of research on the evolution of large technological systems, he rejects both technological determinism (which sees technology as an autonomous force that produces social change) and social constructivism (which views technology as purely a product of social and cultural influences) in favor of a more subtle explanation of the relations between technology and society.

Following Hughes, in a more than thirty-year-old essay that captures some of the heights of post–World War II technological enthusiasm, physicist Alvin Weinberg suggests that we can find shortcuts to the solution of social problems by transforming them into technological ones — since technological problems are much easier to solve. This selection, though dated in many ways, is important for the perspective it represents and for introducing the concept of the "technological fix," which has been widely discussed in subsequent years.

Wendell Berry, meanwhile, rejects not only the technological fix, but even such ubiquitous elements of our technological society as the personal computer, explaining why he does his writing instead by daylight, on a manual typewriter. Finally, Samuel Florman, a practicing engineer as well as a humanist, proposes an alternative approach — a "tragic view" that recognizes the role of technology in human life, including its limits.

The reader looking for unequivocal answers to the problems posed by technology will not find them here. On the whole, the readings in this section, like those in the remainder of the book, raise many more questions than they answer.

1. Does Improved Technology Mean Progress?

LEO MARX

The concepts of technology *and* progress *have been firmly linked in the minds of most Americans for the past 150 years. Only in the past three decades, however, has the question that Leo Marx asks in his essay, "Does Improved Technology Mean Progress?" begun to receive serious attention in our culture. This question is the perfect starting point for* Technology and the Future. *Deceptive in its simplicity, it underlies most of what follows in this book.*

Leo Marx is William R. Kenan Professor of American Cultural History Emeritus at MIT. He is the author of The Machine in the Garden: Technology and the Pastoral Ideal in America *(1964) and is coeditor, with Merritt Roe Smith, of* Does Technology Drive History? *(Cambridge, MA: MIT Press, 1995). He holds a Ph.D. in history of American civilization from Harvard and has taught at that institution and at the University of Minnesota and Amherst College. He has twice been a Guggenheim Fellow and was a Rockefeller Humanities Fellow in 1983–1984. Marx was born in New York City in 1919.*

In this reading (first published in Technology Review *in 1987), he examines how the concept of progress has itself evolved since the early days of the Republic and what that evolution means for understanding the technological choices that confront us today. Improved technology could mean progress, Marx concludes, "But only if we are willing and able to answer the next question: progress toward what?"*

Does improved technology mean progress? If some variant of this question had been addressed to a reliable sample of Americans at any time since the early nineteenth century, the answer of a majority almost certainly would have been an unequivocal "yes." The idea that technological improvements are a primary basis for — and an accurate gauge of — progress has long been a fundamental belief in the United States. In the last half-century, however, that belief has lost some of its credibility. A growing minority of Americans has adopted a skeptical, even negative, view of technological innovation as an index of social progress.

The extent of this change in American attitudes was brought home to me when I spent October 1984 in China. At that time the announced goal of the People's Republic was to carry out (in the popular slogan) "Four Modernizations" — agriculture, science and technology, industry, and the military. What particularly struck our group of Americans was the seemingly unbounded, largely uncritical ardor with which the Chinese were conducting their love affair with

3

Western-style modernization — individualistic, entrepreneurial, or "capitalist," as well as scientific and technological. Like early nineteenth-century visitors to the United States, we were witnessing a society in a veritable transport of improvement: long pent-up, innovative energies were being released, everyone seemed to be in motion, everything was eligible for change. It was assumed that any such change almost certainly would be for the better.

Most of the Chinese we came to know best — teachers and students of American studies — explicitly associated the kind of progress represented by the four modernizations with the United States. This respect for American wealth and power was flattering but disconcerting, for we often found ourselves reminding the Chinese of serious shortcomings, even some terrible dangers, inherent in the Western mode of industrial development. Like the Americans whom European travelers met 150 years ago, many of the Chinese seemed to be extravagantly, almost blindly, credulous and optimistic.

Our reaction revealed, among other things, a change in our own culture and, in some cases, in our own personal attitudes. We came face to face with the gulf that separates the outlook of many contemporary Americans from the old national faith in the advance of technology as the basis of social progress.

The standard explanation for this change includes that familiar litany of death and destruction that distinguishes the recent history of the West: two barbaric world wars, the Nazi holocaust, the Stalinist terror, and the nuclear arms race. It is striking to note how many of the fearful events of our time involve the destructive use or misuse, the unforeseen consequences, or the disastrous malfunction of modern technologies: Hiroshima and the nuclear threat; the damage inflicted upon the environment by advanced industrial societies; and spectacular accidents like Three Mile Island.

Conspicuous disasters have helped to undermine the public's faith in progress, but there also has been a longer-term change in our thinking. It is less obvious, less dramatic and tangible than the record of catastrophe that distinguishes our twentieth-century history, but I believe it is more fundamental. Our very conception — our chief criterion — of progress has undergone a subtle but decisive change since the founding of the Republic, and that change is at once a cause and a reflection of our current disenchantment with technology. To chart this change in attitude, we need to go back at least as far as the first Industrial Revolution.

THE ENLIGHTENMENT BELIEF IN PROGRESS

The development of radically improved machinery (based on mechanized motive power) used in the new factory system of the late eighteenth century coincided with the formulation and diffusion of the modern Enlightenment idea of history as a record of progress. This conception became the fulcrum of the dominant American worldview. It assumes that history, or at least modern history, is driven by the steady, cumulative, and inevitable expansion of human knowledge of and power over nature. The new scientific knowledge and technological power were expected to make possible a comprehensive improvement in all the conditions of life — social, political, moral, and intellectual as well as material.

The modern idea of progress, as developed by its radical French, English, and American adherents, emerged in an era of political revolution. It was a revolutionary doctrine, bonded to the radical struggle for freedom from feudal forms of domination. To ardent republicans like the French philosopher Condorcet, the English chemist Priestley, and Benjamin Franklin, a necessary criterion of progress was the achievement of political and social liberation. They regarded the new sciences and technologies not as ends in themselves, but as instruments for carrying out a comprehensive transformation of society. The new knowledge and power would provide the basis for alternatives to the deeply entrenched authoritarian, hierarchical institutions of *l'ancien régime:* monarchical, aristocratic, and ecclesiastical. Thus in 1813 Thomas Jefferson wrote to John Adams describing the combined effect of the new science and the American Revolution on the minds of Europeans:

> Science had liberated the ideas of those who read and reflect, and the American example had kindled feelings of right in the people. An insurrection has consequently begun, of science, talents, and courage, against rank and birth, which have fallen into contempt. . . . Science is progressive.

Admittedly, the idea of history as endless progress did encourage extravagantly optimistic expectations, and in its most extreme form, it fostered some wildly improbable dreams of the "perfectability of Man" and of humanity's absolute mastery of nature. Yet the political beliefs of the radical republicans of the eighteenth century, such as the principle of making the authority of government dependent upon the consent of the governed, often had the effect of limiting those aspirations to omnipotence.

The constraining effect of such ultimate, long-term political goals makes itself felt, for example, in Jefferson's initial reaction to the prospect of introducing the new manufacturing system to America. "Let our work-shops remain in Europe," he wrote in 1785.

Although a committed believer in the benefits of science and technology, Jefferson rejected the idea of developing an American factory system on the ground that the emergence of an urban proletariat, which he then regarded as an inescapable consequence of the European factory system, would be too high a price to pay for any potential improvement in the American material standard of living. He regarded the existence of manufacturing cities and an industrial working class as incompatible with republican government and the happiness of the people. He argued that it was preferable, even if more costly in strictly economic terms, to ship raw materials to Europe and import manufactured goods. "The loss by the transportation of commodities across the Atlantic will be made up in happiness and permanence of government." In weighing political, moral, and aesthetic costs against economic benefits, he anticipated the viewpoint of the environmentalists and others of our time for whom the test of a technological innovation is its effect on the overall quality of life.

Another instance of the constraining effect of republican political ideals is Benjamin Franklin's refusal to exploit his inventions for private profit. Thus Franklin's reaction when the governor of Pennsylvania urged him to accept a patent for his successful design of the "Franklin stove":

> Governor Thomas was so pleased with the construction of this stove as described in . . . [the pamphlet] that . . . he offered to give me a patent for the sole vending of them for a term of years; but I declined it from a principle which has ever weighed with me on such occasions, namely; viz., *that as we enjoy great advantages from the inventions of others, we should be glad of an opportunity to serve others by any invention of ours, and this we should do freely and generously* [emphasis in original].

What makes the example of Franklin particularly interesting is the fact that he later came to be regarded as the archetypal self-made American and the embodiment of the Protestant work ethic. When Max Weber sought out of all the world *the* exemplar of that mentality for his seminal study, *The Protestant Ethic and the Spirit of Capitalism,* whom did he choose but our own Ben? But Franklin's was a principled and limited self-interest. In his *Autobiography,* he told the story of his rise in the world not to exemplify a merely personal success, but rather to illustrate the achievements of a "rising people." He belonged to that heroic revolutionary phase in the history of the bourgeoisie when that class saw itself as the vanguard of humanity and its principles as universal. He thought of his inventions as designed not for his private benefit but for the benefit of all.

THE TECHNOCRATIC CONCEPT OF PROGRESS

With the further development of industrial capitalism, a quite different conception of technological progress gradually came to the fore in the United States. Americans celebrated the advance of science and technology with increasing fervor, but they began to detach the idea from the goal of social and political liberation. Many regarded the eventual attainment of that goal as having been assured by the victorious American Revolution and the founding of the Republic.

The difference between this later view of progress and that of Jefferson's and Franklin's generation can be heard in the rhetoric of Daniel Webster. He and Edward Everett were perhaps the leading public communicators of this new version of the progressive ideology. When Webster decided to become a senator from Massachusetts instead of New Hampshire, the change was widely interpreted to mean that he had become the quasi-official spokesman for the new industrial manufacturing interests. Thus Webster, who was generally considered the nation's foremost orator, was an obvious choice as the speaker at the dedication of new railroads. Here is a characteristic peroration of one such performance in 1847:

> It is an extraordinary era in which we live. It is altogether new. The world has seen nothing like it before. I will not pretend, no one can pretend, to discern the end; but everybody knows that the age is remarkable for scientific research

into the heavens, the earth, and what is beneath the earth; and perhaps more remarkable still for the application of this scientific research to the pursuits of life. . . . We see the ocean navigated and the solid land traversed by steam power, and intelligence communicated by electricity. Truly this is almost a miraculous era. What is before us no one can say, what is upon us no one can hardly realize. The progress of the age has almost outstripped human belief; the future is known only to Omniscience.

By the 1840s, as Webster's rhetoric suggests, the idea of progress was already being dissociated from the Enlightenment vision of political liberation. He invests the railroad with a quasi-religious inevitability that lends force to the characterization of his language as the rhetoric of the technological sublime. Elsewhere in the speech, to be sure, Webster makes the obligatory bow to the democratic influence of technological change, but it is clear that he is casting the new machine power as the prime exemplar of the overall progress of the age, quite apart from its political significance. Speaking for the business and industrial elite, Webster and Everett thus depict technological innovation as a sufficient cause, *in itself,* for the fact that history assumes the character of continuous, cumulative progress.

At the same time, discarding the radical political ideals of the Enlightenment allowed the idea of technological progress to blend with other grandiose national aspirations. Webster's version of the "rhetoric of the technological sublime" is of a piece with the soaring imperial ambitions embodied in the slogan "Manifest Destiny," and by such tacit military figurations of American development as the popular notion of the "conquest of nature" (including Native Americans) by the increasingly technologized forces of advancing European-American "civilization." These future-oriented themes easily harmonized with the belief in the coming of the millennium that characterized evangelical Protestantism, the most popular American religion at the time. Webster indicates as much when, at the end of his tribute to the new railroad, he glibly brings in "Omniscience" as the ultimate locus of the meaning of progress.

The difference between the earlier Enlightenment conception of progress and that exemplified by Webster is largely attributable to the difference between the groups they represented. Franklin, Jefferson, and the heroic generation of founding revolutionists constituted a distinct, rather unusual social class in that for a short time the same men possessed authority and power in most of its important forms: economic, social, political, and intellectual. The industrial capitalists for whom Daniel Webster spoke were men of a very different stripe. They derived their status from a different kind of wealth and power, and their conception of progress, like their economic and social aspirations, was correspondingly different. The new technology and the immense profits it generated belonged to them, and since they had every reason to assume that they would retain their property and power, they had a vested interest in technological innovation. It is not surprising, under the circumstances, that as industrialization proceeded these men became true believers in technological improvement as the primary basis for — as virtually tantamount to — universal progress.

This dissociation of technological and material advancement from the larger political vision of progress was an intermediate stage in the eventual impoverishment of that radical eighteenth-century worldview. This subtle change prepared the way for the emergence, later in the century, of a thoroughly technocratic idea of progress. It was "technocratic" in that it valued improvements in power, efficiency, rationality as ends in themselves. Among those who bore witness to the widespread diffusion of this concept at the turn of the century were Henry Adams and Thorstein Veblen, who were critical of it, and Andrew Carnegie, Thomas Edison, and Frederick Winslow Taylor and his followers, who lent expression to it. Taylor's theory of scientific management embodies the quintessence of the technocratic mentality, "the idea," as historian Hugh Aitken describes it, "that human activity could be measured, analyzed, and controlled by techniques analogous to those that had proved so successful when applied to physical objects."

The technocratic idea of progress is a belief in the sufficiency of scientific and technological innovation as the basis for general progress. It says that if we can ensure the advance of science-based technologies, the rest will take care of itself. (The "rest" refers to nothing less than a corresponding degree of improvement in the social, political, and cultural conditions of life.) Turning the Jeffersonian ideal on its head, this view makes instrumental values fundamental to social progress, and relegates what formerly were considered primary, goal-setting values (justice, freedom, harmony, beauty, or self-fulfillment) to a secondary status.

In this century, the technocratic view of progress was enshrined in Fordism and an obsessive interest in economies of scale, standardization of process and product, and control of the workplace. This shift to mass production was accompanied by the more or less official commitment of the U.S. government to the growth of the nation's wealth, productivity, and global power, and to the most rapid possible rate of technological innovation as the essential criterion of social progress.

But the old republican vision of progress — the vision of advancing knowledge empowering humankind to establish a less hierarchical, more just and peaceful society — did not disappear. If it no longer inspired Webster and his associates, it lived on in the minds of many farmers, artisans, factory workers, shopkeepers, and small-business owners, as well as in the beliefs of the professionals, artists, intellectuals, and other members of the lower middle and middle classes. During the late nineteenth century, a number of disaffected intellectuals sought new forms for the old progressive faith. They translated it into such political idioms as utopian socialism, the single-tax movement, the populist revolt, Progressivism in cities, and Marxism and its native variants.

THE ROOTS OF OUR ADVERSARY CULTURE

Let me turn to a set of these late-eighteenth-century ideas that was to become the basis for a powerful critique of the culture of advanced industrial society. Usually described as the viewpoint of the "counter-Enlightenment" or the "romantic reaction," these ideas have formed the basis for a surprisingly long-lived adversarial culture.

According to conventional wisdom, this critical view originated in the intellectual backlash from the triumph of the natural sciences we associate with the great discoveries of Galileo, Kepler, Harvey, and Newton. Put differently, this tendency was a reaction against the extravagant claims of the universal, not to say exclusive, truth of "the Mechanical Philosophy." That term derived from the ubiquity of the machine metaphor in the work of Newton and other natural scientists ("celestial mechanics") and many of their philosophic allies, notably Descartes, all of whom tended to conceive of nature itself as a "great engine" and its subordinate parts (including the human body) as lesser machines.

By the late eighteenth century, a powerful set of critical, antimechanistic ideas was being developed by Kant, Fichte, and other German idealists, and by great English poets like Coleridge and Wordsworth. But in their time the image of the machine also was being invested with greater tangibility and social import. The Industrial Revolution was gaining momentum, and as power machinery was more widely diffused in Great Britain, Western Europe, and North America, the machine acquired much greater resonance: it came to represent both the new technologies based on mechanized motive power and the mechanistic mindset of scientific rationalism. Thus the Scottish philosopher and historian Thomas Carlyle, who had been deeply influenced by the new German philosophy, announced in his seminal 1829 essay, "Signs of the Times," that the right name for the dawning era was the "Age of Machinery." It was to be the Age of Machinery, he warned, in every "inward" and "outward" sense of the word, meaning that it would be dominated by mechanical (utilitarian) thinking as well as by actual machines.

In his criticism of this new era, Carlyle took the view that neither kind of "machinery" was inherently dangerous. In his opinion, indeed, they represented *potential* progress as long as neither was allowed to become the exclusive or predominant mode in its respective realm.

In the United States a small, gifted, if disaffected minority of writers, artists, and intellectuals adopted this ideology. Their version of Carlyle's critical viewpoint was labeled "romantic" in reference to its European strains, or "transcendentalist" in its native use. In the work of writers like Emerson and Thoreau, Hawthorne and Melville, we encounter critical responses to the onset of industrialism that cannot be written off as mere nostalgia or primitivism. These writers did not hold up an idealized wilderness, a pre-industrial Eden, as preferable to the world they saw in the making. Nor did they dismiss the worth of material improvement as such. But they did regard the dominant view, often represented (as in Webster's speech) by the appearance of the new machine power in the American landscape, as dangerously shallow, materialistic, and one-sided. Fear of "mechanism," in the several senses of that word — especially the domination of the individual by impersonal systems — colored all of their thought. In their work, the image of the machine-in-the-landscape, far from being an occasion for exultation, often seems to arouse anxiety, dislocation, and foreboding. Henry Thoreau's detailed, carefully composed account of the intrusion of the railroad into the Concord woods is a good example; it bears out his delineation of the new inventions as "improved means to unimproved ends."

This critical view of the relationship between technological means and social ends did not merely appear in random images, phrases, and narrative episodes. Indeed, the whole of *Walden* may be read as a sustained attack on a culture that had allowed itself to become confused about the relationship of ends and means. Thoreau's countrymen are depicted as becoming "the tools of their tools." Much the same argument underlies Hawthorne's satire, "The Celestial Railroad," a modern replay of *Pilgrim's Progress* in which the hero, Christian, realizes too late that his comfortable railroad journey to salvation is taking him to hell, not heaven. Melville incorporates a similar insight into his characterization of Captain Ahab, who is the embodiment of the Faustian aspiration toward domination and total control given credence by the sudden emergence of exciting new technological capacities. Ahab exults in his power over the crew, and he explicitly identifies it with the power exhibited by the new railroad spanning the North American continent. In reflective moments, however, he also acknowledges the self-destructive nature of his own behavior: "Now in his heart, Ahab had some glimpse of this, namely, all my means are sane, my motive and my object mad."

Of course there was nothing new about the moral posture adopted by these American writers. Indeed, their attitude toward the exuberant national celebration of the railroad and other inventions is no doubt traceable to traditional moral and religious objections to such an exaggeration of human powers. In this view, the worshipful attitude of Americans toward these new instruments of power had to be recognized for what it was: idolatry like that attacked by Old Testament prophets in a disguised, new-fashioned form. This moral critique of the debased, technocratic version of the progressive worldview has slowly gained adherents since the mid-nineteenth century, and by now it is one of the chief ideological supports of an adversary culture in the United States.

The ideas of writers like Hawthorne, Melville, and Thoreau were usually dismissed as excessively idealistic, nostalgic, or sentimental, hence impractical and unreliable. They were particularly vulnerable to that charge at a time when the rapid improvement in the material conditions of American life lent a compelling power to the idea that the meaning of history is universal progress. Only in the late twentieth century, with the growth of skepticism about scientific and technological progress, and with the emergence of a vigorous adversary culture in the 1960s, has the standpoint of that earlier eccentric minority been accorded a certain intellectual respect. To be sure, it is still chiefly the viewpoint of a relatively small minority, but there have been times, like the Vietnam upheaval of the 1960s, when that minority has won the temporary support of, or formed a tacit coalition with, a remarkably large number of other disaffected Americans. Much the same antitechnocratic viewpoint has made itself felt in various dissident movements and intellectual tendencies since the 1960s: the antinuclear movements (against both nuclear power and nuclear weaponry); some branches of the environmental and feminist movements; the "small is beautiful" and "stable-state" economic theories, as well as the quest for "soft energy paths" and "alternative (or appropriate) technologies."

TECHNOCRATIC VERSUS SOCIAL PROGRESS

Perhaps this historical summary will help explain the ambivalence toward the ideal of progress expressed by many Americans nowadays. Compared with prevailing attitudes in the United States in the 1840s, when the American situation was more like that of China today, the current mood in this country would have to be described as mildly disillusioned.

To appreciate the reasons for that disillusionment, let me repeat the distinction between the two views of progress on which this analysis rests. The initial Enlightenment belief in progress perceived science and technology to be in the service of liberation from political oppression. Over time that conception was transformed, or partly supplanted, by the now familiar view that innovations in science-based technologies are in themselves a sufficient and reliable basis for progress. The distinction, then, turns on the apparent loss of interest in, or unwillingness to name, the social ends for which the scientific and technological instruments of power are to be used. What we seem to have instead of a guiding political goal is a minimalist definition of civic obligation.

The distinction between two versions of the belief in progress helps sort out reactions to the many troubling issues raised by the diffusion of high technology. When, for example, the introduction of some new labor-saving technology is proposed, it is useful to ask what the purpose of this new technology is. Only by questioning the assumption that innovation represents progress can we begin to judge its worth. The aim may well be to reduce labor costs, yet in our society the personal costs to the displaced workers are likely to be ignored.

The same essential defect of the technocratic mindset also becomes evident when the president of the United States calls upon those who devise nuclear weapons to provide an elaborate new system of weaponry, the Strategic Defense Initiative, as the only reliable means of avoiding nuclear war. Not only does he invite us to put all our hope in a "technological fix," but he rejects the ordinary but indispensable method of international negotiation and compromise.[1] Here again, technology is thought to obviate the need for political ideas and practices.

One final word. I perhaps need to clarify the claim that it is the modern, technocratic worldview of Webster's intellectual heirs, not the Enlightenment view descended from the Jeffersonians, that encourages the more dangerous contemporary fantasies of domination and total control. The political and social aspirations of the generation of Benjamin Franklin and Thomas Jefferson *provided tacit limits to, as well as ends for, the progressive vision of the future.* But the technocratic version so popular today entails a belief in the worth of scientific and technological innovations as ends in themselves.

All of which is to say that we urgently need a set of political, social, and cultural goals comparable to those formulated at the beginning of the industrial era if we are to accurately assess the worth of new technologies. Only such goals can provide the criteria required to make rational and humane choices among alternative technologies and, more important, among alternative long-term policies.

Does improved technology mean progress? Yes, it certainly *could* mean just that. But only if we are willing and able to answer the next question: progress toward what? What is it that we want our new technologies to accomplish? What do we want beyond such immediate, limited goals as achieving efficiencies, decreasing financial costs, and eliminating the troubling human element from our workplaces? In the absence of answers to these questions, technological improvements may very well turn out to be incompatible with genuine, that is to say *social*, progress.

NOTE

1. See Alvin M. Weinberg, "Can Technology Replace Social Engineering?" (Chapter 4), for a discussion of the concept of the "technological fix" — Ed.

2. Technopoly: The Broken Defenses

NEIL POSTMAN

Neil Postman is a technological critic in the tradition of Jacques Ellul, Lewis Mumford, and Paul Goodman. His concern, like those of his predecessors, is with the destructive moral and cultural consequences of technology in modern society. His book Technopoly, *subtitled* The Surrender of Culture to Technology, *is an attempt (in his own words) "to describe when, how, and why technology became a particularly dangerous enemy." Postman recognizes the benefits of technology, acknowledging that "it makes life easier, cleaner, and longer." But he suggests that these benefits are seductive, because they lead us to overlook the negative side of technology — the fact that it "creates a culture without a moral foundation" and undermines the very things that make life worth living. The chapter included here describes how, in Postman's view, bureaucracies have emerged to deal with the information glut in society and how they undermine traditional social institutions.*

Postman is chair of the Department of Culture and Communication at New York University, where he received the Distinguished Professor Award in 1989. He has published numerous books, among the best known of which are Teaching as a Subversive Activity, The Disappearance of Childhood, *and* Amusing Ourselves to Death.

Technopoly is a state of culture. It is also a state of mind. It consists in the deification of technology, which means that the culture seeks its authorization in technology, finds its satisfactions in technology, and takes its orders from technology. This requires the development of a new kind of social order, and of necessity leads to the rapid dissolution of much that is associated with traditional beliefs. Those who feel most comfortable in Technopoly are those who are convinced that technical progress is humanity's supreme achievement and the instrument by which our most profound dilemmas may be solved. They also believe that information is an unmixed blessing, which through its continued and uncontrolled production and dissemination offers increased freedom, creativity, and peace of mind. The fact that information does none of these things — but quite the opposite — seems to change few opinions, for such unwavering beliefs are an inevitable product of the structure of Technopoly. In particular, Technopoly flourishes when the defenses against information break down.

The relationship between information and the mechanisms for its control is fairly simple to describe: Technology increases the available supply of information. As the supply is increased, control mechanisms are strained. Additional control mechanisms are needed to cope with new information. When additional control mechanisms are themselves technical, they in turn further increase the supply of information. When the supply of information is no longer controllable, a general breakdown in psychic tranquillity and social purpose occurs. Without defenses, people have no way of finding meaning in their experiences, lose their capacity to remember, and have difficulty imagining reasonable futures.

One way of defining Technopoly, then, is to say it is what happens to society when the defenses against information glut have broken down. It is what happens when institutional life becomes inadequate to cope with too much information. It is what happens when a culture, overcome by information generated by technology, tries to employ technology itself as a means of providing clear direction and humane purpose. The effort is mostly doomed to failure. Though it is sometimes possible to use a disease as a cure for itself, this occurs only when we are fully aware of the processes by which disease is normally held in check. My purpose here is to describe the defenses that in principle are available and to suggest how they have become dysfunctional.

The dangers of information on the loose may be understood by the analogy I suggested [elsewhere] with an individual's biological immune system, which serves as a defense against the uncontrolled growth of cells. Cellular growth is, of course, a normal process without which organic life cannot survive. But without a well-functioning immune system, an organism cannot manage cellular growth. It becomes disordered and destroys the delicate interconnectedness of essential organs. An immune system, in short, destroys unwanted cells. All societies have institutions and techniques that function as does a biological immune system. Their purpose is to maintain a balance between the old and the new, between novelty and tradition, between meaning and conceptual disorder, and they do so by "destroying" unwanted information.

I must emphasize that social institutions of all kinds function as control mechanisms. This is important to say, because most writers on the subject of social institutions (especially sociologists) do not grasp the idea that any decline in the force of institutions makes people vulnerable to information chaos.[1] To say that life is destabilized by weakened institutions is merely to say that information loses its use and therefore becomes a source of confusion rather than coherence.

Social institutions sometimes do their work simply by denying people access to information, but principally by directing how much weight and, therefore, value one must give to information. Social institutions are concerned with the *meaning* of information and can be quite rigorous in enforcing standards of admission. Take as a simple example a court of law. Almost all rules for the presentation of evidence and for the conduct of those who participate in a trial are designed to limit the amount of information that is allowed entry into the system. In our system, a judge disallows "hearsay" or personal opinion as evidence except under strictly controlled circumstances, spectators are forbidden to express their feelings, a defendant's previous convictions may not be mentioned, juries are not allowed to hear arguments over the admissibility of evidence — these are instances of information control. The rules on which such control is based derive from a theory of justice that defines what information may be considered relevant and, especially, what information must be considered irrelevant. The theory may be deemed flawed in some respects — lawyers, for example, may disagree over the rules governing the flow of information — but no one disputes that information must be regulated in some manner. In even the simplest law case, thousands of events may have had a bearing on the dispute, and it is well understood that, if they were all permitted entry, there could be no theory of due process, trials would have no end, law itself would be reduced to meaninglessness. In short, the rule of law is concerned with the "destruction" of information.

It is worth mentioning here that, although legal theory has been taxed to the limit by new information from diverse sources — biology, psychology, and sociology among them — the rules governing relevance have remained fairly stable. This may account for Americans' overuse of the courts as a means of finding coherence and stability. As other institutions become unusable as mechanisms for the control of wanton information, the courts stand as a final arbiter of truth. For how long, no one knows.

I have referred [elsewhere] to the school as a mechanism for information control. What its standards are can usually be found in a curriculum or, with even more clarity, in a course catalogue. A college catalogue lists courses, subjects, and fields of study that, taken together, amount to a certified statement of what a serious student ought to think about. More to the point, in what is omitted from a catalogue, we may learn what a serious student ought *not* to think about. A college catalogue, in other words, is a formal description of an information management program; it defines and categorizes knowledge, and in so doing systematically excludes, demeans, labels as trivial — in a word, disregards certain kinds of information. That is why it "makes sense" (or, more accurately, used to make sense). By what it includes/excludes it reflects a theory of the purpose and meaning of education. In the university where I teach, you will not find courses in astrology or dianetics or creationism. There is, of course, much available information about these subjects, but the theory of education that sustains the university does not allow such information entry into the formal structure of its courses. Professors and students are denied the opportunity to focus their attention on it, and are encouraged to proceed as if it did not exist. In this way, the university gives expression to its idea of what constitutes legitimate knowledge. At the present time, some accept this idea and some do not, and the resulting controversy weakens the university's function as an information control center.

The clearest symptom of the breakdown of the curriculum is found in the concept of "cultural literacy," which has been put forward as an organizing principle and has attracted the serious attention of many educators.[2] If one is culturally literate, the idea goes, one should master a certain list of thousands of names, places, dates, and aphorisms; these are supposed to make up the content of the literate American's mind. But . . . cultural literacy is not an organizing principle at all; it represents, in fact, a case of calling the disease the cure. The point to be stressed here is that any educational institution, if it is to function well in the management of information, must have a theory about its purpose and meaning, must have the means to give clear expression to its theory, and must do so, to a large extent, by excluding information.

As another example, consider the family. As it developed in Europe in the late eighteenth century, its theory included the premise that individuals need emotional protection from a cold and competitive society. The family became, as Christopher Lasch calls it, a haven in a heartless world.[3] Its program included (I quote Lasch here) preserving "separatist religious traditions, alien languages and dialects, local lore and other traditions." To do this, the family was required to take charge of the socialization of children, the family became a structure, albeit an informal one, for the management of information. It controlled what "secrets" of adult life would be allowed entry and what "secrets" would not. There may be readers who can remember when in the presence of children adults avoided using certain words and did not discuss certain topics whose details and ramifications were considered unsuitable for children to know. A family that does not or cannot control the information environment of its children is barely a family at all, and may lay claim to the name only by virtue of the fact that its members share biological information through DNA. In fact, in many societies a family was just that — a group connected by genetic information, itself controlled through the careful planning of marriages. In the West, the family as an institution for the management of nonbiological information began with the ascendance of print. As books on every conceivable subject became available, parents were forced into the roles of guardians, protectors, nurturers, and arbiters of taste and rectitude. Their function was to define what it means to be a child by excluding from the family's domain information that would undermine its purpose. That the family can no longer do this is, I believe, obvious to everyone.

Courts of law, the school, and the family are only three of several control institutions that serve as part of a culture's information immune system. The political party is another. As a young man growing up in a Democratic household, I was provided with clear instructions on what value to assign to political events and commentary. The instructions did not require explicit statement. They followed logically from theory, which was, as I remember it, as follows: Because people need protection, they must align themselves with a political organization. The Democratic Party was entitled to our loyalty because it represented the social and economic interests of the working class, of which our family, relatives, and neighbors were members (except for one uncle who, though a truck driver, consistently voted Republican and was therefore thought to be either stupid or crazy). The Republican Party represented the interests of the rich, who, by definition, had no concern for us.

The theory gave clarity to our perceptions and a standard by which to judge the significance of information. The general principle was that information provided by Democrats was always to be taken seriously and, in all probability, was both true and useful (except if it came from Southern Democrats, who were helpful in electing presidents but were otherwise never to be taken seriously because of their special theory of race). Information provided by Republicans was rubbish and was useful only to the extent that it confirmed how self-serving Republicans were.

I am not prepared to argue here that the theory was correct, but to the accusation that it was an oversimplification I would reply that all theories are oversimplifications, or at least lead to oversimplification. The rule of law is an oversimplification. A curriculum is an oversimplification. So is a family's conception of a child. That is the function of theories — to oversimplify, and thus to assist believers in organizing, weighting, and excluding information. Therein lies the power of theories. Their weakness is that precisely because they oversimplify, they are vulnerable to attack by new information. When there is too much information to sustain *any* theory, information becomes essentially meaningless.

The most imposing institutions for the control of information are religion and the state. They do their work in a somewhat more abstract way than do courts, schools, families, or political parties. They manage information through the creation of myths and stories that express theories about fundamental questions: why are we here, where have we come from, and where are we headed? I have [elsewhere] alluded to the comprehensive theological narrative of the medieval European world and how its great explanatory power contributed to a sense of well-being and coherence. Perhaps I have not stressed enough the extent to which the Bible also served as an information control mechanism, especially in the moral domain. The Bible gives manifold instructions on what one must do and must not do, as well as guidance on what language to avoid (on pain of committing blasphemy), what ideas to avoid (on pain of committing heresy), what symbols to avoid (on pain of committing idolatry). Necessarily but perhaps unfortunately, the Bible also explained how the world came into being in such literal detail that it could not accommodate new information produced by the telescope and subsequent technologies. The trials of Galileo and, three hundred years later, of Scopes were therefore about the admissibility of certain kinds of information. Both Cardinal Bellarmine and William Jennings Bryan were fighting to maintain the authority of the Bible to control information about the profane world as well as the sacred. In their defeat, more was lost than the Bible's claim to explain the origins and structure of nature. The Bible's authority in defining and categorizing moral behavior was also weakened.

Nonetheless, Scripture has at its core such a powerful mythology that even the residue of that mythology is still sufficient to serve as an exacting control mechanism for some people. It provides, first of all, a theory about the meaning of life and therefore rules on how one is to conduct oneself. With apologies to Rabbi Hillel, who expressed it more profoundly and in the time it takes to stand on one leg, the theory is as follows: There is one God, who created the universe and all that is in it. Although humans can never fully understand God, He has revealed Himself and His will to us throughout history, particularly through His commandments and the testament of the prophets as recorded in the Bible. The greatest of these commandments tells us that humans are to love God and express their love for Him through love, mercy, and justice to our fellow humans. At the end of time, all nations and humans will appear before God to be judged, and those who have followed His commandments will find favor in His sight. Those who have denied God and the commandments will perish utterly in the darkness that lies outside the presence of God's light.

To borrow from Hillel: That is the theory. All the rest is commentary. Those who believe in this theory — particularly those who accept the Bible as the literal word of God — are free to dismiss other theories about the origin and meaning of life and to give minimal weight to the facts on which other theories are based. Moreover, in observing God's laws, and the detailed requirements of their enactment, believers receive guidance about what books they should not read, about what plays and films they should not see, about what music they should not hear, about what subjects their children should not study, and so on. For strict fundamentalists of the Bible, the theory and what follows from it seal them off from unwanted information, and in that way their actions are invested with meaning, clarity, and, they believe, moral authority.

Those who reject the Bible's theory and who believe, let us say, in the theory of Science are also protected from unwanted information. Their theory, for example, instructs them to disregard information about astrology, dianetics, and creationism, which they usually label as medieval superstition or subjective opinion. Their theory fails to give any guidance about moral information and, by definition, gives little weight to information that falls outside the constraints of science. Undeniably, fewer and fewer people are bound in any serious way to Biblical or other religious traditions as a source of compelling attention and authority, the result of which is that they make no moral decisions, only practical ones. This is still another way of defining Technopoly. The term is aptly used for a culture whose available theories do not offer guidance about what is acceptable information in the moral domain.

I trust the reader does not conclude that I am making an argument for fundamentalism of any kind. One can hardly approve, for example, of a Muslim fundamentalism that decrees a death sentence to someone who writes what are construed as blasphemous words, or a Christian fundamentalism that once did the same or could lead to the same. I must hasten to acknowledge, in this context, that it is entirely possible to live as a Muslim, a Christian, or a Jew with a modified and temperate view of religious theory. Here, I am merely making the point that religious tradition serves as a mechanism for the regulation and valuation of information. When religion loses much or all of its binding power — if it is reduced to mere rhetorical ash — then confusion inevitably follows about what to attend to and how to assign it significance.

Indeed, as I write, another great world narrative, Marxism, is in the process of decomposing. No doubt there are fundamentalist Marxists who will not let go of Marx's theory, and will continue to be guided by its prescriptions and constraints. The theory, after all, is sufficiently powerful to have engaged the imagination and devotion of more than a billion people. Like the Bible, the theory includes a transcendent idea, as do all great world narratives. With apologies to a century and a half of philosophical and sociological disputation, the idea is as follows: All forms of institutional misery and oppression are a result of class conflict, since the consciousness of all people is formed by their material situation. God has no interest in this, because there is no God. But there *is* a plan, which is both knowable and beneficent. The plan unfolds in the movement of history itself, which shows unmistakably that the working class, in the end, must triumph. When it does, with or without the help of revolutionary movements, class itself will have disappeared. All will share equally in the bounties of nature and creative production, and no one will exploit the labors of another.

It is generally believed that this theory has fallen into disrepute among believers because information made available by television, films, telephone, fax machines, and other technologies has revealed that the working classes of capitalist nations are sharing quite nicely in the bounties of nature while at the same time enjoying a considerable measure of personal freedom. Their situation is so vastly superior to those of nations enacting Marxist theory that millions of people have concluded, seemingly all at once, that history may have no opinion whatever on the fate of the working class or, if it has, that it is moving toward a final chapter quite different in its point from what Marx prophesied.

All of this is said provisionally. History takes a long time, and there may yet be developments that will provide Marx's vision with fresh sources of verisimilitude. Meanwhile, the following points need to be made: Believers in the Marxist story were given quite clear guidelines on how they were to weight information and therefore to understand events. To the extent that they now reject the theory, they are threatened with conceptual confusion, which means they no longer know who to believe or what to believe. In the West, and especially in the United States, there is much rejoicing over this situation, and assurances are given that Marxism can be replaced by what is called "liberal democracy." But this must be stated more as a question than an answer, for it is no longer entirely clear what sort of story liberal democracy tells.

A clear and scholarly celebration of liberal democracy's triumph is found in Francis Fukuyama's essay "The End of History?" Using a somewhat peculiar definition of history, Fukuyama concludes that there will be no more ideological conflicts, all the competitors to modern liberalism having been defeated. In support of his conclusion, Fukuyama cites Hegel as having come to a similar position in the early nineteenth century, when the principles of liberty and equality, as expressed in the American and French revolutions, emerged triumphant. With the contemporary decline of fascism and communism, no threat now remains. But Fukuyama pays insufficient attention to the changes in meaning of liberal democracy over two centuries. Its meaning in a technocracy is quite different from its meaning in Technopoly; indeed, in Technopoly it comes much closer to what Walter Benjamin called "commodity capitalism." In the case of the United States, the great eighteenth-century revolution was not indifferent to commodity capitalism but was nonetheless infused with profound moral content. The United States was not merely an experiment in a new form of governance; it was the fulfillment of God's plan. True, Adams, Jefferson, and Paine rejected the supernatural elements in the Bible, but they never doubted that their experiment had the imprimatur of Providence. People were to be free but for a purpose. Their God-given rights implied obligations and responsibilities, not only to God but to other nations, to which the new republic would be a guide and a showcase of what is possible when reason and spirituality commingle.

It is an open question whether or not "liberal democracy" in its present form can provide a thought-world of sufficient moral substance to sustain meaningful lives. This is precisely the question that Václav Havel, then newly elected as president of Czechoslovakia, posed in an address to the U.S. Congress. "We still don't know how to put morality ahead of politics, science, and economics," he said. "We are still incapable of understanding that the only genuine backbone of our actions — if they are to be moral — is responsibility. Responsibility to something higher than my family, my country, my firm, my success." What Havel is saying is that it is not enough for his nation to liberate itself from one flawed theory; it is necessary to find another, and he worries that Technopoly provides no answer. To say it in still another way: Francis Fukuyama is wrong. There is another ideological conflict to be fought — between "liberal democracy" as conceived in the eighteenth century, with all its transcendent moral underpinnings, and Technopoly, a twentieth-century thought-world that functions not only without a transcendent narrative to provide moral underpinnings but also without strong social institutions to control the flood of information produced by technology.

Because that flood has laid waste the theories on which schools, families, political parties, religion, nationhood itself are based, American Technopoly must rely, to an obsessive extent, on technical methods to control the flow of information. Three such means merit special attention. They are interrelated but for purposes of clarity may be described separately.

The first is bureaucracy, which James Beniger in *The Control Revolution* ranks as "foremost among all technological solutions to the crisis of control."[4] Bureaucracy is not, of course, a creation of Technopoly. Its history goes back five thousand years, although the word itself did not appear in English until the nineteenth century. It is not unlikely that the ancient Egyptians found bureaucracy an irritation, but it is certain that, beginning in the nineteenth century, as bureaucracies became more important, the complaints against them became more insistent. John Stuart Mill referred to them as "administrative tyranny." Carlyle called them "the Continental nuisance." In a chilling paragraph, Tocqueville warned about them taking hold in the United States:

> I have previously made the distinction between two types of centralization, calling one governmental and the other administrative. Only the first exists in America, the second being almost unknown. If the directing power in American society had both these means of government at its disposal and combined the right to command with the faculty and habit to perform everything itself, if having established the general principles of the government, it entered into the details of their application, and having regulated the great interests of the country, it came down to consider even individual interest, then freedom would soon be banished from the New World.[5]

Writing in our own time, C. S. Lewis believed bureaucracy to be the technical embodiment of the Devil himself:

> I live in the Managerial Age, in a world of "Admin." The greatest evil is not now done in those sordid "dens of crime" that Dickens loved to paint. It is not done even in concentration camps and labour camps. In those we see its final

result. But it is conceived and ordered (moved, seconded, carried, and minuted) in clean, carpeted, warmed, and well-lighted offices, by quiet men with white collars and cut fingernails and smooth-shaven cheeks who do not need to raise their voices. Hence, naturally enough, my symbol for Hell is something like the bureaucracy of a police state or the office of a thoroughly nasty business concern.[6]

Putting these attacks aside for the moment, we may say that in principle a bureaucracy is simply a coordinated series of techniques for reducing the amount of information that requires processing. Beniger notes, for example, that the invention of the standardized form — a staple of bureaucracy — allows for the "destruction" of every nuance and detail of a situation. By requiring us to check boxes and fill in blanks, the standardized form admits only a limited range of formal, objective, and impersonal information, which in some cases is precisely what is needed to solve a particular problem. Bureaucracy is, as Max Weber described it, an attempt to rationalize the flow of information, to make its use efficient to the highest degree by eliminating information that diverts attention from the problem at hand. Beniger offers as a prime example of such bureaucratic rationalization the decision in 1884 to organize time, on a worldwide basis, into twenty-four time zones. Prior to this decision, towns only a mile or two apart could and did differ on what time of day it was, which made the operation of railroads and other businesses unnecessarily complex. By simply ignoring the fact that solar time differs at each mode of a transportation system, bureaucracy eliminated a problem of information chaos, much to the satisfaction of most people. But not of everyone. It must be noted that the idea of "God's own time" (a phrase used by the novelist Marie Corelli in the early twentieth century to oppose the introduction of Summer Time) had to be considered irrelevant. This is important to say, because, in attempting to make the most rational use of information, bureaucracy ignores all information and ideas that do not contribute to efficiency. The idea of God's time made no such contribution.

Bureaucracy is not in principle a social institution; nor are all institutions that reduce information by excluding some kinds or sources necessarily bureaucracies. Schools may exclude dianetics and astrology; courts exclude hearsay evidence. They do so for substantive reasons having to do with the theories on which these institutions are based. But bureaucracy has no intellectual, political, or moral theory — except for its implicit assumption that efficiency is the principal aim of all social institutions and that other goals are essentially less worthy, if not irrelevant. That is why John Stuart Mill thought bureaucracy a "tyranny" and C. S. Lewis identified it with Hell.

The transformation of bureaucracy from a set of techniques designed to serve social institutions to an autonomous meta-institution that largely serves itself came as a result of several developments in the mid- and late nineteenth century: rapid industrial growth, improvements in transportation and communication, the extension of government into ever larger realms of public and business affairs, the increasing centralization of governmental structures. To these were added, in the twentieth century, the information explosion and what we might call the "bureaucracy effect": as techniques for managing information became more nec-essary, extensive, and complex, the number of people and structures required to manage those techniques grew, and so did the amount of information *generated* by bureaucratic techniques. This created the need for bureaucracies to manage and coordinate bureaucracies, then for additional structures and techniques to man-age the bureaucracies that coordinated bureaucracies, and so on — until bureau-cracy became, to borrow . . . Karl Kraus's comment on psychoanalysis, the disease for which it purported to be the cure. Along the way, it ceases to be merely a servant of social institutions and became their master. Bureaucracy now not only solves problems but creates them. More important, it denies what our problems are — and they are always, in the bureaucratic view, problems of effi-ciency. As Lewis suggests, this makes bureaucracies exceedingly dangerous, because, though they were originally designed to process only technical informa-tion, they now are commonly employed to address problems of a moral, social, and political nature. The bureaucracy of the nineteenth century was largely con-cerned with making transportation, industry, and the distribution of goods more efficient. Technopoly's bureaucracy has broken loose from such restrictions and now claims sovereignty over all of society's affairs.

The peril we face in trusting social, moral, and political affairs to bureaucracy may be highlighted by reminding ourselves what a bureaucrat does. As the word's history suggests, a bureaucrat is little else than a glorified counter. The French word *bureau* first meant a cloth for covering a reckoning table, then the table itself, then the room in which the table was kept, and finally the office and staff that ran the entire counting room or house. The word "bureaucrat" has come to mean a person who by training, commitment, and even temperament is indiffer-ent to both the content and the totality of a human problem. The bureaucrat considers the implications of a decision only to the extent that the decision will affect the efficient operations of the bureaucracy, and takes no responsibility for its human consequences. Thus, Adolf Eichmann becomes the basic model and metaphor for a bureaucrat in the age of Technopoly.[7] When faced with the charge of crimes against humanity, he argued that he had no part in the formulation of Nazi political or sociological theory; he dealt only with the technical problems of moving vast numbers of people from one place to another. Why they were being moved and, especially, what would happen to them when they arrived at their destination were not relevant to his job. Although the jobs of bureaucrats in today's Technopoly have results far less horrific, Eichmann's answer is probably given five thousand times a day in America alone: I have no responsibility for the human consequences of my decisions. I am only responsible for the efficiency of my part of the bureaucracy, which must be maintained at all costs.

Eichmann, it must also be noted, was an expert. And expertise is a second important technical means by which Technopoly strives furiously to control information. There have, of course, always been experts, even in tool-using cul-tures. The pyramids, Roman roads, the Strasbourg Cathedral, could hardly have been built without experts. But the expert in Technopoly has two characteristics that distinguish him or her from experts of the past. First, Technopoly's experts tend to be ignorant about any matter not directly related to their specialized area.

The average psychotherapist, for example, barely has even superficial knowledge of literature, philosophy, social history, art, religion, and biology, and is not expected to have such knowledge. Second, like bureaucracy itself (with which an expert may or may not be connected), Technopoly's experts claim dominion not only over technical matters but also over social, psychological, and moral affairs. In the United States, we have experts in how to raise children, how to educate them, how to be lovable, how to make love, how to influence people, how to make friends. There is no aspect of human relations that has not been technicalized and therefore relegated to the control of experts.

These special characteristics of the expert arose as a result of three factors. First, the growth of bureaucracies, which, in effect, produced the world's first entirely mechanistic specialists and thereby gave credence and prestige to the specialist-as-ignoramus. Second, the weakening of traditional social institutions, which led ordinary people to lose confidence in the value of tradition. Third, and underlying everything else, the torrent of information which made it impossible for anyone to possess more than a tiny fraction of the sum total of human knowledge. As a college undergraduate, I was told by an enthusiastic professor of German literature that Goethe was the last person who knew everything. I assume she meant, by this astounding remark, less to deify Goethe than to suggest that by the year of his death, 1832, it was no longer possible for even the most brilliant mind to comprehend, let alone integrate, what was known.

The role of the expert is to concentrate on one field of knowledge, sift through all that is available, eliminate that which has no bearing on a problem, and use what is left to assist in solving a problem. This process works fairly well in situations where only a technical solution is required and there is no conflict with human purposes — for example, in space rocketry or the construction of a sewer system. It works less well in situations where technical requirements may conflict with human purposes, as in medicine or architecture. And it is disastrous when applied to situations that cannot be solved by technical means and where efficiency is usually irrelevant, such as in education, law, family life, and problems of personal maladjustment. I assume I do not need to convince the reader that there are no experts — there can be no experts — in child-rearing and lovemaking and friend-making. All of this is a figment of the Technopolist's imagination, made plausible by the use of technical machinery, without which the expert would be totally disarmed and exposed as an intruder and an ignoramus.

Technical machinery is essential to both the bureaucrat and the expert, and may be regarded as a third mechanism of information control. I do not have in mind such "hard" technologies as the computer — which must, in any case, be treated separately, since it embodies all that Technopoly stands for. I have in mind "softer" technologies such as IQ tests, SATs, standardized forms, taxonomies, and opinion polls. . . . I mention them here because their role in reducing the types and quantity of information admitted to a system often goes unnoticed, and therefore their role in redefining traditional concepts also goes unnoticed. *There is, for example, no test that can measure a person's intelligence.* Intelligence is a general term used to denote one's capacity to solve real-life problems in a variety of novel contexts. It is acknowledged by everyone except experts that each person varies greatly in such capacities, from consistently effective to consistently inef-fective, depending on the kinds of problems requiring solution. If, however, we are made to believe that a test can reveal precisely the quantity of intelligence a per-son has, then, for all institutional purposes, a score on a test becomes his or her intelligence. The test transforms an abstract and multifaceted meaning into a tech-nical and exact term that leaves out everything of importance. One might even say that an intelligence test is a tale told by an expert, signifying nothing. None-theless, the expert relies on our believing in the reality of technical machinery, which means we will reify the answers generated by the machinery. We come to believe that our score *is* our intelligence, or our capacity for creativity or love or pain. We come to believe that the results of opinion polls *are* what people believe, as if our beliefs can be encapsulated in such sentences as "I approve" and "I disapprove."

When Catholic priests use wine, wafers, and incantations to embody spiritual ideas, they acknowledge the mystery and the metaphor being used. But experts of Technopoly acknowledge no such overtones or nuances when they use forms, standardized tests, polls, and other machinery to give technical reality to ideas about intelligence, creativity, sensitivity, emotional imbalance, social deviance, or political opinion. They would have us believe that technology can plainly reveal the true nature of some human condition or belief because the score, sta-tistic, or taxonomy has given it technical form.

There is no denying that the technicalization of terms and problems is a serious form of information control. Institutions can make decisions on the basis of scores and statistics, and there certainly may be occasions where there is no reasonable alternative. But unless such decisions are made with profound skepti-cism — that is, acknowledged as being made for administrative convenience—they are delusionary. In Technopoly, the delusion is sanctified by our granting inordinate prestige to experts who are armed with sophisticated technical machinery. Shaw once remarked that all professions are conspiracies against the laity. I would go further: in Technopoly, all experts are invested with the charisma of priestliness. Some of our priest-experts are called psychiatrists, some psycholo-gists, some sociologists, some statisticians. The god they serve does not speak of righteousness or goodness or mercy or grace. Their god speaks of efficiency, preci-sion, objectivity. And that is why such concepts as sin and evil disappear in Tech-nopoly. They come from a moral universe that is irrelevant to the theology of expertise. And so the priests of Technopoly call sin "social deviance," which is a statistical concept, and they call evil "psychopathology," which is a medical con-cept. Sin and evil disappear because they cannot be measured and objectified, and therefore cannot be dealt with by experts.

As the power of traditional social institutions to organize perceptions and judg-ment declines, bureaucracies, expertise, and technical machinery become the principal means by which Technopoly hopes to control information and thereby provide itself with intelligibility and order

NOTES

1. An empathetic exception among those sociologists who have written on this subject is Arnold Gehlen. See his *Man in the Age of Technology* (New York: Columbia University Press, 1980).

2. Though this term is by no means original with E. D. Hirsch, Jr., its current popularity is attributable to Hirsch's book, *Cultural Literacy: What Every American Needs to Know* (Boston: Houghton Mifflin Co., 1987).
3. This poignant phrase is also the title of one of Lasch's most important books. Christopher Lasch, *Haven in a Heartless World: The Family Besieged* (New York: Basic Books, 1975).
4. James Beniger, *The Control Revolution: Technological and Economic Origins of the Information Society* (Cambridge, Mass., and London: Harvard University Press, 1986), p. 13. Beniger's book is the best source for an understanding of the technical means of eliminating — that is, controlling — information.
5. A. de Tocqueville, *Democracy in America* (New York: Anchor Books [Doubleday & Co., Inc.], 1969), p. 262.
6. C. S. Lewis, *The Screwtape Letters* (New York: Macmillan, 1943), p. x.
7. See H. Arendt, *Eichmann in Jerusalem: A Report on the Banality of Evil* (New York: Penguin Books, 1977).

3. Technological Momentum

THOMAS P. HUGHES

Does technology drive history — that is, does it shape the course of human society? Or does society create — "construct" — technology based on the interactions of individuals, institutions, social classes, and economic and political forces? Those who hold the former view, sometimes called technological determinists, *view technology as a largely autonomous force that produces major social changes in a manner largely outside human control, whereas* social constructivists *contend that the nature of society and of the individuals and organizations that develop technologies shape the characteristics of technological systems.*

Thomas Hughes developed the notion of "technological momentum" as an alternative explanation of the relations between technology and society. Drawing on what he has learned from a long and distinguished career studying the development of technological systems, Hughes contends that reality is more subtle than either the determinists or the constructivists would have us believe. Technological momentum, he claims, presents "a more complex, flexible, time-dependent, and persuasive explanation of technological change." Using examples from his research, much of which has been devoted to electrical power systems, Hughes demonstrates how newer, developing systems are generally more open to societal influences than more mature systems, which are more resistant to external influences and thus more deterministic.

Thomas P. Hughes is professor emeritus in the Department of History and Sociology of Science at the University of Pennsylvania and holds the Torsten Althin Chair at the Royal Institute of Technology in Stockholm, Sweden. He is the author of American Genesis: A Century of Invention and Technological Enthusiasm *(1989) and has twice won the Dexter Prize for the outstanding book on the history of technology.*

The concepts of technological determinism and social construction provide agendas for fruitful discussions among historians, sociologists, and engineers interested in the nature of technology and technological change. Specialists can engage in a general discourse that subsumes their areas of specialization. In this essay I shall offer an additional concept — technological momentum — that will, I hope, enrich the discussion. Technological momentum offers an alternative to technological determinism and social construction. Those who in the past espoused a technological determinist approach to history offered a needed corrective to the conventional interpretation of history that virtually ignored the role of technology in effecting social change. Those who more recently advocated a social construction approach provided an invaluable corrective to an interpretation of history that encouraged a passive attitude toward an overwhelming technology. Yet both approaches suffer from a failure to encompass the complexity of technological change.

All three concepts present problems of definition. Technological determinism I define simply as the belief that technical forces determine social and cultural changes. Social construction presumes that social and cultural forces determine technical change. A more complex concept than determinism and social construction, technological momentum infers that social development shapes and is shaped by technology. Momentum also is time dependent. Because the focus of this essay is technological momentum, I shall define it in detail by resorting to examples.

"Technology" and "technical" also need working definitions. Proponents of technological determinism and of social construction often use "technology" in a narrow sense to include only physical artifacts and software. By contrast, I use "technical" in referring to physical artifacts and software. By "technology" I usually mean technological or sociotechnical systems, which I shall also define by examples.

Discourses about technological determinism and social construction usually refer to society, a concept exceedingly abstract. Historians are wary of defining society other than by example because they have found that twentieth-century societies seem quite different from twelfth-century ones and that societies differ not only over time but over space as well. Facing these ambiguities, I define the social as the world that is not technical, or that is not hardware or technical software. This world is made up of institutions, values, interest groups, social classes, and political and economic forces. As the reader will learn, I see the social and the technical as interacting within technological systems. Technological system, as I shall explain, includes both the technical and the social. I name the world outside of technological systems that shapes them or is shaped by them the "environment." Even though it may interact with the technological system, the environment is not a part of the system because it is not under the control of the system, as are the system's interacting components.

In the course of this essay the reader will discover that I am no technological determinist. I cannot associate myself with such distinguished technological determinists as Karl Marx, Lynn White, and Jacques Ellul. Marx, in moments of simplification, argued that waterwheels ushered in manorialism and that steam engines gave birth to bourgeois factories and society. Lenin added that electrification was the bearer of socialism. White elegantly portrayed the stirrup as the prime mover in a train of cause and effect culminating in the establishment of feudalism. Ellul finds the human-made environment structured by technical systems, as determining in their effects as the natural environment of Charles Darwin. Ellul sees the human-made as steadily displacing the natural — the world becoming a system of artifacts, with humankind, not God, as the artificer.[1]

Nor can I agree entirely with the social constructivists. Wiebe Bijker and Trevor Pinch have made an influential case for social construction in their essay "The Social Construction of Facts and Artifacts."[2] They argue that social, or interest, groups define and giving meaning to artifacts. In defining them, the social groups determine the designs of artifacts. They do this by selecting for survival the designs that solve the problems they want solved by the artifacts and that fulfill desires they want fulfilled by the artifacts. Bijker and Pinch emphasize the interpretive flexibility discernible in the evolution of artifacts: they believe that the various meanings given by social groups to, say, the bicycle result in a number of alternative designs of that machine. The various bicycle designs are not fixed; closure does not occur until social groups believe that the problems and desires they associate with the bicycle are solved or fulfilled.

In summary, I find the Bijker-Pinch interpretation tends toward social determinism, and I must reject it on these grounds. The concept of technological momentum avoids the extremism of both technological determination and social construction by presenting a more complex, flexible, time-dependent, and persuasive explanation of technological change.

TECHNOLOGICAL SYSTEMS

Electric light and power systems provide an instructive example of technological systems. By 1920 they had taken on a messy complexity because of the heterogeneity of their components. In their diversity, their complexity, and their large scale, such mature technological systems resemble the megamachines that Lewis Mumford described in *The Pentagon of Power*.[3] The actor networks of Bruno Latour and Michel Callon also share essential characteristics with technological systems.[4] An electric power system consists of inanimate electrons and animate regulatory boards, both of which, as Latour and Callon suggest, can be intractable if not brought in line or into the actor network.

The Electric Board and Share Company (EBASCO), an American electric utility holding company of the 1920s, provides an example of a mature technological system. Established in 1905 by the General Electric Company, EBASCO controlled, through stock ownership, a number of electric utility companies, and through them a number of technical subsystems — namely electric light and power networks, or grids.[5] EBASCO provided financial, management, and engineering construction services for the utility companies. The inventors, engineers, and manager who were the systems builders of EBASCO saw to it that the services related synergistically. EBASCO management recommended construction that EBASCO engineering carried out and for which EBASCO arranged financing through sale of stocks or bonds. If the utilities lay in geographical proximity, then EBASCO often physically interconnected them through high-voltage power grids. The General Electric Company founded EBASCO and, while not owning a majority of stock in it, substantially influenced its policies. Through EBASCO General Electric learned of equipment needs in the utility industry and then provided them in accord with specifications defined by EBASCO for the various utilities with which it interacted. Because it interacted with EBASCO, General Electric was a part of the EBASCO system. Even though I have labeled this the EBASCO system, it is not clear that EBASCO solely controlled the system. Control of the complex systems seems to have resulted from a consensus among EBASCO, General Electric, and the utilities in the systems.

Other institutions can also be considered parts of the EBASCO system, but because the interconnections were loose rather than tight[6] these institutions are usually not recognized as such. I refer to the electrical engineering departments in engineering colleges, whose faculty and graduate students conducted research or consulted for EBASCO. I am also inclined to include a few of the various state regulatory authorities as parts of the EBASCO system, if their members were greatly influenced by it. If the regulatory authorities were free of this control, then they should be considered a part of the EBASCO environment, not of the system.

Because it had social institutions as components, the EBASCO system could be labeled a sociotechnical system. Since, however, the system had a technical (hardware and software) core, I prefer to name it a technological system, to distinguish it from social systems without technical cores. This privileging of the technical in a technological system is justified in part by the prominent roles played by engineers, scientists, workers, and technical-minded managers in solving the problems arising during the creation and early history of a system. As a system matures, a bureaucracy of managers and white-collar employees usually plays an increasingly prominent role in maintaining and expanding the system, so that it then becomes more social and less technical.

EBASCO AS A CAUSE AND AN EFFECT

From the point of view of technological — better, technical — determinists, the determined is the world beyond the technical. Technical determinists considering EBASCO as a historical actor would focus on its technical core as a cause with many effects. Instead of seeing EBASCO as a technological system with interacting technical and social components, they would see the technical core as causing change in the social components of EBASCO and in society in general. Determinists would focus on the way in which EBASCO's generators, by energizing electric motors on individual production machines, made possible the reorganization of the factory floor in a manner commonly associated with Fordism. Such persons would see street, workplace, and home lighting changing working and leisure hours and affecting the nature of work and play. Determinists would also cite electrical appliances in the home as bringing less — and more — work for women,[7] and the layout of EBASCO's power lines as causing demographic changes. Electric grids such as those presided over by EBASCO brought a new, decentralized regionalism, which contrasted with the industrial, urban-centered society of the steam age.[8] One could extend the list of the effects of electrification enormously.

Yet, contrary to the view of the technological determinists, the social constructivists would find exogenous technical, economic, political, and geographical forces, as well as values, shaping, with varying intensity, the EBASCO system during its evolution. Social constructivists see the technical core of EBASCO as an effect rather than a cause. They could cite a number of instances of social construction. The spread of alternation (polyphase) current after 1900, for instance, greatly affected, even determined, the history of the early utilities that had used direct current, for these had to change their generators and related equipment to alternating current or fail in the face of competition. Not only did such external technical forces shape the technical core of the utilities; economic forces did so as well. With the rapid increase in the U.S. population and the concentration of industry in cities, the price of real estate increased. Needing to expand their generating capacity, EBASCO and other electric utilities chose to build new turbine-driven power plants outside city centers and to transmit electricity by high-voltage lines back into the cities and throughout the area of supply. Small urban utilities became regional ones and then faced new political or regulatory forces as state governments took over jurisdiction from the cities. Regulations also caused technical changes. As the regional utilities of the EBASCO system expanded, they conformed to geographical realities as they sought cooling water, hydroelectric sites, and mine-mouth locations. Values, too, shaped the history of EBASCO. During the Great Depression, the Roosevelt administration singled out utility holding-company magnates for criticism, blaming the huge losses experienced by stock- and bondholders on the irresponsible, even illegal, machinations of some of the holding companies. Partly as a result of this attack, the attitudes of the public toward large-scale private enterprise shifted so that it was relatively easy for the administration to push through Congress the Holding Company Act of 1935, which denied holding companies the right to incorporate utilities that were not physically contiguous.[9]

GATHERING TECHNOLOGICAL MOMENTUM

Neither the proponents of technical determinism nor those of social construction can alone comprehend the complexity of an evolving technological system such as EBASCO. On some occasions EBASCO was a cause; on others it was an effect. The system both shaped and was shaped by society. Furthermore, EBASCO's shaping society is not an example of purely technical determinism, for EBASCO, as we have observed, contained social components. Similarly, social constructivists must acknowledge that social forces in the environment were not shaping simply a technical system, but a technological system, including — as systems invariably do — social components.

The interaction of technological systems and society is not symmetrical over time. Evolving technological systems are time dependent. As the EBASCO system became larger and more complex, thereby gathering momentum, the system became less shaped by and more the shaper of its environment. By the 1920s the EBASCO system rivaled a large railroad company in its level of capital investment, in its number of customers, and in its influence upon local, state, and federal governments. Hosts of electric engineers, their professional organizations, and the engineering schools that trained them were committed by economic interests and their special knowledge and skills to the maintenance and growth of the EBASCO system. Countless industries and communities interacted with

EBASCO utilities because of shared economic interests. These various human and institutional components added substantial momentum to the EBASCO system. Only a historical event of large proportions could deflect or break the momentum of an EBASCO, the Great Depression being a case in point.

CHARACTERISTICS OF MOMENTUM

Other technological systems reveal further characteristics of technological momentum, such as acquired skill and knowledge, special-purpose machines and processes, enormous physical structures, and organizational bureaucracy. During the late nineteenth century, for instance, mainline railroad engineers in the United States transferred their acquired skill and knowledge to the field of intra-urban transit. Institutions with specific characteristics also contributed to this momentum. Professors in the recently founded engineering schools and engineers who had designed and built the railroads organized and rationalized the experience that had been gathered in preparing roadbeds, laying tracks, building bridges, and digging tunnels for mainline railroads earlier in the century. This engineering science found a place in engineering texts and in the curricula of the engineering schools, thus informing a new generation of engineers who would seek new applications for it.

Late in the nineteenth century, when street congestion in rapidly expanding industrial and commercial cities such as Chicago, Baltimore, New York, and Boston threatened to choke the flow of traffic, extensive subway and elevated railway building began as an antidote. The skill and the knowledge formerly expended on railroad bridges were now applied to elevated railway structures; the know-how once invested in tunnels now found application in subways. A remarkably active period of intra-urban transport construction began about the time when the building of mainline railways reached a plateau, thus facilitating the movement of know-how from one field to the other. Many of the engineers who played leading roles in intra-urban transit between 1890 and 1910 had been mainline railroad builders.[10]

The role of the physical plant in the buildup of technological momentum is revealed in the interwar history of the Badische Anilin und Soda Fabrik (BASF), one of Germany's leading chemical manufacturers and a member of the I.G. Farben group. During World War I, BASF rapidly developed large-scale production facilities to utilize the recently introduced Haber-Bosch technique of nitrogen fixation. It produced the nitrogen compounds for fertilizers and explosives so desperately needed by a blockaded Germany. The high-technology process involved the use of high-temperature, high-pressure, complex instrumentation and apparatus. When the blockade and the war were over, the market demand for synthetic nitrogen compounds did not match the large capacity of the high-technology plants built by BASF and other companies during the war. Numerous engineers, scientists, and skilled craftsmen who had designed, constructed, and operated these plants found their research and development knowledge and their construction skills underutilized. Carl Bosch, chairman of the managing board of BASF and one of the inventors of the Haber-Bosch process, had a personal and professional interest in further development and application of high-temperature, high-pressure, catalytic processes. He and other managers, scientists, and engineers at BASF sought additional ways of using the plant and the knowledge created during the war years. They first introduced a high-temperature, high-pressure catalytic process for manufacturing synthetic methanol in the early 1920s. The momentum of the now-generalized process next showed itself in management's decision in the mid-1920s to invest in research and development aimed at using high-temperature, high-pressure catalytic chemistry for the production of synthetic gasoline from coal. This project became the largest investment in research and development by BASF during the Weimar era. When the National Socialists took power, the government contracted for large amounts of the synthetic product. Momentum swept BASF and I.G. Farben into the Nazi system of economic autarky.[11]

When managers pursue economies of scope, they are taking into account the momentum embodied in large physical structures. Muscle Shoals Dam, an artifact of considerable size, offers another example of this aspect of technological momentum. As the loss of merchant ships to submarines accelerated during World War I, the United States also attempted to increase its indigenous supply of nitrogen compounds. Having selected a process requiring copious amounts of electricity, the government had to construct a hydroelectric dam and power station. This was located at Muscle Shoals, Alabama, on the Tennessee River. Before the nitrogen-fixation facilities being built near the dam were completed, the war ended. As in Germany, the supply of synthetic nitrogen compounds then exceeded the demand. The U.S. government was left not only with process facilities but also with a very large dam and power plant.

Muscle Shoals Dam (later named Wilson Dam), like the engineers and managers we have considered, became a solution looking for a problem. How should the power from the dam be used? A number of technological enthusiasts and planners envisioned the dam as the first of a series of hydroelectric projects along the Tennessee River and its tributaries. The poverty of the region spurred them on in an era when electrification was seen as a prime mover of economic development. The problem looking for a solution attracted the attention of an experienced problem solver, Henry Ford, who proposed that an industrial complex based on hydroelectric power be located along 75 miles of the waterway that included the Muscle Shoals site. An alliance of public power and private interests with their own plans for the region frustrated his plan. In 1933, however, Muscle Shoals became the original component in a hydroelectric, flood-control, soil-reclamation, and regional development project of enormous scope sponsored by Senator George Norris and the Roosevelt administration and presided over by the Tennessee Valley Authority. The technological momentum of the Muscle Shoals Dam had carried over from World War I to the New Deal. This durable artifact acted over time like a magnetic field, attracting plans and projects suited to its characteristics. Systems of artifacts are not neutral forces; they tend to shape the environment in particular ways.[12]

USING MOMENTUM

System builders today are aware that technological momentum — or whatever they may call it — provides the durability and the propensity for growth that were associated more commonly in the past with the spread of bureaucracy. Immediately after World War II, General Leslie Groves displayed his system-building instincts and his awareness of the critical importance of technological momentum as a means of ensuring the survival of the system for the production of atomic weapons embodied in the wartime Manhattan Project. Between 1945 and 1947, when others were anticipating disarmament, Groves expanded the gaseous-diffusion facilities for separating fissionable uranium at Oak Ridge, Tennessee; persuaded the General Electric Company to operate the reactors for producing plutonium at Hanford, Washington; funded the new Knolls Atomic Power Laboratory at Schenectady, New York; established the Argonne and Brookhaven National Laboratories for fundamental research in nuclear science; and provided research funds for a number of universities. Under his guiding hand, a large-scale production system with great momentum took on new life in peacetime. Some of the leading scientists of the wartime project had confidently expected production to end after the making of a few bombs and the coming of peace.[13]

More recently, proponents of the Strategic Defense Initiative (SDI), organized by the Reagan administration in 1983, have made use of momentum. The political and economic interests and the organizational bureaucracy vested in this system were substantial — as its makers intended. Many of the same industrial contractors, research universities, national laboratories, and government agencies that took part in the construction of intercontinental ballistic missile systems, National Aeronautics and Space Administration projects, and atomic weapon systems have been deeply involved in SDI. The names are familiar: Lockheed, General Motors, Boeing, TRW, McDonnell Douglas, General Electric, Rockwell, Teledyn, MIT, Stanford, the University of California's Lawrence Livermore Laboratory, Los Alamos, Hanford, Brookhaven, Argonne, Oak Ridge, NASA, the U.S. Air Force, the U.S. Navy, the CIA, the U.S. Army, and others. Political interests reinforced the institutional momentum. A number of congressmen represent districts that receive SDI contracts, and lobbyists speak for various institutions drawn into the SDI network.[14] Only the demise of the Soviet Union as a military threat allowed counterforces to build up sufficient momentum to blunt the cutting edge of SDI.

CONCLUSION

A technological system can be both a cause and an effect; it can shape or be shaped by society. As they grow larger and more complex, systems tend to be more shaping of society and less shaped by it. Therefore, the momentum of technological systems is a concept that can be located somewhere between the poles of technical determinism and social constructivism. The social constructivists have a key to understanding the behavior of young systems; technical determinists come into their own with the mature ones. Technological momentum, however, provides a more flexible mode of interpretation and one that is in accord with the history of large systems.

What does this interpretation of the history of technological systems offer to those who design and manage systems or to the public that might wish to shape them through a democratic process? It suggests that shaping is easiest before the system has acquired political, economic, and value components. It also follows that a system with great technological momentum can be made to change direction if a variety of its components are subjected to the forces of change.

For instance, the changeover since 1970 by U.S. automobile manufacturers from large to more compact automobiles and to more fuel-efficient and less polluting ones came about as a result of pressure brought on a number of components in the huge automobile production and use system. As a result of the oil embargo of 1973 and the rise of gasoline prices, American consumers turned to imported compact automobiles; this, in turn, brought competitive economic pressure to bear on the Detroit manufacturers. Environmentalists helped persuade the public to support, and politicians to enact, legislation that promoted both anti-pollution technology and gas-mileage standards formerly opposed by American manufacturers. Engineers and designers responded with technical inventions and developments.

On the other hand, the technological momentum of the system of automobile production and use can be observed in recent reactions against major environmental initiatives in the Los Angeles region. The host of institutions and persons dependent politically, economically, and ideologically on the system (including gasoline refiners, automobile manufacturers, trade unions manufacturers of appliances and small equipment using internal-combustion engines, and devotees of unrestricted automobile usage) rallied to frustrate change.

Because social and technical components interact so thoroughly in technological systems and because the inertia of these systems is so large, they bring to mind the iron-cage metaphor that Max Weber used in describing the organizational bureaucracies that proliferated at the beginning of the twentieth century.[15] Technological systems, however, are bureaucracies reinforced by technical, or physical, infrastructures which give them ever greater rigidity and mass than the social bureaucracies that were the subject of Weber's attention. Nevertheless, we must remind ourselves that technological momentum, like physical momentum, is not irresistible.

NOTES

1. Lynn White, Jr., *Medieval Technology and Social Change* (Clarendon, 1962); Jacques Ellul, *The Technological System* (Continuum, 1980); Karl Marx, *Capital: A Critique of Political Economy*, ed. F. Engels (1887); *Electric Power Development in the U.S.S.R.*, ed. B. I. Weitz (Moscow: INRA, 1936).
2. The essay is found in *The Social Construction of Technological Systems: New Directions in the Sociology and History of Technology*, ed. W. E. Bijker et al. (MIT Press, 1987).
3. Lewis Mumford, *The Myth of the Machine: II. The Pentagon of Power* (Harcourt Brace Jovanovich, 1970).

4. Bruno Latour, *Science in Action: How to Follow Scientists and Engineers through Society* (Harvard University Press, 1987); Michel Callon, "Society in the Making: The Study of Technology as a Tool for Sociological Analysis," in *The Social Construction of Technological Systems*.

5. Before 1905, General Electric used the United Electric Securities Company to holds its utility securities and to fund its utility customers who purchased GE equipment. See Thomas P. Hughes, *Networks of Power: Electrification in Western Society, 1880–1930* (Johns Hopkins University Press, 1983), pp. 395–396.

6. The concept of loosely and tightly coupled components in systems is found in Charles Perrow's *Normal Accidents: Living with High Risk Technology* (Basic Books, 1984).

7. Ruth Schwartz Cowan, "The 'Industrial Revolution' in the Home," *Technology and Culture* 17 (1976): 1–23.

8. Lewis Mumford, *The Culture of Cities* (Harcourt Brace Jovanovich, 1970), p. 378.

9. More on EBASCO's history can be found on pp. 395–399 of *Networks of Power*.

10. Thomas Parke Hughes, "A Technological Frontier: The Railway," in *The Railroad and the Space Program*, ed. B. Mazlish (MIT Press, 1965).

11. Thomas Parke Hughes, "Technological Momentum: Hydrogenation in Germany 1900–1933," *Past and Present*, August 1969, pp. 106–132.

12. On Muscle Shoals and the TVA, see Preston J. Hubbard's *Origins of the TVA: The Muscle Shoals Controversy, 1920–1932* (Norton, 1961).

13. Richard G. Hewlett and Oscar E. Anderson, Jr., *The New World, 1939–1946* (Pennsylvania State University Press, 1962), pp. 624–638.

14. Charlene Mires, "The Strategic Defense Initiative" (unpublished essay, History and Sociology of Science Department, University of Pennsylvania, 1990).

15. Max Weber, *The Protestant Ethic and the Spirit of Capitalism*, tr. T. Parsons (Unwin-Hyman, 1990), p. 155.

4. Can Technology Replace Social Engineering?

ALVIN M. WEINBERG

Since Alvin Weinberg's essay "Can Technology Replace Social Engineering?" was first published in the mid-1960s, it has become a classic in the literature of technology and society. Indeed, the term Technological Fix, introduced here, has become part of the lexicon of the field. Weinberg, one of the pioneers of large-scale atomic energy R&D and an inveterate technological optimist, argues that technology is capable of finding shortcuts (technological fixes) to the solution of social problems. For example, faced with a shortage of fresh water, he suggests, society can try either social engineering — altering life-styles and the ways people use water — or a technological fix, such as the provision of additional fresh water through nuclear-powered desalting of sea water. The reader should keep in mind that this article dates from 1966. Although aspects are anachronistic and out of tune with contemporary views of technology, society, and politics, the questions it raises are as relevant today as they were more than thirty years ago.

Alvin M. Weinberg is a physicist who joined the World War II Manhattan Project early in his career. He went to Oak Ridge National Laboratory in 1945 and served as its director from 1955 through 1973. He is currently on the staff of Oak Ridge Associated Universities. Weinberg was a member of the President's Science Advisory Committee in 1960–1962 and is the recipient of many awards, including the President's Medal of Science and the Enrico Fermi Award. He was born in Chicago in 1915 and holds A.B., A.M., and Ph.D. degrees from the University of Chicago.

During World War II, and immediately afterward, our federal government mobilized its scientific and technical resources, such as the Oak Ridge National Laboratory, around great technological problems. Nuclear reactors, nuclear weapons, radar, and space are some of the miraculous new technologies that have been created by this mobilization of federal effort. In the past few years there has been a major change in focus of much of our federal research. Instead of being preoccupied with technology, our government is now mobilizing around problems that are largely social. We are beginning to ask what can we do about world population, about the deterioration of our environment, about our educational system, our decaying cities, race relations, poverty. Recent administrations have dedicated the power of a scientifically oriented federal apparatus to finding solutions for these complex social problems.

Social problems are much more complex than are technological problems. It is much harder to identify a social problem than a technological problem: how do we know when our cities need renewing, or when our population is too big, or when our modes of transportation have broken down? The problems are, in a way, harder to identify just because their solutions are never clear-cut: how do we know when our cities are renewed, or our air clean enough, or our transportation convenient enough? By contrast, the availability of a crisp and beautiful technological *solution* often helps focus on the problem to which the new technology is the solution. I doubt that we would have been nearly as concerned with an eventual shortage of energy as we now are if we had not had a neat solution — nuclear energy — available to eliminate the shortage.

There is a more basic sense in which social problems are much more difficult than are technological problems. A social problem exists because many people behave, individually, in a socially unacceptable way. To solve a social problem one must induce social change — one must persuade many people to behave differently than they have behaved in the past. One must persuade many people to have fewer babies, or to drive more carefully, or to refrain from disliking blacks. By contrast, resolution of a technological problem involves many fewer individual decisions. Once President Roosevelt decided to go after atomic energy, it was by comparison a relatively simple task to mobilize the Manhattan Project.

The resolution of social problems by the traditional methods — by motivating or forcing people to behave more rationally — is a frustrating business. People don't behave rationally; it is a long, hard business to persuade individuals to forgo immediate personal gain or pleasure (as seen by the individual) in favor of longer term social gain. And indeed, the aim of social engineering is to invent the social devices — usually legal, but also moral and educational and organizational — that will change each person's motivation and redirect his activities along ways that are more acceptable to the society.

The technologist is appalled by the difficulties faced by the social engineer; to engineer even a small social change by inducing individuals to behave differently is always hard even when the change is rather neutral or even beneficial. For example, some rice eaters in India are reported to prefer starvation to eating wheat that we send to them. How much harder it is to change motivations where the individual is insecure and feels threatened if he acts differently, as illustrated by the poor white's reluctance to accept the black as an equal. By contrast, technological engineering is simple: the rocket, the reactor, and the desalination plants are devices that are expensive to develop, to be sure, but their feasibility is relatively easy to assess, and their success relatively easy to achieve once one understands the scientific principles that underlie them. It is, therefore, tempting to raise the following question: In view of the simplicity of technological engineering, and the complexity of social engineering, to what extent can social problems be circumvented by reducing them to technological problems? Can we identify Quick Technological Fixes for profound and almost infinitely complicated social problems, "fixes" that are within the grasp of modem technology, and which would either eliminate the original social problem without requiring a change in the individual's social attitudes, or would so alter the problem as to make its resolution more feasible? To paraphrase Ralph Nader, to what extent can technological *remedies* be found for social problems without first having to remove the *causes* of the problem? It is in this sense that I ask, "Can technology replace social engineering?"

THE MAJOR TECHNOLOGICAL FIXES OF THE PAST

To better explain what I have in mind, I shall describe how two of our profoundest social problems — poverty and war — have in some limited degree been solved by the Technological Fix, rather than by the methods of social engineering. Let me begin with poverty.

The traditional Marxian view of poverty regarded our economic ills as being primarily a question of maldistribution of goods. The Marxist recipe for elimination of poverty, therefore, was to eliminate profit, in the erroneous belief that it was the loss of this relatively small increment from the worker's paycheck that kept him poverty-stricken. The Marxist dogma is typical of the approach of the social engineer: one tries to convince or coerce many people to forgo their short-term profits in what is presumed to be the long-term interest of the society as a whole.

The Marxian view seems archaic in this age of mass production and automation not only to us, but apparently to many Eastern bloc economists. For the brilliant advances in the technology of energy, of mass production, and of automation have created the affluent society. Technology has expanded our productive capacity so greatly that even though our distribution is still inefficient, and unfair by Marxian precepts, there is more than enough to go around. Technology has provided a "fix" — greatly expanded production of goods — which enables our capitalistic society to achieve many of the aims of the Marxist social engineer without going through the social revolution Marx viewed as inevitable. Technology has converted the seemingly intractable social problem of *widespread* poverty into a relatively tractable one.

My second example is war. The traditional Christian position views war as primarily a moral issue: if men become good, and model them selves after the Prince of Peace, they will live in peace. This doctrine is so deeply ingrained in the spirit of all civilized men that I suppose it is a blasphemy to point out that it has never worked very well — that men have not been good, and that they are not paragons of virtue or even of reasonableness.

Though I realize it is terribly presumptuous to claim, I believe that Edward Teller may have supplied the nearest thing to a Quick Technological Fix to the problem of war. The hydrogen bomb greatly increases the provocation that would precipitate large-scale war — and not because men's motivations have been changed, not because men have become more tolerant and understanding, but rather because the appeal to the primitive instinct of self-preservation has been intensified far beyond anything we could have imagined before the H-bomb was invented. To point out these things today [in 1966], with the United States involved in a shooting war, may sound hollow and unconvincing; yet the desperate and partial peace we have now is much better than a full-fledged exchange of thermonuclear weapons. One cannot deny that the Soviet leaders now recognize the force of H-bombs, and that this has surely contributed to the less militant attitude of the USSR. One can only hope that the Chinese leadership, as it acquires familiarity with H-bombs, will also become less militant. If I were to be asked who has given the world a more effective means of achieving peace, our great religious leaders who urge men to love their neighbors and, thus, avoid fights, or our weapons technologists who simply present men with no rational alternative to peace, I would vote for the weapons technologist. That the peace we get is at best terribly fragile, I cannot deny; yet, as I shall explain, I think technology can help stabilize our imperfect and precarious peace.

THE TECHNOLOGICAL FIXES OF THE FUTURE

Are there other Technological Fixes on the horizon, other technologies that can reduce immensely complicated social questions to a matter of "engineering"? Are there new technologies that offer society ways of circumventing social problems and at the same time do *not* require individuals to renounce short-term advantage for long-term gain?

Probably the most important new Technological Fix is the Intra-Uterine Device for birth control. Before the IUD was invented, birth control demanded very strong motivation of countless individuals. Even with the pill, the individual's motivation had to be sustained day in and day out; should it flag even temporarily, the strong motivation of the previous month might go for naught. But the IUD, being a one-shot method, greatly reduces the individual motivation required the induce a social change. To be sure, the mother must be sufficiently motivated to accept the IUD in the first place, but, as experience in India already seems to show, it is much easier to persuade the Indian mother to accept the IUD once, than it is to persuade her to take a pill every day. The IUD does not completely replace social engineering by technology; and indeed, in some Spanish American cultures where the husband's manliness is measured by the number of children he has, the IUD attacks only part of the problem. Yet, in many other situations, as in India, the IUD so reduces the social component of the problem as to make an impossibly difficult social problem much less hopeless.

Let me turn now to problems that from the beginning have had both technical and social components — broadly, those concerned with conservation of our resources: our environment, our water, and our raw materials for production of the means of subsistence. The social issue here arises because many people by their individual acts cause shortages and, thus, create economic, and ultimately social, imbalance. For example, people use water wastefully, or they insist on moving to California because of its climate, and so we have water shortages; or too many people drive cars in Los Angeles with its curious meteorology, and so Los Angeles suffocates from smog.

The water resources problem is a particularly good example of a complicated problem with strong social and technological connotations. Our management of water resources in the past has been based largely on the ancient Roman device, the aqueduct: every water shortage was to be relieved by stealing water from someone else who at the moment didn't need the water or was too poor or too weak to prevent the steal. Southern California would steal from Northern California, New York City from upstate New York, the farmer who could afford a cloud-seeder from the farmer who could not afford a cloud-seeder. The social engineer insists that such shortsighted expedients have got us into serious trouble; we have no water resources policy, we waste water disgracefully, and, perhaps, in denying the ethic of thriftiness in using water, we have generally undermined our moral fiber. The social engineer, therefore, views such technological shenanigans as being shortsighted, if not downright immoral. Instead, he says, we should persuade or force people to use less water, or to stay in the cold Middle West where water is plentiful instead of migrating to California where water is scarce.

The water technologist, on the other hand, views the social engineer's approach as rather impractical. To persuade people to use less water, to get along with expensive water, is difficult, time consuming, and uncertain in the extreme. Moreover, say the technologists, what right does the water resources expert have to insist that people use water less wastefully? Green lawns and clean cars and swimming pools are part of the good life, American style, . . . and what right do we have to deny this luxury if there is some alternative to cutting down the water we use?

Here we have a sharp confrontation of the two ways of dealing with a complex social issue: the social engineering way, which asks people to behave more "reasonably," and the technologists' way, which tries to avoid changing people's habits or motivation. Even though I am a technologist, I have sympathy for the social engineer. I think we must use our water as efficiently as possible, that we ought to improve people's attitudes toward the use of water, and that everything that can be done to rationalize our water policy will be welcome. Yet as a technologist, I believe I see ways of providing more water more cheaply than the social engineers may concede is possible.

I refer to the possibility of nuclear desalination. The social engineer dismisses the technologist's simpleminded idea of solving a water shortage by transporting more water primarily because, in so doing, the water user steals water from someone else — possibly foreclosing the possibility of ultimately utilizing land now only sparsely settled. But surely water drawn from the sea deprives no one of his share of water. The whole issue is then a technological one; can fresh water be drawn from the sea cheaply enough to have a major impact on our chronically water-short areas like Southern California, Arizona, and the Eastern seaboard?

I believe the answer is yes, though much hard technical work remains to be done. A large program to develop cheap methods of nuclear desalting has been undertaken by the United States, and I have little doubt that within the next ten to twenty years we shall see huge dual-purpose desalting plants springing up on many parched seacoasts of the world.* At first these plants will produce water at municipal prices. But I believe, on the basis of research now in progress at ORNL [Oak Ridge National Laboratory] and elsewhere, water from the sea at a cost acceptable for agriculture — less than ten cents per 1,000 gallons — is eventually in the cards. In short, for areas close to the seacoasts, technology can provide water without requiring a great and difficult-to-accomplish change in people's attitudes toward the utilization of water.

The Technological Fix for water is based on the availability of extremely cheap energy from very large nuclear reactors. What other social consequences can one

*Here, as elsewhere, the reader should bear in mind that the essay dates from the mid-1960s. — Ed.

foresee flowing from really cheap energy eventually available to every country regardless of its endowment of conventional resources? Though we now see only vaguely the outlines of the possibilities, it does seem likely that from very cheap nuclear energy we shall get hydrogen by electrolysis of water, and, thence, the all important ammonia fertilizer necessary to help feed the hungry of the world; we shall reduce metals without requiring cooking coal; we shall even power automobiles with electricity, via fuel cells or storage batteries, thus reducing our world's dependence on crude oil, as well as eliminating our air pollution insofar as it is caused by automobile exhaust or by the burning of fossil fuels. In short, the widespread availability of very cheap energy everywhere in the world ought to lead to an energy autarky in every country of the world; and eventually to an autarky in the many staples of life that should flow from really cheap energy.

WILL TECHNOLOGY REPLACE SOCIAL ENGINEERING?

I hope these examples suggest how social problems can be circumvented or at least reduced to less formidable proportions by the application of the Technological Fix. The examples I have given do not strike me as being fanciful, nor are they at all exhaustive. I have not touched, for example, upon the extent to which really cheap computers and improved technology of communication can help improve elementary teaching without having first to improve our elementary teachers. Nor have I mentioned Ralph Nader's brilliant observation that a safer car, and even its development and adoption by the auto company, is a quicker and probably surer way to reduce traffic deaths than is a campaign to teach people to drive more carefully. Nor have I invoked some really fanciful Technological Fixes: like providing air conditioners and free electricity to operate them for every black family in Watts on the assumption (suggested by Huntington) that race rioting is correlated with hot, humid weather; or the ultimate Technological Fix, Aldous Huxley's soma pills that eliminate human unhappiness without improving human relations in the usual sense.

My examples illustrate both the strength and the weakness of the Technological Fix for social problems. The Technological Fix accepts man's intrinsic shortcomings and circumvents them or capitalizes on them for socially useful ends. The Fix is, therefore, eminently practical and, in the short term, relatively effective. One does not wait around trying to change people's minds: if people want more water, one gets them more water rather than requiring them to reduce their use of water; if people insist on driving autos while they are drunk, one provides safer autos that prevent injuries even after a severe accident.

But the technological solutions to social problems tend to be incomplete and metastable, to replace one social problem with another. Perhaps the best example of this instability is the peace imposed upon us by the H-bomb. Evidently the pax hydrogenica is metastable in two senses: in the short term, because the aggressor still enjoys such an advantage; the long term, because the discrepancy and have-not nations must eventually be resolved if we are to have permanent peace. Yet, for these particular shortcomings, technology has something to offer. To the imbalance between offense and defense, technology says let us devise passive defense that redresses the balance. A world with H-bombs and adequate civil defense is less likely to lapse into thermonuclear war than a world with H-bombs alone, at least if one concedes that the danger of the thermonuclear war mainly lies in the acts of irresponsible leaders. Anything that deters the irresponsible leader is a force for peace: a technologically sound civil defense therefore would help stabilize the balance of terror.

To the discrepancy between haves and have-nots, technology offers the nuclear energy revolution, with its possibility of autarky for haves and have-nots alike. How this might work to stabilize our metastable thermonuclear peace is suggested by the possible politic effect of the recently proposed Israeli desalting plant. The Arab states I should think would be much less set upon destroying the Jordan River Project if the Israelis had a desalination plant in reserve that would nullify the effect of such actions. In this connection, I think countries like ours can contribute very much. Our country will soon have to decide whether to continue to spend 5.5×10^9 per year for space exploration after our lunar landing. Is it too outrageous to suggest that some of this money be devoted to building huge nuclear desalting complexes in the arid ocean rims of the troubled world? If the plants are powered with breeder reactors, the out-of-pocket costs, once the plants are built, should be low enough to make large-scale agriculture feasible in these areas. I estimate that for 4×10^9 per year we could build enough desalting capacity to feed more than ten million new mouths per year (provided we use agricultural methods that husband water), and we would, thereby, help stabilize the metastable, bomb-imposed balance of terror.

Yet, I am afraid we technologists shall not satisfy our social engineers, who tell us that our Technological Fixes do not get to the heart of the problem; they are at best temporary expedients; they create new problems as they solve old ones; to put a Technological Fix into effect requires a positive social action. Eventually, social engineering, like the Supreme Court decision on desegregation, must be invoked to solve social problems. And, of course, our social engineers are right. Technology will never *replace* social engineering. But technology has provided and will continue to provide to the social engineer broader options, to make intractable social problems less intractable; perhaps, most of all, technology will buy time — that precious commodity that converts violent social revolution into acceptable social evolution.

Our country now recognizes and is mobilizing around the great social problems that corrupt and disfigure our human existence. It is natural that in this mobilization we should look first to the social engineer. But, unfortunately, the apparatus most readily available to the government, like the great federal laboratories, is technologically oriented, not socially oriented. I believe we have a great opportunity here; for, as I hope I have persuaded you, many of our seemingly social problems do admit of partial technological solutions. Our already deployed technological apparatus can contribute to the resolution of social questions. I plead, therefore, first for our government to deploy its laboratories, its hardware contractors, and its engineering universities around social problems. And I plead, secondly, for understanding and cooperation between technologist and social engineer. Even with all the help he can get from the technologist, the social engineer's problems are never really solved. It is only by cooperation between technologist and social engineer that we can hope to achieve what is the aim of all technologists and social engineers — a better society, and thereby, a better life, for all of us who are part of society.

5.   Why I Am Not Going to Buy a Computer

WENDELL BERRY

Wendell Berry may be the antithesis of the "technological fixer" Alvin Weinberg describes in the preceding chapter. His short essay — concise and spare — explains why he prefers a 30-year-old manual typewriter to a personal computer or even an electric typewriter. The essay, originally published in New England Review *and* Bread Loaf Quarterly, *was reprinted in* Harper's *and is followed by several letters to the editor that* Harper's *received, together with Berry's response. It is a simple, elegant indictment of centralization, bigness, and consumption-driven technological society that some will resonate with and others will utterly reject.*

A writer and farmer, Wendell Berry lives in Port Royal, Kentucky, and is a former member of the English faculty at the University of Kentucky. "Why I Am Not Going to Buy a Computer" is included in a book of his essays entitled, What Are People For? *Berry's other writings include several novels and collections of short stories, poems, and essays.*

Like almost everybody else, I am hooked to the energy corporations which I do not admire. I hope to become less hooked to them. In my work, I try to be as little hooked to them as possible. As a farmer, I do almost all of my work with horses. As a writer, I work with a pencil or a pen and a piece of paper.

My wife types my work on a Royal standard typewriter bought new in 1956 and as good now as it was then. As she types, she sees things that are wrong and marks them with small checks in the margins. She is my best critic because she is the one most familiar with my habitual errors and weaknesses. She also understands, sometimes better than I do, what *ought* to be said. We have, I think, a literary cottage industry that works well and pleasantly. I do not see anything wrong with it.

A number of people, by now, have told me that I could greatly improve things by buying a computer. My answer is that I am not going to do it. I have several reasons, and they are good ones.

The first is the one I mentioned at the beginning. I would hate to think that my work as a writer could not be done without a direct dependence on strip-mined coal. How could I write conscientiously against the rape of nature if I were, in the act of writing, implicated in the rape? For the same reason, it matters to me that my writing is done in the daytime, without electric light.

I do not admire the computer manufacturers a great deal more than I admire the energy industries. I have seen their advertisements, attempting to seduce struggling or failing farmers into the belief that they can solve their problems by buying yet another piece of expensive equipment. I am familiar with their propaganda campaigns that have put computers into public schools in need of books. That computers are expected to become as common as TV sets in "the future" does not impress me or matter to me. I do not own a TV set. I do not see that computers are bringing us one step nearer to anything that does matter to me: peace, economic justice, ecological health, political honesty, family and community stability, good work.

What would a computer cost me? More money, for one thing, than I can afford, and more than I wish to pay to people whom I do not admire. But the cost would not be just monetary. It is well understood that technological innovation always requires the discarding of the "old model" — the "old model" in this case being not just our old Royal standard, but my wife, my critic, my closest reader, my fellow worker. Thus (and I think this is typical of present-day technological innovation), what would be superseded would be not only something, but somebody. In order to be technologically up to date as a writer, I would have to sacrifice an association that I am dependent upon and that I treasure.

My final and perhaps my best reason for not owning a computer is that I do not wish to fool myself. I disbelieve, and therefore strongly resent, the assertion that I or anybody else could write better or more easily with a computer than with a pencil. I do not see why I should not be as scientific about this as the next fellow: when somebody has used a computer to write work that is demonstrably better than Dante's, and when this better is demonstrably attributable to the use of a computer, then I will speak of computers with a more respectful tone of voice, though I still will not buy one.

To make myself as plain as I can, I should give my standards for technological innovation in my own work. They are as follows:

1. The new tool should be cheaper than the one it replaces.
2. It should be at least as small in scale as the one it replaces.
3. It should do work that is clearly and demonstrably better than the one it replaces.
4. It should use less energy than the one it replaces.
5. If possible, it should use some form of solar energy, such as that of the body.
6. It should be repairable by a person of ordinary intelligence, provided that he or she has the necessary tools.
7. It should be purchasable and repairable as near to home as possible.
8. It should come from a small, privately owned shop or store that will take it back for maintenance and repair.
9. It should not replace or disrupt anything good that already exists, and this includes family and community relationships.

1987

After the forgoing essay, first published in the *New England Review and Bread Loaf Quarterly,* was reprinted in *Harper's,* the *Harper's* editors published the following letters in response and permitted me a reply.

W.B.

LETTERS

Wendell Berry provides writers enslaved by the computer with a handy alternative: Wife — a low-tech energy-saving device. Drop a pile of handwritten notes on Wife and you get back a finished manuscript, edited while it was typed. What computer can do that? Wife meets all of Berry's uncompromising standards for technological innovation: she's cheap, repairable near home, and good for the family structure. Best of all, Wife is politically correct because she breaks a writer's "direct dependence on strip-mined coal."

History teaches us that Wife can also be used to beat rugs and wash clothes by hand, thus eliminating the need for the vacuum cleaner and washing machine, two more nasty machines that threaten the act of writing.

Gordon Inkeles
Miranda, Calif.

I have no quarrel with Berry because he prefers to write with pencil and paper; that is his choice. But he implies that I and others are somehow impure because we choose to write on a computer. I do not admire the energy corporations, either. Their shortcoming is not that they produce electricity but how they go about it. They are poorly managed because they are blind to long-term consequences. To solve this problem, wouldn't it make more sense to correct the precise error they are making rather than simply ignore their product? I would be happy to join Berry in a protest against strip mining, but I intend to keep plugging this computer into the wall with a clear conscience.

James Rhoads
Battle Creek, Mich.

I enjoyed reading Berry's declaration of intent never to buy a personal computer in the same way that I enjoy reading about the belief systems of unfamiliar tribal cultures. I tried to imagine a tool that would meet Berry's criteria for superiority to his old manual typewriter. The clear winner is the quill pen. It is cheaper, smaller, more energy efficient, human powered, easily repaired, and non-disruptive of existing relationships.

Berry also requires that this tool must be "clearly and demonstrably better" than the one it replaces. But surely we all recognize by now that "better" is in the mind of the beholder. To the quill pen aficionado, the benefits obtained from elegant calligraphy might well outweigh all others.

I have no particular desire to see Berry use a word processor; if he doesn't like computers, that's fine with me. However, I do object to his portrayal of this reluctance as a moral virtue. Many of us have found that computers can be an invaluable tool in the fight to protect our environment. In addition to helping me write, my personal computer gives me access to up-to-the-minute reports on the workings of the EPA and the nuclear industry. I participate in electronic bulletin boards on which environmental activists discuss strategy and warn each other about urgent legislative issues. Perhaps Berry feels that the Sierra Club should eschew modern printing technology, which is highly wasteful of energy, in favor of having its members hand-copy the club's magazines and other mailings each month?

Nathaniel S. Borenstein
Pittsburgh, Pa.

The value of a computer to a writer is that it is a tool not for generating ideas but for typing and editing words. It is cheaper than a secretary (or a wife!) and arguably more fuel efficient. And it enables spouses who are not inclined to provide free labor more time to concentrate on *their* own work.

We should support alternatives both to coal-generated electricity and to IBM-style technocracy. But I am reluctant to entertain alternatives that presuppose the traditional subservience of one class to another. Let the PCs come and the wives and servants go seek more meaningful work.

Toby Koosman
Knoxville, Tenn.

Berry asks how he could write conscientiously against the rape of nature if in the act of writing on a computer he was implicated in the rape. I find it ironic that a writer who sees the underlying connectedness of things would allow his diatribe against computers to be published in a magazine that carries ads for the National Rural Electric Cooperative Association, Marlboro, Phillips Petroleum, McDonnell Douglas, and yes, even Smith Corona. If Berry rests comfortably at night, he must be using sleeping pills.

Bradley C. Johnson
Grand Forks, N.D.

WENDELL BERRY REPLIES:

The foregoing letters surprised me with the intensity of the feelings they expressed. According to the writers' testimony, there is nothing wrong with their computers; they are utterly satisfied with them and all that they stand for. My correspondents are certain that I am wrong and that I am, moreover, on the losing side, a side already relegated to the dustbin of history. And yet they grow huffy and condescending over my tiny dissent. What are they so anxious about?

I can only conclude that I have scratched the skin of a technological fundamentalism that, like other fundamentalisms, wishes to monopolize a whole society and, therefore, cannot tolerate the smallest difference of opinion. At the slightest hint of a threat to their complacency, they repeat, like a chorus of toads, the notes sounded by their leaders in industry. The past was gloomy, drudgery ridden, servile, meaningless, and slow. The present, thanks only to purchasable products, is meaningful, bright, lively, centralized, and fast. The future, thanks only to more purchasable products, is going to be even better. Thus consumers become salesmen, and the world is made safer for corporations.

I am also surprised by the meanness with which two of these writers refer to my wife. In order to imply that I am a tyrant, they suggest by both direct statement and innuendo that she is subservient, characterless, and stupid — a mere "device" easily forced to provide meaningless "free labor." I understand that it is impossible to make an adequate public defense of one's private life, and so I will only point out that there are a number of kinder possibilities that my critics have disdained to imagine: that my wife may do this work because she wants to and likes to; that she may find some use and some meaning in it; that she may not work for nothing. These gentlemen obviously think themselves feminists of the most correct and principled sort, and yet they do not hesitate to stereotype and insult, on the basis of one fact, a woman they do not know. They are audacious and irresponsible gossips.

In his letter, Bradley C. Johnson rushes past the possibility of sense in what I said in my essay by implying that I am or ought to be a fanatic. That I am a person of this century and implicated in many practices that I regret is fully acknowledged at the beginning of my essay. I did not say that I proposed to end forthwith all my involvement in harmful technology, for I do not know how to do that. I said merely that I want to limit such involvement and to a certain extent I do know how to do that. If some technology does damage to the world — as two of the [these] letters seem to agree that it does — then why is it not reasonable and indeed moral, to try to limit one's use of that technology? *Of course,* I think that I am right to do this.

I would not think so, obviously, if I agreed with Nathaniel S. Borenstein that "'better' is in the mind of the beholder." But if he truly believes this, I do not see why he bothers with his personal computer's "up-to-the-minute reports on the workings of the EPA and the nuclear industry" or why he wishes to be warned about "urgent legislative issues." According to his system, the "better" in a bureaucratic, industrial, or legislative mind is as good as the "better" in his. His mind apparently is being subverted by an objective standard of some sort, and he had better look out.

Borenstein does not say what he does after his computer has drummed him awake. I assume from his letter that he must send donations to conservation organizations and letters to officials. Like James Rhoads, at any rate, he has a clear conscience. But this is what is wrong with the conservation movement. It has a clear conscience. The guilty are always other people, and the wrong is always somewhere else, that is why Borenstein finds his "electronic bulletin board" so handy. To the conservation movement, it is only production that causes environmental degradation; the consumption that supports the production is rarely acknowledged to be at fault. The ideal of the run-of-the-mill conservationist is to impose restraints upon production without limiting consumption or burdening the consciences of consumers.

But virtually all of our consumption now is extravagant, and virtually all of it consumes the world. It is not beside the point that most electrical power comes from strip-mined coal. The history of the exploitation of the Appalachian coal fields is long, and it is available to readers. I do not see how anyone can read it and plug in any appliance with a clear conscience. If Rhoads can do so, that does not mean that his conscience is clear; it means that his conscience is not working.

To the extent that we consume, in our present circumstances, we are guilty. To the extent that we guilty consumers are conservationists, we are absurd. But what can we do? Must we go on writing letters to politicians and donating to conservation organizations until the majority of our fellow citizens agree with us? Or can we do something directly to solve our share of the problem?

I am a conservationist. I believe wholeheartedly in putting pressure on the politicians and in maintaining the conservation organizations. But I wrote my little essay partly in distrust of centralization. I don't think that the government and the conservation organizations alone will ever make us a conserving society. Why do I need a centralized computer system to alert me to environmental crises? That I live every hour of every day in an environmental crisis I know from all my senses. Why then is not my first duty to reduce, so far as I can, my own consumption?

Finally, it seems to me that none of my correspondents recognizes the innovativeness of my essay. If the use of a computer is a new idea, then a newer idea is not to use one.

6. Technology and the Tragic View

SAMUEL C. FLORMAN

In Part II, which follows this chapter, two writers of an earlier generation engage in a famous debate that, in many ways, epitomizes the bitter divisions between the advocates and critics of technology in the late 1960s and early 1970s. Though no longer tied to the domestic conflict over U.S. participation in the Vietnam War or to the social revolution that was then raging in the United States, these pro- and anti-technology divisions still exist today. However, to treat a subject as complex as the relations of technology and society in such simplistic, for-or-against terms is ultimately less than satisfying. Samuel Florman's insightful essay, "Technology and the Tragic View," taken from his book Blaming Technology, *suggests another approach. Florman draws on the classical Greek concept of tragedy to develop a new perspective on technology. In the tragic view of life, says Florman,*

> *[it] is man's destiny to die, to be defeated by the forces of the universe. But in challenging his destiny, in being brave, determined, ambitious, resourceful, the tragic hero shows to what heights a human being can soar. This is an inspiration to the rest of us. After witnessing a tragedy we feel good, because the magnificence of the human spirit has been demonstrated.*

The tragic view accepts responsibility but does not seek to cast blame. It challenges us to do, with caution, what needs to be done, and to consider at the same time the consequences of not acting. Florman's view is ultimately an affirmation of the value of technology in human life, tempered by a recognition of its limits in sustaining human happiness. It is a uniquely constructive approach to thinking about technology and society and a fitting note on which to close the first section of this book Samuel C. Florman, author of The Existential Pleasures of Engineering, *is a practicing engineer and chairman of Kreisler Borg Florman Construction Company in Scarsdale, New York. His more than one hundred articles dealing with the relationship of technology to general culture have appeared in professional journals and popular magazines. Florman, born in New York City in 1925, is a fellow of the American Society of Civil Engineers and a member of the New York Academy of Sciences. He holds a bachelor's degree and a civil engineer's degree from Dartmouth College and an M.A. in English literature from Columbia University.*

The blaming of technology starts with the making of myths — most importantly, the myth of the technological imperative and the myth of the technocratic elite. In spite of the injunctions of common sense, and contrary to the evidence at hand, the myths flourish.

False premises are followed by confused deductions — a maligning of the scientific view; the assertion that small is beautiful; the mistake about job enrichment; an excessive zeal for government regulation; the hostility of feminists toward engineering; and the wishful thinking of the Club of Rome. These in turn are followed by distracted rejoinders from the technological community, culminating in the bizarre exaltation of engineering ethics.

In all of this it is difficult to determine how much is simple misunderstanding and how much is willful evasion of the truth, a refusal to face up to the harsh realities that underlie life, not only in a technological age, but in every age since the beginning of civilization.

Out of the confusion has come a dialogue of sorts, shaped around views that are deemed "pro"-technology or "anti," "optimistic" or "pessimistic." I believe that we should be thinking in different terms altogether.

House & Garden magazine, in celebration of the American Bicentennial, devoted its July 1976 issue to the topic "American Know-How." The editors invited me to contribute an article, and enticed by the opportunity to address a new audience, plus the offer of a handsome fee, I accepted. We agreed that the title of my piece would be "Technology and the Human Adventure," and I thereupon embarked on a strange adventure of my own.

I thought that it would be appropriate to begin my Bicentennial-inspired essay with a discussion of technology in the time of the Founding Fathers, so I went to the library and immersed myself in the works of Benjamin Franklin, surely the most famous technologist of America's early days. Remembering stories from my childhood about Ben Franklin the clever tinkerer, I expected to find a pleasant recounting of inventions and successful experiments, a cheering tale of technological triumphs. I found such a tale, to be sure, but along with it I found a record of calamities *caused by* the technological advances of his day.

In several letters and essays, Franklin expressed concern about fire, an ever-threatening scourge in Colonial times. Efficient sawmills made it possible to build frame houses, more versatile and economical than log cabins — but less fire-resistant. Advances in transport made it possible for people to crowd these frame houses together in cities. Cleverly conceived fireplaces, stoves, lamps, and warming pans made life more comfortable, but contributed to the likelihood of catastrophic fires in which many lives were lost.

To deal with this problem, Franklin recommended architectural modifications to make houses more fireproof. He proposed the licensing and supervision of chimney sweeps and the establishment of volunteer fire companies, well supplied and trained in the science of firefighting. As is well known, he invented the lightning rod. In other words, he proposed technological ways of coping with the unpleasant consequences of technology. He applied Yankee ingenuity to solve problems arising out of Yankee ingenuity.

In Franklin's writings I found other examples of technological advances that brought with them unanticipated problems. Lead poisoning was a peril. Contaminated rum was discovered coming from distilleries where lead parts had been substituted for wood in the distilling apparatus. Drinking water collected from lead-coated roofs was also making people seriously ill.

The advancing techniques of medical science were often a mixed blessing, as they are today. Early methods of vaccination for smallpox, for example, entailed the danger of the vaccinated person dying from the artificially induced disease. (In a particularly poignant article, Franklin was at pains to point out that his four-year-old son's death from smallpox was attributable to the boy's *not* having been vaccinated and did not result, as rumor had it, from vaccination itself.)

After a while, I put aside the writings of Franklin and turned my attention to American know-how in the nineteenth century. I became engrossed in the story of the early days of steamboat transport. This important step forward in American technology was far from being the unsullied triumph that it appears to be in our popular histories.

Manufacturers of the earliest high-pressure steam engines often used materials of inferior quality. They were slow to recognize the weakening of boiler shells caused by rivet holes, and the danger of using wrought-iron shells together with cast iron heads that had a different coefficient of expansion. Safety valve openings were often not properly proportioned, and gauges had a tendency to malfunction. Even well-designed equipment quickly became defective through the effects of corrosion and sediment. On top of it all, competition for prestige led to racing between boats, and during a race the usual practice was to tie down the safety valve so that excessive steam pressure would not be relieved.

From 1825 to 1830, 42 recorded explosions killed upward of 270 persons. When, in 1830, an explosion aboard the *Helen McGregor* near Memphis killed more than 50 passengers, public outrage forced the federal government to take action. Funds were granted to the Franklin Institute of Philadelphia to purchase apparatus needed to conduct experiments on steam boilers. This was a notable event, the first technological research grant made by the federal government.

The institute made a comprehensive report in 1838, but it was not until 14 years later that a workable bill was passed by Congress providing at least minimal safeguards for the citizenry. Today we may wonder why the process took so long, but at the time Congress was still uncertain about its right, under the interstate commerce provision of the Constitution, to control the activities of individual entrepreneurs.

When I turned from steamboats to railroads I found another long-forgotten story of catastrophe. Not only were there problems with the trains themselves, but the roadbeds, and particularly the bridges, made even the shortest train journey a hazardous adventure. In the late 1860s more than 25 American bridges were collapsing each year, with appalling loss of life. In 1873 the American Society of Civil Engineers set up a special commission to address the problem, and eventually the safety of our bridges came to be taken for granted.

The more I researched the history of American know-how, the more I perceived that practically every technological advance had unexpected and unwanted side effects. Along with each triumph of mechanical genius came an inevitable portion of death and destruction. Instead of becoming discouraged, however, our forebears seemed to be resolute in confronting the adverse consequences of their own inventiveness. I was impressed by this pattern of progress/setback/renewed-creative-effort. It seemed to have a special message for our day, and I made it the theme of my essay for *House & Garden.*

No matter how many articles one has published, and no matter how much one likes the article most recently submitted, waiting to hear from an editor is an anxious experience. In this case, as it turned out, I had reason to be apprehensive. I soon heard from one of the editors who, although she tried to be encouraging, was obviously distressed. "We liked the part about tenacity and ingenuity," she said, "but, oh dear, *all those disasters* — they are so depressing."

I need not go into the details of what follows: the rewriting, the telephone conferences, the rewriting — the gradual elimination of accidents and casualty statistics, and a subtle change in emphasis. I retreated, with some honor intact I like to believe, until the article was deemed to be suitably upbeat.

I should have known that the Bicentennial issue of *House & Garden* was not the forum in which to consider the dark complexities of technological change. My piece was to appear side by side with such articles as "A House That Has Everything," "Live Longer, Look Younger," and "Everything's Coming Up Roses" (devoted to a review of Gloria Vanderbilt's latest designs).

In the United States today magazines like *House & Garden* speak for those, and to those, who are optimistic about technology. Through technology we get better dishwashers, permanent-press blouses, and rust-proof lawn furniture. "Better living through chemistry," the old Du Pont commercial used to say. Not only is *House & Garden* optimistic, that is, hopeful, about technology; it is cheerfully optimistic. There is no room in its pages for failure, or even for struggle, and in this view it speaks for many Americans, perhaps a majority. This is the lesson I learned — or I should say, relearned — in the Bicentennial year.

Much has been written about the shallow optimism of the United States: about life viewed as a Horatio Alger success story or as a romantic movie with a happy ending. This optimism is less widespread than it used to be, particularly as it relates to technology. Talk of nuclear warfare and a poisoned environment tends to dampen one's enthusiasm. Yet optimistic materialism remains a powerful force in American life. The poll-takers tell us that people believe technology is, on balance, beneficial. And we all know a lot of people who, even at this troublesome moment in history, define happiness in terms of their ability to accumulate new gadgets. The business community, anxious to sell merchandise, spares no expense in promoting a gleeful consumerism.

Side by side with what I have come to think of as *House & Garden* optimism, there is a mood that we might call *New York Review of Books* pessimism. Our intellectual journals are full of gloomy tracts that depict a society debased by technology. Our health is being ruined, according to this view, our landscape despoiled, and our social institutions laid waste. We are forced to do demeaning work and consume unwanted products. We are being dehumanized. This is happening because a technological demon has escaped from human control or, in a slightly different version, because evil technocrats are leading us astray.

It is clear that in recent years the resoluteness exhibited by Benjamin Franklin, and other Americans of similarly robust character, has been largely displaced by a foolish optimism on the one hand and an abject pessimism on the other. These two opposing outlooks are actually manifestations of the same defect in the American character. One is the obverse, the "flip side," of the other. Both reflect a flaw that I can best describe as immaturity.

A young child is optimistic, naively assuming that his needs can always be satisfied and that his parents have it within their power to "make things right." A child frustrated becomes petulant. With the onset of puberty a morose sense of disillusionment is apt to take hold. Sulky pessimism is something we associate with the teenager.

It is not surprising that many inhabitants of the United States, a rich nation with seemingly boundless frontiers, should have evinced a childish optimism, and declared their faith in technology, endowing it with the reassuring power of a parent — also regarding it with the love of a child for a favorite toy. It then follows that technological setbacks would be greeted by some with the naive assumption that all would turn out for the best and by others with peevish declarations of despair. Intellectuals have been in the forefront of this childish display, but every segment of society has been caught up in it. Technologists themselves have not been immune. In the speeches of nineteenth-century engineers, we find bombastic promises that make us blush. Today the profession is torn between a blustering optimism and a confused guilt

The past 50 years have seen many hopes dashed, but we can see in retrospect that they were unrealistic hopes. We simply cannot make use of coal without killing miners and polluting the air. Neither can we manufacture solar panels without worker fatalities and environmental degradation. (We assume that it will be less than with coal, but we are not sure.) We cannot build highways or canals or airports without despoiling the landscape. Not only have we learned that environmental dangers are inherent in every technological advance, but we find that we are fated to be dissatisfied with much of what we produce because our tastes keep changing. The sparkling, humming, paved metropolises of science fiction — even if they could be realized — are not, after all, the home to which humankind aspires. It seems that many people find such an environment "alienating." There can never be a technologically based Utopia because we discover belatedly that we cannot agree on what form that Utopia might take.

To express our disillusionment we have invented a new word: "trade-off." It is an ugly word, totally without grace, but it signifies, I believe the beginning of maturity for American society.

It is important to remember that our disappointments have not been limited to technology. (This is a fact that the antitechnologists usually choose to ignore.) Wonderful dreams attended the birth of the New Deal, and later the founding of the United Nations, yet we have since awakened to face unyielding economic and political difficulties. Socialism has been discredited, as was laissez-faire capitalism before it. We have been bitterly disappointed by the labor movement, the educational establishment, efforts at crime prevention, the ministrations of psychiatry, and most recently by the abortive experiments of the so-called counterculture. We have come face to face with *limits* that we had presumed to hope might not exist.

Those of us who have lived through the past 50 years have passed personally from youthful presumptuousness to mature skepticism at the very moment that American society has been going through the same transition. We have to be careful not to define the popular mood in terms of our personal sentiments, but I do not think I am doing that when I observe the multiple disenchantments of our time. We also have to be careful not to deprecate youthful enthusiasm, which is a force for good, along with immaturity, which is tolerable only in the young.

It can be argued that there was for a while good reason to hold out hope for Utopia, since modern science and technology appeared to be completely new factors in human existence. But now that they have been given a fair trial, we perceive their inherent limitations. The human condition is the human condition still.

To persist in saying that we are optimistic or pessimistic about technology is to acknowledge that we will not grow up.

I suggest that an appropriate response to our new wisdom is neither optimism nor pessimism, but rather the espousal of an attitude that has traditionally been associated with men and women of noble character — the tragic view of life.

As a student in high school, and later in college, I found it difficult to comprehend what my teachers told me about comedy and tragedy. Comedy, they said, expresses despair. When there is no hope, we make jokes. We depict people as puny, ridiculous creatures. We laugh to keep from crying.

Tragedy, on the other hand, is uplifting. It depicts heroes wrestling with fate. It is man's destiny to die, to be defeated by the forces of the universe. But in challenging his destiny, in being brave, determined, ambitious, resourceful, the tragic hero shows to what heights a human being can soar. This is an inspiration to the rest of us. After witnessing a tragedy we feel good, because the magnificence of the human spirit has been demonstrated. Tragic drama is an affirmation of the value of life.

Students pay lip service to this theory and give the expected answers in examinations. But sometimes the idea seems to fly in the face of reason. How can we say we feel better after Oedipus puts out his eyes, or Othello kills his beloved wife and commits suicide, than we do after laughing heartily over a bedroom farce?

Yet this concept, which is so hard to grasp in the classroom, where students are young and the environment is serene, rings true in the world where mature people wrestle with burdensome problems.

I do not intend to preach a message of stoicism. The tragic view is not to be confused with world-weary resignation. As Moses Hadas, a great classical scholar of a generation ago, wrote about the Greek tragedians: "Their gloom is not fatalistic pessimism but an adult confrontation of reality, and their emphasis is not on the grimness of life but on the capacity of great figures to adequate themselves to it."[1]

It is not an accident that tragic drama flourished in societies that were dynamic: Periclean Athens, Elizabethan England, and the France of Louis XIV.

For tragedy speaks of ambition, effort, and unquenchable spirit. Technological creativity is one manifestation of this spirit, and it is only a dyspeptic antihumanist who can feel otherwise. Even the Greeks, who for a while placed technologists low on the social scale, recognized the glory of creative engineering. Prometheus is one of the quintessential tragic heroes. In viewing technology through a tragic prism we are at once exalted by its accomplishments and sobered by its limitations. We thus ally ourselves with the spirit of great ages past.

The fate of Prometheus, as well as that of most tragic heroes, is associated with the concept of *hubris*, "overweening pride." Yet pride, which in drama invariably leads to a fall, is not considered sinful by the great tragedians. It is an essential element of humanity's greatness. It is what inspires heroes to confront the universe, to challenge the status quo. Prometheus defied Zeus and brought technological knowledge to the human race. Prometheus was a revolutionary. So were Gutenberg, Watt, Edison, and Ford. Technology is revolutionary. Therefore, hostility toward technology is antirevolutionary, which is to say it is reactionary. This charge is currently being leveled against environmentalists and other enemies of technology. Since antitechnologists are traditionally "liberal" in their attitudes, the idea that they are reactionary confronts us with a paradox.

The tragic view does not shrink from paradox; it teaches us to live with ambiguity. It is at once revolutionary and cautionary. *Hubris*, as revealed in tragic drama, is an essential element of creativity; it is also a tragic flaw that contributes to the failure of human enterprise. Without effort, however, and daring, we are nothing. Walter Kerr has spoken of "tragedy's commitment to freedom, to the unflinching exploration of the possible." "At the heart of tragedy," he writes, "feeding it energy, stands godlike man passionately desiring a state of affairs more perfect than any that now exists."[2]

This description of the tragic hero well serves, in my opinion, as a definition of the questing technologist.

An aspect of the tragic view that particularly appeals to me is its reluctance to place blame. Those people who hold pessimistic views about technology are forever reproaching others, if not individual engineers, then the "technocratic establishment," the "megastate," "the pentagon of power," or some equally amorphous entity. Everywhere they look they see evil intent.

There is evil in the world, of course, but most of our disappointments with technology come when decent people are trying to act constructively. "The essentially tragic fact," says Hegel, "is not so much the war of good with evil as the war of good with good."

Pesticides serve to keep millions of poor people from starving. To use pesticides is good; to oppose them when they create havoc in the food chain is also good. To drill for oil and to transport it across the oceans is good, since petroleum provides life-saving chemicals and heat for homes. To prevent oil spills is also good. Nuclear energy is good, as is the attempt to eliminate radioactivity. To seek safety is a worthy goal; but in a world of limited resources, the pursuit of economy is also worthy. We are constantly accusing each other of villainy when we should be consulting together on how best to solve our common problems.

Although the tragic view shuns blame, it does not shirk responsibility. "The fault, dear Brutus, is not in our stars, but in ourselves. . . ." We are accountable for what we do or, more often, for what we neglect to do. The most shameful feature of the antitechnological creed is that it so often fails to consider the consequences of not taking action. The lives lost or wasted that might have been saved by exploiting our resources are the responsibility of those who counsel inaction. The tragic view is consistent with good citizenship. It advocates making the most of our opportunities; it challenges us to do the work that needs doing.

Life, it may be said, is not a play. Yet we are constantly talking about roles — role-playing, role models, and so forth. It is a primordial urge to want to play one's part. The outlook I advocate sees value in many different people playing many different parts. A vital society, like a meaningful drama, feeds on diversity. Each participant contributes to the body social: scientist, engineer, farmer, craftsman, laborer, politician, jurist, teacher, artist, merchant, entertainer. . . . The pro-growth industrialist and the environmentalist are both needed, and in a strange way they need each other.

Out of conflict comes resolution; out of variety comes health. This is the lesson of the natural world. It is the moral of ecological balance; it is also the moral of great drama. We cannot but admire Caesar, Brutus, and Antony all together. So should we applaud the guardians of our wilderness, even as we applaud the creators of dams and paper mills. I am a builder, but I feel for those who are afraid of building, and I admire those who want to endow all building with grace.

George Steiner, in *The Death of Tragedy* (1961), claimed that the tragic spirit was rendered impotent by Christianity's promise of salvation. But I do not think that most people today are thinking in terms of salvation. They are thinking of doing the best they can in a world that promises neither damnation nor transcendent victories, but instead confronts us with both perils and opportunities for achievement. In such a world the tragic spirit is very much alive. Neither optimism nor pessimism is a worthy alternative to this noble spirit.

We use words to communicate, but sometimes they are not as precise as we pretend, and then we confuse ourselves and each other. "Optimism," "pessimism," "tragic view" — these are mere sounds or scratches on paper. The way we feel is not adequately defined by such sounds or scratches. René Dubos used to write a column for *The American Scholar* that he called "The Despairing Optimist." I seem to recall that he once gave his reasons for not calling it "The Hopeful Pessimist," although I cannot remember what they were. What really counts, I suppose, is not what we say, or even what we feel, but what we want to do.

By saying that I espouse the tragic view of technology I mean to ally myself with those who, aware of the dangers and without foolish illusions about what can be accomplished, still want to move on, actively seeking to realize our constantly changing vision of a more satisfactory society. I mean to oppose those who would evade harsh truths by intoning platitudes. I particularly mean to challenge those who enjoy the benefits of technology but refuse to accept responsibility for its consequences.

Earlier in this essay I mentioned the problems I encountered in preparing an article for *House & Garden,* and I would like to close by quoting the last few lines from that much-rewritten opus. The prose is somewhat florid, but please remember that it was written in celebration of the American Bicentennial:

For all our apprehensions, we have no choice but to press ahead. We must do so, first, in the name of compassion. By turning our backs on technological change, we would be expressing our satisfaction with current world levels of hunger, disease, and privation. Further, we must press ahead in the name of human adventure. Without experimentation and change our existence would be a dull business. We simply cannot stop while there are masses to feed and diseases to conquer, seas to explore and heavens to survey.

The editors of *Home & Garden* thought I was being optimistic. I knew that I was being tragic, but I did not argue the point.

NOTES

1. Moses Hadas, *A History of Greek Literature* (New York: Columbia University Press, 1950), p. 75.
2. Walter Kerr, *Tragedy and Comedy* (New York: Simon and Schuster, 1967), p. 107.

PART II
DEBATING TECHNOLOGY: 1960S STYLE

Chapter 7, Emmanuel Mesthene's essay, "The Role of Technology in Society," and the piece that follows it, "Technology: The Opiate of the Intellectuals" by John McDermott (Chapter 8), constitute a classic debate about the role of technology in society. The articles date from the late 1960s, when the war in Vietnam was in full swing and intellectual and political life in the United States was torn by bitter conflicts between the "establishment" and the "New Left."

The two articles are included here, as they have been in every edition of *Technology and the Future* since 1972, as a means illustrating in sharp relief the different perspectives on technology of the powerful and powerless. Mesthene, a Harvard professor and former RAND Corporation analyst, funded by a large grant from IBM, is comfortable with technology. He and his colleagues feel that technology is something that they can control and use. It is a neutral tool, which can be employed for purposes that are good as well those that are evil, and which often has both positive and negative effects on society.

McDermott, on the other hand, sees technology from the lower rungs of society's ladder. A professor of labor studies writing in the then–radical left *New York Review of Books,* his viewpoint is that of the factory worker struggling to make ends meet rather than the highly paid industry executive. He is the foot soldier slogging through the jungles of Vietnam in a war whose purpose he doesn't understand, rather than the systems analyst comfortably ensconced in the Pentagon or in RAND's Santa Monica headquarters. Technology, seen from McDermott's side of the fence, is hardly a neutral tool; it is the means by which those in power maintain their control of society while perpetuating social injustice.

Some of the illustrations the authors use in these two essays — which were instantly recognizable and conjured up clear images to readers of their day — may be unfamiliar to today's college students. But the issues they raise and the differing perspectives on technology of the rulers and the ruled are as important today as they were three decades ago.

7. The Role of Technology in Society

EMMANUEL G. MESTHENE

Emmanuel Mesthene's essay, "The Role of Technology in Society," originated as the overview section of the fourth annual report of the Harvard Program on Technology and Society, an interdisciplinary program of academic studies funded by a $5 million grant from IBM. Mesthene was the program's director, and this essay was his general statement of what the program had learned, during its first four years, about the implications of technological change for society.

According to Mesthene, technology appears to induce social change in two ways: by creating new opportunities and by generating new problems for individuals and for societies. "It has both positive and negative effects, and it usually has the two at the same time and in virtue of each other." By enlarging the realm of goal choice, or by altering the relative costs associated with different values, technology can induce value change. In all areas, technology is seen to have two faces, one positive and one negative.

Emmanuel G. Mesthene directed the Harvard Program on Technology and Society from 1964 through 1974, following 11 years with the Rand Corporation. He joined Rutgers University in 1974, serving as dean of Livingston College for several years, then as distinguished professor of philosophy and professor of management. Mesthene died in 1990. Among his books are Technological Change: Its Impact on Man and Society *(1970) and* How Language Makes Us Know *(1964).*

SOCIAL CHANGE

Three Unhelpful Views about Technology

While a good deal of research is aimed at discerning the particular effects of technological change on industry, government, or education, systematic inquiry devoted to seeing these effects together and to assessing their implications for contemporary society as a whole is relatively recent and does not enjoy the strong methodology and richness of theory and data that mark more established fields of scholarship. It therefore often has to contend with facile or one-dimensional views about what technology means for society. Three such views, which are prevalent at the present time, may be mildly caricatured somewhat as follows.

The first holds that technology is an unalloyed blessing for man and society. Technology is seen as the motor of all progress, as holding the solution to most of our social problems, as helping to liberate the individual from the clutches of a complex and highly organized society, and as the source of permanent prosperity; in short, as the promise of utopia in our time. This view has its modern origins in the social philosophies of such nineteenth-century thinkers as Saint Simon, Karl Marx, and Auguste Comte. It tends to be held by many scientists and engineers, by many military leaders and aerospace industrialists, by people who believe that man is fully in command of his tools and his destiny, and by many of the devotees of modern techniques of "scientific management."

A second view holds that technology is an unmitigated curse. Technology is said to rob people of their jobs, their privacy, their participation in democratic government, and even, in the end, their dignity as human beings. It is seen as autonomous and uncontrollable, as fostering materialistic values and as destructive of religion, as bringing about a technocratic society and bureaucratic state in which the individual is increasingly submerged, and as threatening, ultimately, to poison nature and blow up the world. This view is akin to historical "back-to-nature" attitudes toward the world and is propounded mainly by artists, literary commentators, popular social critics, and existentialist philosophers. It is becoming increasingly attractive to many of our youth, and it tends to be held, understandably enough, by segments of the population that have suffered dislocation as a result of technological change.

The third view is of a different sort. It argues that technology as such is not worthy of special notice, because it has been well recognized as a factor in social change at least since the Industrial Revolution, because it is unlikely that the social effects of computers will be nearly so traumatic as the introduction of the factory system in eighteenth-century England, because research has shown that technology has done little to accelerate the rate of economic productivity since the 1880s, because there has been no significant change in recent decades in the time periods between invention and widespread adoption of new technology, and because improved communications and higher levels of education make people much more adaptable than heretofore to new ideas and to new social reforms required by technology.

While this view is supported by a good deal of empirical evidence, however, it tends to ignore a number of social, cultural, psychological, and political effects of technological change that are less easy to identify with precision. It thus reflects the difficulty of coming to grips with a new or broadened subject matter by means of concepts and intellectual categories designed to deal with older and different subject matters. This view tends to be held by historians, for whom continuity is an indispensable methodological assumption, and by many economists, who find that their instruments measure some things quite well while those of the other social sciences do not yet measure much of anything.

Stripped of caricature, each of these views contains a measure of truth and reflects a real aspect of the relationship of technology and society. Yet they are oversimplifications that do not contribute much to understanding. One can find empirical evidence to support each of them without gaining much knowledge about the actual mechanism by which technology leads to social change or significant insight into its implications for the future. All three remain too uncritical or too partial to guide inquiry. Research and analysis lead to more differentiated conclusions and reveal more subtle relationships.

* * *

How Technological Change Impinges on Society

It is clearly possible to sketch a more adequate hypothesis about the interaction of technology and society than the partial views outlined [here]. Technological change would appear to induce or "motor" social change in two principal ways. New technology creates new opportunities for men and societies, and it also generates new problems for them. It has both positive and negative effects, and it usually has the two *at the same time and in virtue of each other.* Thus, industrial technology strengthens the economy, as our measures of growth and productivity show. . . . However, it also induces changes in the relative importance of individual supplying sectors in the economy as new techniques of production alter the amounts and kinds of materials, parts and components, energy, and service inputs used by each industry to produce its output. It thus tends to bring about dislocations of businesses and people as a result of changes in industrial patterns and in the structure of occupations.

The close relationship between technological and social change itself helps to explain why any given technological development is likely to have both positive and negative effects. The usual sequence is that (1) technological advance creates a new opportunity to achieve some desired goal; (2) this requires (except in trivial cases) alterations in social organization if advantage is to be taken of the new opportunity, (3) which means that the functions of existing social structures will be interfered with, (4) with the result that other goals, which were served by the older structures, are now only inadequately achieved.

As the Meyer-Kain[1] study has shown, for example, improved transportation technology and increased ownership of private automobiles have increased the mobility of businesses and individuals. This has led to altered patterns of industrial and residential location, so that older unified cities are being increasingly transformed into larger metropolitan complexes. The new opportunities for mobility are largely denied to the poor and black populations of the core cities, however, partly for economic reasons, and partly as a result of restrictions on choice of residence by blacks, thus leading to persistent black unemployment despite a generally high level of economic activity. Cities are thus increasingly unable to perform their traditional functions of providing employment opportunities for all segments of their populations and an integrated social environment that can temper ethnic and racial differences. The new urban complexes are neither fully viable economic units nor effective political organizations able to upgrade and integrate their core populations into new economic and social structures. The resulting instability is further aggravated by modern mass communications technology, which heightens the expectations of the poor and the fears of the well-to-do and adds frustration and bitterness to the urban crisis. . . .

In all such cases, technology creates a new opportunity and a new problem at the same time. That is why isolating the opportunity or the problem and construing it as the whole answer is ultimately obstructive of rather than helpful to understanding.

How Society Reacts to Technological Change

The heightened prominence of technology in our society makes the interrelated tasks of profiting from its opportunities and containing its dangers a major intellectual and political challenge of our time.

Failure of society to respond to the opportunities created by new technology means that much actual or potential technology lies fallow, that is, is not used at all or is not used to its full capacity. This can mean that potentially solvable problems are left unsolved and potentially achievable goals unachieved, because we waste our technological resources or use them inefficiently. A society has at least as much stake in the efficient utilization of technology as in that of its natural or human resources.

There are often good reasons, of course, for not developing or utilizing a particular technology. The mere fact that it can be developed is not sufficient reason for doing so. . . .

But there are also cases where technology lies fallow because existing social structures are inadequate to exploit the opportunities it offers. . . . Community institutions wither for want of interest and participation by residents. City agencies are unable to marshal the skills and take the systematic approach needed to deal with new and intensified problems of education, crime control, and public welfare. Business corporations, finally, which are organized around the expectation of private profit, are insufficiently motivated to bring new technology and management know-how to bear on urban projects where the benefits will be largely social. All these factors combine to dilute what may otherwise be a genuine desire to apply our best knowledge and adequate resources to the resolution of urban tensions and the eradication of poverty in the nation. . . .

Containing the Negative Effects of Technology

The kinds and magnitude of the negative effects of technology are no more independent of the institutional structures and cultural attitudes of society than is realization of the new opportunities that technology offers. In our society, there are individuals or individual firms always on the lookout for new technological opportunities, and large corporations hire scientists and engineers to invent such opportunities. In deciding whether to develop a new technology, individual entrepreneurs engage in calculations of expected benefits and expected costs to themselves, and proceed if the former are likely to exceed the latter. Their calculations do not take adequate account of the probable benefits and costs of the new developments to others than themselves or to society generally. These latter are what economists call external benefits and costs.

The external benefits potential in new technology will thus not be realized by the individual developer and will rather accrue to society as a result of deliberate social action, as has been argued above. Similarly with the external costs. In minimizing only expected costs to himself, the individual decision maker helps to contain only some of the potentially negative effects of the new technology. The external costs and therefore the negative effects on society at large are not of principal concern to him and, in our society, are not expected to be.

Most of the consequences of technology that are causing concern at the present time — pollution of the environment, potential damage to the ecology of the planet, occupational and social dislocations, threats to the privacy and political significance of the individual, social and psychological malaise — are negative externalities of this kind. They are with us in large measure because it has not been anybody's explicit business to foresee and anticipate them. They have fallen between the stools of innumerable individual decisions to develop individual technologies for individual purposes without explicit attention to what all these decisions add up to for society as a whole and for people as human beings. This freedom of individual decision making is a value that we have cherished and that is built into the institutional fabric of our society. The negative effects of technology that we deplore are a measure of what this traditional freedom is beginning to cost us. They are traceable, less to some mystical autonomy presumed to lie in technology, and much more to the autonomy that our economic and political institutions grant to individual decision making. . . .

Measures to control and mitigate the negative effects of technology, however, often appear to threaten freedoms that our traditions still take for granted as inalienable rights of men and good societies, however much they may have been tempered in practice by the social pressures of modern times; the freedom of the market, the freedom of private enterprise, the freedom of the scientist to follow truth wherever it may lead, and the freedom of the individual to pursue his fortune and decide his fate. There is thus set up a tension between the need to control technology and our wish to preserve our values, which leads some people to conclude that technology is inherently inimical to human values. The political effect of this tension takes the form of inability to adjust our decision-making structures to the realities of technology so as to take maximum advantage of the opportunities it offers and so that we can act to contain its potential ill effects before they become so pervasive and urgent as to seem uncontrollable.

To understand why such tensions are so prominent a social consequence of technological change, it becomes necessary to look explicitly at the effects of technology on social and individual values.

VALUES

* * *

Technology as a Cause of Value Change

Technology has a direct impact on values by virtue of its capacity for creating new opportunities. By making possible what was not possible before, it offers individuals and society new options to choose from. For example, space technology makes it possible for the first time to go to the moon or to communicate by satellite and thereby adds those two new options to the spectrum of choices available to society. By adding new options in this way, technology can lead to changes in values in the same way that the appearance of new dishes on the heretofore standard menu of one's favorite restaurant can lead to changes in one's tastes and choices of food. Specifically, technology can lead to value change either (1) by bringing some previously unattainable goal within the realm of choice or (2) by making some values easier to implement than heretofore, that is, by changing the costs associated with realizing them. . . .

One example related to the effect of technological change on values is implicit in our concept of democracy. The ideal we associate with the old New England town meeting is that each citizen should have a direct voice in political decisions. Since this has not been possible, we have elected representatives to serve our interests and vote our opinions. Sophisticated computer technology, however, now makes possible rapid and efficient collection and analysis of voter opinion and could eventually provide for "instant voting" by the whole electorate on any issue presented to it via television a few hours before. It thus raises the possibility of instituting a system of direct democracy and gives rise to tensions between those who would be violently opposed to such a prospect and those who are already advocating some system of participatory democracy.

This new technological possibility challenges us to clarify what we mean by democracy. Do we construe it as the will of an undifferentiated majority, as the resultant of transient coalitions of different interest groups representing different value commitments, as the considered judgment of the people's elected representatives, or as by and large the kind of government we actually have in the United States, minus the flaws in it that we would like to correct? By bringing us face to face with such questions, technology has the effect of calling society's bluff and thereby preparing the ground for changes in its values.

In the case where technological change alters the relative costs of implementing different values, it impinges on inherent contradictions in our value system. To pursue the same example, modern technology can enhance the values we associate with democracy. But it can also enhance another American value — that of "secular rationality," as sociologists call it — by facilitating the use of scientific and technical expertise in the process of political decision making. This can in turn further reduce citizen participation in the democratic process. Technology thus has the effect of facing us with contradictions in our value system and of calling for deliberate attention to their resolution.

* * *

ECONONIC AND POLITICAL ORGANIZATION

The Enlarged Scope of Public Decision Making

When technology brings about social changes (as described in the first section of this essay) that impinge on our existing system of values (in ways reviewed in the second section), it poses for society a number of problems that are ultimately political in nature. The term "political" is used here in the broadest sense: it encompasses all of the decision-making structures and procedures that have to do with the allocation and distribution of wealth and power in society. The political organization of society thus includes not only the formal apparatus of the state but also industrial organizations and other private institutions that play a role in the decision-making process. It is particularly important to attend to the organization of the entire body politic when technological change leads to a blurring of once clear distinctions between the public and private sectors of society and to changes in the roles of its principal institutions.

It was suggested above that the political requirements of our modern technological society call for a relatively greater public commitment on the part of individuals than in previous times. The reason for this, stated most generally, is that technological change has the effect of enhancing the importance of public decision making in society, because technology is continually creating new possibilities for social action as well as new problems that have to be dealt with.

A society that undertakes to foster technology on a large scale, in fact, commits itself to social complexity and to facing and dealing with new problems as a normal feature of political life. Not much is yet known with any precision about the political imperatives inherent in technological change, but one may nevertheless speculate about the reasons why an increasingly technological society seems to be characterized by enlargement of the scope of public decision making.

For one thing, the development and application of technology seems to require large-scale, and hence increasingly complex, social concentrations, whether these be large cities, large corporations, big universities, or big government. In instances where technological advance appears to facilitate reduction of such first-order concentrations, it tends to instead enlarge the relevant *system* of social organization, that is, to lead to increased centralization. Thus, the physical dispersion made possible by transportation and communications technologies, as Meyer and Kain have shown, enlarges the urban complex that must be governed as a unit.

A second characteristic of advanced technology is that its effects cover large distances, in both the geographical and social senses of the term. Both its positive and negative features are more extensive. Horse-powered transportation technology was limited in its speed and capacity, but its nuisance value was also limited, in most cases to the owner and to the occupant of the next farm. The supersonic transport can carry hundreds across long distances in minutes, but its noise and vibration damage must also be suffered willy-nilly by everyone within the limits of a swath 3,000 miles long and several miles wide.

The concatenation of increased density (or enlarged system) and extended technological "distance" means that technological applications have increasingly wider ramifications and that increasingly large concentrations of people and organizations become dependent on technological systems. . . . The result is not only that more and more decisions must be social decisions taken in public ways, as already noted, but that, once made, decisions are likely to have a shorter useful life than heretofore. That is partly because technology is continually altering the spectrum of choices and problems that society faces, and partly because any decision taken is likely to generate a need to take ten more.

These speculations about the effects of technology on public decision making raise the problem of restructuring our decision-making mechanisms — including the system of market incentives — so that the increasing number and importance of social issues that confront us can be resolved equitably and effectively.

* * *

The Promise and Problems of Scientific Decision Making

There are two further consequences of the expanding role of public decision making. The first is that the latest information-handling devices and techniques tend to be utilized in the decision-making process. This is so (1) because public policy can be effective only to the degree that it is based on reliable knowledge about the actual state of the society, and thus requires a strong capability to collect, aggregate, and analyze detailed data about economic activities, social patterns, popular attitudes, and political trends, and (2) because it is recognized increasingly that decisions taken in one area impinge on and have consequences for other policy areas often thought of as unrelated, so that it becomes necessary to base decisions on a model of society that sees it as a system and that is capable of signaling as many as possible of the probable consequences of a contemplated action.

As Professor Alan F. Westin points out, reactions to the prospect of more decision making based on computerized data banks and scientific management techniques run the gamut of optimism to pessimism mentioned in the opening of this essay. Negative reactions take the form of rising political demands for greater popular participation in decision making, for more equality among different segments of the population, and for greater regard for the dignity of individuals. The increasing dependence of decision making on scientific and technological devices and techniques is seen as posing a threat to these goals, and pressures are generated in opposition to further "rationalization" of decision-making processes. These pressures have the paradoxical effect, however, not of deflecting the supporters of technological decision making from their course, but of spurring them on to renewed effort to save the society before it explodes under planlessness and inadequate administration

The paradox goes further, and helps to explain much of the social discontent that we are witnessing at the present time. The greater complexity and the more extensive ramifications that technology brings about in society tend to make social processes increasingly circuitous and indirect. The effects of actions are widespread and difficult to keep track of, so that experts and sophisticated techniques are increasingly needed to detect and analyze social events and to formulate policies adequate to the complexity of social issues. The "logic" of modern decision making thus appears to require greater and greater dependence on the collection and analysis of data and on the use of technological devices and scientific techniques. Indeed, many observers would agree that there is an "increasing relegation of questions which used to be matters of political debate to professional cadres of technicians and experts which function almost independently of the democratic political process."[2] In recent times, that process has been most noticeable, perhaps, in the areas of economic policy and national security affairs.

This "logic" of modern decision making, however, runs counter to that element of traditional democratic theory that places high value on direct participation in the political processes and generates the kind of discontent referred to above. If it turns out on more careful examination that direct participation is becoming less relevant to a society in which the connections between causes and effects are long and often hidden — which is an increasingly "indirect" society, in other words — elaboration of a new democratic ethos and of new democratic processes more adequate to the realities of modern society will emerge as perhaps the major intellectual and political challenge of our time.

The Need for Institutional Innovation

The challenge is, indeed, already upon us, for the second consequence of the enlarged scope of public decision making is the need to develop new institutional forms and new mechanisms to replace established ones that can no longer deal effectively with the new kinds of problems with which we are increasingly faced. Much of the political ferment of the present time — over the problems of technology assessment, the introduction of statistical data banks, the extension to domestic problems of techniques of analysis developed for the military services, and the modification of the institutions of local government — is evidence of the need for new institutions. . . .

CONCLUSION

As we review what we are learning about the relationship of technological and social change, a number of conclusions begin to emerge. We find, on the one hand, that the creation of new physical possibilities and social options by technology tends toward and appears to require the emergence of new values, new forms of economic activity, and new political organizations. On the other hand, technological change also poses problems of social and psychological displacement.

The two phenomena are not unconnected, nor is the tension between them new: man's technical prowess always seems to run ahead of his ability to deal with and profit from it. In America, especially, we are becoming adept at extracting the new techniques, the physical power, and the economic productivity that are inherent in our knowledge and its associated technologies. Yet we have not fully accepted the fact that our progress in the technical realm does not leave our institutions, values, and political processes unaffected. Individuals will be fully integrated into society only when we can extract from our knowledge not only its technological potential but also its implications for a system of values and a social, economic, and political organization appropriate to a society in which technology is so prevalent. . . .

NOTES

1. Unless otherwise noted, studies referred to in this article are described in the Fourth Annual Report (1967–68) of the Harvard University Program on Technology and Society.
2. Harvey Books, "Scientific Concepts and Cultural Changes," in G. Holton, ed., *Science and Culture* (Boston: Houghton Mifflin, 1965), p. 71.

8.   Technology: The Opiate of the Intellectuals

JOHN McDERMOTT

Several months after the report containing Emmanuel Mesthene's article was published by Harvard, a sharply critical review-essay by John McDermott appeared in The New York Review of Books. *McDermott's piece, which follows here, is not a point-by-point analysis or rebuttal of the Mesthene work. Rather, it is McDermott's attempt to critique the entire point of view that he sees as epitomized by Mesthene — "not of a new but of a newly aggressive right-wing ideology in this country." McDermott focuses on a notion he calls* laissez innover, *which holds that technology is a self-correcting system. Mesthene, he claims, finds this principle acceptable because he defines technology abstractly. McDermott himself, however, rejects* laissez innover *because he claims to see specific characteristics in contemporary technology that contradict the abstraction.*

Concentrating on the application of technology to the war in Vietnam, McDermott examines its nature and concludes that "technology, in its concrete, empirical meaning, refers fundamentally to systems of rationalized control over large groups of men, events, and machines by small groups of technically skilled men operating through organized hierarchy." Using this definition, he proceeds to discuss the social effect of modern technology in America, concluding that the ideology of laissez innover *is attractive to those in power since they are in a position to reap technology's benefits while avoiding its costs.*

John McDermott has served on the faculty of the State University of New York at Old Westbury, in the Department of Labor Studies.

I

. . . If religion was formerly the opiate of the masses, then surely technology is the opiate of the educated public today, or at least of its favorite authors. No other single subject is so universally invested with high hopes for the improvement of mankind generally and of Americans in particular. . . .

These hopes for mankind's, or technology's, future, however, are not unalloyed. Technology's defenders, being otherwise reasonable men, are also aware that the world population explosion and the nuclear missile race are also the fruit of the enormous advances made in technology during the past half century or so.

But here too a cursory reading of their literature would reveal widespread though qualified optimism that these scourges too will fall before technology's might. Thus population (and genetic) control and permanent peace are sometimes added to the already imposing roster of technology's promises. What are we to make of such extravagant optimism?

[In early 1968] Harvard University's Program on Technology and Society . . . issued its Fourth Annual Report to the accompaniment of full front-page coverage in *The New York Times* (January 18). Within the brief (fewer than 100) pages of that report and most clearly in the concluding essay by the Program's director, Emmanuel G. Mesthene, one can discern some of the important threads of belief that bind together much current writing on the social implications of technology. Mesthene's essay is worth extended analysis because these beliefs are of interest in themselves and, of greater importance, because they form the basis not of a new but of a newly aggressive right-wing ideology in this country, an ideology whose growing importance was accurately measured by the magnitude of the *Times*'s news report.

. . . Mesthene believes there are two distinct problems in technology's relation to society, a positive one of taking full advantage of the opportunity it offers and the negative one of avoiding unfortunate consequences that flow from the exploitation of those opportunities. Positive opportunities may be missed because the costs of technological development outweigh likely benefits (e.g., Herman Kahn's "Doomsday Machine"). Mesthene seems convinced, however, that a more important case is that in which

> . . . technology lies fallow because existing social structures are inadequate to exploit the opportunities it offers. This is revealed clearly in the examination of institutional failure in the ghetto carried on by [the Program]. . . .

His diagnosis of these problems is generous in the extreme:

> All these factors combine to dilute what may be otherwise a genuine desire to apply our best knowledge and adequate resources to the resolution of urban tensions and the eradication of poverty in the nation.

Moreover, because government and the media ". . . are not yet equipped for the massive task of public education that is needed . . . " if we are to exploit technology more fully, many technological opportunities are lost because of the lack of public support. This too is a problem primarily of "institutional innovation."

Mesthene believes that institutional innovation is no less important in combating the negative effects of technology. Individuals or individual firms that decide to develop new technologies normally do not take "adequate account" of their likely social benefits or costs. His critique is anticapitalist in spirit, but lacks bite, for he goes on to add that

> . . . [most of the negative] consequences of technology that are causing concern at the present time — pollution of the environment, potential damage to the ecology of the planet, occupational and social dislocations, threats to the

privacy and political significance of the individual, social and psychological malaise — are *negative externalities of this kind.* They are with us in large measure because it has not been anybody's explicit business to foresee and anticipate them. [Italics added.]

Mesthene's abstract analysis and its equally abstract diagnosis in favor of "institutional innovation" place him in a curious and, for us, instructive position. If existing social structures are inadequate to exploit technology's full potential, or if, on the other hand, so-called negative externalities assail us because it is nobody's business to foresee and anticipate them, doesn't this say that we should apply technology to this problem too? That is, we ought to apply and organize the appropriate *organizational* knowledge for the practical purpose of solving the problems of institutional inadequacy and "negative externalities." Hence, in principle, Mesthene is in the position of arguing that the cure for technology's problems, whether positive or negative, is still more technology. This is the first theme of the technological school of writers and its ultimate First Principle.

Technology, in their view, is a self-correcting system. Temporary oversight or "negative externalities" will and should be corrected by technological means. Attempts to restrict the free play of technological innovation are, in the nature of the case, self-defeating. Technological innovation exhibits a distinct tendency to work for the general welfare in the long run. *Laissez innover!*

I have so far deliberately refrained from going into any greater detail than does Mesthene on the empirical character of contemporary technology for it is important to bring out the force of the principle of *laissez innover* in its full generality. Many writers on technology appear to deny in their definition of the subject — organized knowledge for practical purposes — that contemporary technology exhibits distinct trends, which can be identified or projected. Others, like Mesthene, appear to accept these trends, but then blunt the conclusion by attributing to technology so much flexibility and "scientific" purity that it becomes an abstraction infinitely malleable in behalf of good, pacific, just, and egalitarian purposes. Thus the analogy to the laissez-faire principle of another time is quite justified. Just as the market or the free play of competition provided in theory the optimum long-run solution for virtually every aspect of virtually every social and economic problem, so too does the free play of technology, according to its writers. Only if technology or innovation (or some other synonym) is allowed the freest possible reign, they believe, will the maximum social good be realized.

What reasons do they give to believe that the principle of *laissez innover* will normally function for the benefit of mankind rather than, say, merely for the belief of the immediate practitioners of technology, their managerial cronies, and for the profits accruing to their corporations? As Mesthene and other writers of his school are aware, this is a very real problem, for they all believe that the normal tendency of technology is, and ought to be, the increasing concentration of decision-making power in the hands of larger and larger scientific-technical bureaucracies. *In principle* their solution is relatively simple, though not often explicitly stated.[1]

Their argument goes as follows: the men and women who are elevated by technology into commanding positions within various decision-making bureaucracies exhibit no generalized drive for power such as characterized, say, the landed gentry of preindustrial Europe or the capitalist entrepreneur of the last century. For their social and institutional position and its supporting culture as well are defined solely by the fact that these men are problem solvers. (Organized knowledge for practical purposes again.) That is, they gain advantage and reward only to the extent that they can bring specific technical knowledge to bear on the solution of specific technical problems. Any more general drive for power would undercut the bases of their usefulness and legitimacy.

Moreover their specific training and professional commitment to solving technical problems creates a bias against ideologies in general, which inhibits any attempts to formulate a justifying ideology for the group. Consequently, they do not constitute a class and have no general interests antagonistic to those of their problem-beset clients. We may refer to all of this as the disinterested character of the scientific-technical decision-maker, or, more briefly and cynically, as the principle of the Altruistic Bureaucrat. . . .

This combination of guileless optimism with scientific tough-mindedness might seem to be no more than an eccentric delusion were the American technology it supports not moving in directions that are strongly antidemocratic. To show why this is so we must examine more closely Mesthene's seemingly innocuous distinction between technology's positive opportunities and its "negative externalities." In order to do this I will make use of an example drawn from the very frontier of American technology, the war in Vietnam.

II

* * *

Advanced technological systems such as those employed in the bombardment of South Vietnam make use not only of extremely complex and expensive equipment but, quite as important, of large numbers of relatively scarce and expensive-to-train technicians. They have immense capital costs; a thousand aircraft of a very advanced type, literally hundreds of thousands of spare parts, enormous stocks of rockets, bombs, shells and bullets, in addition to tens of thousands of technical specialists: pilots, bombardiers, navigators, radar operators, computer programmers, accountants, engineers, electronic and mechanical technicians, to name only a few. In short, they are "capital intensive."

Moreover, the coordination of this immense mass of esoteric equipment and its operators in the most effective possible way depends upon an extremely highly developed technique both in the employment of each piece of equipment by a specific team of operators and in the management of the program itself. Of course, all large organizations standardize their operating procedures, but it is peculiar to advanced technological systems that their operating procedures embody a very high degree of information drawn from the physical sciences, while their managerial procedures are equally dependent on information drawn from the social sciences. We may describe this situation by saying that advanced technological systems are both "technique intensive" and "management intensive."

It should be clear, moreover, even to the most casual observer that such intensive use of capital, technique, and management spills over into almost every area touched by the technological system in question. An attack program delivering 330,000 tons of munitions more or less selectively to several thousand different targets monthly would be an anomaly if forced to rely on sporadic intelligence data, erratic maintenance systems, or a fluctuating and unpredictable supply of heavy bombs, rockets, jet fuel, and napalm tanks. Thus it is precisely because the bombing program requires an intensive use of capital, technique, and management that the same properties are normally transferred to the intelligence, maintenance, supply, coordination and training systems that support it. Accordingly, each of these supporting systems is subject to sharp pressures to improve and rationalize the performance of its machines and men, the reliability of its techniques, and the efficiency and sensitivity of the management controls under which it operates. Within integrated technical systems, higher levels of technology drive out lower, and the normal tendency is to integrate systems.

From this perverse Gresham's Law of Technology follow some of the main social and organizational characteristics of contemporary technological systems: the radical increase in the scale and complexity of operations that they demand and encourage; the rapid and widespread diffusion of technology to new areas; the great diversity of activities that can be directed by central management; an increase in the ambition of management's goals; and, as a corollary, especially to the last, growing resistance to the influence of so-called negative externalities.

Complex technological systems are extraordinarily resistant to intervention by persons or problems operating outside or below their managing groups, and this is so regardless of the "politics" of a given situation. Technology creates its own politics. The point of such advanced systems is to minimize the incidence of personal or social behavior that is erratic or otherwise not easily classified, of tools and equipment with poor performance, of improvisory techniques, and of unresponsiveness to central management. . . .

To define technology so abstractly that it obscures these observable characteristics of contemporary technology — as Mesthene and his school have done — makes no sense. It makes even less sense to claim some magical malleability for something as undefined as "institutional innovation." Technology, in its concrete, empirical meaning, refers fundamentally to systems of rationalized control over large groups of men, events, and machines by small groups of technically skilled men operating through organizational hierarchy. The latent "opportunities" provided by that control and its ability to filter out discordant "negative externalities" are, of course, best illustrated by extreme cases. Hence the most instructive and accurate example should be of a technology able to suppress the humanity of its rank-and-file and to commit genocide as a by-product of its rationality. The Vietnam bombing program fits technology to a "T."

* * *

IV

Among the conventional explanations for the rise and spread of the democratic ethos in Europe and North America in the seventeenth, eighteenth, and nineteenth centuries, the destruction of the gap in political culture between the mass of the population and that of the ruling classes is extremely important. . . .

Similarly, it is often argued that with the expansion and improvement of road and postal systems, the spread of new tools and techniques, the growth in the number and variety of merchants, the consequent invigoration of town life, and other numerous and familiar related developments, the social experience of larger numbers of people became richer, more varied, and similar in fact to those of the ruling class. . . .

The same period also witnessed a growth in the organized means of popular expression. . . .

This description by no means does justice to the richness and variety of the historical process underlying the rise and spread of what has come to be called the democratic ethos. But it does, I hope, isolate some of the important structural elements and, moreover, it enables us to illuminate some important ways in which the new technology, celebrated by Mesthene and his associates for its potential contributions to democracy, contributes instead to the erosion of that same democratic ethos. For if, in an earlier time, the gap between the political cultures of the higher and lower orders of society was being widely attacked and closed, this no longer appears to be the case. On the contrary, I am persuaded that the direction has been reversed and that we now observe evidence of a growing separation between ruling and lower-class culture in America, a separation that is particularly enhanced by the rapid growth of technology and the spreading influence of its *laissez innover* ideologues.

Certainly, there has been a decline in popular literacy, that is to say, in those aspects of literacy that bear on an understanding of the political and social character of the new technology. Not one person in a hundred is even aware of, much less understands, the nature of technologically highly advanced systems such as are used in the Vietnam bombing program. . . .

Secondly, the social organization of this new technology, by systematically denying to the general population experiences that are analogous to those of its higher management, contributes very heavily to the growth of social irrationality in our society. For example, modern technological organization defines the roles and values of its members, not vice versa. An engineer or a sociologist is one who does all those things but only those things called for by the "table of organization" and the "job description" used by his employer. Professionals who seek self-realization through creative and autonomous behavior without regard to the defined goals, needs, and channels of their respective departments have no more place in a large corporation or government agency than squeamish soldiers in the army. . . .

However, those at the top of technology's most advanced organizations hardly suffer the same experience. For reasons that are clearly related to the principle of the Altruistic Bureaucracy the psychology of an individual's fulfillment through work has been incorporated into management ideology. As the pages of *Fortune, Time,* or *Business Week* . . . serve to show, the higher levels of business and government are staffed by men and women who spend killing hours looking after the economic welfare and national security of the rest of us. The rewards of this life are said to be very few: the love of money would be demeaning and, anyway, taxes are said to take most of it; its sacrifices are many, for failure brings economic depression to the masses or gains for communism as well as disgrace to the erring managers. Even the essential high-mindedness or altruism of our managers earns no reward, for the public is distracted, fickle, and, on occasion, vengeful. . . . Hence for these "real revolutionaries of our time," as Walt Rostow has called them, self-fulfillment through work and discipline is the only reward. The managerial process is seen as an expression of the vital personalities of our leaders and the right to it an inalienable right of the national elite.

In addition to all this, their lonely and unrewarding eminence in the face of crushing responsibility, etc., tends to create an air of mystification around technology's managers. . . .

It seems fundamental to the social organization of modern technology that the quality of the social experience of the lower orders of society declines as the level of technology grows no less than does their literacy. And, of course, this process feeds on itself, for with the consequent decline in the real effectiveness and usefulness of local and other forms of organization open to easy and direct popular influence their vitality declines still further, and the cycle is repeated.

The normal life of men and women in the lower and, I think, middle levels of American society now seems cut off from those experiences in which near social means and distant social ends are balanced and rebalanced, adjusted and readjusted. But it is from such widespread experience with effective balancing and adjusting that social rationality derives. To the degree that it is lacking, social irrationality becomes the norm, and social paranoia a recurring phenomenon. . . .

Mesthene himself recognizes that such "negative externalities" are on the increase. His list includes ". . . pollution of the environment, potential damage to the ecology of the planet, occupational and social dislocations, threats to the privacy and political significance of the individual, social and psychological malaise. . . ." Minor matters all, however, when compared to the marvelous opportunities *laissez innover* holds out to us: more GNP, continued free world leadership, supersonic transports, urban renewal on a regional basis, institutional innovation, and the millennial promises of his school.

This brings us finally to the ideologies and doctrines of technology and their relation to what I have argued is a growing gap in political culture between the lower and upper classes in American society. Even more fundamentally than the principles of *laissez innover* and the altruistic bureaucrat, technology in its very definition as the organization of knowledge for practical purposes assumes that the primary and really creative role in the social processes consequent on technological change is reserved for a scientific and technical elite, the elite that presumably discovers and organizes that knowledge. But if the scientific and technical elite and their indispensable managerial cronies are the really creative (and hardworking and altruistic) elements in American society, what is this but to say that the common mass of men are essentially drags on the social weal? This is precisely the implication which is drawn by the *laissez innover* school. Consider the following quotations from an article that appeared in *The New Republic* in December 1967, written by Zbigniew Brzezinski, one of the intellectual leaders of the school.

Brzezinski is describing a nightmare that he calls the "technetronic society" (the word like the concept is a pastiche of technology and electronics). This society will be characterized, he argues, by the application of ". . . the principle of equal opportunity for all but . . . special opportunity for the singularly talented few." It will thus combine ". . . continued *respect* for the popular will with an increasing *role* in the key decision-making institutions of individuals with special intellectual and scientific attainments." (Italics added.) Naturally, "The educational and social systems [will make] it increasingly attractive and easy for those meritocratic few to develop to the fullest of their special potential."

However, while it will be ". . . necessary to require everyone at a sufficiently responsible post to take, say, two years of [scientific and technical] retraining every ten years . . . ," the rest of us can develop a new ". . . interest in the cultural and humanistic aspects of life, *in addition to purely hedonistic preoccupations.*" (Italics added.) The latter, he is careful to point out, "would serve as a social valve, reducing tensions and political frustration."

Is it not fair to ask how much *respect* we carefree pleasure lovers and culture consumers will get from the hard-working bureaucrats, going to night school two years in every ten, while working like beavers in the "key decision-making institutions"? The altruism of our bureaucrats has a heavy load to bear.

Stripped of their euphemisms these are simply arguments that enhance the social legitimacy of the interests of new technical and scientific elites and detract from the interests of the rest of us. . . .

As has already been made clear, the *laissez innover* school accepts as inevitable and desirable the centralizing tendencies of technology's social organization, and they accept as well the mystification that comes to surround the management process. Thus equality of opportunity, as they understand it, has precious little to do with creating a more egalitarian society. On the contrary, it functions as an indispensable feature of the highly stratified society they envision for the future. For in their society of meritocratic hierarchy, equality of opportunity assures that talented young meritocrats (the word is no uglier than the social system it refers to) will be able to climb into the "key decision-making" slots reserved for trained talent, and thus generate the success of the new society, and its cohesion against popular "tensions and political frustration."

The structures that formerly guaranteed the rule of wealth, age, and family will not be destroyed (or at least not totally so). They will be firmed up and rationalized by the perpetual addition of trained (and, of course, acculturated) talent. In technologically advanced societies, equality of opportunity functions as a hierarchical principle, in opposition to the egalitarian social goals it pretends to serve. To the extent that is has already become the kind of "equality" we seek to institute in our society, it is one of the main factors contributing to the widening gap between the cultures of upper- and lower-class America.

V

. . . *Laissez innover* is now the premier ideology of the technological impulse in American society, which is to say, of the institutions that monopolize and profit from advanced technology and of the social classes that find in the free exploitation of *their* technology the most likely guarantee of their power, status, and wealth.

This said, it is important to stress both the significance and limitations of what has in fact been said. Here Mesthene's distinction between the positive opportunities and negative "externalities" inherent in technological change is pivotal; for everything else that I've argued follows inferentially from the actual social meaning of that distinction. As my analysis of the Vietnam bombing program suggested, those technological effects that are sought after as positive opportunities and those that are dismissed as negative externalities are decisively influenced by the fact that this distinction between positive and negative within advanced technological organizations tends to be made among the planners and managers themselves. Within these groups there are, as was pointed out, extremely powerful organizational, hierarchical, doctrinal, and other "*technical*" factors, which tend by design to filter out "irrational" demands from below, substituting for them the "rational" demands of technology itself. As a result, technological rationality is as socially neutral today as market rationality was a century ago. . . .

This analysis lends some weight (though perhaps no more than that) to a number of wide-ranging and unorthodox conclusions about American society today and the directions in which it is tending. . . .

First, and most important, technology should be considered as an institutional system, not more and certainly not less. Mesthene's definition of the subject is inadequate, for it obscures the systematic and decisive social changes, especially their political and cultural tendencies, that follow the widespread application of advanced technological systems. At the same time, technology is less than a social system per se, though it has many elements of a social system, viz., an elite, a group of linked institutions, an ethos, and so forth. Perhaps the best summary statement of the case resides in an analogy — with all the vagueness and imprecision attendant on such things: today's technology stands in relation to today's capitalism as, a century ago, the latter stood to the free market capitalism of the time. . . .

A second major hypothesis would argue that the most important dimension of advanced technological institutions is the social one, that is, the institutions are agencies of highly centralized and intensive social control. Technology conquers nature, as the saying goes. But to do so it must first conquer man. More precisely, it demands a very high degree of control over the training, mobility, and skills of the work force. The absence (or decline) of direct controls or of coercion should not serve to obscure from our view the reality and intensity of the social controls that are employed (such as the internalized belief in equality of opportunity, indebtedness through credit, advertising, selective service channeling, and so on).

Advanced technology has created a vast increase in occupational specialties, many of them requiring many, many years of highly specialized training. It must motivate this training. It has made ever more complex and "rational" the ways in which these occupational specialties are combined in our economic and social life. It must win passivity and obedience to this complex activity. Formerly, technical rationality had been employed only to organize the production of rather simple physical objects, for example, aerial bombs. Now technical rationality is increasingly employed to organize all of the processes necessary to the utilization of physical objects, such as bombing systems. For this reason it seems a mistake to argue that we are in a "postindustrial" age, a concept favored by the *laissez innover* school. On the contrary, the rapid spread of technical in organizational and economic life and, hence, into social life is more aptly described as a second and much more intensive phase of the industrial revolution. One might reasonably suspect that it will create analogous social problems.

Accordingly, a third major hypothesis would argue that there are very profound social antagonisms or contradictions not less sharp or fundamental than those ascribed by Marx to the development of nineteenth-century industrial society. The general form of the contradictions might be described as follows: a society characterized by the employment of advanced technology requires an ever more socially disciplined population, yet retains an ever declining capacity to enforce the required discipline. . . .

These are brief and, I believe, barely adequate reviews of extremely complex hypotheses. But, in outline, each of these contradictions appears to bear on roughly the same group of the American population, a technological underclass. If we assume this to be the case, a fourth hypothesis would follow, namely that technology is creating the basis for new and sharp class conflict in our society. That is, technology is creating its own working and managing classes just as earlier industrialization created its working and owning classes. Perhaps this suggests a return to the kind of class-based politics that characterized the U.S. in the last quarter of the nineteenth century, rather than the somewhat more ambiguous politics that was a feature of the second quarter of this century. I am inclined to think that this is the case, though I confess the evidence for it is as yet inadequate.

This leads to a final hypothesis, namely that *laissez innover* should be frankly recognized as a conservative or right-wing ideology. . . .

The point of this final hypothesis is not primarily to reimpress the language of European politics on the American scene. Rather it is to summarize the fact that many of the forces in American life hostile to the democratic ethos have enrolled under the banner of *laissez innover*. Merely to grasp this is already to take the first step toward a politics of radical reconstruction and against the malaise, irrationality, powerlessness, and official violence that characterize American life today.

NOTE

1. For a more complete statement of the argument that follows, see Suzanne Keller, *Beyond the Ruling Class* (New York: Random House, 1963).

PART III
ALTERNATIVE PERSPECTIVES ON TECHNOLOGY

Is it possible to reshape technological systems in ways that reflect a different set of interests and perspectives than those served by existing mainstream industrial technology? Is it possible to see and direct technological development from a fundamentally different point of view? Those who approach technology from such alternative perspectives are not interested in abstract critiques. Some are concerned with the practical, long-term viability of contemporary industrial society in the face of growing population, resource constraints, and the potential for human actions to cause long-term, possibly irreversible damage to the global environment. Others focus on the equity implications of current technological systems — for example, the impacts of such systems on women and racial minorities. Still others see the need for reforms to the policy-making apparatus by which technological development is governed. All would alter the directions of technological change to better accommodate these alternative perspectives.

Central to the first two readings in this section is the notion of *alternative* or *appropriate* technology. This concept, which in the United States was associated with the counterculture of the 1960s and 1970s, is a way of looking at technology itself rather than at a specific type of hardware. It is a set of design criteria that stress simplicity, individual self-worth and self-reliance, labor intensiveness rather than capital intensiveness, minimum energy use, consistency with environmental quality, and decentralization rather than centralization.

The authors of the first two chapters are two of the best known and most creative thinkers on the subject of technological alternatives: E. F. Schumacher and Paul Goodman. Schumacher's name is practically synonymous with appropriate technology, especially as it applies to Third World development. His essay, "Buddhist Economics," though more than twenty-five years old, is still as thought-provoking as it is original. Paul Goodman's paper, "Can Technology Be Humane?" which actually predates Schumacher's by several years, provides an idea of what the philosophical underpinnings of a really different style of technology might be like.

The next four chapters discuss the redirection of technology from somewhat different angles. Richard Sclove's recent essay, "Technological Politics As If Democracy Really Mattered," updates some of Goodman's ideas and suggests ways in which technological decision making can be made more democratic and technology can be used to create a more democratic society.

Timothy Jenkins takes a fresh look at technology from an African American perspective in his 1997 book (coauthored by Khafra K. Om-Ra-Seti), *Black Futurists in the Information Age.* How can new technologies be made to serve the interests of the black community, he asks, and how can the members of that community seize the initiative?

Australian sociologist Judy Wajcman critiques mainstream technology from a feminist standpoint, suggesting along the way how a technology based on women's values might look. Finally, in one his many provocative essays on technology, Langdon Winner asks whether certain technological systems *by their nature* determine particular arrangements of power and authority among people. Understanding the significance of this and related questions is essential, Winner would argue, to maintaining (or perhaps restoring), democratic control over the course of technological and social development.

9. Buddhist Economics

E. F. SCHUMACHER

More than any other single individual, E. F. Schumacher is responsible for popular-izing the notion of appropriate technology. It may seem strange that a man who was once chief economist of Britain's National Coal Board emerged as intellectual par-ent of a movement that seeks the radical restructuring of the whole essence of eco-nomics, but Schumacher was also a longtime advocate of organic farming, a student of Gandhi, and an activist for political decentralization.

Schumacher was born in Germany in 1911, trained in economics, and came to England as a Rhodes scholar. Like many Germans living in Britain, he was interned for a long time during World War II. Later he was released to do farm work, an experience that strongly influenced his later work. While pursuing a career as a government economist, he became involved in organic farming, became president of the Soil Association, and in 1966 founded the Intermediate Technology Development Group, an organization that promotes small-scale technology tailored to the needs of specific developing countries. Schumacher died in 1977, not long after a visit to the United States in which he was accorded the recognition of a meeting with President Jimmy Carter to discuss his ideas.

His book Small Is Beautiful, *from which the brilliant essay "Buddhist Econom-ics" is taken, became an underground classic soon after its publication in the early 1970s. As effective an introduction as can be found to the ideas of appropriate technology. "Buddhist Economics" provides Schumacher's answer to the question Leo Marx asks in the opening chapter of this book, "Does Improved Technology Mean Progress?"*

"Right Livelihood" is one of the requirements of the Buddha's Noble Eightfold Path. It is clear, therefore, that there must be such a thing as Buddhist economics.

Buddhist countries have often stated that they wish to remain faithful to their heritage. So Burma: "The New Burma sees no conflict between religious values and economic progress. Spiritual health and material well-being are not enemies: they are natural allies."[1] Or "We can blend successfully the religious and spiritual values of our heritage with the benefits of modern technology."[2] Or: "We Bur-mans have sacred duty to conform both our dreams and our acts to our faith. This we shall ever do."[3]

All the same, such countries invariably assume that they can model their eco-nomic development plans in accordance with modern economics, and they call upon modern economists from so-called advanced countries to advise them, to formulate the policies to be pursued, and to construct the grand design for development, the Five-Year Plan or whatever it may be called. No one seems to think that a Buddhist way of life would call for Buddhist economics, just as the modern materialist way of life has brought forth modern economics.

Economists themselves, like most specialists, normally suffer from a kind of metaphysical blindness, assuming that theirs is a science of absolute and invariable truths, without any presuppositions. Some go as far as to claim that economic laws are as free from "metaphysics" or "values" as the law of gravitation. We need not, however, get involved in arguments of methodology. Instead, let us take some fundamentals and see what they look like when viewed by a modern economist and a Buddhist economist.

There is universal agreement that a fundamental source of wealth is human labor. Now, the modern economist has been brought up to consider "labor" or work as little more than a necessary evil. From the point of view of the employer, it is in any case simply an item of cost, to be reduced to a minimum if it cannot be eliminated altogether, say, by automation. From the point of view of the workman, it is a "disutility"; to work is to make a sacrifice of one's leisure and comfort, and wages are a kind of compensation for the sacrifice. Hence the ideal from the point of view of the employer is to have output without employees, and the ideal from the point of view of the employee is to have income without employment.

The consequences of these attitudes both in theory and in practice are, of course, extremely far-reaching. If the ideal with regard to work is to get rid of it, every method that "reduces the work load" is a good thing. The most potent method, short of automation, is the so-called "division of labor," and the classical example is the pin factory eulogized in Adam Smith's *Wealth of Nations*. Here it is not a matter of ordinary specialization, which mankind has practiced from time immemorial, but of dividing up every complete process of production into minute parts, so that the final product can be produced at great speed without anyone having had to contribute more than a totally insignificant and, in most cases, unskilled movement of his limbs.

The Buddhist point of view takes the function of work to be at least threefold: to give a man a chance to utilize and develop his faculties; to enable him to overcome his egocenteredness by joining with other people in a common task; and to bring forth the goods and services needed for a becoming existence. Again, the consequences that flow from this view are endless. To organize work in such a manner that it becomes meaningless, boring, stultifying, or nerve-racking for the worker would be little short of criminal; it would indicate a greater concern with goods than with people, an evil lack of compassion and a soul-destroying degree of attachment to the most primitive side of this worldly existence. Equally, to strive for leisure as an alternative to work would be considered a complete misunderstanding of one of the basic truths of human existence, namely that work and leisure are complementary parts of the same living process and cannot be separated without destroying the joy of work and the bliss of leisure.

From the Buddhist point of view, there are therefore two types of mechanization, which must be clearly distinguished: one that enhances a man's skill and power and one that turns the work of man over to a mechanical slave, leaving man in a position of having to serve the slave. How to tell the one from the other?

"The craftsman himself," says Ananda Coomaraswamy, a man equally competent to talk about the modern West as the ancient East, "can always, if allowed to, draw the delicate distinction between the machine and the tool. The carpet loom is a tool, a contrivance for holding warp threads at a stretch for the pile to be woven round them by the craftsmen's fingers; but the power loom is a machine, and its significance as a destroyer of culture lies in the fact that it does the essentially human part of the work."[4] It is clear, therefore, that Buddhist economics must be very different from the economics of modern materialism, since the Buddhist sees the essence of civilization not in a multiplication of wants but in the purification of human character. Character, at the same time, is formed primarily by a man's work. And work, properly conducted in conditions of human dignity and freedom, blesses those who do it and equally their products. The Indian philosopher and economist J. C. Kumarappa sums the matter up as follows:

> If the nature of the work is properly appreciated and applied, it will stand in the same relation to the higher faculties as food is to the physical body. It nourishes and enlivens the higher man and urges him to produce the best he is capable of. It directs his free will along the proper course and disciplines the animal in him into progressive channels. It furnishes an excellent background for man to display his scale of values and develop his personality.[5]

If a man has no chance of obtaining work he is in a desperate position, not simply because he lacks an income but because he lacks this nourishing and enlivening factor of disciplined work, which nothing can replace. A modern economist may engage in highly sophisticated calculations on whether full employment "pays" or whether it might be more "economic" to run an economy at less than full employment so as to ensure a greater mobility of labor, a better stability of wages, and so forth. His fundamental criterion of success is simply the total quantity of goods produced during a given period of time. "If the marginal urgency of goods is low," says Professor Galbraith in *The Affluent Society,* "then so is the urgency of employing the last man or the last million men in the labor force."[6] And again: "If . . . we can afford some unemployment in the interest of stability — a proposition, incidentally, of impeccably conservative antecedents — then we can afford to give those who are unemployed the goods that enable them to sustain their accustomed standard of living."

From a Buddhist point of view, this is standing the truth on its head by considering goods as more important than people and consumption as more important than creative activity. It means shifting the emphasis from the worker to the product of work, that is, from the human to the subhuman, a surrender to the forces of evil. The very start of Buddhist economic planning would be a planning for full employment, and the primary purpose of this would in fact be employment for everyone who needs an "outside" job: it would not be the maximization of employment nor the maximization of production. Women, on the whole, do not need an "outside" job, and the large-scale employment of women in offices or factories would be considered a sign of serious economic failure. In particular, to let mothers of young children work in factories while the children run wild would be as uneconomic in the eyes of a Buddhist economist as the employment of a skilled worker as a soldier in the eyes of a modern economist.

While the materialist is mainly interested in goods, the Buddhist is mainly interested in liberation. But Buddhism is "The Middle Way" and therefore in no way antagonistic to physical well-being. It is not wealth that stands in the way of liberation but the attachment to wealth; not the enjoyment of pleasurable things but the craving for them. The keynote of Buddhist economics, therefore, is simplicity and nonviolence. From an economist's point of view, the marvel of the Buddhist way of life is the utter rationality of its pattern — amazingly small means leading to extraordinarily satisfactory results.

For the modern economist this is very difficult to understand. He is used to measuring the "standard of living" by the amount of annual consumption, assuming all the time that a man who consumes more is "better off" than a man who consumes less. A Buddhist economist would consider this approach excessively irrational: since consumption is merely a means to human well-being, the aim should be to obtain the maximum of well-being with the minimum of consumption. Thus, if the purpose of clothing is a certain amount of temperature comfort and an attractive appearance, the task is to attain this purpose with the smallest possible effort; that is, with the smallest annual destruction of cloth and with the help of designs that involve the smallest possible input of toil. The less toil there is, the more time and strength are left for artistic creativity. It would be highly uneconomic, for instance, to go in for complicated tailoring, like the modern West, when a much more beautiful effect can be achieved by the skillful draping of uncut material. It would be the height of folly to make material so that it should wear out quickly and the height of barbarity to make anything ugly, shabby or mean. What has just been said about clothing applies equally to all other human requirements. The ownership and the consumption of goods are a means to an end, and Buddhist economics is the systematic study of how to attain given ends with the minimum means.

Modern economics, on the other hand, considers consumption to be the sole end and purpose of all economic activity, taking the factors of production — land, labor, and capital — as the means. The former, in short, tries to maximize human satisfactions by the optimal pattern of consumption, while the latter tries to maximize consumption by the optimal pattern of productive effort. It is easy to see that the effort needed to sustain a way of life that seeks to attain the optimal pattern of consumption is likely to be much smaller than the effort needed to sustain a drive for maximum consumption. We need not be surprised, therefore, that the pressure and strain of living are very much less in, say, Burma than they are in the United States, in spite of the fact that the amount of labor-saving machinery used in the former country is only a minute fraction of the amount used in the latter.

Simplicity and nonviolence are obviously closely related. The optimal pattern of consumption, producing a high degree of human satisfaction by means of a relatively low rate of consumption, allows people to live without great pressure and strain and to fulfill the primary injunction of Buddhist teaching: "Cease to do evil; try to do good." As physical resources are everywhere limited, people satisfying their needs by means of a modest use of resources are obviously less likely to be at each other's throats than people depending upon a high rate of use. Equally, people who live in highly self-sufficient local communities are less likely to get involved in large-scale violence than people whose existence depends on world-wide systems of trade.

From the point of view of Buddhist economics, therefore, production from local resources for local needs is the most rational way of economic life, while dependence on imports from afar and the consequent need to produce for export to unknown and distant peoples is highly uneconomic and justifiable only in exceptional cases and on a small scale just as the modern economist would admit that a high rate of consumption of transport services between a man's home and his place of work signifies a misfortune and not a high standard of life, so the Buddhist economist would hold that to satisfy human wants from faraway sources rather than from sources nearby signifies failure rather than success. The former tends to take statistics showing an increase in the number of tons/miles per head of the population carried by a country's transport system as proof of economic progress, while to the latter — the Buddhist economist — the same statistics would indicate a highly undesirable deterioration in the *pattern* of consumption.

Another striking difference between modern economics and Buddhist economics arises over the use of natural resources. Bertrand de Jouvenel, the eminent French political philosopher, has characterized "Western man" in words that may be taken as a fair description of the modern economist:

> He tends to count nothing as an expenditure, other than human effort; he does not seem to mind how much mineral matter he wastes and, far worse, how much living matter he destroys. He does not seem to realize at all that human life is a dependent part of an ecosystem of many different forms of life. As the world is ruled from towns where men are cut off from any form of life other than human, the feeling of belonging to an ecosystem is not revived. This results in a harsh and improvident treatment of things upon which we ultimately depend, such as water and trees.[7]

The teaching of the Buddha, on the other hand, enjoins a reverent and nonviolent attitude not only to all sentient beings but also, with great emphasis, to trees. Every follower of the Buddha ought to plant a tree every few years and look after it until it is safely established, and the Buddhist economist can demonstrate without difficulty that the universal observation of this rule would result in a high rate of genuine economic development independent of any foreign aid. Much of the economic decay of southeast Asia (as of many other parts of the world) is undoubtedly due to a heedless and shameful neglect of trees.

Modern economics does not distinguish between renewable and nonrenewable materials, as its very method is to equalize and quantify everything by means of a money price. Thus, taking various alternative fuels, like coal, oil, wood, or water-power: the only difference between them recognized by modern economics is relative cost per equivalent unit. The cheapest is automatically the one to be preferred, as to do otherwise would be irrational and "uneconomic." From a Buddhist point of view, of course, this will not do; the essential difference between nonrenewable fuels like coal and oil on the one hand and renewable fuels like wood and water-power on the other cannot simply be overlooked. Nonrenewable goods must be used only if they are indispensable, and then only with the greatest care and the most meticulous concern for conservation. To use them heedlessly or extravagantly is an act of violence, and while complete nonviolence may not be attainable on this earth, there is nonetheless an ineluctable duty on man to aim at the ideal of nonviolence in all he does.

Just as a modern European economist would not consider it a great economic achievement if all European art treasures were sold to America at attractive prices, so the Buddhist economist would insist that a population basing its economic life on nonrenewable fuels is living parasitically, on capital instead of income. Such a way of life could have no permanence and could therefore be justified only as a purely temporary expedient. As the world's resources of nonrenewable fuels — coal, oil, and natural gas — are exceedingly unevenly distributed over the globe and undoubtedly limited in quantity, it is clear that their exploitation at an ever-increasing rate is an act of violence against nature, which must almost inevitably lead to violence between men.

This fact alone might give food for thought even to those people in Buddhist countries who care nothing for the religious and spiritual values of their heritage and ardently desire to embrace the materialism of modern economics at the fastest possible speed. Before they dismiss Buddhist economics as nothing better than a nostalgic dream, they might wish to consider whether the path of economic development outlined by modern economics is likely to lead them to places where they really want to be. Towards the end of his courageous book *The Challenge of Man's Future*, Professor Harrison Brown of the California Institute of Technology gives the following appraisal:

> Thus we see that, just as industrial society is fundamentally unstable and subject to reversion to agrarian existence, so within it the conditions which offer individual freedom are unstable in their ability to avoid the conditions which impose rigid organization and totalitarian control. Indeed, when we examine all of the foreseeable difficulties which threaten the survival of industrial civilization, it is difficult to see how the achievement of stability and the maintenance of individual liberty can be made compatible.[8]

Even if this were dismissed as a long-term view there is the immediate question of whether "modernization," as currently practiced without regard to religious and spiritual values, is actually producing agreeable results. As far as the masses are concerned, the results appear to be disastrous — a collapse of the rural economy, a rising tide of unemployment in town and country, and the growth of a city proletariat without nourishment for either body or soul.

It is in the light of both immediate experience and long-term prospects that the study of Buddhist economics could be recommended even to those who believe that economic growth is more important than any spiritual or religious values. For it is not a question of choosing between "modern growth" and "traditional stagnation." It is a question of finding the right path of development, the Middle Way between materialist heedlessness and traditionalist immobility, in short, of finding "Right Livelihood."

NOTES

1. *The New Burma* (Economic and Social Board, Government of the Union of Burma, 1954).
2. *Ibid.*
3. *Ibid.*
4. Ananda K. Coomaraswamy, *Art and Swadeshi* (Madras: Ganesh & Co.).
5. J. C. Kumarappa, *Economy of Permanence* (Sarva-Seva Sangh Publication, Rajghat, Kashi, 4th ed., 1958).
6. John Kenneth Galbraith, *The Affluent Society* (London: Penguin Books Ltd., 1962).
7. Richard B. Gregg, A *Philosophy of Indian Economic Development* (Ahmedabad: Navajivan Publishing House, 1958).
8. Harrison Brown, *The Challenge of Man's Future* (New York: The Viking Press, 1954).

10. Can Technology Be Humane?

PAUL GOODMAN

In his essay "Technology: The Opiate of the Intellectuals" (which appears in Part II of this book), John McDermott despairs of the possibility of creating a humane technology within our present system. In a footnote to a section not included in this book, he writes, "Any discussion of the reorganization of technology to serve human needs seems, at this point, so Utopian that it robs one of the conviction necessary to shape a believable vision." Paul Goodman, unwilling to accept such a hopeless view, asks in the title of his selection, "Can Technology Be Humane?"

In developing his response to this question, Goodman admits there is no certainty that technology will become humane. Yet, in the classic style of a prophet — partly predictive and partly prescriptive — he asserts that our society is "on the eve of a new protestant Reformation, and no institution or status will go unaffected." In this selection, he offers a number of suggestions for channeling the energies of this Reformation into directions that he sees as critical to its success: prudence in the application of technology, an ecological viewpoint, and decentralization. Although the term appropriate technology *was barely known when Goodman first published this essay in the late 1960s, it is easy to see its roots in his prescription for reshaping technology.*

Paul Goodman (1911–1972) was a philosopher and humanist whose books Growing Up Absurd *established him as "the philosopher of the New Left" in the 1960s. His work ranged widely, from* Communitas *(1947), a classic of community planning written with his brother, Percival Goodman, to* Gestalt Therapy *(1951), written with F. S. Perls and Ralph Hefferline. Goodman was an anarchist and a pacifist, very active in the antiwar movement of the sixties. He wrote theoretical and practical treatises on politics, education, language, and literature, but his own judgment was that his literary work — novels, stories, poems, and plays — was his best. He was born in Manhattan, attended City College of New York, and was trained in philosophy at the University of Chicago.*

On March 4, 1969, there was a "work stoppage" and teach-in initiated by dissenting professors at the Massachusetts Institute of Technology, and followed at thirty other major universities and technical schools across the country, against misdirected scientific research and the abuse of scientific technology. Here I want to consider this event in a broader context than the professors did, indeed as part of a religious crisis. For an attack on the American scientific establishment is an attack on the worldwide system of belief. I think we are on the eve of a new Protestant Reformation, and no institution or status will go unaffected.

March 4 was, of course, only [one] of a series of protests in the [over] twenty-five years since the Manhattan Project to build the atom bomb, during which time the central funding of research and innovation has grown so enormously and its purposes have become so unpalatable. In 1940 the federal budget for research and development was less than 100 million dollars, in 1967, 17 billion.* Hitler's war was a watershed of modern times. We are accustomed, as H. R. Trevor-Roper has pointed out, to write Hitler off as an aberration, of little political significance. But, in fact, the military emergency that he and his Japanese allies created confirmed the worst tendencies of the giant states, till now they are probably irreversible by ordinary political means.

After Hiroshima, there was the conscience-stricken movement of the Atomic Scientists and the founding of their Bulletin. The American Association for the Advancement of Science pledged itself to keep the public informed about the dangerous bearings of new developments. There was the Oppenheimer incident. Ads of the East Coast scientists successfully stopped the bomb shelters, warned about the fallout, and helped produce the test ban. There was a scandal about the bombardment of the Van Allen belt. Scientists and technologists formed a powerful (and misguided) ad hoc group for Johnson in the 1964 election. In some universities, sometimes with bitter struggle, classified contracts have been excluded. There is a Society for Social Responsibility in Science. Rachel Carson's book on the pesticides caused a stir, until the Department of Agriculture rescued the manufacturers and plantation-owners. Ralph Nader has been on his rampage. Thanks to spectacular abuses like smog, strip-mining, asphalting, pesticides, and oil pollution, even ecologists and conservationists have been getting a hearing. Protest against the boom has slowed up the development of the supersonic transport [particularly in the United States]. Most recent has been the concerned outcry against the antiballistic missiles.

The target of protest has become broader and the grounds of complaint deeper. The target is now not merely the military, but the universities, commercial corporations, and government. It is said that money is being given by the wrong sponsors to the wrong people for the wrong purposes. In some of the great schools, such funding is the main support, e.g., at MIT, 90 percent of the research budget is from the government, and 65 percent of that is military.

Inevitably, such funding channels the brainpower of most of the brightest science students, who go where the action is, and this predetermines the course of American science and technology for the foreseeable future. At present nearly 200,000 American engineers and scientists spend all their time making weapons, which is a comment on, and perhaps explanation for, the usual statement that more scientists are now alive than since Adam and Eve. And the style of such research and development is not good. It is dominated by producing hardware, figuring logistics, and devising salable novelties. Often there is secrecy, always nationalism. Since the grants go overwhelmingly through a very few corporations and universities, they favor a limited number of scientific attitudes and preconceptions, with incestuous staffing. There is a premium on "positive results"; surprising "failures" cannot be pursued, so that science ceases to be a wandering dialogue with the unknown.

---

*R&D in the fiscal year 2000 federal budget is estimated at about $78 billion — Ed.

The policy is economically wasteful. A vast amount of brains and money is spent on crash programs to solve often essentially petty problems, and the claim that there is a spin-off of useful discoveries is derisory, if we consider the sums involved. The claim that research is neutral, and it doesn't matter what one works on, is shabby, if we consider the heavy funding in certain directions. Social priorities are scandalous: money is spent on overkill, supersonic planes, brand name identical drugs, annual model changes of cars, new detergents, and color television, whereas water, air space, food, health, and foreign aid are neglected. And much research is morally so repugnant, e.g., chemical and biological weapons, that one dares not humanly continue it.

The state of the behavioral sciences is, if anything, worse. Their claim to moral and political neutrality becomes, in effect, a means of diverting attention from glaring social evils, and they are in fact used — or would be if they worked — for warfare and social engineering, manipulation of people for the political and economic purposes of the powers that be. This is an especially sad betrayal since, in the not-too-distant past, the objective social sciences were developed largely to dissolve orthodoxy, irrational authority, and taboo. They were heretical and intellectually revolutionary, as the physical sciences had been in their own Heroic Age, and they weren't getting government grants.

This is a grim indictment. Even so, I do not think the dissenting scientists understand how deep their trouble is. They still take themselves too much for granted. Indeed, a repeated theme of the March 4, [1969,] complaints was that the science budget was being cut back, especially in basic research. The assumption was that though the sciences are abused, Science would rightly maintain and increase its expensive preeminence among social institutions. Only Science could find the answers.

But underlying the growing dissent there is a historical crisis. There has been a profound change in popular feeling, more than among the professors. Put it this way: Modern societies have been operating as if religion were a minor and moribund part of the scheme of things. But this is unlikely. Men do not do without a system of "meanings" that everybody believes and puts his hope in even if, or especially if, he doesn't know anything about it; what Freud called a "shared psychosis," meaningful because shared, and with the power that resides in dream and longing. In fact, in advanced countries it is science and technology themselves that have gradually and finally triumphantly become the system of mass faith, not disputed by various political ideologies and nationalism that have also been mass religions. Marxism called itself "scientific socialism" as against moral and utopian socialisms; and movements of national liberation have especially promised to open the benefits of industrialization and technological progress when once they have gotten rid of the imperialists.

For three hundred years, science and scientific technology had an unblemished and justified reputation as a wonderful adventure, pouring out practical benefits, and liberating the spirit from the errors of superstition and traditional faith. During this century they have finally been the only generally credited system of explanation and problem-solving. Yet in our generation they have come to seem to many, and to very many of the best of the young, as essentially inhuman, abstract, regimenting, hand-in-glove with Power, and even diabolical. Young people say that science is antilife, it is a Calvinist obsession, it has been a weapon of white Europe to subjugate colored races, and manifestly — in view of recent scientific technology — people who think that way become insane. With science, the other professions are discredited; and the academic "disciplines" are discredited.

The immediate reasons for this shattering reversal of values are fairly obvious. Hitler's ovens and his other experiments in eugenics, the first atom bombs and their frenzied subsequent developments, the deterioration of the physical environment and the destruction of the biosphere, the catastrophes impending over the cities because of technological failures and psychological stress, the prospect of a brainwashed and drugged 1984. Innovations yield diminishing returns in enhancing life. And instead of rejoicing, there is now widespread conviction that beautiful advances in genetics, surgery, computers, rocketry, or atomic energy will surely only increase human woe.

In such a crisis, in my opinion, it will not be sufficient to ban the military from the universities; and it will not even be sufficient, as liberal statesmen and many of the big corporations envisage, to beat the swords into ploughshares and turn to solving problems of transportation, desalinization, urban renewal, garbage disposal, and cleaning up the air and water. If the present difficulty is religious and historical, it is necessary to alter the entire relationship of science, technology, and social needs both in men's minds and in fact. This involves changes in the organization of science, in scientific education, and in the kinds of men who make scientific decisions.

In spite of the fantasies of hippies, we are certainly going to continue to live in a technological world. The question is a different one: is that workable?

PRUDENCE

Whether or not it draws on new scientific research, technology is a branch of moral philosophy, not of science. It aims at prudent goods for the commonweal and to provide efficient means for these goods. At present, however, "scientific technology" occupies a bastard position in the universities, in funding, and in the public mind. It is half tied to the theoretical sciences and half treated as mere know-how for political and commercial purposes. It has no principles of its own. To remedy this — so Karl Jaspers in Europe and Robert Hutchins in America have urged — technology must have its proper place on the faculty as a learned profession important in modern society, along with medicine, law, the humanities, and natural philosophy, learning from them and having something to teach them. As a moral philosopher, a technician should be able to criticize the programs given him to implement. As a professional in a community of learned professionals, a technologist must have a different kind of training and develop a different character than we see at present among technicians and engineers. He should know something of the social sciences, law, the fine arts, and medicine, as well as relevant natural sciences.

Prudence is foresight, caution, utility. Thus it is up to the technologists, not to regulatory agencies of the government, to provide for safety and to think about remote effects. This is what Ralph Nader is saying and Rachel Carson used to ask. An important aspect of caution is flexibility, to avoid the pyramiding catastrophe that occurs when something goes wrong in interlocking technologies, as in urban power failures. Naturally, to take responsibility for such things often requires standing up to the front office and urban politicians, and technologists must organize themselves in order to have power to do it.

Often it is clear that a technology has been oversold, like the cars. Then even though the public, seduced by advertising, wants more, technologists must balk, as any professional does when his client wants what isn't good for him. We are now repeating the same self-defeating congestion with the planes and airports: the more the technology is oversold, the less immediate utility it provides, the greater the costs, and the more damaging the remote effects. As this becomes evident, it is time for technologists to confer with sociologists and economists and ask deeper questions. Is so much travel necessary? Are there ways to diminish it? Instead, the recent history of technology has consisted largely of a desperate effort to remedy situations caused by previous overapplication of technology.

Technologists should certainly have a say about simple waste, for even in an affluent society there are priorities — consider the supersonic transport, which has little to recommend it. But the moon shot has presented the more usual dilemma of authentic conflicting claims. I myself believe that space exploration is a great human adventure, with immense aesthetic and moral benefits, whatever the scientific or utilitarian uses. Yet it is amazing to me that the scientists and technologists involved have not spoken more insistently for international cooperation instead of a puerile race. But I have heard some say that except for this chauvinist competition, Congress would not vote any money at all.

Currently, perhaps the chief moral criterion of a philosophic technology is modesty, having a sense of the whole and not obtruding more than a particular function warrants. Immodesty is always a danger of free enterprise, but when the same disposition is financed by big corporations, technologists rush into production with neat solutions that swamp the environment. This applies to packaging products and disposing of garbage, to freeways that bulldoze neighborhoods, high-rises that destroy landscape, wiping out a species for a passing fashion, strip mining, scrapping an expensive machine rather than making a minor repair, draining a watershed for irrigation because (as in Southern California) the cultivable land has been covered by asphalt. Given this disposition, it is not surprising that we defoliate a forest in order to expose a guerrilla and spray tear gas from a helicopter on a crowded campus.

Since we are technologically overcommitted, a good general maxim in advanced countries at present is to innovate in order to simplify the technical system, but otherwise to innovate as sparingly as possible. Every advanced country is overtechnologized; past a certain point, the quality of life diminishes with new "improvements." Yet no country is rightly technologized, making efficient use of available techniques. There are ingenious devices for unimportant functions, stressful mazes for essential functions, and drastic dislocation when anything goes wrong, which happens with increasing frequency. To add to the complexity, the mass of people tend to become incompetent and dependent on repairmen — indeed, unrepairability except by experts has become a desideratum of industrial design.

When I speak of slowing down or cutting back, the issue is not whether research and making working models should be encouraged or not. They should be, in every direction, and given a blank check. The point is to resist the temptation to apply every new device without a second thought. But the big corporate organization of research and development makes prudence and modesty very difficult; it is necessary to get big contracts and rush into production in order to pay the salaries of the big team. Like other bureaucracies, technological organizations are run to maintain themselves but they are more dangerous because, in capitalist countries, they are in a competitive arena.

I mean simplification quite strictly, to simplify the *technical* system. I am unimpressed by the argument that what is technically more complicated is really economically or politically simpler, e.g., by complicating the packaging we improve the supermarkets; by throwing away the machine rather than repairing it, we give cheaper and faster service all around; or even by expanding the economy with trivial innovations, we increase employment, allay discontent, save on welfare. Such ideas may be profitable for private companies or political parties, but for society they have proved to be an accelerating rat race. The technical structure of the environment is too important to be a political or economic pawn; the effect on the quality of life is too disastrous; and the hidden social costs are not calculated — the auto graveyards, the torn-up streets, the longer miles of commuting, the advertising, the inflation, etc. As I pointed out in *People or Personnel*, a country with a fourth of our per capita income, like Ireland, is not necessarily less well off; in some respects it is much richer, in some respects a little poorer. If possible, it is better to solve political problems by political means. For instance, if teaching machines and audiovisual aids are indeed educative, well and good; but if they are used just to save money on teachers, then not good at all — nor do they save money.

Of course, the goals of right technology must come to terms with other values of society. I am not a technocrat. But the advantage of raising technology to be a responsible learned profession with its own principles is that it can have a voice in the debate and argue for its proper contribution to the community. Consider the important case of modular sizes in building, or prefabrication of a unit bathroom: these conflict with the short-run interests of manufacturers and craft-unions, yet to deny them is technically an abomination. The usual recourse is for a government agency to set standards; such agencies accommodate to interests that have a strong voice, and at present technologists have no voice.

The crucial need for technological simplification, however, is not in the advanced countries — which can afford their clutter and probably deserve it — but in underdeveloped countries which must rapidly innovate in order to diminish disease, drudgery, and deepening starvation. They cannot afford to make mistakes. It is now widely conceded that the technological aid we have given to such areas according to our own high style — a style usually demanded by the native ruling groups — has done more harm than good. Even when, as frequently if not usually, aid has been benevolent, without strings attached, not military, and not dumping, it has nevertheless disrupted ways of life, fomented tribal wars, accelerated urbanization, decreased the food supply, gone wasted for lack of skills to use it, developed a do-nothing élite.

By contrast, a group of international scientists called Intermediate Technology argue that what is needed is techniques that use only native labor, resources, traditional customs, and teachable know-how, with the simple aim of remedying drudgery, disease, and hunger, so that people can then develop further in their own style. This avoids cultural imperialism. Such intermediate techniques may be quite primitive, on a level unknown among us for a couple of centuries, and yet they may pose extremely subtle problems, requiring exquisite scientific research and political and human understanding, to devise a very simple technology. Here is a reported case (which I trust I remember accurately): In Botswana, a very poor country, pasture was overgrazed, but the economy could be salvaged if the land were fenced. There was no local material for fencing, and imported fencing was prohibitively expensive. The solution was to find the formula and technique to make posts out of mud, and a pedagogic method to teach people how to do it.

In *The Two Cultures*, C. P. Snow berated the humanists for their irrelevance when two-thirds of mankind are starving and what is needed is science and technology. They have perhaps been irrelevant; but unless technology is itself more humanistic and philosophical, it is of no use. There is only one culture.

Finally, let me make a remark about amenity as a technical criterion. It is discouraging to see the concern about beautifying a highway and banning billboards, and about the cosmetic appearance of the cars, when there is no regard for the ugliness of bumper-to-bumper traffic and the suffering of the drivers. Or the concern for preserving a historical landmark while the neighborhood is torn up and the city has no shape. Without moral philosophy, people have nothing but sentiments.

ECOLOGY

The complement to prudent technology is the ecological approach to science. To simplify the technical system and modestly pinpoint our artificial intervention in the environment makes it possible for the environment to survive in its complexity evolved for a billion years, whereas the overwhelming instant intervention of tightly interlocked and bulldozing technology has already disrupted many of the delicate sequences and balances. The calculable consequences are already frightening, but of course we don't know enough, and won't in the foreseeable future, to predict the remote effects of much of what we have done. The only possible conclusion is to be prudent; when there is serious doubt, to do nothing.

Cyberneticists — I am thinking of Gregory Bateson — come to the same cautious conclusion. The use of computers has enabled us to carry out crashingly inept programs on the bases of willful analyses. But we have also become increasingly alert to the fact that things respond, systematically, continually, cumulatively; they cannot simply be manipulated or pushed around. Whether bacteria or weeds or bugs or the technologically unemployed or unpleasant thoughts, they cannot be eliminated and forgotten; repressed, the nuisances return in new forms. A complicated system works most efficiently if its parts readjust themselves decentrally, with a minimum of central intervention or control, except in case of breakdown. Usually there is an advantage in a central clearinghouse of information about the gross total situation, but decision and execution require more minute local information. The fantastically simulated moon landing hung on a last split-second correction on the spot. In social organization, deciding in headquarters means relying on information that is cumulatively abstract and irrelevant, and chain-of-command execution applies standards that cumulatively do not fit the concrete situation. By and large it is better, given a sense of the whole picture, for those in the field to decide what to do and do it.

But with organisms too, this has long been the bias of psychosomatic medicine, the Wisdom of the Body, as Cannon called it. To cite a classical experiment of Ralph Hefferline of Columbia: a subject is wired to suffer an annoying regular buzz, which can be delayed and finally eliminated if he makes a precise but unlikely gesture, say by twisting his ankle in a certain way; then it is found that he adjusts quicker if he is *not* told the method and it is left to his spontaneous twitching than if he is told and tries deliberately to help himself. He adjusts better without conscious control, his own or the experimenter's.

Technological modesty, fittingness, is not negative. It is the ecological wisdom of cooperating with Nature rather than trying to master her. (The personification of "Nature" is linguistic wisdom.) A well-known example is the long-run superiority of partial pest-control in farming by using biological deterrents rather than chemical ones. The living defenders work harder, at the right moment, and with more pinpointed targets. But let me give another example because it is so lovely — though I have forgotten the name of my informant: A tribe in Yucatan educates its children to identify and pull up all weeds in the region; then what is left is a garden of useful plants that have chosen to be there and now thrive.

In the life sciences there is at present a suggestive bifurcation in methodology. The rule is still to increase experimental intervention, but there is also a considerable revival of old-fashioned naturalism, mainly watching and thinking, with very modest intervention. Thus, in medicine, there is new diagnostic machinery, new drugs, spectacular surgery; but there is also a new respect for family practice with psychosomatic background, and a strong push, among young doctors and students, for a social-psychological and sociological approach, aimed at preventing disease and building up resistance. In psychology, the operant conditioners multiply and refine their machinery to give maximum control of the organism and the environment (I have not heard of any dramatic discoveries, but perhaps they have escaped me). On the other hand, the most interesting psychology in recent years has certainly come from animal naturalists, e.g., pecking order, territoriality, learning to control aggression, language of the bees, overcrowding among rats, trying to talk to dolphins.

On a fair judgment, both contrasting approaches give positive results. The logical scientific problem that arises is, What is there in the nature of things that makes a certain method, or even moral attitude, work well or poorly in a given case? This question is not much studied. Every scientist seems to know what "the" scientific method is.

Another contrast of style, extremely relevant at present, is that between Big Science and old-fashioned shoestring science. There is plenty of research, with corresponding technology, that can be done only by Big Science; yet much, and perhaps most, of science will always be shoestring science, for which it is absurd to use the fancy and expensive equipment that has gotten to be the fashion.

Consider urban medicine. The problem, given a shortage of doctors and facilities, is how to improve the level of mass health, the vital statistics, and yet to practice medicine, which aims at the maximum possible health for each person. Perhaps the most efficient use of Big Science technology for the general health would be compulsory biennial checkups, as we inspect cars, for early diagnosis and to forestall chronic conditions with accumulating costs. Then an excellent machine would be a total diagnostic bus to visit the neighborhoods, as we do [with] chest X-rays. On the other hand, for actual treatment and especially for convalescence, the evidence seems to be that small, personalized hospitals are best. And to revive family practice, maybe the right idea is to offer a doctor a splendid suite in a public housing project.

Our contemporary practice makes little sense. We have expensive technology stored in specialists' offices and big hospitals, really unavailable for mass use in the neighborhoods; yet every individual, even if he is quite rich, finds it almost impossible to get attention to himself as an individual whole organism in his setting. He is sent from specialist to specialist and exists as a bag of symptoms and a file of test scores.

In automating there is an analogous dilemma of how to cope with masses of people and get economies of scale, without losing the individual at great consequent human and economic cost. A question of immense importance for the immediate future is, Which functions should be automated or organized to use business machines, and which should not? This question also is not getting asked, and the present disposition is that the sky is the limit for extraction, refining, manufacturing, processing, packaging, transportation, clerical work, ticketing, transactions, information retrieval, recruitment, middle management, evaluation, diagnosis, instruction, and even research and invention Whether the machines can do all these kinds of jobs and more is partly an empirical question, but it also partly depends on what is meant by doing a job. Very often, e.g., in college admissions, machines are acquired for putative economies (which do not eventuate); but the true reason is that an overgrown and overcentralized organization cannot be administered without them. The technology conceals the essential trouble, e.g., that there is no community of scholars and students are treated like things. The function is badly performed, and finally the system breaks down anyway. I doubt that enterprises in which interpersonal relations are important are suited to much programming.

But worse, what can happen is that the real function of the enterprise is subtly altered so that it is suitable for the mechanical system (F..g., "information retrieval" is taken as an adequate replacement for critical scholarship.) Incommensurable factors, individual differences, the local context, the weighting of evidence are quietly overlooked though they may be of the essence. The system, with its subtly transformed purposes, seems to run very smoothly; it is productive, and it is more and more out of line with the nature of things and the real problems. Meantime it is geared in with other enterprises of society, e.g., major public policy may depend on welfare or unemployment statistics, which, as they are tabulated, are blind to the actual lives of poor families. In such a case, the particular system may not break down, the whole society may explode.

I need hardly point out that American society is peculiarly liable to the corruption of inauthenticity, busily producing phony products. It lives by public relations, abstract ideals, front politics, show-business communications, mandarin credentials. It is preeminently overtechnologized. And computer technologists especially suffer for the euphoria of being in a new and rapidly expanding field. It is so astonishing that the robot can do the job at all or seem to do it, that it is easy to blink at the fact that it is doing it badly or isn't really doing quite that job.

DECENTRALIZATION

The current political assumption is that scientists and inventors, and even social scientists, are "value-neutral," but their discoveries are "applied" by those who make decisions for the nation. Counter to this, I have been insinuating a kind of Jeffersonian democracy or guild socialism, that scientists and inventors and other workmen are responsible for the uses of the work they do, and ought to be competent to judge these uses and have a say in deciding them. They usually are competent. To give a striking example, Ford assembly-line workers, according to Harvey Swados, who worked with them, are accurately critical of the glut of cars, but they have no way to vent their dissatisfactions with their useless occupation except to leave nuts and bolts to rattle in the body.

My bias is also pluralistic. Instead of the few national goals of a few decision-makers, I propose that there are many goals of many activities of life, and many professions and other interest groups each with its own criteria and goals that must be taken into account. A society that distributes power widely is superficially conflictful but fundamentally stable.

Research and development ought to be widely decentralized, the national fund for them being distributed through thousands of centers of initiative and decision. This would not be chaotic. We seem to have forgotten that for four hundred years Western science majestically progressed with no central direction whatever, yet with exquisite international coordination, little duplication, almost nothing getting lost, in constant communication despite slow facilities. The reason was simply that all scientists wanted to get on with the same enterprise of testing the boundaries of knowledge, and they relied on one another.

What is noteworthy is that something similar holds also in invention and innovation, even in recent decades when there has been such a concentration of funding and apparent concentration of opportunity. The majority of big advances have still come from independents, partnerships, and tiny companies. (Evidence published by the Senate Subcommittee on Antitrust and Monopoly, May 1965.) To name a few, jet engines, xerography, automatic transmission, cellophane, air-conditioning, quick freeze, antibiotics, and tranquilizers. The big technological teams must have disadvantages that outweigh their advantages, like lack of single-mindedness, poor communications, awkward scheduling. Naturally, big corporations have taken over the innovations, but the Senate evidence is that 90 percent of the government subsidy has gone for last-stage development for production, which they ought to have paid out of their own pockets.

We now have a theory that we have learned to learn, and that we can program technical progress, directed by a central planning board. But this doesn't make it so. The essence of the new still seems to be that nobody has thought of it, and the ones who get ideas are those in direct contact with the work. *Too precise* a preconception of what is wanted discourages creativity more than it channels it; and bureaucratic memoranda from distant directors don't help. This is especially true when, as at present, so much of the preconception of what is wanted comes from desperate political anxiety in emergencies. Solutions that emerge from such an attitude rarely strike out on new paths, but rather repeat traditional thinking with new gimmicks; they tend to compound the problem. A priceless advantage of widespread decentralization is that it engages more minds, and more mind, instead of a few panicky (or greedy) corporate minds.

A homespun advantage of small groups, according to the Senate testimony, is that co-workers can talk to one another, without schedules, reports, clock-watching, and face-saving.

An important hope from decentralizing science is to develop knowledgeable citizens, and provide not only a bigger pool of scientists and inventors but also a public better able to protect itself and know how to judge the enormous budgets asked for. The safety of the environment is too important to be left to scientists, even ecologists. During the last decades of the nineteenth century and the first decade of the twentieth, the heyday of public faith in the beneficent religion of science and invention, say from Pasteur and Huxley to Edison and the Wright brothers, philosophers of science had a vision of a "scientific way of life," one in which people would be objective, respectful of evidence, accurate, free of superstition and taboo, immune to irrational authority, experimental. All would be well, is the impression one gets from Thomas Huxley, if everybody knew the splendid Ninth Edition of the *Encyclopaedia Britannica* with its articles by Darwin and Clerk Maxwell. Veblen put his faith in the modesty and matter-of-factness of engineers to govern. Sullivan and Frank Lloyd Wright spoke for an austere functionalism and respect for the nature of materials and industrial processes. Patrick Geddes thought that new technology would finally get us out of the horrors of the Industrial Revolution and produce good communities. John Dewey devised a system of education to rear pragmatic and experimental citizens to be at home in the new technological world rather than estranged from it. Now fifty years later, we are in the swamp of a scientific and technological environment and there are more scientists alive, etc., etc. But the mention of the "scientific way of life" seems like black humor.

Many of those who have grown up since 1945 and have never seen any other state of science and technology assume that rationalism itself is totally evil and dehumanizing. It is probably more significant than we like to think that they go in for astrology and the Book of Changes, as well as inducing psychedelic dreams by technological means. Jacques Ellul, a more philosophic critic, tries to show that technology is necessarily overcontrolling, standardizing, and voraciously inclusive, so that there is no place for freedom. But I doubt that any of this is intrinsic to science and technology. The crude history has been, rather, that they have fallen willingly under the dominion of money and power. Like Christianity or communism, the scientific way of life has never been tried.

THE NEW REFORMATION

To satisfy the March 4 dissenters, to break the military-industrial corporations and alter the priorities of the budget, would be to restructure the American economy almost to a revolutionary extent. But to meet the historical crisis of science at present, for science and technology to become prudent, ecological, and decentralized requires a change that is even more profound, a kind of religious transformation. Yet there is nothing untraditional in what I have proposed; prudence, ecology, and decentralization are indeed the high tradition of science and technology. Thus the closest analogy I can think of is the Protestant Reformation, a change of moral allegiance, liberation from the Whore of Babylon, return to the pure faith.

Science has long been the chief orthodoxy of modern times and has certainly been badly corrupted, but the deepest flaw of the affluent societies that has alienated the young is not, finally, their imperialism, economic injustice, or racism, bad as these are, but their nauseating phoniness, triviality, and wastefulness, the cultural and moral scandal that Luther found when he went to Rome in 1510. And precisely science, which should have been the wind of truth to clear the air, has polluted the air, helped to brainwash, and provided weapons for war. I doubt that most young people today have even heard of the ideal of the dedicated researcher, truculent and incorruptible, and unrewarded, for instance the "German scientist" that Sinclair Lewis described in *Arrowsmith*. Such a figure is no longer believable. I don't mean, of course, that he doesn't exist; there must be thousands of him, just as there were good priests in 1510.

The analogy to the Reformation is even more exact if we consider the school system, from educational toys and Head Start up through the universities. This system is manned by the biggest horde of monks since the time of Henry VIII. It is the biggest industry in the country. I have heard the estimate that 40 percent of the national product is in the Knowledge Business. It is mostly hocus-pocus. Yet the belief of parents in this institution is quite delusional and school diplomas are in fact the only entry to licensing and hiring in every kind of job. The abbots of this system are the chiefs of science, e.g., the National Science Foundation, who talk about reform but work to expand the school budgets, step up the curriculum, and inspire the endless catechism of tests.

These abuses are international, as the faith is. For instance, there is no essential difference between the military-industrial or the school systems of the Soviet Union and the United States. There are important differences in way of life and standard of living, but the abuses of technology are very similar: pollution, excessive urbanization, destruction of the biosphere, weaponry, and disastrous foreign aid. Our protesters naturally single out our own country, and the United States is the most powerful country, but the corruption we are speaking of is not specifically American nor even capitalist; it is a disease of modern times.

But the analogy is to the Reformation, it is not to primitive Christianity or some other primitivism, the abandonment of technological civilization. There is indeed much talk about the doom of Western civilization, and a few Adamites actually do retire into the hills; but for the great mass of mankind, and myself, that's not where it's at. There is not the slightest interruption to the universalizing of Western Civilization, including most of its delusions, into the so-called Third World. (If the atom bombs go off, however?)

Naturally the exquisitely interesting question is whether or not this Reformation will occur, how to make it occur, against the entrenched worldwide system of corrupt power that is continually aggrandizing itself. I don't know. In my analogy I have deliberately been choosing the date 1510, Luther in Rome, rather than 1517 when, in the popular story, he nailed his Theses on the cathedral door. There are everywhere contradictory signs and dilemmas. The new professional and technological class is more and more entangled in the work, statuses, and rewards of the system, and yet this same class, often the very same people, are more and more Protestant. On the other hand, the dissident young, who are unequivocally for radical change, are so alienated from occupation, function, knowledge, or even concern, that they often seem to be simply irrelevant to the underlying issues of modern times. The monks keep "improving" the schools and getting bigger budgets to do so, yet it is clear that high schools will be burned down, twelve-year-olds will play truant in droves, and the taxpayers are already asking what goes on and voting down the bonds.

The interlocking of technologies and all other institutions makes it almost impossible to reform policy in any part; yet this very interlocking that renders people powerless, including the decision-makers, creates a remarkable resonance and chain reaction if any determined group, or even determined individual, exerts force. In the face of overwhelmingly collective operations like space exploration, the average man must feel that local or grassroots efforts are worthless, there is no science but Big Science, and no administration but the State. And yet there is a powerful surge of localism, populism, and community action, as if people were determined to be free even if it makes no sense. A mighty empire is stood off by a band of peasants, and *neither* can win — this is even more remarkable than if David beats Goliath; it means that neither principle is historically adequate. In my opinion, these dilemmas and impasses show that we are on the eve of a transformation of conscience.

11. Technological Politics As If Democracy Really Mattered

RICHARD SCLOVE

"Of all the social impacts of technology," writes Richard Sclove in the following selection, "perhaps the most worrisome are the adverse effects on democracy." Technologies as diverse as microwave ovens, air conditioning, and urban sewage systems all have aspects that can prove detrimental to human communities and to democracy. Sclove has no desire to reject all technology outright, however. Rather, he would like us "to become more discriminating in how we design, choose, and use technologies" — a course that might force us to give democracy priority over short-run economic goals.

How would democratic technologies look? Sclove proposes a set of design criteria. He gives examples, including several from Scandinavian nations, of technologies that meet these criteria. And he suggests some of the ways in which our political system and the nation's R&D enterprise might contribute to the development and promotion of democratic technologies. Sclove's essay comes from the "progressive left" political tradition. Some might regard it as hopelessly idealistic, particularly in view of current political trends in the United States that seem to run in the opposite direction. Nevertheless, it is a provocative piece that should give readers from all parts of the political spectrum much food for thought.

Richard Sclove, executive director of the Loka Institute in Amherst, Massachusetts, is the author of Democracy and Technology *(Guilford Press, 1995). He is also the founder of the Federation of Activists on Science and Technology Network (FASTnet). Sclove, whose education combines a B.A. in environmental studies with a graduate degree in nuclear engineering and Ph.D. in political science from MIT, founded the Loka Institute in 1987 as a vehicle to carry on his work, which is dedicated to making science and technology more responsive to democratically decided social and environmental concerns. He is a popular lecturer and serves as a consultant to a variety of organizations.*

A century and a half ago Alexis de Tocqueville described a politically exuberant United States in which steaming locomotives could not restrain citizens' enthusiasm to involve themselves in politics and community life:

> In some countries the inhabitants seem unwilling to avail themselves of the political privileges which the law gives them; it would seem that they set too high a value upon their time to spend it on the interests of the community; and they shut themselves up in a narrow selfishness. . . . But if an American were

condemned to confine his activity to his own affairs, he would be robbed of one half of his existence; he would feel an immense void in the life which he is accustomed to lead, and his wretchedness would be unbearable.[1]

That is not today's United States, in which a bare majority of eligible voters participate in presidential elections while usually even fewer engage in local politics.[2] The causes of Americans' political disengagement are complex, but one culprit, more significant and intricate than commonly believed, is technology. Consider an instructive story from across the Atlantic.

During the early 1970s running water was installed in the houses of Ibieca, a small village in northeast Spain. With pipes running directly to their homes, Ibiecans no longer had to fetch water from the village fountain. Families gradually purchased washing machines, and women stopped gathering to scrub laundry by hand at the village washbasin. Arduous tasks were rendered technologically superfluous, but village social life was unexpectedly altered. The public fountain and washbasin, once scenes of vigorous social interaction, became nearly deserted. Men began losing their sense of familiarity with the children and donkeys that once helped them haul water. Women stopped gathering at the washbasin to intermix scrubbing with politically empowering gossip about men and village life. In hindsight the installation of running water helped break down the Ibiecans' strong bonds — with one another, with their animals, and with the land — that had knit them together as a community.[3] Painful in itself, such loss of community carries a specific political cost as well: as social ties weaken, so does a people's capacity to mobilize for political action.[4]

Is this a parable for our time? Like Ibiecans, we acquiesce in seemingly benign or innocuous technological changes. Ibiecans opted for technological innovations promising convenience, productivity, and economic growth. But they did not anticipate the hidden costs: greater inequality, social alienation, and steps toward community disintegration and political disempowerment. Does technological change invariably embody a Faustian trade-off between economic reward and sociopolitical malaise? No, not invariably. But the best hope for escaping such trade-offs is to develop a full-blown democratic politics of technology — something that even political progressives have not begun to conceive.

* * *

TECHNOLOGY AND DEMOCRACY

The approach to technology policy proposed here is grounded morally in the belief that people should be able to shape the basic social circumstances of their lives. It is aimed at organizing society along relatively equal and participatory lines, at achieving a system of egalitarian decentralization and confederation that Rutgers political scientist Benjamin Barber calls "strong democracy."[5] Historic examples of strong democracy include New England town meetings, the confederation of self-governing Swiss villages and cantons, and the tradition of trial by a jury of peers. Strong democracy also is apparent in the methods or aspirations of various social movements, such as the late nineteenth-century American Farmers Alliance, the 1960s civil rights movement, and the 1980s uprising of Solidarity in Poland.[6] In each of these cases ordinary people claimed the rights and responsibilities of active citizenship.

If citizens ought to be empowered to participate in determining their society's basic structure and if technologies *are* an important part of that structure, it follows that technological design and practice should be democratized. Substantively, technologies must be compatible with our fundamental interest in strong democracy. And procedurally, people from all walks of life must have expanding opportunities to shape the evolving technological order.

DESIGN CRITERIA FOR DEMOCRATIC TECHNOLOGIES

Table 1 presents some criteria for distinguishing among technologies based on their compatibility with democracy. The criteria are labeled "provisional" because they are neither complete nor definitive. Rather, they are intended to provoke political debate that can lead to an improved set of criteria.

Each criterion is intended to fulfill the institutional requirements for strong democracy: democratic community, democratic work, or democratic politics.[7] Technological decisions should attend initially and foremost to strengthening democracy, because democracy provides the necessary circumstances for deciding freely and fairly what other considerations must be taken into account in technological (and non-technological) decision making. Until we do this, technologies will continue to hinder the advancement of other social objectives in subtle yet significant ways.

A series of examples can help explain these criteria and the feasibility of designing technologies that can satisfy them. Before proceeding, however, one clarifying note is in order. Each of the following examples illustrates a worthy social and democratic goal in its own right. However, isolated technological changes of this sort cannot be expected to represent a significant improvement in the overall democratization of society. The latter result will require multiple democratic design criteria, applied simultaneously to diverse technologies by citizens who employ broadly democratized processes of technological decision making. In other words, all the elements of a complete democratic politics of technology should converge at one time.

Criterion A: Technology and Democratic Community

Egalitarian community life is important to strong democracy because it enhances citizens' mutual respect, shared understanding, political equality, and social commitment. It empowers individuals within collectivities to challenge unjust concentrations of power. Unfortunately, diverse technological developments have contributed to the decline of community. The noise and danger of automobile traffic, detached single-family homes, air conditioning, and television all have

Table 1.   A Provisional System of Design Criteria for Democratic Technologies

TOWARD DEMOCRATIC COMMUNITY:
A. Seek a balance among communitarian/cooperative, individualized, and inter-community technologies. Avoid technologies that establish authoritarian social relationships.

TOWARD DEMOCRATIC WORK:
B. Seek a diverse array of flexibly schedulable, self-actualizing technological practices. Avoid meaningless, debilitating, or otherwise autonomy-impairing technological practices.

TOWARD DEMOCRATIC POLITICS:
C. Seek technologies that can enable disadvantaged individuals and groups to participate fully in social and political life. Avoid technologies that support illegitimately hierarchical power relations between groups, organizations, or polities.

TO SECURE DEMOCRATIC SELF-GOVERNANCE:
D. Keep the potentially adverse consequences (e.g., environmental or social harms) of technologies within the boundaries of local political jurisdictions.
E. Seek local economic self-reliance. Avoid technologies that promote dependency and loss of local autonomy.
F. Seek technologies (including an architecture of public space) compatible with globally aware, egalitarian political decentralization and federation.

TO PERPETUATE DEMOCRATIC SOCIAL STRUCTURES:
G. Avoid technologies that are ecologically unsustainable or destructive of human health, survival, and the perpetuation of democratic institutions.

isolated families away from one another and undermined a sense of collective purpose. This has been exacerbated by the loss of public spaces (with, for instance, town commons being supplanted by shopping malls).[8]

Are these plausible alternatives? Zurich, Switzerland, has promoted a partial antidote by providing neighborhoods with legal advice and architectural assistance aimed at increasing community interaction.[9] Thanks to the program, neighbors have begun to remove backyard fences; to build new walkways, gardens, and other community facilities; and generally to refashion a system of purely private yards into a well-balanced blend of private, semipublic, and public spaces.[10]

A housing movement born in Denmark in the mid-1960s seeks, more ambitiously, to integrate desirable aspects of traditional village life with such contemporary realities as urbanization, smaller families, single-parent or working-parent households, and greater sexual equality. The result is "co-housing" — resident-planned communities ranging today from 6 to 80 households. More than 100 such communities now exist in Denmark and the Netherlands, and they are spreading to the United States and elsewhere.

The Trudeslund co-housing community, located near Copenhagen, comprises thirty-three families. Homes for each family cluster along two garden-lined pedestrian streets and are surrounded by ample open space and forested areas. Each home has its own kitchen, living room, and bedrooms, though these rooms have been somewhat downsized so that the savings can be used to construct and maintain common facilities. The latter include picnic tables, sandboxes, a parking lot, and, most importantly, a "common house" with a large kitchen and dining room, playrooms, a darkroom, a workshop room, a laundry room, and a community store. Each night residents have the option of eating in the common dining room; cooking responsibilities rotate among all adults in the community (which means everyone cooks one evening a month). Because the community is designed to have residents walk past the common house on the way from the parking lot to any house, the common house becomes a natural gathering spot.

Trudeslund is successful by many measures. The common facilities save time and money, day care and baby-sitting flow naturally from the pattern of community life, social interaction flourishes without sacrificing privacy, and safety and conviviality both prosper by banishing cars to the outskirts of the community. Over time cooperation has grown, with resident families choosing to purchase and share collectively tools, a car, a sailboat, and a vacation home. Rather than becoming insular, residents are actively involved in social and political life outside Trudeslund, with the common house serving as an organizing base for other activities.[11]

Insofar as mutual respect and equality are fundamental democratic values, an egalitarian community represents a democratic gain in its own right. Moreover, if one could envision creating an interacting network of such communities, one could expect to see greater respect, tolerance, and commonality emerging *between* communities, with beneficial implications for democratization on a broader scale.[12]

Criterion B: Democratic Work

Social scientists have hypothesized that the quality of our work life influences our moral development and our readiness to function as engaged citizens — that is, as active participants in a strong democracy.[13] Technology, in turn, plays a critical role in shaping our work experiences. Some years ago sociologist and one-time union organizer Robert Schrank discussed alternative work arrangements with a group of union representatives at the General Motors Corporation. After describing several experiments in Scandinavian factories that permitted more interesting work routines and greater worker involvement in the day-to-day decision making, Schrank asked the men to imagine how they might redesign their own factories if given a chance. Their response was skeptical and unenthusiastic. Later Schrank reflected: "[T]he frame of reference of these workers was the linear assembly line as they experienced it. Even to think beyond that seemed difficult."[14]

Linear assembly lines not only tend to restrict possibilities for worker self-management, conviviality, and meaningful work but also to impair the ability of workers to envision technological alternatives. Schrank, however, was eventually able to show the GM workers more democratic automobile manufacturing technologies that have been in use for some years. For example, an innovative Volvo factory in Kalmar, Sweden, uses independently movable electronic dollies — each carrying an individual auto chassis — in place of a traditional assembly line. The dollies enable small teams of workers to plan and vary their daily routines for assembling automobile subsystems.[15]

A more creative and self-managed workplace "is democratically desirable in itself. But it also can help workers develop the moral commitment, skills, and confidence to participate politically beyond the workplace.

Criterion C: Technology and Power

While political equality is essential for strong democracy, all contemporary political systems encompass groups whose opportunities for participating in social and political life are circumscribed. Today's technologies help reproduce this inequitable constellation of power. For instance, the technologies and architecture with which women must cope every day often help exclude them from the corridors of power. "Labor-saving" appliances "liberate" many wives to do housework that was once performed by other family members. (During the bygone era of open hearth cooking, for example, men chopped wood and children hauled water, thus contributing more equally to household maintenance.)[16] Likewise, modern neighborhood designs often isolate women socially, heighten their risk of physical abuse, and limit their opportunities to organize child care. The typical suburb lacks sidewalks, common gathering spaces, or the opportunity to work within a short distance of home.[17] Most public-transit systems have been designed without regard to women's typical social responsibilities. How is a mother supposed to get a baby carriage up onto a traditional bus or down the steps of a New York City subway station?[18] Many workplaces have jobs stereotyped as female that carry special risks of isolation, domination, stress, or harm. Secretaries and key-punch operators, who are preponderantly female, suffer unusually high levels of stress-related emotional and physical disorders. The marketing techniques of the mass media often degrade women and erect punishingly unattainable beauty standards.[19]

All of these consequences of technology limit women's opportunities to participate on equal terms in social and political life — including technological decision making. To explain these results, one need not invoke theories of misogyny or conspiracy (although the temptation may be strong). Generally it seems more plausible to blame the indifference and insensitivity of male-dominated institutions and design professions, in which women's evaluations of their own needs rarely qualify as even a discussion topic.

Criterion D: Translocal Harms

Local self-governance is a key building block for strong democracy. The average citizen can exert much more influence locally than nationally, and local political equality and autonomy provide crucial opportunities for citizens to influence translocal politics.

Technologies can affect a community's ability to govern itself in several ways. For example, a technology that harms people in neighboring communities can provoke intercommunity conflict, which in turn can precipitate intervention by higher political authorities that subverts local self-governance. In the late nineteenth and early twentieth centuries, American cities imported clean water, or filtered and treated incoming water, while discharging raw sewage into rivers and lakes. Various methods of sewage treatment were known or under development, but few cities adopted them (unless the raw sewage caused local harm). As the buildup of sewage increased illness and death in downstream communities, state governments passed preemptive laws protecting water quality, established state boards of health to help administer the laws, and created new regional governmental authorities ("special districts") charged with integrating and managing the systems of water supply and sewage treatment. The result of this state intervention was that water quality and public health dramatically improved — but local autonomy dramatically declined. Indeed, regional water management set a precedent that influenced the development of institutions governing transportation, electrification, and telephone communication. The failure of municipal governments to assume technological responsibility toward neighboring communities wound up subverting their own autonomy and the tradition of local self-governance.[20]

Today a related pattern continues to play out as large corporations repeatedly use cross-border pollution as a rationale to justify environmental regulation at ever higher levels of political aggregation (shifting, that is, from local to state, national, and ultimately international authorities). When "successful," this reallocation of power has transposed environmental decision making to arenas relatively inaccessible to grassroots participation, where corporations have secured weak environmental standards that preempt stronger standards favored at the local level. This logic helps to explain industry support for the 1970 U.S. Clean Air Act and for the 1990 amendments to the Montreal Protocol (a treaty that regulates emissions of industrial chemicals hazardous to the earth's atmospheric ozone shield).[21] The erosion of local authority to control pollution has thus led to a violation of Criterion G in Table 1 — "seek ecological sustainability."

Criterion E: Local Economic Self-Reliance

How can citizens meaningfully decide the fate of their community if economic survival depends on institutions or forces utterly beyond their control? Just as a measure of local political autonomy is essential for strong democracy, so, in turn, is a measure of local and regional economic self-reliance essential for political autonomy. Many modern technologies, however, can subvert self-reliance.

A century ago London differed from other leading world cities in eschewing reliance on a single major electric company, large generating plants, or even a city-wide electric grid. Instead there were dozens of small electric companies scattered throughout London — some privately owned, some public — deploying a diverse array of small-scale electrical generating technologies. Was London just back-wards and irrational, as engineers from elsewhere commonly supposed? Not obvi-ously. London's electric companies operated at a profit and provided reliable and affordable power adapted to local needs. London's borough governments, perceiv-ing their own political significance and autonomy as inextricable from the infra-structures upon which they depended economically, consistently opposed Parliamentary efforts to consolidate the grid. The boroughs favored a highly decen-tralized electrical system that each could control more easily.[22]

For analogous reasons, a number of American cities, towns, and neighbor-hoods have begun to develop locally owned businesses oriented toward produc-tion for nearby markets. The Rocky Mountain Institute has developed an analytical process, along with supporting instructional materials, which a growing number of towns in economic difficulty are using to reduce their consumption of imported energy, water, and food (rather than to depend on distant supplies) and to reinvest local capital (rather than to put it in the hands of bankers thousands of miles away).[23] Once these communities are more secure against distant market forces or multinational corporate decisions, they are more empowered to con-ceive and undertake local democratic initiatives.[24]

This strategy of self-reliance contrasts strikingly with the prevalent strategy used by communities — self-defeating when it is not futile — of using conces-sionary tax breaks, waivers on environmental standards or the promise of low wages to try to entice geographically fickle corporations. While generally decry-ing these corporate inducements, most proposed progressive technological strate-gies nonetheless remain preoccupied with advancing U.S. international competitiveness in ways that will assuredly *erode* local self-reliance. [25]

DEMOCRATIC DESIGN VERSUS PROGRESSIVE PROPOSALS

Several of the preceding examples suggest an important deficiency in the familiar progressive call to "rebuild America's crumbling technological infrastructure."[26] If our infrastructure needs repair or modernization, shouldn't we rebuild it in ways amenable to local democratic governance? For instance, there are technolo-gies for managing industrial and municipal waste and conserving energy that can be deployed and administered with extensive local involvement.[27] Facilities to store solar energy for heating homes and buildings, as pioneered in Scandinavia, comprise another example of neighborhood-scale technology. Indeed, unless localities regain more control of their own infrastructures, there will be dimin-ished incentive for the kind of grassroots political involvement essential to strong democracy. People only will participate in local politics when they have the power to affect important local decisions.

Another significant feature of all the preceding criteria is that they are designed to work together as a complementary system applied to an entire technological order. This too can improve the technology policies advocated by progressives. For instance, advocates of workplace democracy aim admirably to fulfill Criteria A and B, but generally fail to inquire whether the resulting goods and services are socially benign.[28] If we competitively and democratically produce democratically dubious technologies — say, chemical weapons, or certain consumer electronics like Walkmen that erode social interaction and solidarity — are we really making progress?[29]

Similarly, in an era of growing popular concern over acid rain, atmospheric ozone depletion, and global warming, few doubt the necessity of devising more ecologically sustainable technologies (Criterion G). Yet environmentalists sometimes imagine that sustainability alone is a sufficient basis for technological design.[30] To see the incompleteness here, recall the old sewage system configurations that both protected public health *and* subverted local self-governance, or consider Singapore's relatively stringent environmental policies that are coupled with a starkly authoritarian political regime.[31] In evaluating technology, we must learn to take into account all technologies, all their focal and nonfocal effects, and all the manifold ways in which technologies influence political relations.

TOWARD A DEMOCRATIC POLITICS OF TECHNOLOGY

Democratic design criteria are essential to a democratic politics of technology, but only if coupled with institutions for greater popular involvement in all domains of technological decision making. This suggests the need to establish new opportunities for popular participation to contest and apply the design criteria (in communities, workplaces, and other social realms), to set research and development (R&D) priorities, and to govern important technological systems. For instance, perhaps corporate R&D tax credits could be scaled up if a business introduces a democratic process or uses democratic design criteria to guide its R&D.

Our basic goal must be to open, democratize, and partly decentralize pertinent government agencies, to create avenues for worker and community involvement in corporate R&D and strategic planning, and to strengthen the capabilities of public institutions to monitor and, as needed, guide the political and social consequences of technology. We also need political strategies to accomplish these objectives, preferably built on popular movements and technological initiatives that already exist.[32]

One pertinent example of how to democratize technological decision making began in the early 1970s, when natural gas was found beneath the frigid and remote northwest corner of Canada. Energy companies soon proposed building a high-pressure, chilled pipeline across thousands of miles of wilderness, the traditional home of the Inuit (Eskimos) and various Indian tribes. At that point a government ministry, anticipating significant environmental and social repercussions, initiated a public inquiry under the supervision of a respected Supreme Court justice, Thomas R. Berger.

The MacKenzie Valley Pipeline Inquiry opened its preliminary hearings to any Canadian who felt remotely affected by the proposal. Berger and his staff developed a novel format to encourage a thorough, open, and accessible inquiry. Formal, quasi-judicial hearings were held that combined conventional expert testimony with cross-examination. Berger also conducted a series of informal "community hearings." Traveling 17,000 miles to 35 remote villages and settlements, the

MacKenzie Inquiry took testimony from nearly 1,000 native witnesses. And it provided funding to disadvantaged groups to support travel and legal counsel for more competent participation. The Canadian Broadcasting Company carried daily radio summaries of all the hearings in English and in six native languages.

One of the MacKenzie Inquiry's important lessons was that laypeople can produce useful social *and* technical information. According to one technical adviser:

> Input from nontechnical people played a key role in the Inquiry's deliberations over even the most highly technical and specialized scientific and engineering subjects. . . . [The final report] discusses the biological vulnerability of the Beaufort Sea based not only on the evidence of the highly trained biological experts who testified at the formal hearings but also on the views of the Inuit hunters who spoke at the community hearings. . . . [Moreover,] when discussion turned to . . . complex socioeconomic issues of social and cultural impact, [native] land claims, and local business involvement — it became apparent that the people who live their lives with the issues are in every sense the experts. . . . Their perceptions provided precisely the kind of information necessary to make an impact assessment.[33]

Quoting generously from expert and citizen witnesses, Berger's final report became a national best-seller. Within months the original pipeline proposal was rejected, and the Canadian Parliament instead approved an alternate route paralleling the existing Alaska Highway.[34] One can fault the MacKenzie Inquiry for depending so much on the democratic sensibilities and good faith of one man — Judge Berger — rather than empowering the affected native groups to play a role in formulating the conclusions. But the process was nevertheless vastly more open and egalitarian than comparable decisionmaking efforts in other industrial societies.[35]

There are many other prototypes for institutions or processes that enable greater popular involvement in technological decisions. For instance, the nascent Community Health Decisions (CHD) movement has developed grassroots procedures to forge popular consensus on ethical principles governing medical policy and technology. One of the accomplishments of the movement has been to organize dozens of community meetings throughout Oregon to debate proposed reforms in the state's health care system.[36] The CHD movement could provide a model for future forums in which citizens debate more general democratic design criteria for technology.

In several states, including Maine, Washington, and California, coalitions of peace activists, labor unions, business leaders, community groups, and government officials have created democratic processes to wean regional economies away from their dependence on military production. For example, responding to grassroots pressure, the state of Washington has established a citizen advisory group that monitors military spending in the state, assesses post–Cold War economic needs and opportunities, and promulgates action plans to help defense-dependent communities diversify their productive base.[37] This shows how a region can use social criteria to evaluate and redirect an entire technological order.

During the past twenty years the Dutch have developed a network of street corner "science shops," supported by nearby university staff and students, where citizen groups receive free assistance to address social issues with technical components. One science shop helped a local environmental group document the contamination of heavy metals in vegetables, which pressured the Dutch government to sponsor a major cleanup in metalworking plants. The science shops have empowered citizens to participate in technological decision making so successfully that they have prompted similar efforts throughout much of Western Europe.[38]

Traditional Amish communities, often misperceived as technologically naive or backwards, have pioneered popular deliberative processes for screening technologies based on their cumulative social impacts, in effect attending to many of the criteria listed in Table 1. One of their methods is to place the adoption of a new technology on probation for one year to discover what the social effects might be. For instance, Amish dairy communities in east-central Illinois ran a one-year trial with diesel-powered bulk milk tanks before judging them socially acceptable; other Amish communities used social trials to prohibit once-probationary household telephones or personal computers.[39]

The preceding examples are, of course, atypical. Most technological choices are made by experts, bureaucratic machination, or unregulated market interactions. But the exceptions provide crucial evidence that, given the right institutional circumstances, lay citizens can make reasonable technological decisions reflecting their own priorities. Even federal agencies, such as the Office of Technology Assessment, the National Science Foundation, and the National Institutes of Health (NIH), have occasionally supported or incorporated citizen participation in their decisionmaking procedures.[40] For instance, the NIH has used both expert and lay advisory panels to evaluate research proposals. The experts judge the scientific merits, while laypeople help weigh the social value, political import, or ethical propriety. One can envision a wide range of private or public institutions using such models to develop a new system of democratic procedures for choosing among technological alternatives.

PARTICIPATORY RESEARCH, DEVELOPMENT, AND DESIGN

Democratic processes for technological choice and oversight are vital, yet hardly worth the effort unless participants have a broad range of alternative technologies from which to choose. Hence it is essential to weave democracy into the fabric of technological research, development, and design (RD&D).[41] Consider four examples of how this has been done.

Democratic Design of Workplace Technology

In Scandinavia during the early 1980s unionized newspaper-graphics workers — in collaboration with sympathetic university researchers, a Swedish government laboratory, and a state-owned publishing company — succeeded in inventing a form of computer software unique in its day. Instead of following trends toward routinized or mechanized newspaper layout, this software contained some of the capabilities later embodied in desktop publishing programs that enable printers and graphic artists to exercise considerable creativity in page design.[42] Known as UTOPIA, this project demonstrated how broadened participation in the RD&D process could lead to a design innovation that, in turn, supported one condition of democracy — creative work (Criterion B).

UTOPIA is less ambitious than several other attempts at participatory design within the workplace. For example, in the 1970s workers at Britain's Lucas Aerospace Corporation sought not only to democratize their own work processes but also to produce more socially useful products.[43] But UTOPIA demonstrated that workers could go beyond just developing prototypes. It also should be noted that this instance of collaboration between workers and technical experts — initially limited to a single technology within a single industry — occurred under unusually favorable social and political conditions. Sweden's workforce is 85 percent unionized, and the nation's pro-labor Social Democratic party has held power during most of the past 50 years.

Participatory Architecture

Compared with the relatively few examples of participatory design of machinery, appliances, or technical infrastructure, there is a rich history of citizen participation in architectural design. One example is the "Zone Sociale" at the Catholic University of Louvain Medical School in Brussels. In 1969 students insisted that new university housing mitigate the alienating architecture of the adjacent hospital. Architect Lucien Kroll established an open-ended, participatory design process that elicited intricate organic forms (e.g., support pillars shaped like gnarled tree trunks), richly diverse patterns of social interaction (e.g., a nursery school situated near administrative offices and a bar), and a dense network of pedestrian paths, gardens, and public spaces. Walls and floors of dwellings were movable, so that students could design their own living spaces. Construction workers were given design principles and constraints rather than finalized blueprints, and they were encouraged to create and display their own sculptures. Initially baffled by the level of spontaneity and playfulness, the project's structural engineers gradually adapted themselves to the diversity of competent participants.

Everything proceeded splendidly for some years until the university administration became alarmed at the extent to which they could not control the process. When the students were away on vacation, they fired Kroll and halted further construction.[44]

Feminist Design

What would happen if women played a greater part in RD&D? One answer comes from feminists who have long been critical of housing designs and urban layouts that reinforce the social isolation and the low, unpaid status of women as housewives.[45] If women were more actively engaged in community design, they might set up more shared neighborhood facilities for day care, laundry, or food preparation, or they might locate homes, workplaces, stores, and public facilities more closely together. Realized examples of feminist design exist in London, Stockholm, and Providence, Rhode Island.[46]

Another approach has been pioneered by an artist and former overworked mother named Frances Gabe, who devoted several decades to inventing a self-cleaning house. "In Gabe's house," according to author Jan Zimmerman, "dishes are washed in the cupboard, clothes are cleaned in the closets, and the rest of the house sparkles after a humid misting and blow dry!"[47]

Other feminists have established women's computer networks and designed alternatives to dreary female office work and to transportation networks insensitive to women's needs.[48] An explicit feminist complaint against current reproductive technologies — such as infertility treatments, surrogate mothering, hysterectomy, and abortion — is that women have played a negligible role in guiding the medical RD&D agendas which have imposed on women agonizing moral dilemmas that might otherwise be averted or structured differently.[49]

Barrier-Free Design

During the past two decades there has been substantial innovation in the design of "barrier-free" equipment, buildings, and public spaces responsive to the needs of people with physical disabilities. Much of the impetus came from disabled citizens who organized themselves to assert their needs or helped invent design solutions. For example, prototypes of the Kurzweil Reading Machine, which uses computer voice-synthesis to read typed text aloud, were tested by over 150 blind users. In an eighteen-month period these users made over a hundred recommendations, many of which were incorporated into later versions of the device.[50]

Technology by the People

All these examples of participatory design demonstrate that it is possible to have a much wider range of people participating in technological research, development, and design.[51] Moreover, participatory design broadens the menu of technological choices. But many participatory design exercises also have encountered fierce opposition from powerful institutions — opposition engendered, not because the exercises were failing, but because they were succeeding.

Still, some advocates of participatory RD&D have elected to state their case entirely in terms of the material interests of the nonparticipants. Others have noted the contribution that participation can make to improved productivity or to better design solutions. These are all fair and reasonable arguments. What is rarely articulated is the specific moral argument that the opportunity to participate in RD&D should be a matter of right, because it is essential to individual moral autonomy, to human dignity, and to democratic self-governance.

A powerful moral case for participatory design has been made by people with disabilities who have demanded barrier-free design. The movement's achievements are now apparent in the profusion of ramps and modified rest rooms in public places (responsive to Criterion C), and they will soon become even more apparent with the promulgation of new regulations under the Americans with Disabilities Act of 1990. The movement not only opposes antidemocratic design but also has a constructive, hopeful thrust. Nonmarket, democratic design criteria — often formulated and applied by disabled laypeople — are now being used to define individual and collective needs, including access to public spaces. Moreover, participants do not evaluate just one technology at a time — the norm in conventional technology assessment — but entire technological and architectural environments. When the range of democratic criteria broadens and when the participants expand beyond the disabled population, we will be well on our way toward ensuring that our technology is compatible with democracy.

CONCLUSION

Current technological orders are generally short on communitarian or cooperative activities, and long on isolation and authoritarianism (violating Criterion A). Work is frequently stultifying and tends to impair moral growth and political efficacy (violating Criterion B). Illegitimate power asymmetries are reproduced through technological means (violating Criterion C.)

The opportunity to engage in a vibrant civic life is often preempted by shopping malls, suburban subdivisions, unconstrained automobilization, and an explosive proliferation in home entertainment devices. Thus we have diminished access to local mediating institutions or to public spaces that could support democratic empowerment within the broader society (violating Criteria A and F). The need to manage translocal harms, coupled with widespread dependence on centrally managed technological systems and with the growing integration of the global economy, has helped render local governments relatively powerless, thereby reducing anyone's incentive to participate (violating Criteria D, E, and F). Meanwhile, there is little compensating incentive to engage directly in national politics, which television reduces to a passive spectator sport, where powerful corporations exert disproportionate influence, where deep questions of social structure are slighted, and where the average citizen has negligible effect.

While it is not always easy to establish causal connections running from structural deficiencies to other social ills, it hardly seems conceivable that weak community ties, atrophied local political capabilities, and authoritarian and degraded work processes have had no influence upon illiteracy, stress, illness, divorce rates, teen pregnancy, crime, drug abuse, psychological disorders, and so on. Perhaps, as de Tocqueville foresaw, many of us *do* sometimes feel shut up in a narrow selfishness, robbed of one half of our existence, left with an immense void in our lives.

Progressive technological strategists face a dilemma. We can couch our nostrums in terms of prevailing economic goals like competitiveness and try to win short-run victories. Or we can strive for a world worthy of our ideals. But we can no longer pretend that the progressive policies so far proposed for improving national economic performance, any more than conservative policies, are going to avoid exacerbating the United States' most profound social and political maladies. Has not the time arrived to mobilize for a democratic politics of technology?

NOTES

1. Alex De Tocqueville, *Democracy in America*, ed. Phillips Bradley, rev. ed. (1848; reprint, New York: Vintage Books, 1954), Vol. 1, p. 260.
2. John J. Kushma, "Participation and the Democratic Agenda: Theory and Praxis," in Marc V. Levine et al. *The State and Democracy: Revitalizing America's Government* (New York: Routledge, 1988), pp. 14–48. According to the Harwood Group, many Americans would like to be move involved in public affairs, but feel locked out of the current system. See *Citizens and Politics: A View from Main Street America* (Dayton, OH: The Kettering Foundation, 1991).
3. Susan Friend Harding, *Remaking Ibieca: Rural Life in Aragon under Franco* (Chapel Hill: University of North Carolina Press, 1984).
4. Samuel Bowles and Herbert Gintis, *Democracy and Capitalism: Property, Community, and the Contradictions of Modern Social Thought* (New York: Basic Books, 1986). The converse causal tie between community strength and political empowerment is suggested, for instance, by solidaristic Amish communities' success in resisting mandatory public schooling, military conscription, and participation in the federal social security system. See Donald B. Kraybill, *The Riddle of Amish Culture* (Baltimore: Johns Hopkins University Press, 1989).
5. Benjamin Barber, *Strong Democracy: Participatory Politics for a New Age* (Berkeley: University of California Press, 1984).
6. See, for example, Sara M. Evans and Harry C. Boyte, *Free Spaces: The Sources of Democratic Change in America* (New York: Harper and Row, 1986).
7. For the complete derivation and justification for these and additional democratic design criteria, see Richard E. Sclove, *Democracy and Technology* (New York: Guilford Press, 1995).
8. See, for example, Kenneth T. Jackson, *Crabgrass Frontier: The Suburbanization of the United States* (New York: Oxford University Press, 1985); and Barber, *Strong Democracy* pp. 267–273, 306–6.
9. I define technology broadly as material artifacts and the practices or beliefs that accompany their creation or use. Hence I regard architecture and community planning as a subdomain of technology.
10. Dolores Hayden, *Redesigning the American Dream: The Future of Housing, Work, and Family Life* (New York: W. W. Norton, 1984), pp. 189–91.
11. Kathryn McCamant and Charles Durrett, *Cohousing: A Contemporary Approach to Housing Ourselves* (Berkeley, CA: Habitat Press, 1988).
12. Some supporting evidence can be found in the emerging international network of "sister cities." See, for example, Michael Shuman, "From Charity to Justice," *Bulletin of Municipal Foreign Policy* 2:4 (Autumn 1988), pp. 50–59.
13. Edward S. Greenberg, *Workplace Democracy: The Political Effects of Participation* (Ithaca: Cornell University Press, 1986); William M. Lafferty, "Work as a Source of Political Learning among Wage-Laborers and Lower-Level Employees," in *Political Learning in Adulthood: A Sourcebook of Theory and Research*, ed. Roberta S. Sigel (Chicago: University of Chicago Press, 1989), pp. 102–42; Melvin L. Kohn et al., "Position in the Class Structure and Psychological Functioning in the United States, Japan, and Poland," *American Journal of Sociology*, 95:4 (January 1990), pp. 964–1008.
14. Robert Schrank, *Ten Thousand Working Days* (Cambridge, MA: MIT Press, 1978), p. 226.

15. Ibid., pp. 221–27. On remaining democratic shortcomings in the Volvo factories, see Stephen Hill, *Competition and Control at Work: The New Industrial Sociology* (Cambridge, MA: MIT Press, 1981), pp. 39 and 104–5. For further recent examples of both democratic and nondemocratic workplace technology, see Shoshana Zuboff, *In the Age of the Smart Machine: The Future of Work and Power* (New York: Basic Books, 1988).

16. See Ruth Schwartz Cowan, *More Work for Mother: The Ironies of Household Technology from the Open Hearth to the Microwave* (New York: Basic Books, 1983).

17. Hayden, *Redesigning the American Dream*; Ray Oldenburg, *The Great Good Place: Cafes, Coffee Shops, Community Centers, Beauty Parlors, General Stores, Bars, Hangouts, and How They Get You though the Day* (New York: Paragon House, 1989).

18. See Women and Transport Forum, "Women on the Move: How Public Is Public Transport?" in *Technology and Women's Voices: Keeping in Touch*, ed. Cheris B. Kramarae (New York: Routledge & Kegan Paul, 1988), pp. 116–34.

19. Barbara Drygulski Wright, *Women, Work, and Technology: Transformations* (Ann Arbor: University of Michigan Press, 1987); Naomi Wolf, *The Beauty Myth: How Images of Beauty Are Used against Women* (New York: William Morrow, 1991).

20. See Joel A. Tarr, "Sewerage and the Development of the Networked City in the United States, 1850–1930," in *Technology and the Rise of the Networked City*, ed. Joel A. Tarr and Gabriel Dupuy (Philadelphia: Temple University Press, 1988), pp. 159–85; and Gerald E. Frug, "The City as a Legal Concept," *Harvard Law Review*, 93:6 (April 1980), pp. 1057–1154.

21. See Samuel P. Hays, *Beauty, Health, and Permanence: Environmental Politics in the United States, 1955–1985* (Cambridge: Cambridge University Press, 1987), pp. 443–45, 456–57; Gareth Porter and Janet Welsh Brown, *Global Environmental Politics* (Boulder, CO: Westview Press, 1991), pp. 64, 66; Wolfgang Sachs, "Environment and Development: The Story of a Dangerous Liaison," *The Ecologist*, 21:6 (November/December 1991), pp. 252–57. Local ability to pressure corporations to reduce pollution could be much advanced by supportive legislation such as the Environmental Bill of Rights proposed in Samuel Bowles, David M. Gordon, and Thomas E. Weisskopf, *Beyond the Wasteland: A Democratic Alternative to Economic Decline* (Garden City: Anchor Press/Doubleday, 1983), pp. 346–46.

22. Thomas Parke Hughes, *Networks of Power: Electrification in Western Society, 1880–1930* (Baltimore: Johns Hopkins University Press, 1983), Chapter 9.

23. See Robert Gilman, "Four Steps to Self-Reliance: The Story behind Rocky Mountain Institute's Economic Renewal Project," *In Context*, 14 (Autumn 1986), pp. 41–46; Barbara A. Cole, *Business Opportunities Casebook* (Snowmass, CO: Rocky Mountain Institute, 1988); and David Morris, "Self-Reliant Cities: The Rise of the New City-States," in *Resettling America: Energy, Ecology, and Community*, ed. Gary J. Coates (Andover, MA: Brick Housing Publishing Co., 1981), pp. 240–62.

24. See John Gaventa, *Power and Powerlessness: Quiescence and Rebellion in an Appalachian Valley* (Urbana: University of Illinois Press, 1980), Chapter 8; and Frug, "The City as a Legal Concept."

25. See, for example, Stephen S. Cohen and John Zysman, *Manufacturing Matters: The Myth of the Post-Industrial Economy* (New York: Basic Books, 1987); Michael L. Dertouzos, Richard K. Lester, Robert M. Solow, and the MIT Commission on Industrial Competitiveness, *Made in America: Regaining the Productive Edge* (Cambridge, MA: MIT Press, 1989); Lester C. Thurow, *The Zero-Sum Solution: Building a World-Class American Economy* (New York: Simon & Schuster, 1985); and Joel S. Yudken and Michael Black, "Targeting National Needs: A New Direction for Science and Technology Policy," *World Policy Journal*, 7:2 (Spring 1990), pp. 282–83. While sharply critical of economic nationalism, Robert B. Reich's *The Work of Nations* (New York: Vintage Books, 1992) assumes increased integration into an ever more intensively globalized economy. On the importance of granting greater local power over national self-reliance, see Ann J. Tickner, *Self-Reliance versus Power Politics: The American and Indian Experiences in Building Nation States* (New York: Columbia University Press, 1987).

26. See, for example, Bowles et al., *Beyond the Wasteland*; Yudken and Black, "Targeting National Needs"; and Robert B. Reich, "The Real Economy," *Atlantic Monthly*, 267:2, (February 1991), pp. 35–52.

27. Amory B. Lovins, *Soft Energy Paths: Toward a Durable Peace* (Cambridge, MA: Ballinger, 1977); National Center for Appropriate Technology, *Wastes to Resources: Appropriate Technologies for Sewage Treatment and Conversion*, DOE/CE/15095-2 (Washington, DC: US. Government Printing Office, July 1983); Ken Darrow and Mike Saxenian, *Appropriate Technology Sourcebook: A Guide to Practical Books for Village and Small Community Technology* (Stanford, CA: Volunteers in Asia, 1986); Valjean McLenighan, *Sustainable Manufacturing: Saving Jobs, Saving the Environment* (Chicago: Center for Neighborhood Technology, 1990).

28. See, for example, Michael J. Piore and Charles F. Sabel, *The Second Industrial Divide: Possibilities for Prosperity* (New York: Basic Books, 1984); Cohen and Zysman, *Manufacturing Matters*.

29. David F. Noble's deservedly influential essay, "Social Choice in Machine Design: The Case of Automatically Controlled Machine Tools," lauds Norwegian factory worker involvement in technology choices that helped workers maintain autonomy and creativity. True enough, but the factory in question was a state-owned weapons production plant. In *Case Studies on the Labor Process*, ed. Andrew Zimbalist (New York: Monthly Review Press, 1979), pp. 18–50.

30. See, for example, John Todd and Nancy Jack Todd, *Bioshelters, Ocean Arks, City Farming: Ecology as the Basis of Design* (San Francisco: Sierra Club Books, 1984).

31. Stan Sesser, "A Reporter at Large: A Nation of Contradictions," *The New Yorker*, 13 January 1992, pp. 37–68.

32. See Richard E. Sclove, "The Nuts and Bolts of Democracy: Toward a Democratic Politics of Technological Design," in *Critical Perspectives on Non-Academic Science and Engineering*, ed. Paul T. Durbin (Bethlehem, PA: Lehigh University Press, 1991), pp. 239–62; and Sclove, *Technology and Freedom*.

33. D. J. Gamble, "The Berger Inquiry: An Impact Assessment Process," *Science*, 199:4332 (3 March 1978), pp. 950–51.

34. Ibid., pp. 946–52; Thomas R. Berger, *Northern Frontier, Northern Homeland: The Report of the MacKenzie Valley Pipeline Inquiry*, 2 vols. (Ottawa: Minister of Supply and Services, Canada, 1977); Organisation for Economic Cooperation and Development (OECD), *Technology on Trial. Public Participation in Decision-Making Related to Science and Technology* (Paris: OECD, 1979).

35. See, for example, Barry M. Casper and Paul David Wellstone, *Powerline: The First Battle of America's Energy War* (Amherst: University of Massachusetts Press, 1981); David Dickson, *The New Politics of Science* (Chicago: University of Chicago Press, 1988).

36. Bruce Jennings et al., "Grassroots Bioethics Revisited: Health Care Priorities and Community Values," *Hastings Center Report* 20:5 (September/October 1990), pp. 16–23.

37. Kevin J. Cassidy, "Defense Conversion: Economic Planning and Democratic Participation," *Science, Technology, and Human Values*, 17:3 (Summer 1992), pp. 334–48.

38. Seth Shulman, "Mr. Wizard's Wetenschapswinkel," *Technology Review*, 91:5 (July 1988), pp. 8–9.

39. On Amish technological decision making see, for example, Marc A. Olshan, "Modernity, the Folk Society, and the Old Order Amish: An Alternative Interpretation," *Rural Sociology*, 46:2 (Summer 1981), pp. 297–309; Victor Stoltzfus, "Amish Agriculture: Adaptive Strategies for Economic Survival of Community Life," *Rural Sociology*, 38:2 (Fall 1973), pp. 196–206; Kraybill, *The Riddle of the Amish Culture*.

40. See for example, U.S. Congress, Office of Technology Assessment, *Coastal Effects of Offshore Energy Systems* (Washington, DC: U.S. Government Printing Office, 1976); Rachelle Hollander, "Institutionalizing Public Service Science: Its Perils and Promise," in *Citizen Participation in Science Policy*, ed. James C. Petersen (Amherst: University of Massachusetts Press, 1984), pp. 75–95.

41. For additional arguments in support of participatory design, see Richard E. Sclove, "The Nuts and Bolts of Democracy: Democratic Theory and Technological Design," in

Democracy in Technological Society, ed. Langdon Winner (Dordrecht: Kluwer Academic Publisher, 1992), pp. 132–57.

42. Andrew Martin, "Unions, the Quality of Work, and Technological Change in Sweden," in *Worker Participation and the Politics of Reform,* ed. Carmen Sirianni (Philadelphia: Temple University Press, 1987), pp. 99–139.

43. Hilary Wainwright and Dave Elliott, *The Lucas Plan. A New Trade Unionism in the Making?* (London: Allison and Busby, 1982).

44. Lucien Kroll, "Anarchitecture," in *The Scope of Social Architecture,* ed. Richard C. Hatch (New York: Van Nostrand Reinhold, 1984), pp. 166–85.

45. Hayden, *Redesigning the American Dream,* Chapter 4.

46. Ibid., pp. 163–70.

47. Jan Zimmerman, *Once Upon the Future: A Woman's Guide to Tomorrow's Technology* (New York: Pandora, 1986), pp. 36–37.

48. Wright, *Women, Work, and Technology;* Kramarae, *Technology and Women's Voices.*

49. See Sarah Franklin and Maureen McNeil, "Reproductive Futures: Recent Literature and Current Feminist Debates on Reproductive Technologies," *Feminist Studies,* 14:3 (Fall 1988), pp. 545–60.

50. See Michael Hingson, "The Consumer Testing Project for the Kurzweil Reading Machine for the Blind," pp. 89–90, and Raymond Kurzweil, "The Development of the Kurzweil Reading Machine," pp. 94–96, in Virginia W. Stern and Martha Ross Redden, eds., *Technology for Independent Living: Proceedings of the 1980 Workshops on Science and Technology for the Handicapped* (Washington, DC: American Association for the Advancement of Science, 1982).

51. For a number of additional examples, see Sclove, "The Nuts and Bolts of Democracy: Toward a Democratic Politics of Technological Design," or contact the Loka Institute, P.O. Box 355, Amherst, MA 01004; e-mail: Loka@amherst.edu.

12.   Black Futurists in the Information Age

TIMOTHY L. JENKINS

The new technologies of the information age offer great promise to African Americans, according to Timothy L. Jenkins. They present the prospect of a more level playing field on which ideas can stand or fall on their own merits, regardless of the economic power of those who propose them, and out of which a freer and more egalitarian society can evolve. But such an outcome is not foreordained. In fact, there are many reasons to believe that information age technologies could bring new woes to already disadvantaged minorities. "Left to their own devices," says Jenkins, "minorities are most likely to be the major road kill of the Information Super-highway."

Black Futurists in the Information Age, from which this selection is taken, is intended as a wake-up call to black leadership in the United States. Jenkins and volume coauthor Khafra K. Om-Ra-Seti would have these leaders move from being gatekeepers — mediators of information from other areas of society — to gatecrashers — "opening up new lines of thinking and new avenues of public policy." They call for no less than a scientific and technological revolution in the African American world, advising its leaders to focus their attention on economic and technology progress.

Timothy L. Jenkins is chairman and CEO of Unlimited Vision, Inc., a multimedia firm. He was instrumental in creating the first all-black on-line forum on the Internet. Jenkins holds a J.D. degree from Yale University Law School and served as chief lobbyist for the Student Nonviolent Coordinating Committee for five years.

THE FAR SIDE OF THE MOUNTAIN

It has been a source of amazement and alarm that, in spite of the roar of public attention surrounding the advent of the Information Age as the explosive successor to the industrial era, the leadership of the African American community has yet to broadly interpret the Age's far reaching implications for the vital interests of their constituents. The delinquency of their silence has been all the more profound because of the palpable evidence that without major interventions, the utopian predictions of the Information Age for the society as a whole will paradoxically result in a doomsday scenario for the masses of black people. Alternatively, a clear understanding of the broad implications and susceptibilities of these tools of modern communications, coupled with information science, have the clear potential to foster unheard-of strategies of liberation. The burden of [the book from which this essay was excerpted] has been to articulate a new vision for African Americans in the Information Age.

The benefit and the burden of being black in America arise from the ability and the necessity to view the same things the rest of society sees differently. This difference is born of bitter experience, that popular propaganda is seldom predicated on the best interests of black people in particular or humanity in general. Moreover, black people harbor a justifiable skepticism that the larger society is equipped to interpret or even understand the best interests of those elements of the population it has excluded from so many of its inner sanctums. Ironically, by the very reason of such exclusion, the social perceptions black leaders hold sometimes allow them insights that are clearer and more reliable reflections of reality for the larger society as well. Contributing factors in the black/white leadership divide come from the material differences in their resources and power. In almost every sphere of life, the historic status of Blacks increases their vulnerability. Statistics affirm these differences in economics, education, health, social mobility, and even in certain areas of historical and philosophical aspirations.

Because of these increased vulnerabilities, many stresses that the majority easily survives exceed the level of tolerance for blacks. In this sense, observing the effects of certain conditions on blacks may predict the later ramifications on the general public. Black people, suffering economically in the early stages of the Information Age, may be like the canary in a coal mine, forecasting climactic dangers before they become a general manifestation. Thus, as the euphoria sweeps the nation regarding the exciting expectations of the Information Age, African Americans must sound the alarm on the dangers of systematic exclusion.

On the surface, every reason exists to celebrate the proliferation of Information Age technologies. But it does not follow that information by itself can guarantee an improved quality of life or more secure democratic rights. Nor do the international migrations of information industries assure that the result will not be the lowest common denominator in wages and jobs. The propagandists insist that universally available information leads inexorably toward democracy, but they seldom acknowledge the mega-disparities that exist in the corporate versus citizens' ability to gather, manipulate, and interpret information in politically relevant ways.

Confronted by these pressing issues, black leaders must now move forward in a new role with specific agendas, promoting the development and advocacy of reform policies and programs that can wisely pick and choose among the probable social effects of the Information Age. The result could be an early wake-up call for our nation, hopefully before the negative effects of tele-cybernetics become irreversible. By fulfilling their role, black leaders can move from being gatekeepers to gatecrashers, opening up new lines of thinking and new avenues of public policy. The beneficiaries of their interventions will not only be blacks, but workers of all races, ages, and their institutions. By the same token, if, at the end of the day, technology will only provide an economic haven for the brightest and the best of us — regardless of race — then we will have cold and shallow comfort in the toll that this direction will have on our society. If those of us who care exercise influence sufficient to force the agenda of our interest on the application of technology, then we should have our fortunes rise with the whole of mankind.

It is still too early to know which will be the predominant result. In the meantime, we must do all in our power to assure that we are technically aware of technology's positives and negatives, as each public decision is made in response to the rapidly changing world of *The Age of Light*. And woe be unto us if Marshall McLuhan was right when he said "the medium is the message," for most of us are likely to be left out of understanding or enjoying a vital economic connection with either.

In the final analysis, the essence of technology ought to be service. Judged from that perspective, it remains to be seen whether the interests of the black community are served or sacrificed. Absent purposeful leadership involvement, either could be true. The deciding factor will be the extent to which those who both understand and influence the direction of technology take into account the peculiar interests of the black community, as they may well harbinger society's interests in general. If its prime effect is to reduce the labor force to an absolute minimum in order to maximize profits or to allow jobs to follow tax breaks and the lowest wages wherever they might lead, then technology, while benefiting some, will have failed us all!

DEDICATED TO THE FUTURE

This [chapter] is, therefore, dedicated to the future — not an inevitable future — but rather the future that we can design. Never before has there been a time when so much could be achieved in leveling the playing field of life through pluralistic imagination and commercial creativity, as modern, computer-driven technological genius has now made possible. But we will first have to be open to a personal as well as an institutional *need to change*, before we can use technology to counteract social, economic, and intellectual inertia on the matters of race and ethnicity in America. Indeed, the refusal to open our minds to the discomfort of change may be the largest obstacle yet to our ultimate empowerment through technology.

In spite of its many positive potentials, the unfolding of the decade that closes the twentieth century and opens the twenty-first is at best neutral. With equal facility, this epoch can irrevocably alter for good or ill the intellectual and economic disparities born of race, as well as spatial and social realities. The exercise of values in our allocation of relevant technological resources will be the critical challenge.

The factor that makes these next ten years [1997–2007] so critical are both the unprecedented pace of emergent telecommunications and computer innovations, as well as the recognition that, unlike the agricultural and industrial revolutions, those who are left behind this time may never be able to catch up again. Moreover, the Information Age promises to impact monumentally on every area of human life, especially our social and commercial organizations, where the impact will be far-reaching and pervasive. Emergent technologies will be the keys for determining economic and employment opportunity, freedom of expression, educational attainment and meaningful political participation; all of which are tantamount to deciding who will exercise predominant power for the next hundred years. As such, we stand on the threshold of the invention of what may well become a new worldwide class distinction, or technological caste system.

While the coming of this New Age is a matter of prolific study and investigation in all of these areas, ironically it has been left to the fringe elements of the nation's counterculture to examine its revolutionary implications for America's black, red, and brown minorities. Indeed, if one were to judge by mainstream portrayals of high-tech beneficiaries, it would be easy to conclude that cultural "homogeneity" is to be the uniform requirement of the next century, rather than an increase in diversity implicit in the national demographic shifts in which the minorities of today will become the population majority of tomorrow. Overwhelmingly, the computer icons, advertisements, spokespersons and media campaigns are standardized to look, feel and act like their industrial creators, resulting in their not being user-friendly to minorities or their unique cultural interests. We have not only seen the creation of the Information Age invisible man, but also the invisible interests and concerns of racial and ethnic diversity excluded from high-tech images. As a result, *Star Treks I* and *II* notwithstanding, we might be led subliminally to conclude that the future belongs to only the information industry's chosen few rather than the whole population.

Article 17 of the Universal Declaration of Human Rights asserts that access to technology is a fundamental entitlement, yet nowhere is such an "entitlement" given universal access. Accordingly, those of us who have been to a different mountain and seen a different promised land must now declare a different vision. Ours is a vision in which American society as well as world culture, through the marvels of technology, open themselves up to beneficial change based on a deeper and more intimate understanding of the creative differences of which they are comprised. With an appreciation for the enormity of the coming change in information access, this decade represents the last, best hope to challenge the patterns of social exclusion from the past being extended and reinforced by technology into the future. The information and telecommunications revolution promises brand new games, which require that *we invent new rules* by which they can be played for life quality improvements rather than mere quantitative accelerations. Only then can the inherent power for change — implicit in high-technology communications — yield results that alleviate rather than further degrade our communities. In essence, we as black people must shape and mold the emergent Information Age revolution into our own image, and establish values and morals that are consistent with our historical traditions, to ultimately benefit the world. For example, it will not be appropriate to follow the pattern of mindlessly creating video games on CD-ROM that simply entertain people in the sport of killing the enemy. We need to rethink the possibilities of such tools, so they can help to produce a generation of enlightened people!

Alas, any hope of playing by a set of new rules, demands intellectual as well as behavioral modifications of today's leadership, not only on explicit matters of race and ethnicity in America, but the ingenuous ways in which seemingly neutral trends can help to perpetuate inequalities. In spite of the loudest protests to the contrary, minority group leaders and majority group power holders have both grown used to slow dancing with each other, while they are increasingly distanced from the growing economic and social insecurities that plague their constituents. Although it tends to be less frequently noted, educated white elites often display as little real appreciation for the material and emotional needs lying below them as certain miseducated elite black escapees from the ghetto. Hence, the expressions of political and editorial surprise at the electoral revolts that have occurred throughout the nation in recent years, when blue collar constituencies have rejected predicted group behavior and voted with the opposition, or when opinion polls fly in the face of predictions from would-be pundits and opinion makers.

The establishment just doesn't get it; the majority of people feel betrayed by both their leaders and institutions. Almost nowhere, except in dark alleys, poorly lit parking lots or celebrated talk shows, does the world of most black leaders and white power holders come together with the alienated underclass and its seething social rebellion. These social and economic distances are seriously exacerbated by mainstream communication barriers that provide little or no ongoing dialogue. The heated debates regarding black rap lyrics, as well as the librettos of white heavy metal ballads, vividly illustrate the symptoms of such class warfare.

For the first time, however, walking in another class's shoes is becoming feasible. On-line computer networks can offer a new town hall. Desktop publishing promises a new public forum. Civic teleconferencing can become a new vehicle for group dialogue. Distance learning will allow a classroom to be worldwide. No longer must music, art, and theater suffer an unnatural fence. The libraries and museums of the world can be available to the most remote corners of the earth for the first time in history. Diagnostic health care can now be distributed without regard to distance between patients and national hospital specialists. Soon, with everyone able to be his or her own publisher, the means for truth-telling as an everyday Internet exchange, rather than the occasional moment, can be at hand. While the uncensored picture that emanates from down under may not always be exactly pretty, it at least promises to be far more honest and realistic than the polished products of editorial middlemen with their own hidden agendas.

Few will deny that the instant presence of television has made a tremendous difference politically during the past thirty years, whether evidenced in the civil rights marches or the fall of the Berlin Wall. By way of parallel, the problem will now be assuring that unrestrained market forces alone are not the only forces left to determine individual and group access to knowledge or set the speed limits of the Information Superhighway. This calls for the development of enlightened public policies that balance the bargaining power among the players and provide a level playing field. On such a playing field the merits of an idea will be able to withstand the onslaught of superior economic power, and this can lead to a freer and more egalitarian society than the cash register alone is likely to foster.

But before we get euphoric over these grand *possibilities*, we need the sobering recognition that such progress is not a self-evident truth nor a historical imperative. On the contrary, if the old rules of means tests, class advantage, ethnicity and geographical preferences are applied to these new technologies, the result will not only be the perpetuation of existing disparities, but their indelible reinforcement. And based on emerging patterns to date, the perpetuation of the old rules is clearly at work. Low income children are half as likely to have access to computers at home or in school. Students at historically black colleges and universities are substantially less likely to have high-tech facilities, equipment, and technological programs of equal quality. Minority workers are disproportionately relegated to the tedious, low end of automated systems, if they have any access at all. The geographical areas slated to enjoy entree to these marvelous new and costly communications systems are those least likely to include minority or low income households. In this regard, it is useful to be reminded that the majority of the world's population has yet to be able to place its first telephone call. In the United States population pockets exist that have actually lost ground in their access to telephones in the ears from 1985 to 1995, and many of these are in the very cities that boast the most advanced forms of progress in telecommunications.

All of this suggests that this new information and communications revolution could easily bypass the minority communities of America just like the infamous interstate highways of old, providing few or no meaningful access ramps unless they are carefully designed into the plans taking shape now. Indeed it has been graphically suggested that, left to their own devices, minorities are most likely to be the major *road kill* of the Information Superhighway, with jobs flowing abroad, while those remaining in the country have unreachable high-tech entry requirements or offer a new form of house-bound peonage without hard-won worker fringe benefits or long-term job security. All of this makes the coming decade of pivotal importance, for the next ten years will determine who goes up and who goes down on the technology seesaw. Because we share a stake in the design of the future, we must exercise the option to modify these outcomes based on direct participation in the decision-making processes that are bringing about the construction of the new Information Superhighway. But to do this we must first reinvent our leaders.

One of the most astonishing discoveries we encountered [in the research for the book from which this article was excepted] was the private sector indifference shown by the various Fortune 500 computer hardware, software, and telecommunications companies; there is essentially a lack of concern not only toward the underserved information needs of black people in general, but also toward the $450 billion appeal of the African American market. Having participated in or been aware of efforts to induce such companies to expand their high-tech marketing outreach into minority consumer niches, with only three exceptions, we have witnessed a response that has been uniformly negative. When approached, such companies retort that either blacks aren't interested in high-tech telecommunication devices and computers, or those that are so inclined can be readily reached through a generalized mainstream outreach.

This behavior flies in the face of the great weight of professional marketing in other areas, which shows the importance of special niche market identification and promotion. Such indifference also underestimates the extent to which upper income black consumers not only exceed the general population in brand name loyalties, but also in the mainstream consumption of sophisticated electronic equipment. The consumer areas in question include CDs, hi-fi and stereo equipment buying, as well as VCRs and video cameras; all of which aggregated to a $6 billion electronic market among minorities in 1994, well above the comparable per capita expenditure of the general U. S population. Indeed, the black market penetration of VCRs is greater than that for the household population as a whole. Consider what this might imply for CD-ROM products and other software capable of appealing to this same audience.

In a larger sense, this backward corporate attitude poses an additional threat to the long-term economic and social health of the nation based on technology diffusion. Corporate negativity toward the high-tech minority market suggests the specter of an ever increasing racial and ethnic divide in technology usage, due to ineffective promotion among minorities, leading to a permanently uneven computer and telecommunication diffusion throughout the population to the [detriment of the nation through] a less competitive workforce and less just society. All of this is to underscore the fact that, left to the traditional market forces of today, those *who know* and those *who know-not* will translate to a schism of those employable or unemployable along racial and ethnic lines comparable to a distinction of class or caste. One would have hoped for a more forward looking response from that very segment of the economy that prides itself most on its creative alliance with the future. But alas, even the industrial gatekeepers who stand to collect the tolls to the Information Superhighway have shown themselves unwilling to attract additional road traffic from the minority community. This only reinforces the urgency for the black community's internal mobilization to assure its access to the Information Superhighway and the policies that shape its path, as Malcolm X once said, "by any means necessary."

LOOKING BACK TO MOVE FORWARD

The Adinkra peoples of West Africa have a symbol called Sankofa, of a bird in full flight with its head turned backward. Sankofa signifies the truth that no people can know where it is going if it cannot look backward from whence it came. This may be the classic recognition of all culture. Visionary black leadership will be of critical importance in how we chart our future course. Therefore, we need to be reminded of some of the historic leadership strengths and weaknesses in our community to be able to discern the one from the other in the future. Because of the peculiar ways in which our traditions of leadership have been fashioned, such hegemony may itself represent a temporary impasse to the free flow of benefits from the info-revolution. Such an examination may also identify patterns and practices that are no longer affordable in the face of current requirements. At the same time, it can highlight unique strengths to which we must hold and carry forward for future progress.

From Colonial days to the present, black leadership has primarily been a matter of damage control or the juggling of crises. Limited to operating with inadequate resources against superior material odds, faced with an ever present urgency that defied long-term planning and originally surrounded by a con-stituency with limited understanding, black leaders developed peculiar leadership styles. For most, day-to-day survival was the highest common denominator. Their coping with leadership responsibilities without any management tutelage was like having to learn to read without either a dictionary or the formal rules of grammar. Trial and error mixed with innate talent and personal fortitude often led to highly subjective, if not dogmatic, management styles.

Understandably, not only did the cult of personality sometimes become a prob-lem, but also the requirement for self-reliance was frequently at war with democ-ratic procedures. Moreover, the role of leadership carried with it the conflicting need to project one set of characteristics to black constituents and another to the hostile white world outside the community. Accordingly, it remained for black leaders historically to adapt to special balancing acts for survival.

The traditional procession of leaders has been first preachers, then teachers, and lastly doctors and lawyers. Each succeeding wave of such leaders has had to master the means of walking in two directions at once and the ability to "hit straight licks with crooked sticks" in order to meet the approval of two racially antagonistic audiences for their every act. Preachers were the first to be mutually acceptable in both worlds because they could disguise their temporal leadership as otherworldly guidance. Teachers became acceptable because they were usually controllable public employees. Lawyers and doctors were safe agents of change in the eyes of a dominant majority because of the constraints of their essentially conservative professional guilds. Along the way sprinkles of more radical writers, entrepreneurs or labor leaders have come to the fore, but for the most part, the traditional professions historically comprised the dominant leadership profiles within the black community. This is not to deny that sports, theater, and screen celebrities were briefly elevated to leadership roles, rather it is to recognize that the principal flow of direction associated with large scale membership and affinity groups with mass self-help agendas has come from the same basic professional core, which for the most part had the credentials of higher education as the pre-requisite for its status. Through the accident of such education passed on to their children, an almost hereditary leadership class developed, which has benignly perpetuated itself from the employment differentiations of old until now, with the ever present potential for gradual estrangement from its constituency.

Such leadership has accordingly mastered those messianic arts and crafts required of [it]. Typically some measure of entrepreneurship and personal eco-nomic success, along with a mastery of oratory and audience appeal, were their principal instruments of influence. They exercised persuasion as charismatic spokespersons or grievance-brokers with power centers. Serving as middlemen and -women between two worlds, the perpetuation of their own leadership roles was sometimes as subtle a goal as the objective improvement of their followers. This irony has been aptly described in such works as Carter G. Woodson's *The Mis-education of the Negro,* W. E. B. DuBois's early treatise, *The Philadelphia Negro,* E. Franklin Frazier's *Black Bourgeoisie,* and other analytic works that fol-lowed these pioneering publications.

Historically, this duality was maintained easily when the discriminations faced were palpable and universal both in law as well as in fact, as so vividly described in Gunnar Myrhdal's *American Dilemma*. But with the incremental and sometimes sweeping changes brought about by a steady march of victories over *de jure* segregation and discrimination born of civil rights protests, litigation and legislation, a new set of inequality challenges, not easily addressed by the traditional leadership styles, arose; the creation of a veritable *"Underclass,"* the name first given the phenomena by Douglas Glasgow in his seminal book of the same name. This signaled the demarcation of a new substrata of characteristics reinforcing the factor of race as a barrier to advancement such as welfare dependence, unemployability, and the alienation from middle class ideals, values, and aspirations.

With this metamorphosis has come a kind of leadership dislocation, whereby the alternate traditions of managed protest and accommodation (which had been the black leadership's hallmarks from precolonial days) are less certain or marginally applicable strategies. Now the issues are not petitioning for or even obtaining equality before the law, but obtaining equality *in fact*. With this bold reality has come the need for greater empowerment from within the black community, based on the mechanisms of self-reliance and self-improvement.

In spite of this need for a shift in emphasis, too often the traditional leadership in the black community has continued to emphasize *pro forma* legal remedies, which leave factual inequities beyond their reach. The cynical suggested that this resistance to change was more the result of conflicting interests between traditional leaders and those outside their social and economic class. But a more charitable view is that established leaders may have inadvertently either lost touch with the full weight of the social and economic forces newly confronting their constituents, or be at an intellectual loss for better strategies. The leadership's personal misperceptions may be further influenced by their own relatively stable economic circumstances, which are at stark variance with the increasing numbers of those for whom they would speak. These are problems easily addressed by honest dialogue and the reconsideration of the facts, but first they must be jointly acknowledged.

Because of the many bad experiences of hostile "divide and conquer" strategies as well as leadership assassinations (both real and figurative), a general reluctance to criticize or even challenge leadership figures from within the community has arisen. Those with the temerity to challenge such blind silence frequently have become objects of criticism themselves, branded as disloyalists or worse, agents provocateur for sinister as well as invisible racist forces. Such conspiracy theories are all the more easily promoted when partisan, regional, and monetary considerations are part of the mix. The resulting differences have led to additional strains when both sides have resorted to name calling, and mutual castigation of one another's motives, rather than addressing relevant issues objectively or collaboratively. This caused even further confusion, with the suggestion that many of the traditional civil rights remedies disproportionately benefit the traditional reformers rather than their down-and-out constituencies. Hence, we witness the pro and con affirmative action arguments addressed by Tony Brown in his book, *Black Lies White Lies*, as part of this ongoing dialogue. In addition, demagogues aplenty have practiced patterns of factual denial that have made race and racial inequality the sole culprit for every conceivable social ill in the black community, whether substance abuse, the high rates of crime, school dropout rates, low reading scores, teenage pregnancies, job unreadiness, [or] other social pathologies. These often radical voices have promoted a fatalistic generic excuse for failures, rather than their being attributed to personal inadequacies capable of reform and correction.

As if this were not sufficiently confusing, now comes a new breed of minstrel-like propagandists and politicians from the right, whose profession it is to heap self-blame on blacks for each and every one of their social pathologies. For these neo-apologists, the *holocaust* of slavery either never existed, or if it did, it was primarily the fratricidal African's fault. Equally unfortunate, these distorted voices have been adopted by major political conservatives as their favorite Negroes and given talk shows, widespread media access, highly visible political appointments and the like. Throughout this process, the practice is to rely on the time-honored tools of hyperbolic rhetoric, *ad hominem,* and emotionalism, at the cost of clarity, precision, and objective debate on racial matters. Although thoughtful analysts, thinkers, and writers have existed in the black community throughout, these more measured voices have seldom had a platform off-campus or beyond the pages of scholarly journals and outside the covers of thick volumes in fine print.

Sadly, not enough of the existing cadre of brand-name leadership in the black community are describable in terms of the future analytic needs. Too often they are content with their select roles as middlemen and -women within the power centers. Some are seduced with personal benefits or benefits for those who mirror themselves, without comparable attention to those below them economically and socially with different needs. They are too preoccupied with an assured leadership status throughout their lifetime to be concerned with development of a leadership transition system within their institutions, which prepares younger and equally capable leaders to take on leadership roles after their timely retirement.

Many among this current black leadership generation, like their role models before them, have little or no appreciation for the discipline of managing information in the work they pursue. To many, personal [and] institutional decisions are indistinguishable. Few of them consult quantitative data as a required tool for strategy development. Their preference is for speculation, intuition, subjective past experience, and anecdotal information. They are content to employ statistical data only for rhetorical effect, without ever documenting the factual basis for their citations. Take for example the frequently mouthed shibboleth that, "there are more black men in prisons than there are enrolled in higher education." To the contrary there are far more blacks in colleges and universities and only a minority in confinement, but it is more dramatic to use shock rhetoric over the truth. An information-based, scientific approach to leadership would prevent such excess.

A rigorous review of the institutions and organizations of the black community reveals a consistent absence of other systems controls common to modern institutional management. Typically this improvised approach has left key leadership figures open to willful charges of graft or financial irregularities, even when there can be no showing of criminal intent. From Marcus Garvey to the latest sensation of *laid-back* approaches to financial accountability, these problems seem to be endemic to black institutions.

One finds similar disregard in personnel matters and staff planning. The functions of recruitment, hiring, evaluation, compensation, promotion, and dismissal in staff procedures cannot be assumed as a matter of formal routine. Typically, whatever exists the way of written policies are rife with exceptions. All too frequently, nepotism, sexism, conflicts of interest, technical incompetence, and marginal productivity are shown a blind eye in favor of personal loyalties, congenial personalities and all absolving "good intentions," reminiscent of Sterling Brown's indulgent encomium, "he mean good, even if he do so doggone po!" Because of the absence of planned maintenance, human resources and capital equipment are frequently consumed prematurely, rather than refurbished and scheduled for upgrading or timely replacement to maximize their useful lives. As a result, age-old crisis management is constantly required to meet what could be routine occurrences, leading to uncertainty, program disruptions, and recurring episodes of organizational disruption.

Similarly, local public agencies controlled by people who profess a commitment to high-minded service objectives sometimes reflect the same shortcomings. These occasionally destabilized institutions include housing authorities, welfare agencies, churches, colleges and universities, labor unions, civic and social organizations, health centers, public school systems, business enterprises, professional organizations and a myriad of charitable activities. The ultimate price of this approach to management and operations is less effective organizations and institutions. It comes as no small wonder then that most of our leadership has been taken unawares by the revolutionary sweep of information systems and the managerial implications they generate. In large part, the crux of the problem is a lack of awareness of the necessary connection between valid information management and desired outcomes. While not universally applicable, having participated in all these activities for many years, we are embarrassed by the truth of this as well as the inveterate resistance to improvement by the very leaders who would benefit most from reform. Unless reformed from within, such leadership itself will be a principal impediment to community development and advancement. And unless reformed, such leadership will be unable to lead the black community into the Information Age.

Criticism of such practices should not be taken as personal attacks or forbidden in the name of aiding and abetting our enemies. Investigative journalism or oversight of leadership is just as indispensable within the black community as society at large. Writers must not be expected to play the ancient role of the African "praise singers," highlighting or magnifying accomplishments and following a code of silence on anything negative. The results will only be continued widespread organizational dysfunction in a community trapped in the denial of its procedural problems, given to a collective avoidance of the responsibility for internal reform, and prone to attributing any and all shortcomings on the single external cause of racism. Most importantly, denial will serve to stifle the diffusion of information systems throughout our institutions.

With the coming of program analysis, better communications, and information systems to the black community, many of these historic proclivities will be objectively challenged. Simple computer generated spreadsheets of comparative daily, weekly, monthly, quarterly, annual and biannual financial and performance results, correlated to particular organizational units or individuals, will be able to objectify mission accomplishments alongside particularized costs. Structured reporting relationships and formal report dissemination, as well as documented peer reviews and quantitative evaluations as standard management procedures based on objective criteria and accountabilities, will go a long way to overcome subjective indulgences that cost productivity. The customary distribution of routine information to all appropriately interested parties will further enhance checks and balances on personal excesses and lead to greater confidence in the operations of the institutions we own and care about.

All of these management and information tools, while routine throughout the broader society, are still in their infancy in too many organizations and institutions within the black community. When these are newly introduced, they should not just come on the heels of a major scandal or after protracted litigation or bureaucratic guerrilla warfare. Instead, they should be routine assurances of willingly adopted group accountability consistent with modern management. In all of this, the tools of personal computers and telecommunications offer important improvements. . . .

Furthermore, with the coming of the Information Age's instant media blend of news as entertainment, a heightened mischief will result from having community spokespersons and organizations that easily lend themselves to sit-com caricatures for managerial incompetence. Therefore, an urgent need exists to identify and promote a new paradigm in community leadership of those who can master the newly available information tools and the management capacities they offer. Moreover, given the increasing complexities of the economic, social, and political issues facing the community, we are compelled to seek and promote new voices which speak in factual, managerial, and quantitative terms as additional spokespersons. Existing leaders need to attract these new voices as valuable assets for their effectiveness.

Our leaders need to be aware of the new high-tech avenues through which to talk sense with the masses and to enable these new players to assist in that mission. Equally important are the means to simplify and present complex data and concepts through desktop publishing so that the man in the street can understand, as Marvin Gaye would say, "what's going on." The support of black technologists must be mobilized to combat the distortions of the right-wing on complex social, economic, and political issues. We need a different type of black talk show participant than those most frequently called upon now. Fiery sound bites need to be replaced with sober analysis of the kind that only information analysts can provide. While either possibility might not have been feasible with the gatekeeper controls of traditional media (with its inherently high costs and exclusivity due to scarcity), it is now highly possible with the technological explosion of multimedia outlets.

Revolutionary multimedia systems and state-of-the-art telecommunications technologies include the low costs for the production and distribution of videos, upscale publications, color coded graphs, CD-ROM presentations, animation, E-mail, on-line networks, teleconferencing as well as the rapid transmission of personal computer data and text. Using, state-of-the-art Internet and World Wide Web electronic delivery techniques can mean less time and less censorship of these new voices. . . . these are the new means by which the *old gatekeepers can be turned into gatecrashers*. All of this means that traditional leadership talent must now be enhanced by additional technology training and exposure, to be able to understand and relate to different, more analytic, and more quantitatively verifiable requirements with which to influence public policy as well as manage community institutions. Also, they need to seek out and work with those holding such technological training and talents as a matter of routine.

While the community might well be content with an evolutionary approach to making the managerial and system reforms discussed in this book, national political realities foreclose that genteel option. With the coming of the 104th Congress of the United States on November 6, 1994, many of the public policy assumptions in favor of continued external support for African American interests were turned upside down. For example, a public monopoly for primary and secondary education, which had been the mainstay for upward mobility, is no longer a foregone conclusion. Unending welfare support can no longer be the economic staple for one third of the black community. The expectation of affirmative action to address past inequities through access to higher education, jobs, and public procurement contracts seems to be on its deathbed. The steady increase in elective political power through national, state, and local office holders may be in jeopardy of a Second Reconstruction era.

The steady erosion of economic viability in our high density urban centers sounds parallel alarms. The aggravated tendency toward one-party politics within and without our communities poses a long-term threat of our political isolation. The loss of employment opportunities for unskilled, or even skilled labor as it has been known traditionally, promises a worldwide shift in unemployment and employability likely to be catastrophic to certain segments of the black workforce, and threatens permanent *Depression-like* conditions. These are the external factors that give added impetus to the need to reexamine the ways in which leadership is exhibited and exercised within the black community. With such broad-sweeping changes in required perspectives, traditional leadership types will need to undergo a radical metamorphosis to understand the rules of management, systems analysis, computer literacy, multimedia, and telecommunications, as well as their importance to understanding the domestic connection to worldwide labor and capital markets.

Hopefully, this will also call attention to the necessity for a more dedicated effort to recycle the purchasing power and economic resources within the black community to replace the diminished resources artificially supplied from outside sources. Indeed, the lessening of support from public spending, external philanthropy, and remedial public policy ought to now lead to the resurgence of long forgotten economic self-reliance, which fell dormant when the walls of segregation began to crumble. While much of our leadership's energy has routinely made the case for greater external public and private support, too little emphasis has been devoted to recycling our own $450 billion in earnings and consumer power to provide the response to community self needs. Effecting this shift in emphasis away from external dependency to internal self-help will require a massive and deep reordering of leadership priorities.

Through C-Span, CNN and other twenty-four-hour vehicles of instant access to congressional and state and local legislative proceedings, the leadership role as information middlemen will naturally erode. As a result, only value-added interpreters who can build upon commonly known information with new and meaningful understandings and strategies will be able to justify attention or a popular following.

With this proliferation of media outlets, even in the face of more highly concentrated ownership patterns devolving to a handful of international mega-corporations, there will undoubtedly emerge more cost-effective means through which diverse voices can be heard. This will be the inevitable result of media channel supply exceeding the demand for its use. But to succeed effectively in accessing these new modes of expression, will require higher sophistication than that commonly available among our traditional leaders.

Additional forms of leadership must arise to address the issues critical to the competitive interests of the black community. High-tech educators and entrepreneurs, finance brokers, as well as systems managers and planners, are needed in countless locations throughout black society. For the most part, these will be professionals and who have grown up in the Information Age, learned state-of-the-art computer tools of work, and had an opportunity for hands-on experience within the belly of one of the major commercial structures that are at the center of the Information Age. These will be the very people least likely to have had leadership roles in the old paradigm.

This new generation of role models must see themselves as more than conspicuous consumers, with a recognition of the interaction of their material resources and skills with the security and well-being of the black masses. Hopefully they will be more inclined to participate out of self-interest in the social and economic uplift of that third of the population falling below the poverty-line than many of their miseducated predecessors were typically willing to do. This new generation of *haves* will be the backbone for reform in public education as well as the invention of private means of education through alternative education systems, and will craft the paths by which black youth can be prepared for modern employment through applied forms of learning technology. The coming generation will see church resources as more than private holdings, and connect them with community renewal projects. They will also be able to negotiate better terms by which jobs and business opportunities are coupled with the grant of consumer patronage. Finally, this new generation must appreciate the age-old reality that one cannot take without giving back lest the source of the bounty not be renewable. In addition, this new generation leadership must be at pains to groom their own successors as soon as they assume office, lest the ruin of discontinuity undermine every new level of their accomplishments. The education of successors requires a role reversal for those who are the first to get in to racially restricted positions. Leaders must see themselves as pathfinders for others, instead of barring the door after themselves to assure their continued uniqueness and prestige.

Contrary to the doomsday predictions of some, black people can have confidence in the revitalization required by these changes in circumstances. Based on a bedrock of self-esteem through accomplishments during the worst of times in yesteryear, our community has what it takes to reinvent its institutions and restore the ladders of hope that sustained past progress. Drug addiction and the other attendant pathologies are the symptoms, not the disease. The disease is the despairing inability to fashion the realistic course of survival through self-controlled improvement. Too little has also been devoted to naming those who are the detractors within our ranks for their contribution to the plight of the village. Now this misdirected practice of silent indulgence must stop. It must stop now, not just because of the internal ethical appeals that have been heard for the past fifty years, but because of the imminent cutoff of prior support that was coming by external hands.

The challenge is to use this pivotal decade that spans the end of this century and the beginning of the next to replace the old style of gatekeeping with a new role of gatecrashers to the throughway to the future known as the Information Superhighway. It means retooling the educational engines of our communities. It means assuring internal economic benefit from the billions of dollars that mark the black community as the twelfth largest economy in the world. It means zero tolerance for waste and dysfunctional self-seeking of select institutional leadership. It calls for a deeper celebration of self that is not predicated on a put-down or even a protest against others, but calls for constructive criticism. It means a new message of concern and participation in educational development and communal parenting for our lost youth.

Fortunately the genius of modern-day science and technology of the Information Age offers tools needed for this kind of broad-sweeping change. The demand is that we step up and seize the opportunities inherent in the world reordering that will inevitably result through the communications revolution and the industrial, economic and social ripples resulting in its wake. We must replace rhetoric with analysis, mere opinions with factual documentation, speculation with studied probabilities, procrastination with real-time initiatives, the historical with the futuristic, the haphazard with the calculated, the emotional with the deliberative, and even representation must be replaced by the direct participation of the actual stakeholders themselves, through ongoing and direct means of communications. Our organizational behavior will not change, however, if the people at the top are not personally knowledgeable, committed, and actively given to the demonstration of modern managerial leadership. Simply giving lip service to the importance of computers in information and management sciences will simply generate lip service in response.

Equally important is the assurance that senior executives have the understanding and ability to manage others who are using these new tools. In learning what is and is not possible with personal computers, executives learn to gauge what they can expect from others. The great generals are those familiar with the perspective of the foot soldiers. The object is to make the tools of this complex new world an enhancement to intuition, not its denial. The reinvention of our leadership is a two way street; it will also introduce something new to the world of cybernetics, computational science, and enhanced multimedia applications. For too long such scientific innovations have simply been viewed in quantitative terms to make life faster and more materially profitable without improving goals, purposes or quality.

Because the historic strength of black leadership has been the advocacy of values, it should use this skill to refine the interpretation of cybernetics. By doing so, black people can give a voice and direction that goes beyond engineering for engineering's sake. In this way different and more people-oriented discussions can emerge to complement the language of science. Such a blend of sensitivity with knowledge is what much of the world of cybernetics has repeatedly shown to be lacking. It has known a great deal about how, but not enough about why. Black leadership is ideally positioned to add a *high-touch* of the world of high-tech. By high-touch we mean a personal and caring dimension that assures equal access, affordability, and applications for technology relevant to the disadvantaged elements of society.

13.   Feminist Perspectives on Technology

JUDY WAJCMAN

The study of the relationship between gender and technology has received increasing attention in recent years as feminists (both scholars and activists) have become concerned with the impact of new technology on women's lives and work, while "social constructivist" researchers on technology (see Chapter 3) have begun to examine how women's roles have influenced the evolution of technologies. This selection, "Feminist Perspectives on Technology" by Judy Wajcman, provides an overview of this area of study.

In order to understand the relationship between women and technology, it is important, first of all, to distinguish between science and technology and to be sensitive to the different layers of meaning of "technology." Women have contributed to the development of technology not just in terms of their conventional inventive activity but in terms of other kinds of activities in which they have engaged, but which may not have been recognized as "technological" in a gender-stereotyped view of technology. The emerging sociology of technology lacks a gender dimension, which Wajcman aims to provide both by the conceptual analysis presented here (and in her book, Feminism Confronts Technology, from which this essay is taken), and by her own sociological research.

Judy Wajcman is a professor of sociology at the Research School of Social Sciences at the Australian National University in Canberra. She has been a research fellow at the Industrial Relations Research Unit at the University of Warwick in England, where she studied the differing experiences of men and women who are senior managers. She has been active in the women's movement in both Britain and Australia. In addition, she is coeditor, with Donald MacKenzie, of The Social Shaping of Technology *(1985).*

FROM SCIENCE TO TECHNOLOGY

While there has been a growing interest in the relationship of science to society over the last decade, there has been an even greater preoccupation with the relationship between technology and social change. Debate has raged over whether the "white heat of technology" is radically transforming society and delivering us into a postindustrial age. A major concern of feminists has been the impact of new technology on women's lives, particularly on women's work. The introduction of word processors into the office provided the focus for much early research.

The recognition that housework was also work, albeit unpaid, led to studies on how the increasing use of domestic technology in the home affected the time spent on housework. The exploitation of Third World women as a source of cheap labor for the manufacture of computer components has also been scrutinized. Most recently there has been a vigorous debate over developments in reproductive technology and the implications for women's control over their fertility.

Throughout these debates there has been a tension between the view that technology would liberate women — from unwanted pregnancy, from housework and from routine paid work — and the obverse view that most new technologies are destructive and oppressive to women. For example, in the early seventies, Shulamith Firestone (1970) elaborated the view that developments in birth technology held the key to women's liberation through removing from them the burden of biological motherhood. Nowadays there is much more concern with the negative implications of the new technologies, ironically most clearly reflected in the highly charged debate over the new reproductive technologies.

A key issue here is whether the problem lies in men's domination of technology, or whether the technology is in some sense inherently patriarchal. If women were in control, would they apply technology to more benign ends? In the following discussion on gender and technology, I will explore these and related questions.

An initial difficulty in considering the feminist commentary on technology arises from its failure to distinguish between science and technology. Feminist writing on science has often construed science purely as a form of knowledge, and this assumption has been carried over into much of the feminist writing on technology. However just as science includes practices and institutions, as well as knowledge, so too does technology. Indeed, it is even more clearly the case with technology because technology is primarily about the creation of artifacts. This points to the need for a different theoretical approach to the analysis of the gender relations of technology from that being developed around science.

Perhaps this conflation of technology with science is not surprising given that the sociology of scientific knowledge over the last ten years has contested the idea of a noncontroversial distinction between science and technology. John Staudenmaier (1985, pp. 83–120) comments that although the relationship between science and technology has been a major theme in science and technology studies, the discussion has been plagued by a welter of conflicting definitions of the two basic terms. The only consensus to have emerged is that the way in which the boundaries between science and technology are demarcated, and how they are related to each other, change from one historical period to another.

In recent years, however, there has been a major reorientation of thinking about the form of the relationship between science and technology. The model of the science–technology relationship that enjoyed widespread acceptance over a long period was the traditional hierarchical model, which treats technology as applied science. This view that science discovers and technology applies this knowledge in a routine, uncreative way is now in steep decline. "One thing which practically any modern study of technological innovation suffices to show is that far from applying, and hence depending upon, the culture of natural science, technologists possess their own distinct cultural resources, which provide the principal basis for their innovative activity" (Barnes and Edge, 1982, p. 149). Technologists build on, modify and extend existing technology but they do this by a creative and imaginative process. And part of the received culture technologists inherit in the course of solving their practical problems is nonverbal; nor can it be conveyed adequately by the written word. Instead it is the individual practitioner who transfers practical knowledge and competence to another. In short, the current model of the science–technology relationship characterizes science and technology as distinguishable subcultures in an interactive symmetrical relationship.

Leaving aside the relationship between technology and science, it is most important to recognize that the word "technology" has at least three different layers of meaning. Firstly, "technology" is a form of knowledge, as Staudenmaier emphasizes.[1] Technological "things" are meaningless without the "know-how" to use them, repair them, design them and make them. That know-how often cannot be captured in words. It is visual, even tactile, rather than simply verbal or mathematical. But it can also be systematized and taught, as in the various disciplines of engineering.

Few authors however would be content with this definition of technology as a form of knowledge. "Technology" also refers to what people do as well as what they know. An object such as a car or a vacuum cleaner is a technology, rather than an arbitrary lump of matter, because it forms part of a set of human activities. A computer without programs and programmers is simply a useless collection of bits of metal, plastic and silicon. "Steelmaking," say, is a technology; but this implies that the technology includes what steelworkers do, as well as the furnaces they use. So "technology" refers to human activities and practices. And finally, at the most basic level, there is the "hardware" definition of technology, in which it refers to sets of physical objects, for example, cars, lathes, vacuum cleaners and computers.

In practice the technologies dealt with here cover all three aspects, and often it is not useful to separate them further. My purpose is not to attempt to refine a definition. These different layers of meaning of "technology" are worth bearing in mind in what follows.

The rest of this [essay] will review the theoretical literature on gender and technology, which in many cases mirrors the debates about science outlined above. However, feminist perspectives on technology are more recent and much less theoretically developed than those that have been articulated in relation to science. One clear indication of this is the preponderance of edited collections that have been published in this area.[2] As with many such collections, the articles do not share a consistent approach or cover the field in a comprehensive fashion. Therefore I will be drawing out strands of argument from this literature rather than presenting the material as coherent positions in a debate.

HIDDEN FROM HISTORY

To start with, feminists have pointed out the dearth of material on women and technology, especially given the burgeoning scholarship in the field of technology studies. Even the most perceptive and humanistic works on the relationship between technology, culture and society rarely mention gender. Women's contributions have by and large been left out of technological history. Contributions to *Technology and Culture*, the leading journal of the history of technology, provide one accurate barometer of this. Joan Rothschild's (1983, pp. xii–xiv) survey of the journal for articles on the subject of women found only four in twenty-four years of publishing. In a more recent book about the journal, Staudenmaier (1985, p. 180) also notes the extraordinary bias in the journal towards male figures and the striking absence of a women's perspective. The history of technology represents the prototype inventor as male. So, as in the history of science, an initial task of feminists has been to uncover and recover the women hidden from history who have contributed to technological developments.

There is now evidence that during the industrial era, women invented or contributed to the invention of such crucial machines as the cotton gin, the sewing machine, the small electric motor, the McCormick reaper, and the Jacquard loom (Stanley, 1992). This sort of historical scholarship often relies heavily on patent records to recover women's forgotten inventions. It has been noted that many women's inventions have been credited to their husbands because they actually appear in patent records in their husbands' name. This is explained in terms of women's limited property rights, as well as the general ridicule afforded women inventors at that time (Pursell, 1981; Amram, 1984; Griffiths, 1985). Interestingly, it may be that even the recovery of women inventors from patent records seriously underestimates their contribution to technological development. In a recent article on the role of patents, Christine MacLeod (1987) observes that prior to 1700 patents were not primarily about the recording of the actual inventor, but were instead sought in the name of financial backers.[3] Given this, it is even less surprising that so few women's names are to be found in patent records.

For all but a few exceptional women, creativity alone was not sufficient. In order to participate in the inventive activity of the Industrial Revolution, capital as well as ideas were necessary. It was only in 1882 that the Married Women's Property Act gave English women legal possession and control of any personal property independently of their husbands. Dot Griffiths (1985) argues that the effect of this was to virtually exclude women from participation in the world of the inventor–entrepreneur. At the same time women were being denied access to education and specifically to the theoretical grounding in mathematics and mechanics upon which so many of the inventions and innovation of the period were based. As business activities expanded and were moved out of the home, middle-class women were increasingly left to a life of enforced leisure. Soon the appropriate education for girls became "accomplishments" such as embroidery and music — accomplishments hardly conducive to participation in the world of the inventor–entrepreneur. In the current period, there has been considerable interest in the possible contributions that Ada Lady Lovelace, Grace Hopper and other women may have made to the development of computing. Recent histories of computer programming provide substantial evidence for the view that women played a major part.[4]

To fully comprehend women's contributions to technological development, however, a more radical approach may be necessary. For a start, the traditional conception of technology too readily defines technology in terms of male activities. As I have pointed out above, the concept of technology is itself subject to historical change, and different epochs and cultures had different names for what we now think of as technology. A greater emphasis on women's activities immediately suggests that females, and in particular black women, were among the first technologists. After all, women were the main gatherers, processors and storers of plant food from earliest human times onward. It was therefore logical that they should be the ones to have invented the tools and methods involved in this work such as the digging stick, the carrying sling, the reaping knife and sickle, pestles and pounders. In this vein, Autumn Stanley (1992) illustrates women's early achievements in horticulture and agriculture, such as the hoe, the scratch plow, grafting, hand pollination, and early irrigation.

If it were not for the male bias in most technology research, the significance of these inventions would be acknowledged. As Ruth Schwartz Cowan notes:

> The indices to the standard histories of technology . . . do not contain a single reference, for example, to such a significant cultural artifact as the baby bottle. Here is a simple implement . . . which has transformed a fundamental human experience for vast numbers of infants and mothers, and been one of the more controversial exports of Western technology to underdeveloped countries — yet it finds no place in our histories of technology. (1979, p. 52)

There is important work to be done not only in identifying women inventors, but also in discovering the origins and paths of development of "women's sphere" technologies that seem often to have been considered beneath notice.

A TECHNOLOGY BASED ON WOMEN'S VALUES?

During the eighties, feminists have begun to focus on the gendered character of technology itself. Rather than asking how women could be more equitably treated within and by a neutral technology, many feminists now argue that Western technology itself embodies patriarchal values. This parallels the way in which the feminist critique of science evolved from asking the "woman question" in science to asking the more radical "science question" in feminism. Technology, like science, is seen as deeply implicated in the masculine project of the domination and control of women and nature.[5] Just as many feminists have argued for a science based on women's values, so too has there been a call for a technology based on women's values. In Joan Rothschild's (1983) preface to a collection on feminist perspectives on technology, she says that: "Feminist analysis has sought to show how the subjective, intuitive, and irrational can and do play a key role in our science and technology." Interestingly, she cites an important male figure in the field, Lewis Mumford, to support her case. Mumford's linking of subjective impulses, life-generating forces and a female principle is consistent with such a feminist analysis, as is his endorsement of a more holistic view of culture and technological developments.

Other male authors have also advocated a technology based on women's values. Mike Cooley is a well-known critic of the current design of technological systems and he has done much to popularize the idea of human-centered technologies. In *Architect or Bee?* (1980, p. 43) he argues that technological change has "male values" built into it: "the values of the White Male Warrior, admired for his strength and speed in eliminating the weak, conquering competitors and ruling over vast armies of men who obey his every instruction. . . . Technological change is starved of the so-called female values such as intuition, subjectivity, tenacity and compassion." Cooley sees it as imperative that more women become involved in science and technology to challenge and counteract the built-in male values: that we cease placing the objective above the subjective, the rational above the tacit, and the digital above analogical representation. In *The Culture of Technology*. Arnold Pacey (1983) devotes an entire chapter to "Women and Wider Values." He outlines three contrasting sets of values involved in the practice of technology-firstly, those stressing virtuosity, secondly, economic values and thirdly, user or need-oriented values. Women exemplify this third "responsible" orientation, according to Pacey, as they work with nature in contrast to the male interest in construction and the conquest of nature.

Ironically the approach of these male authors is in some respects rather similar to the eco-feminism that became popular among feminists in the eighties. This marriage of ecology and feminism rests on the "female principle," the notion that women are closer to nature than men and that the technologies men have created are based on the domination of nature in the same way that they seek to dominate women. Eco-feminists concentrated on military technology and the ecological effects of other modern technologies. According to them, these technologies are products of a patriarchal culture that "speaks violence at every level" (Rothschild, 1983, p. 126). An early slogan of the feminist antimilitarist movement, "Take the Toys from the Boys," drew attention to the phallic symbolism in the shape of missiles. However, an inevitable corollary of this stance seemed to be the representation of women as inherently nurturing and pacifist. The problems with this position have been outlined [here] in relation to science based on women's essential values. We need to ask how women became associated with these values. The answer involves examining the way in which the traditional division of labor between women and men has generally restricted women to a narrow range of experience concerned primarily with the private world of the home and family.

Nevertheless, the strength of these arguments is that they go beyond the usual conception of the problem as being women's exclusion from the processes of innovation and from the acquisition of technical skills. Feminists have pointed to all sorts of barriers — in social attitudes, girls' education and the employment policies of firms — to account for the imbalance in the number of women in engineering. But rarely has the problem been identified as the way engineering has been conceived and taught. In particular, the failure of liberal and equal opportunity policies has led authors such as Cynthia Cockburn (1985) to ask whether women actively resist entering technology. Why have the women's training initiatives designed to break men's monopoly of the building trades, engineering and information technology not been more successful? Although schemes to channel women into technical trades have been small scale, it is hard to escape the conclusion that women's response has been tentative and perhaps ambivalent.

I share Cockburn's view that this reluctance "to enter" is to do with the sex-stereotyped definition of technology as an activity appropriate for men. As with science the very language of technology, its symbolism, is masculine. It is not simply a question of acquiring skills, because these skills are embedded in a culture of masculinity that is largely coterminous with the culture of technology. Both at school and in the workplace this culture is incompatible with femininity. Therefore, to enter this world, to learn its language, women have first to forsake their femininity.

TECHNOLOGY AND THE DIVISION OF LABOR

I will now turn to a more historical and sociological approach to the analysis of gender and technology. This approach has built on some theoretical foundations provided by contributors to the labor process debate of the 1970s. Just as the radical science movement had sought to expose the class character of science, these writers attempted to extend the class analysis to technology. In doing so, they were countering the theory of "technological determinism" that remains so widespread.

According to this account, changes in technology are the most important cause of social change. Technologies themselves are neutral and impinge on society from the outside; the scientists and technicians who produce new technologies are seen to be independent of their social location and above sectional interests. Labor process analysts were especially critical of a technicist version of Marxism in which the development of technology and productivity is seen as the motor force of history. This interpretation represented technology itself as beyond class struggle.

With the publication of Harry Braverman's *Labor and Monopoly Capital* (1974), there was a revival of interest in Marx's contribution to the study of technology, particularly in relation to work. Braverman restored Marx's critique of technology and the division of labor to the center of his analysis of the process of capitalist development. The basic argument of the labor process literature that developed was that capitalist–worker relations are a major factor affecting the technology of production within capitalism. Historical case studies of the evolution and introduction of particular technologies documented the way in which they were deliberately designed to deskill and eliminate human labor.[6] Rather than technical inventions developing inexorably, machinery was used by the owners and managers of capital as an important weapon in the battle for control over production. So, like science, technology was understood to be the result of capitalist social relations.

This analysis provided a timely challenge to the notion of technological determinism and, in its focus on the capitalist division of labor, it paved the way for development of a more sophisticated analysis of gender relations and technology. However, the labor process approach was gender-blind because it interpreted the social relations of technology in exclusively class terms. Yet, as has been well established by the socialist feminist current in this debate, the relations of production are constructed as much out of gender divisions as class divisions. Recent writings (Cockburn , 1983, 1985; Faulkner and Arnold, 1985; McNeil, 1987) in this historical vein see women's exclusion from technology as a consequence of the gender division of labor and the male domination of skilled trades that developed under capitalism. In fact, some argue that prior to the Industrial Revolution women had more opportunities to acquire technical skills, and that capitalist technology has become more masculine than previous technologies.

I have already described how, in the early phases of industrialization, women were denied access to ownership of capital and access to education. Shifting the focus, these authors show that the rigid pattern of gender divisions that developed within the working class in the context of the new industries laid the foundation for the male dominance of technology. It was during this period that manufacturing moved into factories, and home became separated from paid work. The advent of powered machinery fundamentally challenged traditional craft skills because tools were literally taken out of the hands of workers and combined into machines. But as it had been men who on the whole had technical skills in the period before the Industrial Revolution, they were in a unique position to maintain a monopoly over the new skills created by the introduction of machines.

Male craft workers could not prevent employers from drawing women into the new spheres of production. So instead they organized to retain certain rights over technology by actively resisting the entry of women to their trades. Women who became industrial laborers found themselves working in what were considered to be unskilled jobs for the lowest pay. "It is the most damning indictment of skilled working-class men and their unions that they excluded women from membership and prevented them gaining competences that could have secured them a decent living" (Cockburn, 1985, p39). This gender division of labor within the factory meant that the machinery was designed by men with men in mind, either by the capitalist inventor or by skilled craftsmen. Industrial technology from its origins thus reflects male power as well as capitalist domination.

The masculine culture of technology is fundamental to the way in which the gender division of labor is still being reproduced today. By securing control of key technologies, men are denying women the practical experience upon which inventiveness depends. I noted earlier the degree to which technical knowledge involves tacit, intuitive knowledge and "learning by doing." New technology typically emerges not from sudden flashes of inspiration but from existing technology, by a process of gradual modification to, and new combinations of, that existing technology. Innovation is to some extent an imaginative process, but that imagination lies largely in seeing ways in which existing devices can be improved, and in extending the scope of techniques successful in one area into new areas. Therefore giving women access to formal technical knowledge alone does not provide the resources necessary for invention. Experience of existing technology is a precondition for the invention of new technology.

The nature of women's inventions, like that of men's, is a function of time, place and resources. Segregated at work and primarily confined to the private sphere of household, women's experience has been severely restricted and therefore so too has their inventiveness: An interesting illustration of this point lies in the fact that women who were employed in the munitions factories during the First World War are on record as having redesigned the weaponry they were making.[7] Thus, given the opportunity, women have demonstrated their inventive capacity in what now seems the most unlikely of contexts.

MISSING: THE GENDER DIMENSION IN THE SOCIOLOGY OF TECHNOLOGY

The historical approach is an advance over essentialist positions that seek to base a new technology on women's innate values. Women's profound alienation from technology is accounted for in terms of the historical and cultural construction of technology as masculine. I believe that women's exclusion from, and rejection of, technology is made more explicable by an analysis of technology as a culture that expresses and consolidates relations among men. If technical competence is an integral part of masculine gender identity, why should women be expected to aspire to it?

Such an account of technology and gender relations, however, is still at a general level.[8] There are few cases where feminists have really got inside the "black box" of technology to do detailed empirical research, as some of the most recent sociological literature has attempted. Over the last few years, a new sociology of technology has emerged, which is studying the invention, development, stabilization and diffusion of specific artifacts.[9] It is evident from this research that technology is not simply the product of rational technical imperatives. Rather, political choices are embedded in the very design and selection of technology.

Technologies result from a series of specific decisions made by particular groups of people in particular places at particular times for their own purposes. As such, technologies bear the imprint of the people and social context in which they developed. David Noble (1984, p. xiii) expresses this point succinctly as follows: "Because of its very concreteness, people tend to confront technology as an irreducible brute fact, a given, a first cause, rather than as hardened history, frozen fragments of human and social endeavor." Technological change is a process subject to struggles for control by different groups. As such, the outcomes depend primarily on the distribution of power and resources within society.

There is now an extensive literature on the history of technology and the economics of technological innovation. Labor historians and sociologists have investigated the relationship between social change and the shaping of production processes in great detail and have also been concerned with the influence of technological form upon social relations. The sociological approach has moved away from studying the individual inventor and from the notion that technological innovation is a result of some inner technical logic. Rather, it attempts to show the effects of social relations on technology that range from fostering or inhibiting particular technologies, through influencing the choice between competing paths of technical development, to affecting the precise design characteristics of particular artifacts. Technological innovation now requires major investment and has become a collective, institutionalized process. The evolution of a technology is thus the function of a complex set of technical, social, economic, and political factors. An artifact may be looked on as the "congealed outcome of a set of negotiations, compromises, conflicts, controversies and deals that were put together between opponents in rooms filled with smoke, lathes or computer terminals" (Law, 1987, p. 406)

Because social groups have different interests and resources, the development process brings out conflicts between different views of the technical requirements of the device. Accordingly, the stability and form of artifacts depend on the capacity and resources that the salient social groups can mobilize in the course of the development process. Thus in the technology of production, economic and social class interests often lie behind the development and adoption of devices. In the case of military technology, the operation of bureaucratic and organizational interests of state decision making will be identifiable. Growing attention is now being given to the extent to which the state sponsorship of military technology shapes civilian technology.

So far, however, little attention has been paid to the way in which technological objects may be shaped by the operation of gender interests. This blindness to gender issues is also indicative of a general problem with the methodology adopted by the new sociology of technology. Using a conventional notion of technology, these writers study the social groups that actively seek to influence the form and direction of technological design. What they overlook is the fact that the absence of influence from certain groups may also be significant. For them, women's absence from observable conflict does not indicate that gender interests are being mobilized. For a social theory of gender, however, the almost complete exclusion of women from the technological community points to the need to take account of the underlying structure of gender relations. Preferences for different technologies are shaped by a set of social arrangements that reflect men's power in the wider society. The process of technological development is socially structured and culturally patterned by various social interests that lie outside the immediate context of technological innovation.

More than ever before technological change impinges on every aspect of our public and private lives, from the artificially cultivated food that we eat to the increasingly sophisticated forms of communication we use. Yet, in common with the labor process debate, the sociology of technology has concentrated almost exclusively on the relations of paid production, focusing in particular on the early stages of product development. In doing so [it has] ignored the spheres of reproduction, consumption and the unpaid production that takes place in the home. By contrast, feminist analysis points us beyond the factory gates to see that technology is just as centrally involved in these spheres.

Inevitably perhaps, feminist work in this area has so far raised as many questions as it has answered. Is technology valued because it is associated with masculinity or is masculinity valued because of the association with technology? How do we avoid the tautology that "technology is masculine because men do it"? Why is women's work undervalued? Is there such a thing as women's knowledge? Is it different from "feminine intuition"? Can technology be reconstructed around women's interests? These are the questions that abstract analysis has so far failed to answer. The character of salient interests and social groups will differ depending on the particular empirical sites of technology being considered. Thus we need to look in more concrete and historical detail at how, in specific areas of work and personal life, gender relations influence the technological enterprise. . . . [In the book from which this excerpt is drawn I stress] that a gendered approach to technology cannot be reduced to a view which treats technology as a set of neutral artifacts manipulated by men in their own interests. While it is the case that men dominate the scientific and technical institutions, it is perfectly plausible that there will come a time when women are more fully represented in these institutions without transforming the direction of technological development. To cite just one instance, women are increasingly being recruited into the American space-defense program but we do not hear their voices protesting about its preoccupations. Nevertheless, gender relations are an integral constituent of the social organization of these institutions and their projects. It is impossible to divorce the gender relations that are expressed in, and shape technologies from, the wider social structures that create and maintain them. In developing a theory of the gendered character of technology, we are inevitably in danger of either adopting an essentialist position that sees technology as inherently patriarchal, or losing sight of the structure of gender relations through an overemphasis on the historical variability of the categories of "women" and "technology." [My work seeks] to chart another course.

NOTES

1. Staudenmaier (1985, pp. 103–20) outlines four characteristics of technological knowledge — scientific concepts, problematic data, engineering theory, and technological skill.
2. A good cross-section of this material can be found in Trescott (1979); Rothschild (1983); Faulkner and Arnold (1985); McNeil (1987); Kramarae (1988). McNeil's book is particularly useful as it contains a comprehensive bibliography, which is organized thematically.
3. MacLeod (1987) suggests that although George Ravenscroft is credited in the patent records with being the "heroic" inventor of lead-crystal glass, he was rather the purchaser or financier of another's invention. This study alerts us to the danger of assuming that patent records have always represented the same thing.
4. For a biography of Lady Lovelace, which takes issue with the view of her as a major contributor to computer programming, see Stein (1985). However, both Kraft (1977) and more recently Giordano (1988) have documented the extensive participation of women in the development of computer programming.
5. Technology as the domination of nature is also a central theme in the work of critical theorists, such as Marcuse, for whom it is capitalist relations (rather than patriarchal relations) that are built into the very structure of technology. "Not only the application of technology but technology itself is domination (of nature and men) — methodical, scientific, calculated,

calculating control. Specific purposes and interests of domination are not foisted upon technology 'subsequently' and from the outside; they enter the very construction of the technical apparatus" (Marcuse, 1968, pp. 223–4).

6. This point is elaborated in Chapter 2 of *Feminism Confronts Technology*. See also Part Two of MacKenzie and Wajcman (1985) for a collection of these case studies.
7. Amram (1984) provides a selection of the patents granted to women during the First World War.
8. Cockburn's (1983, 1985) work is one important exception discussed at greater length in Chapter 2 of *Feminism Confronts Technology*.
9. For an introduction to this literature, see MacKenzie and Wajcman (1985); Bijker, Hughes and Pinch (1987).

REFERENCES

Amram, F. 1984. The Innovative Woman. *New Scientist,* 24 May 1984, 10–12.

Barnes, Barry, and David Edge, eds. 1982. *Science in Context: Readings in the Sociology of Science.* Milton Keynes, England: Open University Press/Cambridge, MA: MIT Press.

Bijker, Wiebe E., Thomas P. Hughes, and Trevor J. Pinch, eds. 1987. *The Social Construction of Technological Systems.* Cambridge, MA: MIT Press.

Braverman, Harry. 1974. *Labor and Monopoly Capital: The Degradation of Work in the Twentieth Century.* New York: Monthly Review Press.

Cockburn, Cynthia. 1983. *Brothers: Male Dominance and Technical Change.* London: Pluto Press.

Cockburn, Cynthia. 1985. *Machinery of Dominance: Women, Men, and Technical Know-How.* London: Pluto Press.

Cooley, Mike. 1980. *Architect or Bee? The Human/Technology Relationship.* Slough, England: Langley Technical Services.

Cowan, Ruth S. 1979. From Virginia Dare to Virginia Slims: Women and Technology in American Life. *Technology and Culture* 20; 51–63.

Faulkner, Wendy, and Erik Arnold, eds. 1985. *Smothered by Invention: Technology in Women's Lives.* London: Pluto Press.

Firestone, Shulamith. 1970. *The Dialectic of Sex.* New York: William Morrow & Co.

Giordano, R. 1988. *The Social Context of Innovation: A Case History of the Development of COBOL Programming Language.* Columbia University Department of History.

Griffiths, Dot. 1985. The Exclusion of Women from Technology. In Faulkner and Arnold, op. cit.

Kraft, P. 1977. *Programmers and Managers: The Routinization of Computer Programming in the United States.* New York: Springer Verlag.

Kramarae, Chris, ed. 1988. *Technology and Women's Voices.* New York: Routledge & Kegan Paul.

Law, John. 1987. Review Article: The Structure of Sociotechnical Engineering — A Review of the New Sociology of Technology. *Sociological Review* 35; 404–425.

MacKenzie, Donald, and Judy Wajcman, eds. 1985. *The Social Shaping of Technology: How the Refrigerator Got Its Hum.* Milton Keynes, England: Open University Press.

MacLeod, Christine. 1987. Accident or Design? George Ravenscroft's Patent and the Invention of Lead-Crystal Glass. *Technology and Culture* 28, 4:776–803.

McNeil, Maureen, ed. 1987. *Gender and Expertise.* London: Free Association Books.

Marcuse, H. 1968. *Negations.* London: Allen Lane.

Noble, David. 1984. *Forces of Production: A Social History of Industrial Automation.* New York: Knopf.

Pacey, Arnold. 1983. *The Culture of Technology.* Oxford, England: Basil Blackwell/Cambridge, MA: MIT Press.

Pursell, C. 1981. Women Inventors in America. *Technology and Culture* 22, 3:545–549.

Rothschild, Joan, ed. 1983. *Machina ex Dea: Feminist Perspectives on Technology.* New York: Pergamon Press.

Stanley, Autumn. 1992. *Mothers and Daughters of Invention: Notes for a Revised History of Technology.* Metuchen, NJ: Scarecrow Press.

Staudenmaier, John M. 1985. *Technology Storytellers: Reweaving the Human Fabric.* Cambridge, MA: MIT Press.

Stein, D. 1985. *Ada: A Life and Legacy.* Cambridge, MA: MIT Press.

Trescott, Martha M., ed. 1979. *Dynamos and Virgins Revisited: Women and Technological Change in History.* Metuchen, NJ: Scarecrow.

14.　Do Artifacts Have Politics?

LANGDON WINNER

Do the properties of technological systems embody specific kinds of power and authority relationships? Are nuclear power systems inherently centralizing and authoritarian? Are solar power systems, as some of their advocates claim, more democratic and consistent with the values of pluralistic societies? Langdon Winner looks for answers to questions such as these in the following essay, originally published in a 1980 symposium issue of the journal Daedalus *devoted to "Modern Technology: Problem or Opportunity?" Winner believes that, indeed, technological choices do have political consequences. He cites many examples, including a particularly egregious one: Robert Moses designed bridges over his parkways on Long Island too low for buses in order to keep members of the urban lower classes (who couldn't afford private automobiles) from crowding the suburban parks and beaches.*

"Technologies," Winner concludes, "are ways of building order in our world," which, by their nature, influence the way people live and work over long periods of time. We need to study and understand their consequences and to develop means of making technological choices in a more open and participatory fashion if we are to maintain a democratic society.

A prolific writer whose works have appeared in both scholarly and popular publications and who served as contributing editor to Rolling Stone *magazine from 1969 to 1971, Langdon Winner is professor of political science in the Department of Science and Technology Studies at Rensselaer Polytechnic Institute (RPI) in Troy, New York. Prior to coming to RPI in 1985, he taught at the Massachusetts Institute of Technology, the University of Leiden (in the Netherlands), and the University of California at Berkeley and at Santa Cruz. Among Winner's books are* Autonomous Technology *(1977) and* The Whale and the Reactor *(1988).*

In controversies about technology and society, there is no idea more provocative than the notion that technical things have political qualities. At issue is the claim that the machines, structures, and systems of modern material culture can be accurately judged not only for their contributions of efficiency and productivity, not merely for their positive and negative environmental side effects, but also for the ways in which they can embody specific forms of power and authority. Since ideas of this kind have a persistent and troubling presence in discussions about the meaning of technology, they deserve explicit attention.[1]

Writing in *Technology and Culture* almost two decades ago, Lewis Mumford gave classic statement to one version of the theme, arguing that "from late neolithic times in the Near East, right down to our own day, two technologies have recurrently existed side by side: one authoritarian, the other democratic, the first system-centered, immensely powerful, but inherently unstable, the other man-centered, relatively weak, but resourceful and durable."[2] This thesis stands at the heart of Mumford's studies of the city, architecture, and the history of technics, and mirrors concerns voiced earlier in the works of Peter Kropotkin, William Morris, and other nineteenth-century critics of industrialism. More recently, antinuclear and prosolar energy movements in Europe and America have adopted a similar notion as a centerpiece in their arguments. Thus environmentalist Denis Hayes concludes, "The increased deployment of nuclear power facilities must lead society toward authoritarianism. Indeed, safe reliance upon nuclear power as the principal source of energy may be possible only in a totalitarian state." Echoing the views of many proponents of appropriate technology and the soft energy path, Hayes contends that "dispersed solar sources are more compatible than centralized technologies with social equity, freedom and cultural pluralism."[3]

An eagerness to interpret technical artifacts in political language is by no means the exclusive property of critics of large-scale high-technology systems. A long lineage of boosters have insisted that the "biggest and best" that science and industry made available were the best guarantees of democracy, freedom, and social justice. The factory system, automobile, telephone, radio, television, the space program, and of course nuclear power itself have all at one time or another been described as democratizing, liberating forces. David Lilienthal, in *T.V.A.: Democracy on the March*, for example, found this promise in the phosphate fertilizers and electricity that technical progress was bringing to rural Americans during the 1940s.[4] In a recent essay, *The Republic of Technology*, Daniel Boorstin extolled television for "its power to disband armies, to cashier presidents, to create a whole new democratic world — democratic in ways never before imagined, even in America."[5] Scarcely a new invention comes along that someone does not proclaim it the salvation of a free society.

It is no surprise to learn that technical systems of various kinds are deeply interwoven in the conditions of modern politics. The physical arrangements of industrial production, warfare, communications, and the like have fundamentally changed the exercise of power and the experience of citizenship. But to go beyond this obvious fact and to argue that certain technologies *in themselves* have political properties seems, at first glance, completely mistaken. We all know that people have politics, not things. To discover either virtues or evils in aggregates of steel, plastic, transistors, integrated circuits, and chemicals seems just plain wrong, a way of mystifying human artifice and of avoiding the true sources, the human sources of freedom and oppression, justice and injustice. Blaming the hardware appears even more foolish than blaming the victims when it comes to judging conditions of public life.

Hence, the stern advice commonly given those who flirt with the notion that technical artifacts have political qualities: What matters is not technology itself, but the social or economic system in which it is embedded. This maxim, which in a number of variations is the central premise of a theory that can be called the social determination of technology, has an obvious wisdom. It serves as a needed corrective to those who focus uncritically on such things as "the computer and its social impacts" but who fail to look behind technical things to notice the social circumstances of their development, deployment, and use. This view provides an antidote to naive technological determinism — the idea that technology develops as the sole result of an internal dynamic, and then, unmediated by any other influence, molds society to fit its patterns. Those who have not recognized the ways in which technologies are shaped by social and economic forces have not gotten very far.

But the corrective has its own shortcomings; taken literally, it suggests that technical *things* do not matter at all. Once one has done the detective work necessary to reveal the social origins — power holders behind a particular instance of technological change — one will have explained everything of importance. This conclusion offers comfort to social scientists: it validates what they had always suspected, namely, that there is nothing distinctive about the study of technology in the first place. Hence, they can return to their standard models of social power — those of interest group politics, bureaucratic politics, Marxist models of class struggle, and the like — and have everything they need. The social determination of technology is, in this view, essentially no different from the social determination of, say, welfare policy or taxation.

There are, however, good reasons technology has of late taken on a special fascination in its own right for historians, philosophers, and political scientists; good reasons the standard models of social science only go so far in accounting for what is most interesting and troublesome about the subject. In another place I have tried to show why so much of modern social and political thought contains recurring statements of what can be called a theory of technological politics, an odd mongrel of notions often crossbred with orthodox liberal, conservative, and socialist philosophies.[6] The theory of technological politics draws attention to the momentum of large-scale sociotechnical systems, to the response of modern societies to certain technological imperatives, and to the all too common signs of the adaptation of human ends to technical means. In so doing it offers a novel framework of interpretation and explanation for some of the more puzzling patterns that have taken shape in and around the growth of modern material culture. One strength of this point of view is that it takes technical artifacts seriously. Rather than insist that we immediately reduce everything to the interplay of social forces, it suggests that we pay attention to the characteristics of technical objects and the meaning of those characteristics. A necessary complement to, rather than a replacement for, theories of the social determination of technology, this perspective identifies certain technologies as political phenomena in their own right. It points us back, to borrow Edmund Husserl's philosophical injunction, *to the things themselves.*

In what follows I shall offer outlines and illustrations of two ways in which artifacts can contain political properties. First are instances in which the invention, design, or arrangement of a specific technical device or system becomes a way of settling an issue in a particular community. Seen in the proper light, examples of this kind are fairly straightforward and easily understood. Second are cases of what can be called inherently political technologies, man-made systems that appear to require, or to be strongly compatible with, particular kinds of political relationships. Arguments about cases of this kind are much more troublesome and closer to the heart of the matter. By "politics," I mean arrangements of power and authority in human associations as well as the activities that take place within those arrangements. For my purposes, "technology" here is understood to mean all of modern practical artifice,[7] but to avoid confusion I prefer to speak of technolog*ies*, smaller or larger pieces or systems of hardware of a specific kind. My intention is not to settle any of the issues here once and for all, but to indicate their general dimensions and significance.

TECHNICAL ARRANGEMENTS AS FORMS OF ORDER

Anyone who has traveled the highways of America and has become used to the normal height of overpasses may well find something a little odd about some of the bridges over the parkways on Long Island, New York. Many of the overpasses are extraordinarily low, having as little as nine feet of clearance at the curb. Even those who happened to notice this structural peculiarity would not be inclined to attach any special meaning to it. In our accustomed way of looking at things like roads and bridges we see the details of form as innocuous, and seldom give them a second thought.

It turns out, however, that the two hundred or so low-hanging overpasses on Long Island were deliberately designed to achieve a particular social effect. Robert Moses, the master builder of roads, parks, bridges, and other public works from the 1920s to the 1970s in New York, had these overpasses built to specifications that would discourage the presence of buses on his parkways. According to evidence provided by Robert A. Caro in his biography of Moses, the reasons reflect Moses's social-class bias and racial prejudice. Automobile-owning whites of "upper" and "comfortable middle" classes, as he called them, would be free to use the parkways for recreation and commuting. Poor people and blacks, who normally used public transit, were kept off the roads because the twelve-foot-tall buses could not get through the overpasses. One consequence was to limit access of racial minorities and low-income groups to Jones Beach, Moses's widely acclaimed public park. Moses made doubly sure of this result by vetoing a proposed extension of the Long Island Railroad to Jones Beach.[8]

As a story in recent American political history, Robert Moses's life is fascinating. His dealings with mayors, governors, and presidents, and his careful manipulation of legislatures, banks, labor unions, the press, and public opinion are all matters that political scientists could study for years. But the most important and enduring results of his work are his technologies, the vast engineering projects that give New York much of its present form. For generations after Moses has gone and the alliances he forged have fallen apart, his public works, especially the highways and bridges he built to favor the use of the automobile over the development of mass transit, will continue to shape that city. Many of his monumental structures of concrete and steel embody a systematic social inequality, a way of engineering relationships among people that, after a time, becomes just another part of the landscape. As planner Lee Koppleman told Caro about the low bridges on Wantagh Parkway, "The old son-of-a-gun had made sure that buses would *never* be able to use his goddamned parkways."[9]

Histories of architecture, city planning, and public works contain many examples of physical arrangements that contain explicit or implicit political purposes. One can point to Baron Haussmann's broad Parisian thoroughfares, engineered at Louis Napoleon's direction to prevent any recurrence of street fighting of the kind that took place during the revolution of 1848. Or one can visit any number of grotesque concrete buildings and huge plazas constructed on American university campuses during the late 1960s and early 1970s to defuse student demonstrations. Studies of industrial machines and instruments also turn up interesting political stories, including some that violate our normal expectations about why technological innovations are made in the first place. If we suppose that new technologies are introduced to achieve increased efficiency, the history of technology shows that we will sometimes be disappointed. Technological change expresses a panoply of human motives, not the least of which is the desire of some to have dominion over others, even though it may require an occasional sacrifice of cost-cutting and some violence to the norm of getting more from less.

One poignant illustration can be found in the history of nineteenth-century industrial mechanization. At Cyrus McCormick's reaper manufacturing plant in Chicago in the middle 1880s, pneumatic molding machines, a new and largely untested innovation, were added to the foundry at an estimated cost of $500,000. In the standard economic interpretation of such things, we would expect that this step was taken to modernize the plant and achieve the kind of efficiencies that mechanization brings. But historian Robert Ozanne has shown why the development must be seen in a broader context. At the time, Cyrus McCormick II was engaged in a battle with the National Union of Iron Molders. He saw the addition of the new machines as a way to "weed out the bad element among the men," namely, the skilled workers who had organized the union local in Chicago.[10] The new machines, manned by unskilled labor, actually produced inferior castings at a higher cost than the earlier process. After three years of use the machines were, in fact, abandoned, but by that time they had served their purpose — the destruction of the union. Thus, the story of these technical developments at the McCormick factory cannot be understood adequately outside the record of workers' attempts to organize, police repression of the labor movement in Chicago during that period, and the events surrounding the bombing at Haymarket Square. Technological history and American political history were at that moment deeply intertwined.

In cases like those of Moses's low bridges and McCormick's molding machines, one sees the importance of technical arrangements that precede the *use* of the things in question. It is obvious that technologies can be used in ways that enhance the power, authority, and privilege of some over others, for example, the use of television to sell a candidate. To our accustomed way of thinking, technologies are seen as neutral tools that can be used well or poorly, for good, evil, or something in between. But we usually do not stop to inquire whether a given device might have been designed and built in such a way that it produces a set of consequences logically and temporally *prior* to any of its professed uses. Robert Moses's bridges, after all, were used to carry automobiles from one point to another; McCormick's machines were used to make metal castings; both technologies, however, encompassed purposes far beyond their immediate use. If our moral and political language for evaluating technology includes only categories having to do with tools and uses, if it does not include attention to the meaning of the designs and arrangements of our artifacts, then we will be blinded to much that is intellectually and practically crucial.

Because the point is most easily understood in the light of particular intentions embodied in physical form, I have so far offered illustrations that seem almost conspiratorial. But to recognize the political dimensions in the shapes of technology does not require that we look for conscious conspiracies or malicious intentions. The organized movement of handicapped people in the United States during the 1970s pointed out the countless ways in which machines, instruments, and structures of common use — buses, buildings, sidewalks, plumbing fixtures, and so forth — made it impossible for many handicapped persons to move about freely, a condition that systematically excluded them from public life. It is safe to say that designs unsuited for the handicapped arose more from long-standing neglect than from anyone's active intention. But now that the issue has been raised for public attention, it is evident that justice requires a remedy. A whole range of artifacts are now being redesigned and rebuilt to accommodate this minority.

Indeed, many of the most important examples of technologies that have political consequences are those that transcend the simple categories of "intended" and "unintended" altogether. These are instances in which the very process of technical development is so thoroughly biased in a particular direction that it regularly produces results counted as wonderful breakthroughs by some social interests and crushing setbacks by others. In such cases it is neither correct nor insightful to say, "Someone intended to do somebody else harm." Rather, one must say that the technological deck has been stacked long in advance to favor certain social interests, and that some people were bound to receive a better hand than others.

The mechanical tomato harvester, a remarkable device perfected by researchers at the University of California from the late 1940s to the present, offers an illustrative tale. The machine is able to harvest tomatoes in a single pass through a row, cutting the plants from the ground, shaking the fruit loose, and in the newest models sorting the tomatoes electronically into large plastic gondolas that hold up to twenty-five tons of produce headed for canning. To accommodate the rough motion of these "factories in the field," agricultural researchers have bred new varieties of tomatoes that are hardier, sturdier, and less tasty. The harvesters replace the system of handpicking, in which crews of farmworkers would pass through the fields three or four times putting ripe tomatoes in lug boxes and saving immature fruit for later harvest.[11] Studies in California indicate that the machine reduces costs by approximately five to seven dollars per ton as compared to hand-harvesting.[12] But the benefits are by no means equally divided in the agricultural economy. In fact, the machine in the garden has in this instance been the occasion for a thorough reshaping of social relationships of tomato production in rural California.

By their very size and cost, more than $50,000 each to purchase, the machines are compatible only with a highly concentrated form of tomato growing. With the introduction of this new method of harvesting, the number of tomato growers declined from approximately four thousand in the early 1960s to about six hundred in 1973, yet with a substantial increase in tons of tomatoes produced. By the late 1970s an estimated thirty-two thousand jobs in the tomato industry had been eliminated as a direct consequence of mechanization.[13] Thus, a jump in productivity to the benefit of very large growers has occurred at a sacrifice to other rural agricultural communities.

The University of California's research and development on agricultural machines like the tomato harvester is at this time the subject of a lawsuit filed by attorneys for California Rural Legal Assistance, an organization representing a group of farmworkers and other interested parties. The suit charges that University officials are spending tax monies on projects that benefit a handful of private interests to the detriment of farmworkers, small farmers, consumers, and rural California generally, and asks for a court injunction to stop the practice. The University has denied these charges, arguing that to accept them "would require elimination of all research with any potential practical application."[14]

As far as I know, no one has argued that the development of the tomato harvester was the result of a plot. Two students of the controversy, William Friedland and Amy Barton, specifically exonerate both the original developers of the machine and the hard tomato from any desire to facilitate economic concentration in that industry.[15] What we see here instead is an ongoing social process in which scientific knowledge, technological invention, and corporate profit reinforce each other in deeply entrenched patterns that bear the unmistakable stamp of political and economic power. Over many decades agricultural research and development in American land-grant colleges and universities has tended to favor the interests of large agribusiness concerns.[16] It is in the face of such subtly ingrained patterns that opponents of innovations like the tomato harvester are made to seem "antitechnology" or "antiprogress." For the harvester is not merely the symbol of a social order that rewards some while punishing others; it is in a true sense an embodiment of that order.

Within a given category of technological change there are, roughly speaking, two kinds of choices that can affect the relative distribution of power, authority, and privilege in a community. Often the crucial decision is a simple "yes or no" choice — are we going to develop and adopt the thing or not? In recent years many local, national, and international disputes about technology have centered on "yes or no" judgments about such things as food additives, pesticides, the building of highways, nuclear reactors, and dam projects. The fundamental choice about an ABM or an SST is whether or not the thing is going to join society as a piece of its operating equipment. Reasons for and against are frequently as important as those concerning the adoption of an important new law.

A second range of choices, equally critical in many instances, has to do with specific features in the design or arrangement of a technical system after the decision to go ahead with it has already been made. Even after a utility company wins permission to build a large electric power line, important controversies can remain with respect to the placement of its route and the design of its towers; even after an organization has decided to institute a system of computers, controversies can still arise with regard to the kinds of components, programs, modes of access, and other specific features the system will include. Once the mechanical tomato harvester had been developed in its basic form, design alteration of critical social significance — the addition of electronic sorters, for example — changed the character of the machine's effects on the balance of wealth and power in California agriculture. Some of the most interesting research on technology and politics at present focuses on the attempt to demonstrate in a detailed, concrete fashion how seemingly innocuous design features in mass transit systems, water projects, industrial machinery, and other technologies actually mask social choices of profound significance. Historian David Noble is now studying two kinds of automated machine tool systems that have different implications for the relative power of management and labor in the industries that might employ them. He is able to show that, although the basic electronic and mechanical components of the record/playback and numerical control systems are similar, the choice of one design over another has crucial consequences for social struggles on the shop floor. To see the matter solely in terms of cost-cutting, efficiency, or the modernization of equipment is to miss a decisive element in the story.[17]

From such examples I would offer the following general conclusions. The things we call "technologies" are ways of building order in our world. Many technical devices and systems important in everyday life contain possibilities for many different ways of ordering human activity. Consciously or not, deliberately or inadvertently, societies choose structures for technologies that influence how people are going to work, communicate, travel, consume, and so forth over a very long time. In the processes by which structuring decisions are made, different people are differently situated and possess unequal degrees of power as well as unequal levels of awareness. By far the greatest latitude of choice exists the very first time a particular instrument, system, or technique is introduced. Because choices tend to become strongly fixed in material equipment, economic investment, and social habit, the original flexibility vanishes for all practical purposes once the initial commitments are made. In that sense technological innovations are similar to legislative acts or political foundings that establish a framework for public order that will endure over many generations. For that reason, the same careful attention one would give to the rules, roles, and relationships of politics must also be given to such things as the building of highways, the creation of television networks, and the tailoring of seemingly insignificant features on new machines. The issues that divide or unite people in society are settled not only in the institutions and practices of politics proper, but also, and less obviously, in tangible arrangements of steel and concrete, wires and transistors, nuts and bolts.

INHERENTLY POLITICAL TECHNOLOGIES

None of the arguments and examples considered thus far address a stronger, more troubling claim often made in writings about technology and society — the belief that some technologies are by their very nature political in a specific way. According to this view, the adoption of a given technical system unavoidably brings with it conditions for human relationships that have a distinctive political cast — for example, centralized or decentralized, egalitarian or inegalitarian, repressive or liberating. This is ultimately what is at stake in assertions like those of Lewis Mumford that two traditions of technology, one authoritarian, the other democratic, exist side by side in Western history. In all the cases I cited the technologies are relatively flexible in design and arrangement, and variable in their effects. Although one can recognize a particular result produced in a particular setting, one can also easily imagine how a roughly similar device or system might have been built or situated with very much different political consequences. The idea we must now examine and evaluate is that certain kinds of technology do not allow such flexibility, and that to choose them is to choose a particular form of political life.

A remarkably forceful statement of one version of this argument appears in Friedrich Engels's little essay "On Authority," written in 1872. Answering anarchists who believed that authority is an evil that ought to be abolished altogether, Engels launches into a panegyric for authoritarianism, maintaining, among other things, that strong authority is a necessary condition in modern industry. To advance his case in the strongest possible way, he asks his readers to imagine that the revolution has already occurred. "Supposing a social revolution dethroned the capitalists, who now exercise their authority over the production and circulation of wealth. Supposing, to adopt entirely the point of view of the anti-authoritarians, that the land and the instruments of labour had become the collective property of the workers who use them. Will authority have disappeared or will it have only changed its form?"[18]

His answer draws upon lessons from three sociotechnical systems of his day, cotton-spinning mills, railways, and ships at sea. He observes that, on its way to becoming finished thread, cotton moves through a number of different operations at different locations in the factory. The workers perform a wide variety of tasks, from running the steam engine to carrying the products from one room to another. Because these tasks must be coordinated, and because the timing of the work is "fixed by the authority of the steam," laborers must learn to accept a rigid discipline. They must, according to Engels, work at regular hours and agree to subordinate their individual wills to the persons in charge of factory operations. If they fail to do so, they risk the horrifying possibility that production will come to a grinding halt. Engels pulls no punches. "The automatic machinery of a big factory," he writes, "is much more despotic than the small capitalists who employ workers ever have been."[19]

Similar lessons are adduced in Engels's analysis of the necessary operating conditions for railways and ships at sea. Both require the subordination of workers to an "imperious authority" that sees to it that things run according to plan. Engels finds that, far from being an idiosyncracy of capitalist social organization, relationships of authority and subordination arise "independently of all social organization, [and] are imposed upon us together with the material conditions under which we produce and make products circulate." Again, he intends this to be stern advice to the anarchists who, according to Engels, thought it possible simply to eradicate subordination and superordination at a single stroke. All such schemes are nonsense. The roots of unavoidable authoritarianism are, he argues, deeply implanted in the human involvement with science and technology. "If man, by dint of his knowledge and inventive genius, has subdued the forces of nature, the latter avenge themselves upon him by subjecting him, insofar as he employs them, to a veritable despotism independent of all social organization."[20]

Attempts to justify strong authority on the basis of supposedly necessary conditions of technical practice have an ancient history. A pivotal theme in the *Republic* is Plato's quest to borrow the authority of *technē* and employ it by analogy to buttress his argument in favor of authority in the state. Among the illustrations he chooses, like Engels, is that of a ship on the high seas. Because large sailing vessels by their very nature need to be steered with a firm hand, sailors must yield to their captain's commands; no reasonable person believes that ships can be run democratically. Plato goes on to suggest that governing a state is rather like being captain of a ship or like practicing medicine as a physician. Much the same conditions that require central rule and decisive action in organized technical activity also create this need in government.

In Engels's argument, and arguments like it, the justification for authority is no longer made by Plato's classic analogy, but rather directly with reference to technology itself. If the basic case is as compelling as Engels believed it to be, one would expect that, as a society adopted increasingly complicated technical systems as its material basis, the prospects for authoritarian ways of life would be greatly enhanced. Central control by knowledgeable people acting at the top of a rigid social hierarchy would seem increasingly prudent. In this respect, his stand in "On Authority" appears to be at variance with Karl Marx's position in Volume One of *Capital*. Marx tries to show that increasing mechanization will render obsolete the hierarchical division of labor and the relationships of subordination that, in his view, were necessary during the early stages of modern manufacturing. The "Modern Industry," he writes, ". . . sweeps away by technical means the manufacturing division of labor, under which each man is bound hand and foot for life to a single detail operation. At the same time, the capitalistic form of that industry reproduces this same division of labour in a still more monstrous shape; in the factory proper, by converting the workman into a living appendage of the machine.[21] In Marx's view, the conditions that will eventually dissolve the capitalist division of labor and facilitate proletarian revolution are conditions latent in industrial technology itself. The differences between Marx's position in *Capital* and Engels's in his essay raise an important question for socialism: What, after all, does modern technology make possible or necessary in political life? The theoretical tension we see here mirrors many troubles in the practice of freedom and authority that have muddied the tracks of socialist revolution.

Arguments to the effect that technologies are in some sense inherently political have been advanced in a wide variety of contexts, far too many to summarize
here. In my reading of such notions, however, there are two basic ways of stating
the case. One version claims that the adoption of a given technical system actually *requires* the creation and maintenance of a particular set of social conditions
as the operating environment of that system. Engels's position is of this kind. A
similar view is offered by a contemporary writer who holds that "if you accept
nuclear power plants, you also accept a techno-scientific-industrial-military elite.
Without these people in charge, you could not have nuclear power."[22] In this
conception, some kinds of technology require their social environments to be
structured in a particular way in much the same sense that an automobile
requires wheels in order to run. The thing could not exist as an effective operating entity unless certain social as well as material conditions were met. The
meaning of "required" here is that of practical (rather than logical) necessity.
Thus, Plato thought it a practical necessity that a ship at sea have one captain
and an unquestioningly obedient crew.

A second, somewhat weaker, version of the argument holds that a given kind
of technology is strongly *compatible with,* but does not strictly require, social and
political relationships of a particular stripe. Many advocates of solar energy now
hold that technologies of that variety are more compatible with a democratic,
egalitarian society than energy systems based on coal, oil, and nuclear power; at
the same time they do not maintain that anything about solar energy requires
democracy. Their case is, briefly, that solar energy is decentralizing in both a technical and political sense: technically speaking, it is vastly more reasonable to
build solar systems in a disaggregated, widely distributed manner than in large-
scale centralized plants; politically speaking, solar energy accommodates the
attempts of individuals and local communities to manage their affairs effectively
because they are dealing with systems that are more accessible, comprehensible,
and controllable than huge centralized sources. In this view, solar energy is desirable not only for its economic and environmental benefits, but also for the salu-
tary institutions it is likely to permit in other areas of public life.[23]

Within both versions of the argument there is a further distinction to be made
between conditions that are *internal* to the workings of a given technical system
and those that are *external* to it. Engels's thesis concerns internal social relations
said to be required within cotton factories and railways, for example; what such
relationships mean for the condition of society at large is for him a separate question. In contrast, the solar advocate's belief that solar technologies are compatible with democracy pertains to the way they complement aspects of society
removed from the organization of those technologies as such.

There are, then, several different directions that arguments of this kind can
follow. Are the social conditions predicated said to be required by, or strongly
compatible with, the workings of a given technical system? Are those conditions
internal to that system or external to it (or both)? Although writings that address
such questions are often unclear about what is being asserted, arguments in this
general category do have an important presence in modern political discourse.
They enter into many attempts to explain how changes in social life take place in

the wake of technological innovation. More importantly, they are often used to buttress attempts to justify or criticize proposed courses of action involving new technology. By offering distinctly political reasons for or against the adoption of a particular technology, arguments of this kind stand apart from more commonly employed, more easily quantifiable claims about economic costs and benefits, environmental impacts, and possible risks to public health and safety that technical systems may involve. The issue here does not concern how many jobs will be created, how much income generated, how many pollutants added, or how many cancers produced. Rather, the issue has to do with ways in which choices about technology have important consequences for the form and quality of human associations.

If we examine social patterns that comprise the environments of technical systems, we find certain devices and systems almost invariably linked to specific ways of organizing power and authority. The important question is: Does this state of affairs derive from an unavoidable social response to intractable properties in the things themselves, or is it instead a pattern imposed independently by a governing body, ruling class, or some other social or cultural institution to further its own purposes?

Taking the most obvious example, the atom bomb is an inherently political artifact. As long as it exists at all, its lethal properties demand that it be controlled by a centralized, rigidly hierarchical chain of command closed to all influences that might make its workings unpredictable. The internal social system of the bomb must be authoritarian; there is no other way. The state of affairs stands as a practical necessity independent of any larger political system in which the bomb is embedded, independent of the kind of regime or character of its rulers. Indeed, democratic states must try to find ways to ensure that the social structures and mentality that characterize the management of nuclear weapons do not "spin off" or "spill over" into the polity as a whole.

The bomb is, of course, a special case. The reasons very rigid relationships of authority are necessary in its immediate presence should be clear to anyone. If, however, we look for other instances in which particular varieties of technology are *widely perceive* to need the maintenance of a special pattern of power and authority, modern technical history contains a wealth of examples.

Alfred D. Chandler in *The Visible Hand,* a monumental study of modern business enterprise, presents impressive documentation to defend the hypothesis that the construction and day-to-day operation of many systems of production, transportation, and communication in the nineteenth and twentieth centuries require the development of a particular social form — a large-scale, centralized, hierarchical organization administered by highly skilled managers. Typical of Chandler's reasoning is his analysis of the growth of the railroads.

> Technology made possible fast, all-weather transportation; but safe, regular, reliable movement of goods and passengers, as well as the continuing maintenance and repair of locomotives, rolling stock, and track, roadbed, stations, roundhouses, and other equipment, required the creation of a sizable administrative organization. It meant the employment of a set of managers to supervise

these functional activities over an extensive geographical area; and the appointment of an administrative command of middle and top executives to monitor, evaluate, and coordinate the work of managers responsible for the day-to-day operations.[24]

Throughout his book Chandler points to ways in which technologies used in the production and distribution of electricity, chemicals, and a wide range of industrial goods "demanded" or "required" this form of human association. "Hence, the operational requirements of railroads demanded the creation of the first administrative hierarchies in American business."[25]

Were there other conceivable ways of organizing these aggregates of people and apparatus? Chandler shows that a previously dominant social form, the small traditional family firm, simply could not handle the task in most cases. Although he does not speculate further, it is clear that he believes there is, to be realistic, very little latitude in the forms of power and authority appropriate within modern sociotechnical systems. The properties of many modern technologies — oil pipelines and refineries, for example — are such that overwhelmingly impressive economies of scale and speed are possible. If such systems are to work effectively, efficiently, quickly, and safely, certain requirements of internal social organization have to be fulfilled; the material possibilities that modern technologies make available could not be exploited otherwise. Chandler acknowledges that as one compares sociotechnical institutions of different nations, one sees "ways in which cultural attitudes, values, ideologies, political systems, and social structure affect these imperatives."[26] But the weight of argument and empirical evidence in *The Visible Hand* suggests that any significant departure from the basic pattern would be, at best, highly unlikely.

It may be that other conceivable arrangements of power and authority, for example, those of decentralized, democratic worker self-management, could prove capable of administering factories, refineries, communications systems, and railroads as well as or better than the organizations Chandler describes. Evidence from automobile assembly teams in Sweden and worker-managed plants in Yugoslavia and other countries is often presented to salvage these possibilities. I shall not be able to settle controversies over this matter here, but merely point to what I consider to be their bone of contention. The available evidence tends to show that many large, sophisticated technological systems are in fact highly compatible with centralized, hierarchical managerial control. The interesting question, however, has to do with whether or not this pattern is in any sense a requirement of such systems, a question that is not solely an empirical one. The matter ultimately rests on our judgments about what steps, if any, are practically necessary in the workings of particular kinds of technology and what, if anything, such measures require of the structure of human associations. Was Plato right in saying that a ship at sea needs steering by a decisive hand and that this could only be accomplished by a single captain and an obedient crew? Is Chandler correct in saying that the properties of large-scale systems require centralized, hierarchical managerial control?

To answer such questions, we would have to examine in some detail the moral claims of practical necessity (including those advocated in the doctrines of economics) and weigh them against moral claims of other sorts, for example, the notion that it is good for sailors to participate in the command of a ship or that workers have a right to be involved in making and administering decisions in a factory. It is characteristic of societies based on large, complex technological systems, however, that moral reasons other than those of practical necessity appear increasingly obsolete, "idealistic," and irrelevant. Whatever claims one may wish to make on behalf of liberty, justice, or equality can be immediately neutralized when confronted with arguments to the effect: "Fine, but that's no way to run a railroad" (or steel mill, or airline, or communications system, and so on). Here we encounter an important quality in modern political discourse and in the way people commonly think about what measures are justified in response to the possibilities technologies make available. In many instances, to say that some technologies are inherently political is to say that certain widely accepted reasons of practical necessity — especially the need to maintain crucial technological systems as smoothly working entities — have tended to eclipse other sorts of moral and political reasoning.

One attempt to salvage the autonomy of politics from the bind of practical necessity involves the notion that conditions of human association found in the internal workings of technological systems can easily be kept separate from the polity as a whole. Americans have long rested content in the belief that arrangements of power and authority inside industrial corporations, public utilities, and the like have little bearing on public institutions, practices, and ideas at large. That "democracy stops at the factory gates" was taken as a fact of life that had nothing to do with the practice of political freedom. But can the internal politics of technology and the politics of the whole community be so easily separated? A recent study of American business leaders, contemporary exemplars of Chandler's "visible hand of management," found them remarkably impatient with such democratic scruples as "one man, one vote." If democracy doesn't work for the firm, the most critical institution in all of society, American executives ask, how well can it be expected to work for the government of a nation — particularly when that government attempts to interfere with the achievements of the firm? The authors of the report observe that patterns of authority that work effectively in the corporation become for businessmen "the desirable model against which to compare political and economic relationships in the rest of society."[27] While such findings are far from conclusive, they do reflect a sentiment increasingly common in the land: what dilemmas like the energy crisis require is not a redistribution of wealth or broader public participation but, rather, stronger, centralized public management — President Carter's proposal for an Energy Mobilization Board and the like.

An especially vivid case in which the operational requirements of a technical system might influence the quality of public life is now at issue in debates about the risks of nuclear power. As the supply of uranium for nuclear reactors runs out, a proposed alternative fuel is the plutonium generated as a by-product in reactor cores. Well-known objections to plutonium recycling focus on its unacceptable economic costs, its risks of environmental contamination, and its dangers in regard to the international proliferation of nuclear weapons. Beyond these concerns, however, stands another, less widely appreciated set of hazards — those that involve the sacrifice of civil liberties. The widespread use of plutonium as a fuel increases the chance that toxic substance might be stolen by terrorists, [members of] organized crime, or other persons. This raises the prospect, and not a trivial one, that extraordinary measures would have to be taken to safeguard plutonium from theft and to recover it if ever the substance were stolen. Workers in the nuclear industry as well as ordinary citizens outside could well become subject to background security checks, covert surveillance, wiretapping, informers, and even emergency measures under martial law — all justified by the need to safeguard plutonium.

Russell W. Ayres's study of the legal ramifications of plutonium recycling concludes: "With the passage of time and the increase in the quantity of plutonium in existence will come pressure to eliminate the traditional checks the courts and legislatures place on the activities of the executive and to develop a powerful central authority better able to enforce strict safeguards." He avers that "once a quantity of plutonium had been stolen, the case for literally turning the country upside down to get it back would be overwhelming." Ayres anticipates and worries about the kinds of thinking that, I have argued, characterize inherently political technologies. It is still true that, in a world in which human beings make and maintain artificial systems, nothing is "required" in an absolute sense. Nevertheless, once a course of action is underway, once artifacts like nuclear power plants have been built and put in operation, the kinds of reasoning that justify the adaptation of social life to technical requirements pop up as spontaneously as flowers in the spring. In Ayres's words, "Once recycling begins and the risks of plutonium theft become real rather than hypothetical, the case for governmental infringement of protected rights will seem compelling."[28] After a certain point, those who cannot accept the hard requirements and imperatives will be dismissed as dreamers and fools.

* * *

The two varieties of interpretation I have outlined indicate how artifacts can have political qualities. In the first instance we noticed ways in which specific features in the design or arrangement of a device or system could provide a convenient means of establishing patterns of power and authority in a given setting. Technologies of this kind have a range of flexibility in the dimensions of their material form. It is precisely because they are flexible that their consequences for society must be understood with reference to the social actors able to influence which designs and arrangements are chosen. In the second instance we examined ways in which the intractable properties of certain kinds of technology are strongly, perhaps unavoidably, linked to particular institutionalized patterns of power and authority. Here, the initial choice about whether or not to adopt something is decisive in regard to its consequences. There are no alternative physical designs or arrangements that would make a significant difference; there are, furthermore, no genuine possibilities for creative intervention by different social systems — capitalist or socialist — that could change the intractability of the entity or significantly alter the quality of its political effects.

To know which variety of interpretation is applicable in a given case is often what is at stake in disputes, some of them passionate ones, about the meaning of technology for how we live. I have argued a "both/and" position here, for it seems to me that both kinds of understanding are applicable in different circumstances. Indeed, it can happen that within a particular complex of technology — a system of communication or transportation, for example — some aspects may be flexible in their possibilities for society, while other aspects may be (for better or worse) completely intractable. The two varieties of interpretation I have examined here can overlap and intersect at many points.

These are, of course, issues on which people can disagree. Thus, some proponents of energy from renewable resources now believe they have at last discovered a set of intrinsically democratic, egalitarian, communitarian technologies. In my best estimation, however, the social consequences of building renewable energy systems will surely depend on the specific configurations of both hardware and the social institutions created to bring that energy to us. It may be that we will find ways to turn this silk purse into a sow's ear. By comparison, advocates of the further development of nuclear power seem to believe that they are working on a rather flexible technology whose adverse social effects can be fixed by changing the design parameters of reactors and nuclear waste disposal systems. For reasons indicated above, I believe them to be dead wrong in that faith. Yes, we may be able to manage some of the "risks" to public health and safety that nuclear power brings. But as society adapts to the more dangerous and apparently indelible features of nuclear power, what will be the long-range toll in human freedom?

My belief that we ought to attend more closely to technical objects themselves is not to say that we can ignore the contexts in which those objects are situated. A ship at sea may well require, as Plato and Engels insisted, a single captain and obedient crew. But a ship out of service, parked at the dock, needs only a caretaker. To understand which technologies and which contexts are important to us, and why, is an enterprise that must involve both the study of specific technical systems and their history as well as a thorough grasp of the concepts and controversies of political theory. In our times people are often willing to make drastic changes in the way they live to accord with technological innovation at the same time they would resist similar kinds of changes justified on political grounds. If for no other reason than that, it is important for us to achieve a clearer view of these matters than has been our habit so far.

NOTES

1. I would like to thank Merritt Roe Smith, Leo Marx, James Miller, David Noble, Charles Weiner, Sherry Turkle, Loren Graham, Gail Stuart, Dick Sclove, and Stephen Graubard for their comments and criticisms on earlier drafts of this essay. My thanks also to Doris Morrison of the Agriculture Library of the University of California, Berkeley, for her bibliographical help.

2. Lewis Mumford, "Authoritarian and Democratic Technics," *Technology and Culture*, 5 (1964): 1–8.
3. Denis Hayes, *Rays of Hope: The Transition to a Post-Petroleum World* (New York: W. W. Norton, 1977), pp. 71, 159.
4. David Lilienthal, *T.V.A.: Democracy on the March* (New York: Harper and Brothers, 1944), pp. 72–83.
5. Daniel J. Boorstin, *The Republic of Technology* (New York: Harper & Row, 1978), p. 7.
6. Langdon Winner, *Autonomous Technology: Technics-out-of-Control as a Theme in Political Thought* (Cambridge, Mass.: M.I.T. Press, 1977).
7. The meaning of "technology" I employ in this essay does not encompass some of the broader definitions of that concept found in contemporary literature, for example, the notion of "technique" in the writings of Jacques Ellul. My purposes here are more limited. For a discussion of the difficulties that arise in attempts to define "technology," see Winner, *Autonomous Technology*, pp. 8–12.
8. Robert A. Caro, *The Power Broker: Robert Moses and the Fall of New York* (New York: Random House, 1974), pp. 318, 481, 514, 546, 951–958.
9. Ibid., p. 952.
10. Robert Ozanne, *A Century of Labor–Management Relations at McCormick and International Harvester* (Madison: University of Wisconsin Press, 1967), p. 20.
11. The early history of the tomato harvester is told in Wayne D. Rasmussen, "Advances in American Agriculture: The Mechanical Tomato Harvester as a Case Study," *Technology and Culture*, 9 (1968): 531–543.
12. Andrew Schmitz and David Seckler, "Mechanized Agriculture and Social Welfare: The Case of the Tomato Harvester," *American Journal of Agricultural Economics*, 52 (1970): 569–577.
13. William H. Friedland and Amy Barton, "Tomato Technology," *Society*, 13:6 (September/October 1976). See also William H. Friedland, *Social Sleepwalkers: Scientific and Technological Research in California Agriculture*, University of California, Davis, Department of Applied Behavioral Sciences, Research Monograph No. 13, 1974.
14. *University of California Clip Sheet*, 54:36, May 1, 1979.
15. Friedland and Barton, "Tomato Technology."
16. A history and critical analysis of agricultural research in the land-grant colleges is given in James Hightower, *Hard Tomatoes, Hard Times* (Cambridge, Mass.: Schenkman, 1978).
17. David Noble, "Social Change in Machine Design: The Case of Automatically Controlled Machine Tools," in *Case Studies in the Labor Process* (New York: Monthly Review Press, 1981).
18. Friedrich Engels, "On Authority" in *The Marx-Engels Reader*, 2nd ed., ed. Robert Tucker (New York: W. W. Norton, 1978), p. 731.
19. Ibid.
20. Ibid., pp. 732, 731.
21. Karl Marx, *Capital*, vol. 1, 3rd ed., trans. Samuel Moore and Edward Aveling (New York: The Modern Library, 1906), p. 530.
22. Jerry Mander, *Four Arguments for the Elimination of Television* (New York: William Morrow, 1978), p. 44.
23. See, for example, Robert Argue, Barbara Emanuel, and Stephen Graham, *The Sun Builders: A People's Guide to Solar, Wind and Wood Energy in Canada* (Toronto: Renewable Energy in Canada, 1978). "We think decentralization is an implicit component of renewable energy; this implies the decentralization of energy systems, communities and of power. Renewable energy doesn't require mammoth generation sources or disruptive transmission corridors. Our cities and towns, which have been dependent on centralized energy supplies, may be able to achieve some degree of autonomy, thereby controlling and administering their own energy needs" (p. 16).
24. Alfred D. Chandler, Jr., *The Visible Hand: The Managerial Revolution in American Business* (Cambridge, Mass.: Belknap, Harvard University Press, 1977), p. 244.

25. Ibid.
26. Ibid., p. 500.
27. Leonard Silk and David Vogel, *Ethics and Profits: The Crisis of Confidence in American Business* (New York: Simon and Schuster, 1976), p. 191.
28. Russell W. Ayres, "Policing Plutonium: The Civil Liberties Fallout," *Harvard Civil Rights–Civil Liberties Law Review*, 10 (1975): 443, 413–414, 374.

PART IV
ENVISIONING THE FUTURE THROUGH TECHNOLOGY

Technological progress often serves as a prism through which we attempt to predict (or imagine) what the future will be like. The tradition of looking at the future in terms of how its technology will look goes back at least to the nineteenth-century and probably earlier. The imaginations of science fiction writers from Jules Verne to Greg Bear and William Gibson have given us pictures of future societies shaped largely by their technologies. "Futurama"-type exhibits at World's Fairs throughout the twentieth-century reinforced similar popular images, often with a corporate agenda behind them. And films — from Fritz Lang's *Metropolis* to *Star Wars* — have perhaps been the most effective means of creating and communicating images of the future in the past several decades.

More recently, futurists have become much more sophisticated and have developed forecasting techniques that involve projecting social and demographic trends and building scenarios that seek to describe a range of possible futures. This shift in how we look at the future parallels the evolution of thinking on technology and society from technological determinism to social constructivism to a middle ground that incorporates elements of both. (See Part I for more on these concepts.) Understanding the value and limits of forecasts is an important part of the study of technology and society. The selections in Part IV are intended to provide an opportunity to think about forecasts of technology and of the future and to cultivate both an appreciation and a healthy skepticism of both.

The first article presents a unique opportunity to compare a thirty-three-year-old forecast of the year 2000 with today's reality. Herman Kahn and Anthony Wiener's essay, "The Year 2000: A View from 1967," came out of the work of the American Academy of Arts and Sciences' Commission on the Year 2000. The authors were both from the Hudson Institute, a futurist think tank in Croton-on-Hudson, New York, that was so intimately connected to Kahn's persona that contemporaries often referred to it as "Herman-on-Hudson." In this chapter, the authors develop what they call a basic multifold trend of socioeconomic and political elements and factor in their forecasts of technological development. The result perhaps tells us more about 1967 than it does about 2000.

In the second piece, journalist Herb Brody looks at predictions of commercial technology development and explains why these prognostications are so often wrong. Brody's view is that the self-interest of the predictors often blinds them to trends that can (and frequently do) undermine the validity of their predictions. The following chapter provides a remarkable example of such foresight, or rather, its lack. In it, historian Paul Ceruzzi conducts a kind of retrospective technology assessment, looking at early expectations of the usefulness and impact of computers and finding them remarkably myopic.

Finally, in the last article in Part IV, veteran futurist Joseph Coates and his colleagues discuss the assumptions that they used (in the mid-1990s) to build fifteen scenarios of the year 2025. The title of their book, *2025: Scenarios of U.S. and Global Society Reshaped by Science and Technology*, suggests the extent to which their views of the future are based on expectations about technology. We'll take a look at how well they did in the seventeenth edition of this book, circa 2027.

15.   The Year 2000: A View from 1967

HERMAN KAHN AND ANTHONY J. WIENER

The question of what the world would be like in the year 2000 was a source of fascination throughout much of the late twentieth-century. One of the many studies, projects, task forces, and commissions that undertook to forecast the state of the world at the turn of the millennium was the Commission on the Year 2000, a group of some thirty-eight prominent scholars assembled by the American Academy of Arts and Sciences in the mid-1960s and supported by the Carnegie Corporation. Among the members of the commission was Herman Kahn, noted futurist and director of the Hudson Institute. Kahn was charged by the group with developing a series of papers that explored alternative futures in order to provide a framework for the commission's discussions. The selection that follows is an excerpt from the summary paper Kahn published together with his associate, Anthony Wiener, in the summer 1967 issue of the academy's journal Daedalus. *In it, we have an opportunity to look back a generation and see how people (presumably experts) envisioned the world we are living in today.*

Kahn and Wiener first examine what they call the "basic multifold trend," separating what they believe are the major trends of Western society over the past several hundred years into thirteen elements — including, for example, "institutionalization of change, especially research, development, innovation, and diffusion," "increasing affluence and (recently) leisure," and "urbanization and (soon) the growth of megalopolises." They proceed to list 100 areas in which they believe technological innovation is likely to occur. On the basis of these trends and projections, they develop a number of scenarios about the world in the year 2000. The reader will find much that is familiar in these scenarios — and a good deal that is not.

Prior to founding the Hudson Institute in 1961, Herman Kahn, was for thirteen years, a senior physicist and military analyst at the Rand Corporation. He was famous (some would say, infamous) for his coldly rational analyses of the consequences of nuclear war, including the baroque On Thermonuclear War *(1960),* Thinking about the Unthinkable *(1962), and* On Escalation: Metaphors and Scenarios *(1965). Together with two colleagues, he established the Hudson Institute as a research organization "dedicated to thinking about the future from a contrarian point of view." Kahn died in 1983. Anthony J. Wiener was, at the time the article was published, chairman of the research management council at the Hudson Institute.*

The pace at which various technological, social, political, and economic changes are taking place has reduced the relevance of experience as a guide to public-policy judgments. Scientists, engineers, and managers who deal directly with modern technology and who are also interested in broad policy issues often overestimate the likely social consequences of technological development and go to extremes of optimism and pessimism, while those more oriented to the cultural heritage often bank too heavily on historical continuity and social inertia. The problem, of course, is to sort out what changes from what continues and to discern what is continuous in the changes themselves.

* * *

THE BASIC MULTIFOLD TREND

The basic trends of Western society, most of which can be traced back hundreds of years, have a common set of sources in the rationalization and secularization of society. For analytic purposes, we shall separate these basic trends into thirteen rubrics, though obviously one might wish to group them into fewer and more abstract categories or to refine the analysis by identifying or distinguishing many more aspects. As basic trends, these elements seem very likely to continue at least for the next thirty-three years, though some may saturate or begin to recede beyond that point.

There is a basic, long-term, multifold trend toward:

1. Increasingly Sensate (empirical, this-worldly, secular, humanistic, pragmatic, utilitarian, contractual, epicurean, or hedonistic) cultures
2. Bourgeois, bureaucratic, "meritocratic," democratic (and nationalistic?) elites
3. Accumulation of scientific and technological knowledge
4. Institutionalization of change, especially research, development, innovation, and diffusion
5. Worldwide industrialization and modernization
6. Increasing affluence and (recently) leisure
7. Population growth
8. Decreasing importance of primary occupations
9. Urbanization and (soon) the growth of megalopolises
10. Literacy and education
11. Increased capability for mass destruction
12. Increasing tempo of change
13. Increasing universality of these trends

Speculations about the future have ranged from the literary speculations of Jules Verne and Edward Bellamy to the humanistic and philosophical writing of Jacob Burckhardt, Arnold Toynbee, and Pitirim Sorokin. Although the observations and philosophical assumptions have differed greatly, some of the empirical observations or contentions have had much in common. Thus when Sorokin finds a circular pattern of Idealistic, Integrated, and Sensate cultures, his categories bear comparison to what Edward Gibbon noted of Rome on a more descriptive level. If both the more theoretical and the more empirical observations are treated merely as *heuristic metaphors*, regardless of their authors' diverse intentions, they may suggest possible patterns for the future without confining one to too narrow or too rigid a view. Metaphoric and heuristic use of these concepts broadens the range of speculations; one can then pick and choose from these speculations as the evidence is developed. Nevertheless, in using concepts this way, there is an obvious risk not only of superficiality and oversimplification but also of excessive or premature commitment to some idiosyncratic view. In this paper we shall illustrate only a few elements of the multifold trend.

THE INCREASINGLY SENSATE CULTURE

The use of the term *Sensate*, derived from Pitirim Sorokin, is best explained in contrast with Sorokin's other concepts: "Integrated" (or "Idealistic"), "Ideational," and "Late Sensate."[1] One can characterize Ideational art by such terms as transcendental, supersensory, religious, symbolic, allegoric, static, worshipful, anonymous, traditional, and immanent. Idealistic or Integrated art can usually be associated with such adjectives as heroic, noble, uplifting, sublime, patriotic, moralistic, beautiful, flattering, and educational, while Sensate art would be worldly, naturalistic, realistic, visual, illusionistic, everyday, amusing, interesting, erotic, satirical, novel, eclectic, syncretic, fashionable, technically superb, impressionistic, materialistic, commercial, and professional. Finally, there are tendencies toward what would be called Late Sensate, characterized as underworldly, expressing protest or revolt, over-ripe, extreme, sensation-seeking, titillating, depraved, faddish, violently novel, exhibitionistic, debased, vulgar, ugly, debunking, nihilistic, pornographic, sarcastic, or sadistic.

Sensate, of course, does not intend a connotation of sensual or sensational; a word such as *worldly, humanistic,* or *empirical* would have been equally useful for our purposes.

. . . In the United States today, for example, there is clearly a strong split between a large group of intellectuals and the government on many issues. Public-opinion polls seem to indicate that although these intellectuals hold a "progressive" consensus and dominate discussion in many serious journals, they are not representative of the country. In particular, the high culture can be thought of as secular humanist, and the public as more religious and less humanist.

Western culture as a whole is clearly Sensate and possibly entering a Late Sensate stage. The Sensate trend goes back seven or eight centuries, but its progress has not been uninterrupted. The Reformation, the Counter-Reformation, the Puritan era in England, some aspects of the later Victorian era, and to some degree such phenomena as Stalinism, Hitlerism, and Fascism — all represented, at least at the time, currents counter to the basic trend of an increasingly Sensate culture. Nevertheless, the long-term, all-embracing Sensate trend expanded from the West and now covers virtually the entire world. Whether this will continue for the next thirty-three or sixty-six years is an open question. If the obvious implications of the description of Late Sensate culture are valid, the long-term tendencies toward Late Sensate must stabilize or even reverse if the system is not to be profoundly modified.

BOURGEOIS, BUREAUCRATIC, "MERITOCRATIC," DEMOCRATIC (AND NATIONALISTIC?) ELITES

By *bourgeois* we mean holding economic values and ideologies of the kind that characterized the new middle classes that emerged from the breakup of feudal society — values of personal and family achievement, financial prudence, economic calculation, commercial foresight, and "business" and professional success as a moral imperative. (The emergence of "bourgeois" elites in this sense is vividly described in such works as Max Weber's *The Protestant Ethic* and R. H. Tawney's *Religion and the Rise of Capitalism.*) Though Karl Marx and Friedrich Engels might have been surprised, it is now clear that these values can, and perhaps must, also be present in socialist or Communist economies, especially if they are industrialized and "revisionist." By *democratic* we mean having a popular political base; this can also be totalitarian or tyrannical in the classical sense, provided it is not merely imposed from above and that there is some economic mobility and relative equality in access to opportunity. Bureaucratic and meritocratic administrations also characterize modern industrial societies, whether capitalist or Communist.

Bourgeois democracy tends to rest on some form of "Social contract" concept of the relationship between the people and their government. The people "hire" and "fire" their governments, and no group has theocratic (Ideational) or aristocratic (Integrated) claims on the government. Clearly, democratic government is also an expression of democratic ideology — it is sustained by the idea of the consent of the governed. The idea is contractual; and the factors of sacredness, occultness, or charisma are restricted.

Nationalistic values are also associated with the rise of the middle class. Kings used nationalism to gain allies among the middle class against the nobles, the church, the emperor, or enemy states. The nationalist idea later involved a recognition that the people (the nation) have the contractual right to government of (and by) their own kind and eventually to self-government — or that the right to govern has to be justified as representing the will of the people and serving the general welfare. Even the totalitarian nationalism of Mussolini, Hitler, Stalin, and the Japanese officer corps usually made its basic appeal to and found its greatest response in the middle class (or, in the case of the Japanese, the agrarian middle class).

One can argue that the long-term nationalist trend is on the decline today, at least in what might be thought of as the NATO area, though this remains in many ways an open issue. (The West European nations could conceivably become more nationalist in the future, and a European political community might emerge that would be nationalist in the sense that "Europe becomes the "nation.") In any case, Late Sensate culture carries implications of cosmopolitanism and pacifism and lack of particularist ethics or loyalties, except on a shifting, contractual basis. Nevertheless, it is probably safe to argue that over the next thirty-three years nationalism will increase in most of the underdeveloped and developing worlds, at least in the minimal sense that modern systems of public education and mass communication will integrate even the most peripheral groups into the common language and culture.

SCIENCE AND TECHNOLOGY

In order to provide a quick impression of science and technology (with an emphasis on technology) in the last third of the twentieth century, we list one hundred areas in which technological innovation will almost certainly occur.

Each item is important enough to make, by itself, a significant change. The difference might lie mainly in being spectacular (for example, transoceanic rocket transportation in twenty or thirty minutes, rather than supersonic in two or three hours); in being ubiquitous (widespread use of paper clothes); in enabling a large number of different things to be done (super materials); in effecting a general and significant increase in productivity (cybernation); or simply in being important to specific individuals (convenient artificial kidneys). It could be argued reasonably that each of these warrants the description technological innovation, revolution, or breakthrough. None is merely an obvious minor improvement on what currently exists.

We should note that the one hundred areas are not ordered randomly. Most people would consider the first twenty-five unambiguous examples of progress. A few would question even these, since lasers and masers, for example, might make possible a particularly effective ballistic missile defense and, thus, accelerate the Soviet-American arms race. Similarly, the expansion of tropical agriculture and forestry could mean a geographical shift in economic and military power, as well as a dislocation of competitive industries. Nevertheless, there probably would be a consensus among readers that the first twenty-five areas do represent progress — at least for those who are in favor of "Progress."

The next twenty-five areas are clearly controversial; many would argue that government policy might better restrain or discourage innovation or diffusion here. These "controversial areas" raise issues of accelerated nuclear proliferation, loss of privacy, excessive governmental or private power over individuals, dangerously vulnerable, deceptive, and degradable overcentralization, inherently dangerous new capabilities, change too cataclysmic for smooth adjustment, or decisions that are inescapable, yet at the same time too complex and far-reaching to be safely trusted to anyone's individual or collective judgment.

The last fifty items are included because they are intrinsically interesting and to demonstrate that a list of one hundred items of "almost certain" and "very significant" innovation can be produced fairly easily.

ONE HUNDRED TECHNICAL INNOVATIONS LIKELY IN THE NEXT THIRTY-THREE YEARS

1. Multiple applications of lasers and masers for sensing, measuring, communicating, cutting, heating, welding, power transmission, illumination, destructive (defensive), and other purposes
2. Extremely high-strength or high-temperature structural materials
3. New or improved super-performance fabrics (papers, fibers, and plastics)
4. New or improved materials for equipment and appliances (plastics, glasses, alloys, ceramics, intermetallics, and cermets)
5. New airborne vehicles (ground-effect machines, VTOL and STOL, superhelicopters, giant supersonic jets)
6. Extensive commercial application of shaped charges
7. More reliable and longer-range weather forecasting
8. Intensive or extensive expansion of tropical agriculture and forestry
9. New sources of power for fixed installations (for example, magnetohydrodynamic, thermionic, and thermoelectric, radioactive)
10. New sources of power for ground transportation (storage-battery, fuel-cell propulsion or support by electromagnetic fields, jet engine, turbine)
11. Extensive and intensive world-wide use of high-altitude cameras for mapping, prospecting, census, land use, and geological investigations
12. New methods of water transportation (large submarines, flexible and special-purpose "container ships," more extensive use of large automated single-purpose bulk cargo ships)
13. Major reduction in hereditary and congenital defects
14. Extensive use of cyborg techniques (mechanical aids or substitutes for human organs, sense, limbs)
15. New techniques for preserving or improving the environment
16. Relatively effective appetite and weight control
17. New techniques in adult education
18. New improved plants and animals
19. Human "hibernation" for short periods (hours or days) for medical purposes
20. Inexpensive "one of a kind" design and procurement through use of computerized analysis and automated production
21. Controlled super-effective relaxation and sleep
22. More sophisticated architectural engineering (geodesic domes, thin shells, pressurized skins, esoteric materials)
23. New or improved uses of the oceans (mining, extraction of minerals, controlled "farming," source of energy)
24. Three-dimensional photography, illustrations, movies, and television
25. Automated or more mechanized housekeeping and home maintenance
26. Widespread use of nuclear reactors for power
27. Use of nuclear explosives for excavation and mining, generation of power, creation of high-temperature/high-pressure environments, or for a source of neutrons or other radiation

28. General use of automation and cybernation in management and production
29. Extensive and intensive centralization (or automatic interconnection) of current and past personal and business information in high-speed data processors
30. Other new and possibly pervasive techniques for surveillance, monitoring, and control of individuals and organizations
31. Some control of weather or climate
32. Other (permanent or temporary) changes or experiments with the overall environment (for example, the "permanent" increase in C-14 and temporary creation of other radioactivity by nuclear explosions, the increasing generation of CO_2 in the atmosphere, projects Starfire, West Ford, Storm Fury, and so forth)
33. New and more reliable "educational" and propaganda techniques for affecting human behavior — public and private
34. Practical use of direct electronic communication with and stimulation of the brain
35. Human hibernation for relatively extensive periods (months to years)
36. Cheap and widely available or excessively destructive central war weapons and weapons systems
37. New and relatively effective counterinsurgency techniques (and perhaps also insurgency techniques)
38. New kinds of very cheap, convenient, and reliable birth-control techniques
39. New, more varied, and more reliable drugs for control of fatigue, relaxation, alertness, mood, personality, perceptions, and fantasies
40. Capability to choose the sex of unborn children
41. Improved capability to "change" sex
42. Other genetic control or influence over the "basic constitution" of an individual
43. New techniques in the education of children
44. General and substantial increase in life expectancy, postponement of aging, and limited rejuvenation
45. Generally acceptable and competitive synthetic foods and beverages (carbohydrates, fats, proteins, enzymes, vitamin, coffee, tea, cocoa, liquor)
46. "High quality" medical care for underdeveloped areas (for example, use of referral hospitals, broad-spectrum antibiotics, artificial blood plasma)
47. Design and extensive use of responsive and super-controlled environments for private and public use (for pleasurable, educational, and vocational purposes)
48. "Nonharmful" methods of "overindulging"
49. Simple techniques for extensive and "permanent" cosmetological changes (features, "figures," perhaps complexion, skin color, even physique)
50. More extensive use of transplantation of human organs

51. Permanent manned satellite and lunar installations — interplanetary travel
52. Application of space life systems or similar techniques to terrestrial installations
53. Permanent inhabited undersea installations and perhaps even colonies
54. Automated grocery and department stores
55. Extensive use of robots and machines "slaved" to humans
56. New uses of underground tunnels for private and public transportation
57. Automated universal (real time) credit, audit, and banking systems
58. Chemical methods for improved memory and learning
59. Greater use of underground buildings
60. New and improved materials and equipment for buildings and interiors (variable transmission glass, beating and cooling by thermoelectric effect, electroluminescent and phosphorescent lighting)
61. Widespread use of cryogenics
62. Improved chemical control of some mental illness and some aspects of senility
63. Mechanical and chemical methods for improving human analytical ability more or less directly
64. Inexpensive and rapid techniques for making tunnels and underground cavities in earth or rock
65. Major improvements in earth moving and construction equipment generally
66. New techniques for keeping physically fit or acquiring physical skills
67. Commercial extraction of oil from shale
68. Recoverable boosters for economic space launching
69. Individual flying platforms
70. Simple inexpensive video recording and playing
71. Inexpensive high-capacity, world-wide, regional, and local (home and business) communication (using satellites, lasers, light pipes, and so forth)
72. Practical home and business use of "wired" video communication for both telephone and television (possibly including retrieval of taped material from libraries or other sources) and rapid transmission and reception of facsimiles (possibly including news, library material, commercial announcements, instantaneous mail delivery, other printouts)
73. Practical large-scale desalinization
74. Pervasive business use of computers for the storage, processing, and retrieval of information
75. Shared-time (public and interconnected) computers generally available to home and business on a metered basis
76. Other widespread use of computers for intellectual and professional assistance (translation, teaching, literary research, medical diagnosis, traffic control, crime detection, computation, design, analysis, and, to some degree, as a general intellectual collaborator)
77. General availability of inexpensive transuranic and other esoteric elements
78. Space defense systems
79. Inexpensive and reasonably effective ground-based ballistic missile defense

80. Very low-cost buildings for home and business use
81. Personal "pagers" (perhaps even two-way pocket phones) and other personal electronic equipment for communication, computing, and data-processing
82. Direct broadcasts from satellites to home receivers
83. Inexpensive (less than $20), long-lasting, very small, battery-operated television receivers
84. Home computers to "run" the household and communicate with outside world
85. Maintenance-free, long-life electronic and other equipment
86. Home education via video and computerized and programmed learning
87. Programmed dream
88. Inexpensive (less than 1 cent a page) rapid, high-quality black and white reproduction; followed by colored, highly detailed photography reproduction
89. Widespread use of improved fluid amplifiers
90. Conference television (both closed-circuit and public communication systems)
91. Flexible penology without necessarily using prisons (by use of modern methods of surveillance, monitoring, and control)
92. Common use of individual power source for lights, appliances, and machines
93. Inexpensive world-wide transportation of humans and cargo
94. Inexpensive road-free (and facility-free) transportation
95. New methods for teaching languages rapidly
96. Extensive genetic control for plants and animals
97. New biological and chemical methods to identify, trace, incapacitate, or annoy people for police and military uses
98. New and possibly very simple methods of lethal biological and chemical warfare
99. Artificial moons and other methods of lighting large areas at night
100. Extensive use of "biological processes" in the extraction and processing of minerals

SOME PERSPECTIVES ON CHANGE

* * *

Perhaps the most significant aspect of the middle third of the twentieth century has been the sustained economic growth achieved in the post–World War II era. This has raised the real possibility of the worldwide industrialization and of the emergence in more advanced industrial nations of what has been called a postindustrial culture. Some of this economic growth clearly derives from a growing sophistication in governmental economic policies. As even the "classical" economist Milton Friedman recently said, "We all are Keynesians today, and we are all post-Keynesians as well." If this were not true, and the postwar world had been marked by the same violent swings between prosperity and depression as the interwar world, we would not now take such a sanguine view of future economic prospects. Today [1967] it is widely believed that, except possibly for China, almost all the Communist and capitalist governments are coming to understand how to keep their economies reasonably stable and growing; both the capitalists and the Marxists are, in this sense, "revisionist."

While we reject the so-called convergence theory, in which it is argued that Communism and capitalism will come to resemble each other so closely that they will be practically indistinguishable, it is clear that they are borrowing from each other — with the Marxists, however, doing more of the explicit borrowing. The current governmental success in economics and planning is a major cause of the emergence of mass-consumption societies in Western Europe, the United States, Japan, and Australia, and is one reason why such societies can be expected to emerge rapidly in the Soviet Union and Eastern Europe.

It is still an open question, however, whether the same thing can be achieved in communal societies (such as China is striving to be) and in the less developed nations generally. But at least two groups of less developed nations are now doing so well economically that it is reasonable to think of them as undergoing a kind of "second" industrial revolution. Thus, those parts of Europe that were left behind by the industrial revolution, or that were "transplanted," are now beginning to catch up.

Even more impressive are the growth rates in the Sinic cultures of the world outside China (including Malaysia and perhaps the Philippines, but possibly not Thailand). These countries seem able to sustain growth rates of about 8 percent, except for the Philippines with 5 percent. Wherever the Chinese and their culture have gone in the world, they have done well, except in China. Until about 1800, China was, except for periodic interregna, an eminent culture in the world. It may once again be coming out of an interregnum, but whether or not it will achieve its "normal" status must now be judged unlikely or at best an open question.

The second third of the twentieth century ended with two super-powers, five large powers, three intermediate powers, and about 120 small powers. This structure and hierarchy seems likely to characterize the next decade or two as well. In fact, listing Japan and West Germany as the two largest of the five "large" powers is even more appropriate for the mid-seventies than for today.

THE LAST THIRD OF THE TWENTIETH CENTURY

Continuation of long-term multifold trend

Emergence of postindustrial society

Worldwide capability for modern technology

Need for worldwide zoning ordinances and other restraints

High (1 to 10 percent) growth rates in GNP per capita

Increasing emphasis on "Meaning and purpose"

Much turmoil in the "new" and possibly in the industrializing nations

Some possibility for sustained "nativist," messianic, or other mass movements

Second rise of Japan

Some further rise of Europe and China

Emergence of new intermediate powers: Brazil, Mexico, Pakistan, Indonesia, East Germany, Egypt

Some decline (relative) of United States and Soviet Union

A possible absence of stark "life and death" political and economic issues in the "old nations"

Except for the possible emergence of what we call, following Daniel Bell, the postindustrial society, the listing is "surprise-free": It assumes the continuation of the multifold trend, but excludes precisely the kinds of dramatic or surprising events that dominated the first two-thirds of the century. More specifically, the "surprise-free" projection rules out *major changes in the old nations* that might be caused by such possibilities as invasion and war; civil strife and revolution; famine and pestilence; despotism (persecution) and natural disaster; depression or economic stagnation; the development of "inexpensive" doomsday or near-doomsday machines and nuclear "six-gun" weapons technology; resurgence of Communism or a revival of Fascism along with a racial, North–South, rich–poor, East–West dichotomy; an economically dynamic China with 10 percent annual growth rate, and a politically dynamic United States, Soviet Union, Japan, or Brazil; development of the United Nations or other worldwide organizations, and possible regional or other multinational organizations; new religious philosophies or other mass movements; and a psychologically upsetting impact of the new techniques, ideas, and philosophies.

If the basic long-term multifold trend continues or is accelerated during the next thirty-three years, and there are no surprising but not-impossible disruptions of the sort listed [here], then a postindustrial society seems likely to develop in the affluent parts of the world.

In a postindustrial world, per-capita income is about fifty times that in a preindustrial society. Most "economic" activities are tertiary and quaternary [knowledge-based] rather than primary or secondary; business firms are, consequently, no longer the major source of innovation. There is an effective floor on income and welfare, and efficiency is not a primary consideration. There is widespread cybernation, a typical "doubling time" for social change of three to thirty years, and a common technological foundation for a world society. Work-oriented, achievement-oriented, advancement-oriented values and "national interest" values erode, and Sensate, secular, humanistic, perhaps self-indulgent, criteria become central, as do the intellectual institutions. Continuing education is widespread, and there is rapid improvement in educational techniques.

NOTE

1. Pitirim A. Sorokin, *Social and Cultural Dynamics,* Vol. 4 (New York, 1962), p. 737 ff.

16.   Great Expectations: Why Technology Predictions Go Awry

HERB BRODY

Predicting the course of technology development is essential to assessing the technology's potential impacts on society and, ultimately, to controlling it. Yet forecasts of technology development are often wildly inaccurate. Technologies expected to have enormous potential disappear with hardly a trace, while others, largely unheralded, come to play highly significant roles in society.

Why technology predictions go wrong is the subject of this essay, which comes from Technology Review, *a monthly magazine published at the Massachusetts Institute of Technology. The author, Herb Brody, is a journalist with a degree in physics and a career interest in science, technology, and society. Brody writes that a critical look at technology predictions requires that one know who is making the predictions and what his or her motives are. Market surveys can be poor guides by which to judge the prospects of truly revolutionary technologies. Furthermore, the course of one technology can be strongly influenced by developments in other fields. Ironically, while Brody is largely correct in his overall argument, many of the technologies that he describes as having "fizzled" have taken off in the years since the article was written.*

Herb Brody has been senior editor at Technology Review *since 1990, prior to which he served as managing editor at* Laser Focus, *associate managing editor at* High Technology, *and senior editor at* PC/Computing. *Among his writings are articles on factory automation in Japan, "smart house" technology, and the use of personal computers by disabled persons.*

Imagine a world where solar cells and nuclear fusion provide megawatts of pollution-free electricity, the average factory bristles with sophisticated robots, videotex terminals rival the TV set for attention in most households, automobiles run on batteries, and computers manipulate information in the form of light waves rather than electric pulses.

That's the world of today as envisioned by technological forecasters only a few years ago. In reality, of course, manufacturers have bought only a modest quantity of robots, videotex sputtered,[1] solar electricity remains too expensive for all but a handful of applications, and electric cars and nuclear fusion seem, as always, to be at least a decade from practicality. Along the way, other technologies have sneaked into prominence while hardly registering a blip on prognosticators' early-warning radars.

No one can be blamed for not predicting the future with pinpoint accuracy. But ever since the first steamboats were derided as "Fulton's folly," experts' technology forecasts have amounted to a chronicle of wildly missed cues and squandered opportunities. The rapid replacement of vacuum tubes by semiconductors surprised even those close to the industry. Meanwhile, after years of hype, developers of voice recognition have yet to deliver a system that can handle more than a few dozen words of continuous speech.

Such errors in prediction lead to technological fads that can disrupt the orderly allocation of R&D resources. Hyped technologies "become very glamorous for a while, and a lot of good people rush into the field," says Robert Lucky, executive director for communications science research at Bell Labs. Even after a glamour technology's difficulties become clearer, scientists often stay in the field anyway. The result is a pool of scientists whose mission has vanished.

But erroneous forecasts can affect more than individual careers. The evaluation of a technology's future success plays an ever larger part in determining the nation's research agenda as universities depend more heavily on industry for research funding. Government standard-setting agencies have a particularly large stake in knowing how technology will move. Before regulators can set a standard for high-definition television, for example, they need to decide whether HDTV is likely to be piped into homes via fiber optics, in which case the video signal could be much richer than if broadcast over already crowded airwaves.

Are faulty forecasts inevitable? To an extent, perhaps. But certain kinds of mistakes tend to recur. By looking at these patterns, companies and policymakers may be able to judge more intelligently the course of today's embryonic technologies and allocate resources more productively.

MISLEADING MISSIONARIES

Rosy predictions often originate with people who have a financial stake in a new technology. And since their bullish statements of technical potential are often misleadingly packaged as precise market forecasts, unwary businesses and investors often suffer.

To develop something new, you have to believe in it. Developers must convince others of the bright prospects as well. An entrepreneur needs financiers. Scientists in a large corporation need advocates high enough in the hierarchy to allocate funds. And government-supported researchers at universities and national labs have an obvious incentive to overstate their progress and understate the problems that lie ahead: the better the chances for success, the more money an agency is willing to shell out. The result is a climate of raised, and sometimes unrealistic, expectations.

Technological breakthroughs can especially skew the vision of normally level-headed planners. "There's a lot of optimism and speculation," says Ian Wilson, a senior management consultant at SRI International. "Then the problem turns out to be complex." The development of high-temperature superconductors provides a recent example. After intense press coverage that proclaimed the imminent coming of levitated trains, intercontinental power transmission, and superfast electronic switches, the novel superconductors turned out to fall far short of immediate commercial practicality. Says Wilson: "History should have drummed this lesson into our heads by now, but we keep making the same mistake."

Similarly, researchers working on nuclear fusion have kept up a steady barrage of "breakthrough" reports since the mid-1970s. But despite bursts of progress, the magic break-even point — at which a reactor produces more energy than it consumes — remains elusive.

Market-forecasting firms feed the tendency to overestimate a technology's near-term promise. Companies such as Dataquest, Frost & Sullivan, and Business Communications regularly publish reports analyzing the business potential of existing and emerging technologies. Over the past decade, outfits like these have foretold billion-dollar markets for artificial intelligence, videotex, and virtually every other new technology that laboratories have reported.

Followers of these rosy visions have met a sorry fate. Numerous firms started up in the early 1980s, for example, to mine the supposedly large and growing market for industrial robots. Many received financing from venture capital firms hungry for short-term paybacks. But manufacturers either declined to modernize or opted for conventional automation instead, stranding the robotics startups. Artificial intelligence went through a similar cycle. Glowing pronouncements of AI's potential to reshape computing inspired a wave of new ventures. When the technology stalled getting out of the laboratory, the budding AI "industry" crashed.

One reason for the consistently inflated predictions is that market researchers survey the wrong people. Typically they ask the companies that make a technology how much of it they are selling and how much they expect to sell. It's clear why vendors are a favorite source: they are easy to identify, and their business plans often incorporate sales forecasts with just the sort of numerical estimates that excite researchers.

But such polls will almost always be skewed. Technology companies — particularly entrepreneurial firms in an emerging field — tend to exhibit an almost missionary zeal about their endeavors. "Vendors believe their own propaganda," says Steven Weissman, senior research editor at BIS CAP International, a Waltham, Mass., firm that follows the computer graphics industry. "You can almost never trust their numbers." Market researchers can create more realistic projections by studying a new technology's potential buyers, who have less of a stake in its success. But the universe of customers is much larger and harder to reach than the universe of sellers. Cost-conscious market researchers usually don't bother.

Weissman cites the advent of CD-ROMs, or compact disc read-only memories. Each CD-ROM disc, identical in appearance to audio CDs, can hold almost 700 megabytes — enough for 275,000 pages of text, or thousands of images. In the mid-1980s, market researchers proclaimed that CD-ROMs were inevitable companions to large numbers of personal computers. But computer users preferred magnetic hard disks, which, unlike CD-ROMs, are erasable and which retrieve data much more rapidly. The CD-ROM advantage in memory capacity has diminished greatly, too, as computer memories have grown from the 10 megabytes common in 1984 to 100 megabytes or more on some of today's machines.

The media have acted as willing accomplices in disseminating overblown fore-casts. The business press, always on the lookout for the next hot technology trend, seizes on an inflated forecast as the basis for a news story. Analysts who go out on a limb with a forecast are cast as "the experts" and cited repeatedly.

Once printed in a reputable publication, forecasts take on a life of their own, and other publications quote them as authoritative. The myth of a huge robot market, for example, grew in large part out of statements by Prudential-Bache vice-president Laura Conigliaro, whose figures echoed throughout dozens of newspaper and magazine stories. Conigliaro's erroneous assumptions about man-ufacturers' needs took on the weight of truth in the retelling.

Such optimistic predictions find a receptive audience in business. They satisfy a need of companies and investors to identify potentially profitable technological breakthroughs. And those within a company who advocate pursuing a certain technology will pointedly seek data that back up their hunches. Even companies that have already committed themselves to a technology value the reassurance of an enthusiastic report from an independent firm. "The higher my numbers, the more reports I can sell," admits Weissman.

SELLING TODAY'S TECHNOLOGY SHORT

Technological forecasts tend to go astray partly because they underestimate the possibilities for advances in existing technology. "Theoretically, it's been possible for the past 25 years for computers to eliminate photographic film," says Alexan-der MacLachlan, senior vice-president for R&D at DuPont. But, he points out, continuing chemical refinements have kept silver-halide film in the center of the picture despite a strong challenge from electronic imaging media.

Chip manufacture is another case in point. Today the production of virtually all integrated circuits involves optical lithography, in which light is projected through a mask onto a silicon wafer to form an intricate pattern of transistors and interconnecting wires. To pack more transistors on a chip — and hence increase its computational power or memory capacity — the lithography process must be able to create higher-resolution images.

During the 1970s, conventional wisdom held that optical lithography would soon run out of steam. "People believed there were fundamental reasons that optics would be unable to produce chips with feature dimensions smaller than about 1 micron," says Marc Brodsky, director of technical planning for IBM's Research Division. (A micron is a millionth of a meter.)

The optical process, it was widely thought, would give way to lithography using X-rays, which have much shorter wavelengths than light and so, in principle, can be focused more sharply. But instead of winding down, optical lithography has undergone continuous refinement. And while chips keep getting more densely packed, semiconductor makers have yet to abandon their tried and true tech-niques. Optical lithography is expected to carry chips down to feature dimensions of a third or a quarter of a micron, says Brodsky.

An exotic class of electronic switches called Josephson junctions offers a classic case of an entrenched technology outpacing upstart challengers. IBM worked for 15 years on these devices, which use an ultrathin layer of superconducting material to achieve switching speeds far faster than the silicon transistors available during the 1970s. But the junctions' advantage slowly dissipated as silicon chips got faster and faster. "Nobody thought that the improvements in silicon would last so long," explains Brodsky. By the time IBM researchers had overcome the major problems of Josephson junctions, advances in silicon had erased the once compelling need for the new technology.

Another electronic revolution continually postponed is the advent of gallium-arsenide chips. These high-speed devices are already widely used in microwave and opto-electronic equipment, as well as in some space and military systems, where gallium arsenide's ability to function despite exposure to nuclear radiation is prized. During the 1980s, bright prospects for gallium-arsenide chips spurred the formation of a miniature industry, largely with money from venture capital firms hoping to score big by backing the next Intel. But gallium-arsenide developers have so far failed to overtake swiftly improving silicon. "We've been hearing for 10 years that silicon is running out of gas," says Bell Labs' Lucky. "People forget that there are always an army of people working on improving an old technology and only a handful of people working on a new technology."

UNDERESTIMATING THE REVOLUTIONS

Although consumer technology is probably the thorniest arena in which to prophesy, one enduring caveat is that consumers are unwilling to spend a lot of money on something only slightly superior to what they already have, especially if it's also less convenient. Quadraphonic sound, for example, forced audiophiles to rearrange their living rooms to provide seating in the small zone of optimal quadraphonic effect — and for all that, the music sounded only a little bit better. Small wonder the technology quickly disappeared.

In another misreading of consumers' appetites, high hopes abounded in the early 1980s among purveyors of home information services. One forecast in 1980 estimated that 5 percent of all U.S. households would be hooked into videotex by 1985. Consumers would supposedly relish the ability to go on-line with their computers and shop, browse through encyclopedias, and read the latest news, weather, and stock market summaries.

Knight-Ridder spent $60 million setting up a videotex service that never made money and was ultimately abandoned. Technology per se was not the problem — all the necessary computer and telecommunication power existed. Instead, videotex marketers badly misunderstood how people want to use their home computers. There are more efficient ways to do just about everything that videotex provides. Newspapers, printed encyclopedias, and shopping catalogs are superior for most people's purposes. Unlike businesses that deal with financial markets and other late-breaking news, consumers at home rarely demand up-to-the-minute information on anything.

While companies like RCA and Knight-Ridder have lost money by backing a loser, other businesses have made the opposite mistake: failing to pursue a winner. A common mistake is the tendency to evaluate emerging technologies as if they were direct replacements for something familiar. "New things are viewed in the clothing of the old," says James Utterback, a professor of engineering at MIT's Sloan School of Management. The difficulty with this, says Utterback, is that "old things are optimized for what they do already."

When the transistor came out of Bell Labs in the late 1940s, for example, its main use was thought to be as an electronic amplifier in radios. Few saw the potential of the new devices to replace vacuum tubes in digital computers, which were still in their infancy. At the time, many believed that these primitive computers were so potent that the world would never need more than a few dozen of them. Of course, it has been in computing that transistors — first as discrete components, later as devices on integrated circuit chips — have had their most profound impact.

Any truly revolutionary technology defies easy prediction. Until the late 1970s, for example, computer designers focused on building ever bigger and more powerful machines. Few foresaw what has turned out to be the technology's defining trend: the evolution toward personal machines using packaged software. "If you asked computer users in 1970 what they wanted, they'd have probably wished that Cobol [a programming language for mainframe computers] was a little easier to use," says Michael Rappa, a professor of management at the Sloan School. "The idea of a desktop computer with a graphical interface like that of the Macintosh would have seemed idiotic."

Indeed, virtually all the elements of today's personal computers existed in the mid-1970s. IBM reportedly concluded, from its study of what computer users said they wanted, that PCs would appeal only to a small group of hobbyists. Xerox, too, forfeited its headstart in desktop computers because management thought the market was too small to be worth the company's while.

One reason for such problems is that the commercial success of a new technology often depends on factors outside the control of its developer. Videodisc players, for example, failed to take root as a popular consumer appliance despite enthusiastic predictions in the late 1970s. Although RCA invested heavily to market its SelectaVision videodisc system, which played prerecorded programs, sales never approached the mass-market RCA had counted on. In 1989 the company abandoned the product and took a $175 million write-off.

Why did the videodisc fail while the videocassette recorder has enjoyed spectacular success? Certainly the VCR's ability to record programs for later viewing provided an obvious advantage. But millions of people who buy VCRs never figure out how to program the machines to record; they rent movies instead. In fact, the VCR owes much of its success to the advent of video stores. Just as Lotus 1-2-3 gave businesspeople a reason to buy a personal computer, the availability of a large number of movies at low cost justified the purchase of a VCR. RCA, by contrast, counted on videodisc owners to build up a library of discs that they would view repeatedly, even though most people want to watch a movie only once.

If retailers had had the idea of renting out videodiscs 10 years ago, disc players would probably now be much more prevalent in homes. After all, the players entered the market substantially cheaper than VCRs, which were then priced in the luxury range. And the picture from a videodisc is markedly superior to that from a tape.

COPING WITH UNCERTAINTY

Given that technology forecasting is a precarious science, some experts advise organizations not to pay much attention to predictions. "The illusion of knowing what's going to happen is worse than not knowing," contends MIT's Utterback. Rather than basing their strategy on flawed visions of the future, he says, managers and policymakers should make sure their organizations are agile enough to respond to technological changes as they occur.

Yet organizations with a financial interest in knowing the future of technology need not abandon prediction altogether, says SRI's Wilson. "Not everything is uncertain." He suggests a middle ground. Rather than predicting a single outcome, a forecaster should paint several scenarios of the future, each hinging on different assumptions. These scenarios, says Wilson, would suggest a "portfolio of technologies that will bound the envelope of uncertainty." Decision makers can speculate on the potential impact of each scenario on the organization's goals and on the technologies needed to reach those goals.

The fate of many energy technologies, for example, depends on the strength of the international environmental movement, particularly the effort to stem emissions of greenhouse gases. Nonfossil energy, notably solar and nuclear, will probably receive more urgent attention — and greater government funding — if the greenhouse warnings hold up to scrutiny. Organizations, says Wilson, should continually tune their planning as current events render scenarios more or less likely.

The uneven record of past predictions suggests a few other guidelines for avoiding costly and embarrassing mistakes:

- Watch developments in related fields. Ten years ago, laser printers cost $10,000 or more. The technology for inexpensive laser printers came not from the printer industry but from Canon, which developed the laser units for photocopiers.
- Discount predictions based on information from vested interests. Investors, management, and the media repeatedly disregard this seemingly obvious advice. Interested parties include not only the companies that stand to make money from a technology but also scientists whose funding grows and wanes with the level of public excitement and who are also distant from the marketplace. "Researchers can be pretty naive about what's a good idea," says, Phil Brodsky, Monsanto's director of corporate research.
- Expect existing technologies to continue improving. And don't expect people to abandon what they have for something new that is 10 percent better.

- Beware of predictions based on simple trend extrapolation. Telling the future by looking at the past assumes that conditions remain constant. This is like driving a car by looking in the rear-view mirror.
- Distinguish between technological forecasts and market predictions. It is one thing to say that new gallium-arsenide chips will be able to operate faster than silicon chips — that is a matter of physics and engineering. But to predict that the market for gallium-arsenide chips will reach a given level in a given year hinges on many hard-to-predict factors, such as the difficulty of handling the material in mass production, the demand for computers, and progress in competing technologies. People often deduce market impact from technology predictions without giving these other factors their due.
- Give innovation time to diffuse. Truly innovative technologies typically take 10 to 25 years to enter widespread use. This is true even for computer and telecommunications technologies that seem to have come out of nowhere: fax machines first appeared in the 1940s, and fiber optics have been around since the 1960s.
- Pay attention to the infrastructure on which a technology's success depends. Lee De Forest invented the vacuum tube in 1906, but radio broadcasting did not begin until 1921; developing techniques to mass-produce the tubes reliably took 15 years. Any attempt today to figure when TVs will be hanging on living room walls must begin with an analysis of the technology available for making flat-panel displays — slim imaging devices that weigh less and consume less power than the cathode-ray tubes used in conventional TVs and computer terminals.

There's certainly plenty of material for would-be technology seers to practice on. Neural-network computers, shirt-pocket telephones, hypermedia, computer-generated virtual realities, intelligent highway systems — all have their enthusiasts who tell of impending "revolutions." Which promises will be fulfilled and which broken?

Following the principles outlined here will help bring some order to the confusing torrent of technology predictions. But at bottom, prophesy is still a gamble. Bell Labs' Lucky likens technology development to the manipulations of a Ouija board. "Everybody's got their hands on it," he says, "but it always feels like somebody else is moving it."

NOTE

1. But the Internet didn't — Ed.

17.   An Unforeseen Revolution: Computers and Expectations, 1935–1985

PAUL CERUZZI

A good illustration of some of Herb Brody's points is contained in Paul Ceruzzi's essay, which looks back at the early forecasts of the societal impact of computers. Ceruzzi writes that the computer pioneers of the 1940s assumed that perhaps half a dozen of the new machines would serve the world's needs for the foreseeable future! As Joseph Corn notes in the introduction to his book, (Imagining Tomorrow), *where this reading was first published, this "dazzling failure of prophecy," is explained by the fact that most of the computer pioneers were physicists who viewed the new devices as equipment for their experiments and found it hard to imagine that their inventions might be applied to entirely different fields, such as payroll processing and graphic arts. The impact of computers on society has been staggering, and it is sobering to realize how little of this impact was anticipated by those most responsible for developing and introducing this new technology.*

Paul Ceruzzi is a curator in the Department of Space History at the National Air and Space Museum in Washington, D.C. He is the author of Beyond the Limits: Flight Enters the Computer Age *(Cambridge, MA: MIT Press, 1989).*

The "computer revolution" is here. Computers seem to be everywhere: at work, at play, and in all sorts of places in between. There are perhaps half a million large computers in use in America today [in 1986], 7 or 8 million personal computers, 5 million programmable calculators, and millions of dedicated microprocessors built into other machines of every description.

The changes these machines are bringing to society are profound, if not revolutionary. And, like many previous revolutions, the computer revolution is happening very quickly. The computer as defined today did not exist in 1950. Before World War II, the word *computer* meant a human being who worked at a desk with a calculating machine, or something built by a physics professor to solve a particular problem, used once or twice, and then retired to a basement storeroom. Modern computers — machines that do a wide variety of things, many having little to do with mathematics or physics — emerged after World War II from the work of a dozen or so individuals in England, Germany, and the United States. The "revolution," however one may define it, began only when their work became better known and appreciated.

The computer age dawned in the United States in the summer of 1944, when a Harvard physics instructor named Howard Aiken publicly unveiled a giant electromechanical machine called the Mark I. At the same time, in Philadelphia, J. Presper Eckert, Jr., a young electrical engineer, and John Mauchly, a physicist, were building the ENIAC, which, when completed in 1945, was the world's first machine to do numerical computing with electronic rather than mechanical switches.

Computing also got underway in Europe during the war. In 1943 the British built an electronic machine that allowed them to decode intercepted German radio messages. They built several copies of this so-called Colossus, and by the late 1940s general-purpose computers were being built at a number of British institutions. In Germany, Konrad Zuse, an engineer, was building computers out of used telephone equipment. One of them, the Z4, survived the war and had a long and productive life at the Federal Technical Institute in Zurich.

These machines were the ancestors of today's computers. They were among the first machines to have the ability to carry out any sequence of arithmetic operations, keep track of what they had just done, and adjust their actions accordingly. But machines that only solve esoteric physics problems or replace a few human workers, as those computers did, do not a revolution make. The computer pioneers did not foresee their creations as doing much more than that. They had no glimmering of how thoroughly the computer would permeate modern life. The computer's inventors saw a market restricted to few scientific, military, or large-scale business applications. For them, a computer was akin to a wind tunnel: a vital and necessary piece of apparatus, but one whose expense and size limited it to a few installations.

For example, when Howard Aiken heard of the plans of Eckert and Mauchly to produce and market a more elegant version of the ENIAC, he was skeptical. He felt they would never sell more than a few of them, and he stated that four or five electronic digital computers would satisfy all the country's computing needs.[1] In Britain in 1951, the physicist Douglas Hartree remarked: "We have a computer here in Cambridge; there is one in Manchester and one at the [National Physical Laboratory]. I suppose there ought to be one in Scotland, but that's about all."[2] Similar statements appear again and again in the folklore of computing.[3] This perception clearly dominated early discussions about the future of the new technology.[4] At least two other American computer pioneers, Edmund Berkeley and John V. Atanasoff, also recall hearing estimates that fewer than ten computers would satisfy all of America's computing needs.[5]

By 1951 about half a dozen electronic computers were running, and in May of that year companies in the United States and England began producing them for commercial customers. Eckert and Mauchly's dream became the UNIVAC — a commercial electronic machine that for a while was a synonym for *computer*, as *Scotch Tape* is for cellophane tape or *Thermos* is for vacuum bottles. It was the star of CBS's television coverage of the 1952 presidential election, when it predicted, with only a few percent of the vote gathered, Eisenhower's landslide victory over Adlai Stevenson. With this election, Americans in large numbers suddenly became aware of this new and marvelous device. Projects got underway at universities and government agencies across the United States and Europe to build computers. Clearly, there was a demand for more than just a few of the large-scale machines.

But not many more. The UNIVAC was large and expensive, and its market was limited to places like the U.S. Census Bureau, military installations, and a few large industries. (Only the fledgling aerospace industry seemed to have an insatiable appetite for those costly machines in the early years.) Nonetheless, UNIVAC and its peers set the stage for computing's next giant leap, from one-of-a-kind special projects built at universities to mass-produced products designed for the world of commercial and business data processing, banking, sales, routine accounting, and inventory control.

Yet, despite the publicity accorded the UNIVAC, skepticism prevailed. The manufacturers were by no means sure of how many computers they could sell. Like the inventors before them, the manufacturers felt that only a few commercial computers would saturate the market. For example, an internal IBM study regarding the potential market for a computer called the Tape Processing Machine (a prototype of which had been completed by 1951) estimated that there was a market for no more than 25 machines of its size.[6] Two years later, IBM developed a smaller computer for business use, the Model 650, which was designed to rent for $3,000 a month — far less than the going price for large computers like the UNIVAC, but nonetheless a lot more than IBM charged for its other office equipment. When it was announced in 1953, those who were backing the project optimistically foresaw a market for 250 machines. They had to convince others in the IBM organization that this figure was not inflated.[7]

As it turned out, businesses snapped up the 650 by the thousands. It became the Model T of computers, and its success helped establish IBM as the dominant computer manufacturer it is today. The idea finally caught on that a private company could manufacture and sell computers — of modest power, and at lower prices than the first monsters — in large quantities. The 650 established the notion of the computer as a machine for business as well as for science, and its success showed that the low estimates of how many computers the world needed were wrong.

Why the inventors and the first commercial manufacturers underestimated the computer's potential market by a wide margin is an interesting question for followers of the computer industry and for historians of modern technology. There is no single cause that accounts for the misperception. Rather, three factors contributed to the erroneous picture of the computer's future: a mistaken feeling that computers were fragile and unreliable; the institutional biases of those who shaped policies toward computer use in the early days; and an almost universal failure, even among the computer pioneers themselves, to understand the very nature of computing (how one got a computer to do work, and just how much work it could do).

It was widely believed that computers were unreliable because their vacuum-tube circuits were so prone to failure. Large numbers of computers would not be built and sold, it was believed, because their unreliability made them totally unsuitable for routine use in a small business or factory. (Tubes failed so frequently they were plugged into sockets, to make it easy to replace them. Other electronic components were more reliable and so were soldered in place.) Eckert and Mauchly's ENIAC had 18,000 vacuum tubes. Other electronic computers got by with fewer, but they all had many more than most other electronic equipment of the day. The ENIAC was a room-sized Leviathan whose tubes generated a lot of heat and used great quantities of Philadelphia's electric power. Tube failures were indeed a serious problem, for if even one tube blew out during a computation it might render the whole machine inoperative. Since tubes are most likely to blow out within a few minutes after being switched on, the ENIAC's power was left on all the time, whether it was performing a computation or not.

Howard Aiken was especially wary of computers that used thousands of vacuum tubes as their switching elements. His Mark I, an electromechanical machine using parts taken from standard IBM accounting equipment of the day, was much slower but more rugged than computers that used vacuum tubes. Aiken felt that the higher speeds vacuum tubes offered did not offset their tendency to burn out. He reluctantly designed computers that used vacuum tubes, but he always kept the numbers of tubes to a minimum and used electromechanical relays wherever he could.[8] Not everyone shared Aiken's wariness, but his arguments against using vacuum-tube circuits were taken seriously by many other computer designers, especially those whose own computer projects were shaped by the policies of Aiken's Harvard laboratory.

That leads to the next reason for the low estimates: Scientists controlled the early development of the computer, and they steered post-war computing projects away from machines and applications that might have a mass market. Howard Aiken, John von Neumann, and Douglas Hartree were physicists or mathematicians, members of a scientific elite. For the most part, they were little concerned with the mundane payroll and accounting problems that business faced every day. Such problems involved little in the way of higher mathematics, and their solutions contributed little to the advancement of scientific knowledge. Scientists perceived their own place in society as an important one but did not imagine that the world would need many more men like themselves. Because their own needs were satisfied by a few powerful computers, they could not imagine a need for many more such machines. Even at IBM, where commercial applications took precedence, scientists shaped the perceptions of the new invention. In the early 1950s the mathematician John von Neumann was a part-time consultant to the company, where he played no little role in shaping expectations for the new technology.

The perception of a modest and limited future for electronic computing came, most of all, from misunderstandings of its very nature. The pioneers did not really understand how humans would interact with machines that worked at the speed of light, and they were far too modest in their assessments of what their inventions could really do. They felt they had made a breakthrough in numerical calculating, but they missed seeing that the breakthrough was in fact a much bigger one. Computing turned out to encompass far more than just doing complicated sequences of arithmetic. But just how much more was not apparent until much later, when other people gained familiarity with computers. A few examples of objections raised to computer projects in the early days will make this clear.

When Howard Aiken first proposed building an automatic computer, in 1937, his colleagues at Harvard objected. Such a machine, they said, would lie idle most of the time, because it would soon do all the work required of it. They were clearly thinking of his proposed machine in terms of a piece of experimental apparatus constructed by a physicist; after the experiment is performed and the results gathered, such an apparatus has no further use and is then either stored or dismantled so that the parts can be reused for new experiments. Aiken's proposed "automatic calculating machine," as he called it in 1937, was perceived that way. After he had used it to perform the calculations he wanted it to perform, would the machine be good for anything else? Probably not. No one had built computers before. One could not propose building one just to see what it would look like; a researcher had to demonstrate the need for a machine with which he could solve a specific problem that was otherwise insoluble. Even if he could show that only with the aid of a computer could he solve the problem, that did not necessarily justify its cost.[9]

Later on, when the much faster electronic computers appeared, this argument surfaced again. Mechanical computers had proved their worth, but some felt that electronic computers worked so fast that they would spew out results much faster than human beings could assimilate them. Once again, the expensive computer would lie idle, while its human operators pondered over the results of a few minutes of its activity. Even if enough work was found to keep an electronic computer busy, some felt that the work could not be fed into the machine rapidly enough to keep its internal circuits busy.[10]

Finally, it was noted that humans had to program a computer before it could do any work. Those programs took the form of long lists of arcane symbols punched into strips of paper tape. For the first electronic computers, it was mostly mathematicians who prepared those tapes. If someone wanted to use the computer to solve a problem, he was allotted some time during which he had complete control over the machine; he wrote the program, fed it into the computer, ran it, and took out the results. By the early 1950s, computing installations saw the need for a staff of mathematicians and programmers to assist the person who wanted a problem solved, since few users would be expected to know the details of programming each specific machine. That meant that every computer installation would require the services of skilled mathematicians, and there would never be enough of them to keep more than a few machines busy. R. F. Clippinger discussed this problem at a meeting of the American Mathematical Society in 1950, stating: "In order to operate the modern computing machine for maximum output, a staff of perhaps twenty mathematicians of varying degrees of training are required. There is currently such a shortage of persons trained for this work, that machines are not working full time."[11] Clippinger forecast a need for 2,000 such persons by 1960, implying that there would be a mere 100 computers in operation by then.

These perceptions, which lay behind the widely held belief that computers would never find more than a limited (though important) market in the industrialized world, came mainly from looking at the new invention strictly in the context of what it was replacing: calculating machines and their human operators. That context was what limited the pioneers' vision.

Whenever a new technology is born, few see its ultimate place in society. The inventors of radio did not foresee its use for broadcasting entertainment, sports, and news; they saw it as a telegraph without wires. The early builders of automobiles did not see an age of "automobility"; they saw a "horseless carriage." Likewise, the computer's inventors perceived its role in future society in terms of the functions it was specifically replacing in contemporary society. The predictions that they made about potential applications for the new invention had to come from the context of "computing" that they knew. Though they recognized the electronic computer's novelty, they did not see how it would permit operations fundamentally different from those performed by human computers.

Before there were digital computers, a mathematician solved a complex computational problem by first recasting it into a set of simpler problems, usually involving only the four ordinary operations of arithmetic — addition, subtraction, multiplication, and division. Then he would take this set of more elementary problems to human computers, who would do the arithmetic with the aid of mechanical desktop calculators. He would supply these persons with the initial input data, books of logarithmic and trigonometric tables, paper on which to record intermediate results, and instructions on how to proceed. Depending on the computer's mathematical skill, the instructions would be more or less detailed. An unskilled computer had to be told, for example, that the product of two negative numbers is a positive number; someone with more mathematical training might need only a general outline of the computation.[12]

The inventors of the first digital computers saw their machines as direct replacements for this system of humans, calculators, tables, pencils and paper, and instructions. We know this because many early experts on automatic computing used the human computing process as the standard against which the new electronic computers were compared. Writers of early textbooks on "automatic computing" started with the time a calculator took to multiply two ten-digit numbers. To that time they added the times for the other operations: writing and copying intermediate results, consulting tables, and keying in input values. Although a skilled operator could multiply two numbers in 10 or 12 seconds, in an 8-hour day he or she could be expected to perform only 400 such operations, each of which required about 72 seconds.[13] The first electronic computers could multiply two ten-digit decimal numbers in about 0.003 second; they could copy and read internally stored numbers even faster. Not only that, they never had to take a coffee break, stop for a meal, or sleep; they could compute as long as their circuits were working.

Right away, these speeds radically altered the context of the arguments that electronic components were too unreliable to be used in more than a few computers. It was true that tubes were unreliable, and that the failure of even one during a calculation might vitiate the results. But the measure of reliability was the number of operations between failures, not the absolute number of hours the machine was in service. In terms of the number of elementary operations it could do before a tube failed, a machine such as ENIAC turned out to be quite reliable after all. If it could be kept running for even one hour without a tube failure, during that hour it could do more arithmetic than the supposedly more reliable mechanical calculators could do in weeks. Eventually the ENIAC's operators were able to keep it running for more than 20 hours a day, 7 days a week.

Computers were reliable enough long before the introduction of the transistor provided a smaller and more rugged alternative to the vacuum tube.

So an electronic computer like the ENIAC could do the equivalent of about 30 million elementary operations in a day — the equivalent of the work of 75,000 humans, By that standard, five or six computers of the ENIAC's speed and size could do the work of 400,000 humans. However, measuring electronic computing power by comparing it with that of humans makes no sense. It is like measuring the output of a steam engine in "horsepower." For a 1- or 2-horsepower engine the comparison is appropriate, but it would be impossible to replace a locomotive with an equivalent number of horses. So it is with computing power. But the human measure was the only one the pioneers knew. Recall that between 1945 and 1950 the ENIAC was the only working electronic computer in the United States. At its public dedication in February 1946, Arthur Burks demonstrated the machine's powers to the press by having it add a number to itself over and over again — an operation that reporters could easily visualize in terms of human abilities. Cables were plugged in, switches set, and a few numbers keyed in. Burks then said to the audience, "I am now going to add 5,000 numbers together," and pushed a button on the machine. The ENIAC took about a second to add the numbers.[14]

Almost from the day the first digital computers began working, they seldom lay idle. As long as they were in working order, they were busy, even long after they had done the computations for which they were built.

As electronic computers were fundamentally different from the human computers they replaced, they were also different from special-purpose pieces of experimental apparatus. The reason was that the computer, unlike other experimental apparatus, was programmable. That is, the computer itself was not just "a machine," but at any moment it was one of an almost infinite number of machines, depending on what its program told it to do. The ENIAC's users programmed it by plugging in cables from one part of the machine to another (an idea borrowed from telephone switchboards). This rewiring essentially changed it into a new machine for each new problem it solved. Other early computers got their instructions from punched strips of paper tape; the holes in the tape set switches in the machine, which amounted to the same kind of rewiring effected by the ENIAC's plugboards. Feeding the computer a new strip of paper tape transformed it into a completely different device that could do something entirely different from what its designers had intended it to do. Howard Aiken designed his Automatic Sequence Controlled Calculator to compute tables of mathematical functions, and that it did reliably for many years. But in between that work it also solved problems in hydrodynamics, nuclear physics, and even economics.[15]

The computer, by virtue of its programmability, is not a machine like a printing press or a player piano — devices that are configured to perform a specific function.[16] By the classical definition, a machine is a set of devices configured to perform a specific function: one employs motors, levers, gears, and wire to print newspapers; another uses motors, levers, gears, and wire to play a prerecorded song. A computer is also made by configuring a set of devices, but its function is not implied by that configuration. It acquires its function only when someone programs it. Before that time it is an abstract machine, one that can do "anything." (It can even be made to print a newspaper or play a tune.) To many people accustomed to the machines of the Industrial Revolution, a machine having such general capabilities seemed absurd, like a toaster that could sew buttons on a shirt. But the computer was just such a device; it could do many things its designers never anticipated.

The computer pioneers understood the concept of the computer as a general-purpose machine, but only in the narrow sense of its ability to solve a wide range of mathematical problems. Largely because of their institutional backgrounds, they did not anticipate that many of the applications computers would find would require the sorting and retrieval of non-numeric data. Yet outside the scientific and university milieu, especially after 1950, it was just such work in industry and business that underlay the early expansion of the computer industry. Owing to the fact that the first computers did not do business work, the misunderstanding persisted that anything done by a computer was somehow more "mathematical" or precise than that same work, done by other means. Howard Aiken probably never fully understood that a computer could not only be programmed to do different mathematical problems but could also do problems having little to do with mathematics. In 1956 he made the following statement: ". . . if it should ever turn out that the basic logics of a machine designed for the numerical solution of differential equations coincide with the logics of a machine intended to make bills for a department store, I would regard this as the most amazing coincidence that I have ever encountered."[17] But the logical design of modern computers for scientific work in fact coincides with the logical design of computers for business purposes. It is a "coincidence," all right, but one fully intended by today's computer designers.

The question remained whether electronic computers worked too fast for humans to feed work into them. Engineers and computer designers met the problem of imbalance of speeds head-on, by technical advances at both the input and output stages of computing. To feed in programs and data, they developed magnetic tapes and disks instead of tedious plugboard wiring or slow paper tape. For displaying the results of a computation, high-speed line printers, plotters, and video terminals replaced the slow and cumbersome electric typewriters and card punches used by the first machines.

Still, the sheer bulk of the computer's output threatened to inundate the humans who ultimately wanted to use it. But that was not a fatal fault, owing (again) to the computer's programmability. Even if in the course of a computation a machine handles millions of numbers, it need not present them all as its output. The humans who use the computer need only a few numbers, which the computer's program itself can select and deliver. The program may not only direct the machine to solve a problem; it also may tell the machine to select only the "important" part of the answer and suppress the rest.

Ultimately, the spread of the computer beyond physics labs and large government agencies depended on whether people could write programs that would solve different types of problems and that would make efficient use of the high internal speed of electronic circuits. That challenge was not met by simply training and hiring armies of programmers (although sometimes it must have seemed that way). It was met by taking advantage of the computer's ability to store its programs internally. By transforming the programming into an activity that did not require mathematical training, computer designers exploited a property of the machine itself to sidestep the shortage of mathematically trained programmers.

Although the computer pioneers recognized the need for internal program storage, they did not at first see that such a feature would have such a significant effect on the nature of programming. The idea of storing both the program and data in the same internal memory grew from the realization that the high speed at which a computer could do arithmetic made sense only if it got its instructions at an equally high speed. The plugboard method used with the ENIAC got instructions to the machine quickly but made programming awkward and slow for humans. In 1944 Eckert proposed a successor to the ENIAC (eventually called the EDVAC whose program would be supplied not by plugboards but by instructions stored on a high-speed magnetic disk or drum.

In the summer of 1944, John von Neumann first learned (by chance) of the ENIAC project, and within a few months he had grasped that giant machine's fundamentals — and its deficiencies, which Eckert and Mauchly hoped to remedy with their next computer. Von Neumann then began to develop a general theory of computing that would influence computer design to the present day.[18] In a 1945 report on the progress of the EDVAC he stated clearly the concept of the stored program and how a computer might be organized around it.[19] Von Neumann was not the only one to do that, but it was mainly from his report and others following it that many modern notions of how best to design a computer originated.

For von Neumann, programming a digital computer never seemed to be much of an intellectual challenge; once a problem was stated in mathematical terms, the "programming" was done. The actual writing of the binary codes that got a computer to carry out that program was an activity he called coding, and from his writings it is clear that he regarded the relationship of coding to programming as similar to that of typing to writing. That "coding" would be as difficult as it turned out to be, and that there could emerge a profession devoted to that task, seems not to have occurred to him. That was due in part to von Neumann's tremendous mental abilities and in part to the fact that the problems that interested him (such as long-range weather forecasting and complicated aspects of fluid dynamics)[20] required programs that were short relative to the time the computer took to digest the numbers. Von Neumann and Herman Goldstine developed a method (still used today) of representing programs by flow charts. However, such charts could not be fed directly into a machine. Humans still had to do that, and for those who lacked von Neumann's mental abilities the job remained as difficult as ever.

The intermediate step of casting a problem in the form of a flow chart, whatever its benefits, did not meet the challenge of making it easy for nonspecialists to program a computer. A more enduring method came from reconsidering, once again, the fact that the computer stored its program internally.

In his reports on the EDVAC, von Neumann had noted the fact that the computer could perform arithmetic on (and thus modify) its instructions as if they were data, since both were stored in the same physical device.[21] Therefore, the computer could give itself new orders. Von Neumann saw this as a way of getting a computer with a modest memory capacity to generate the longer sequences of instructions needed to solve complex problems. For von Neumann, that was a way of condensing the code and saving space.

However, von Neumann did not see that the output of a computer program could be, rather than numerical information, another program. That idea seemed preposterous at first, but once implemented it meant that users could write computer programs without having to be skilled mathematicians. Programs could take on forms resembling English and other natural languages. Computers then would translate these programs into long complex sequences of ones and zeroes, which would set their internal switches. One even could program a computer by simply selecting from a "menu" of commands (as at an automated bank teller) or by paddles and buttons (as on a computerized video game). A person need not even be literate to program.

That innovation, the development of computer programs that translated commands simple for humans to learn into commands the computer needs to know, broke through the last barrier to the spread of the new invention.[22] Of course, the widespread use of computers today owes a lot to the technical revolution that has made the circuits so much smaller and cheaper. But today's computers-on-a-chip, like the "giant brains" before them, would never have found a large market had a way not been found to program them. When the low-cost, mass-produced integrated circuits are combined with programming languages and applications packages (such as those for word processing) that are fairly easy for the novice to grasp, all limits to the spread of computing seem to drop away. Predictions of the numbers of computers that will be in operation in the future become meaningless.

What of the computer pioneers' early predictions? They could not foresee the programming developments that would spread computer technology beyond anything imaginable in the 1940s. Today, students with pocket calculators solve the mathematical problems that prompted the pioneers of that era to build the first computers. Furthermore, general-purpose machines are now doing things, such as word processing and game playing, that no one then would have thought appropriate for a computer. The pioneers did recognize that they were creating a new type of machine, a device that could do more than one thing depending on its programming. It was this understanding that prompted their notion that a computer could do "anything." Paradoxically, the claim was more prophetic than they could ever have known. Its implications have given us the unforeseen computer revolution amid which we are living.

NOTES

1. Harold Bergstein, "An Interview with Eckert and Mauchly," *Datamation* 8, no. 4 (1962), pp. 25–30.
2. Simon Lavington, *Early British Computers* (Bedford, Mass.: Digital Press, 1980), p. 104.

3. See, for example, John Wells, "The Origins of the Computer Industry: A Case Study in Radial Technological Change," Ph.D. Diss., Yale University, 1978, pp. 93, 96, 119; Robert N. Noyce, "Microelectronics," *Scientific American* 237 (September 1977), p. 674; Edmund C. Berkeley, "Sense and Nonsense about Computers and Their Applications," in *Proceedings of World Computer Pioneer Conference,* Llandudno, Wales, 1970, also in Phillip J. Davis and Reuben Hersh (eds.), *The Mathematical Experience* (New York: Houghton Mifflin, 1981).

4. See, for example, the proceedings of two early conferences: *Symposium on Large-Scale Digital Calculation Machinery, Annals of Harvard University Computation Laboratory,* vol. 16, 1949; *The Moore School Lecturers: Theory and Techniques for Design of Electronic Digital Computers,* lectures given at Moore School of Electrical Engineering, University of Pennsylvania, 1946 (Cambridge, Mass.: MIT Press, 1986).

5. Georgia G. Mollenhoff, "John V. Atanasoff, DP Pioneer," *Computerworld* 8, no. 11 (1974), pp. 1, 13.

6. Byron E. Phelps, *The Beginnings of Electronic Computation,* IBM Corporation Technical Report TR-00.2259, Poughkeepsie, N.Y., 1971, p. 19.

7. Cuthbert C. Hurd, "Early IBM Computers: Edited Testimony," *Annals of the History of Computing* 3 (1981), pp. 162–82.

8. Anthony Oettinger, "Howard Aiken," *Communications* ACM 5 (1962), pp. 298–99, 352.

9. Henry Tropp, "The Effervescent Years: A Retrospective," *IEEE Spectrum* 11 (February 1974), pp. 70–81.

10. For an example of this argument, and a refutation of it, see John von Neumann, *Collected Works,* vol. 5 (Oxford: Pergamon, 1961), pp. 182, 365.

11. R. F. Clippinger, "Mathematical Requirements of the Personnel of a Computing Laboratory," *American Mathematical Monthly* 57 (1950), p. 439; Edmund Berkeley, *Giant Brains, or Machines that Think* (New York: Wiley, 1949), pp. 108–9.

12. Ralph J. Slutz, "Memories of the Bureau of Standards SEAC," in N. Metropolis, J. Howlett, and G. Rota (eds.), *A History of Computing in the Twentieth Century* (New York: Academic, 1980), pp. 471–77.

13. In a typical computing installation of the 1930s, humans worked, with mechanical calculators that could perform the four elementary operations of arithmetic, on decimal numbers having up to ten digits, taking a few seconds per operation. Although the machines were powered by electric motors, the arithmetic itself was always done by mechanical parts — gears, wheels, racks, and levers. The machines were sophisticated and complex, and they were not cheap; good ones cost hundreds of dollars. For a survey of early mechanical calculators and early computers, see Francis J. Murray, *Mathematical Machines,* vol. 1: *Digital Computers* (New York: Columbia University Press, 1961); see also Engineering Research Associates, *High-Speed Computing Devices* (New York: McGraw-Hill, 1950; Cambridge, Mass.: MIT Press, 1984).

14. Quoted in Nancy Stern, *From ENIAC to UNIVAC* (Bedford, Mass.: Digital Press, 1981), p. 87.

15. Oettinger, "Howard Aiken."

16. Abbott Payson Usher, *A History of Mechanical Inventions,* second edition (Cambridge, Mass.: Harvard University Press, 1966), p. 117.

17. Howard Aiken, "The Future of Automatic Computing Machinery," in *Elektronische Rechenmaschinen und Informationsverabeitung,* proceedings of a symposium, published in *Nachrichtentechnische Fachberichte,* no. 4 (Braunschweig: Vieweg, 1956), pp. 32–34.

18. Herman H. Goldstine, *The Computer from Pascal to von Neumann* (Princeton University Press, 1972), p. 182.

19. Von Neumann's "First Draft of a Report on the EDVAC" was circulated in typescript for many years. It was not meant to be published, but it nonetheless had an influence on nearly every subsequent computer design. The complete text has been published for the first time as an appendix to Nancy Stern's *From ENIAC to UNIVAC.*

20. Von Neumann, *Collected Works*, vol. 5, pp. 182, 236.
21. Martin Campbell-Kelley, "Programming the EDVAC," *Annals of the History of Computing 2* (1980), p. 15.
22. For a discussion of the concept of high-level programming languages and how they evolved, see H. Wexelblatt (ed.), *History of Programming Languages* (New York: Academic, 1981), especially the papers on FORTRAN, BASIC, and ALGOL.

18. One Hundred Seven Assumptions about the Future

JOSEPH F. COATES, JOHN B. MAHAFFIE, AND ANDY HINES

The year 2000 may have arrived, but the allure of knowing the future remains. In this chapter, another group of futurists takes on the task of forecasting the future world, in this case the world of 2025. Like Kahn and Wiener in the opening chapter of Part IV, Joseph Coates and two colleagues from the Washington, D.C.–based consulting firm of Coates & Jarratt, Inc., looked at social and demographic trends as well as forecasts of scientific and technological developments and built a set of scenarios about the world of the next generation. Unlike the scenarios of many previous studies of the future, however, Coates and his colleagues have organized their ideas under topical areas, such as information, energy, environment, housing, transportation, and health. The approach is intended to serve businesspersons and other leaders in thinking about how current trends will affect their areas of concern. This chapter is an excerpt from the book's first chapter and presents the assumptions on which the scenarios, which are far too long and detailed to include here — they fill nearly 500 pages — are based.

Joseph F. Coates, president of Coates & Jarratt, Inc., is a well-known thinker, writer, and speaker on the future. Prior to founding Coates & Jarrett, Inc., in 1979 he held positions at the National Science Foundation and the Office of Technology Assessment, an arm of the U.S. Congress. He is the author of numerous articles and three books. John B. Mahaffie, vice president of Coates & Jarratt, Inc., has been with the company since 1987. He is also an author and speaker on futures studies. Andy Hines was an associate with Coates & Jarratt, Inc., for six years.

2025 [the book from which the excerpt is taken] emerged from the second phase of a project conducted by Coates and Jarratt, Inc., a Washington, D.C., think tank specializing in the study of the future. The first phase of the project, completed in 1993, organized and analyzed forecasts made from 1970 through 1992 in virtually every subdiscipline of science, technology, and engineering.

A *forecast* is a simple or complex look at the qualities and probabilities of a future event or trend. Futurists differentiate between the *forecast*, which is generally not point-specific to time or place, and the *prediction*, a specific, usually quantitative statement about some future outcome.

In the second phase of the project we created fresh forecasts, examining how diverse technologies from brain science to information technology might interact to influence every aspect of life in the year 2025. Those forecasts are the topic [of the book from which this selection was taken]. They appear in the subsequent chapters [of that book] as scenarios of 2025. To build these scenarios we assume specific scientific, technological, demographic, social, and other changes will occur. These assumptions are included in this [selection].

Assumptions about the future are not like assumptions in a geometry exercise; they are not abstract statements from which consequences can be drawn with mathematical certitude and precision. They are highly probable statements about the future, forming a framework around which less certain ideas can be tested. We need to make assumptions about the future in order to plan it, prepare for it, and prevent undesired events from happening. Here, we built 15 scenarios of 2025 based on 107 assumptions that we made about the future.

Some of these statements are drawn from the project. Others, such as the estimates of future population, come from public or highly credible private statistical and mathematical analyses of trends. Still others result from integrating a wide range of material; one such assumption is that we will be moving toward a totally managed globe. To present the underlying arguments supporting each of these highly reliable statements (which amount to forecasts) would require a massive introductory section. We have, therefore, presented these statements about the future as simply and in as straightforward a manner as possible.

A few of these assumptions have a native, or goals-oriented, aspect to them. The assumption, for example, that per capita energy consumption in the advanced nations will fall to 66 percent of the 1990 level is definitely not a trend extrapolation but a judgment about the confluence of social, political, economic, environmental, technological, and other concerns. Readers are urged to formulate and review alternatives that might characterize the next 30 years and test how those alternatives affect any other thoughts, concepts, beliefs, or conclusions about the future.

What follows is an inventory of high-probability statements about the year 2025 in three categories:

A. Scientific discoveries and research, and technological developments and applications.

B. Contextual, that is, those factors forming the social, economic, political, military, environmental, and other factors that will shape or influence scientific and technological developments. These contextual areas form the environment for the introduction and maturation of new products, processes, and services in society.

C. Twenty-four additional high-probability statements that have slightly less probability of occurring.

These high-probability forecasts, especially the first 83, become assumptions in understanding how any particular area may develop under the influence of new scientific, technological, social, political, or economic developments. It would be nice to suggest that these developments are inevitable, but few developments are. Nonetheless, the convergence of evidence indicates that these 107 developments are of such high likelihood that they form an intellectual substructure for thinking about any aspect of the year 2025.

* * *

MANAGING OUR WORLD

1. Movement toward a *totally managed environment* will be substantially advanced at national and global levels. Oceans, forests, grasslands, and water supplies will make up major areas of the managed environment. Macroengineering — planetary-scale civil works — will make up another element of that managed environment. Finally, the more traditional business and industrial infrastructure — telecommunications, manufacturing facilities, and so on — will be a part of managed systems and subsystems.

    Note that total management does not imply full understanding of what is managed. But expanding knowledge will make this management practical. Total management also does not imply total control over these systems.

2. Everything will be smart, that is, responsive to its external or internal environment. This will be achieved either by embedding microprocessors and associated sensors in physical devices and systems or by creating materials that are responsive to physical variables such as light, heat, noise, odors, and electromagnetic fields, or by a combination of these two strategies.

MANAGING HUMAN HEALTH

3. All human diseases and disorders will have their linkages, if any, to the human genome identified. For many diseases and disorders, the intermediate biochemical processes that lead to the expression of the disease or disorder and its interactions with a person's environment and personal history will also be thoroughly explored.

4. In several parts of the world, the understanding of human genetics will lead to explicit programs to enhance people's overall physical and mental abilities — not just to prevent diseases.

5. The chemical, physiological, and genetic bases of human behavior will be generally understood. Direct, targeted interventions for disease control and individual human enhancement will be commonplace. Brain-mind manipulation technologies to control or influence emotions, learning, sensory acuity, memory, and other psychological states will be in widespread use.

6. In-depth personal medical histories will be on record and under full control of the individual in a medical smart card or disk.

7. More people in advanced countries will be living to their mid-80s while enjoying a healthier, fuller life.

8. Custom-designed drugs such as hormones and neurotransmitters (chemicals that control nerve impulses) will be as safe and effective as those produced naturally within humans or other animals.

9. Prostheses (synthetic body parts or replacements) with more targeted drug treatments will lead to radical improvements for people who are injured, impaired, or have otherwise degraded physical or physiological capabilities.

MANAGING ENVIRONMENT AND RESOURCES

10. Scientists will work out the genomes of prototypical plants and animals, including insects and microorganisms. This will lead to more refined management, control, and manipulation of their health and propagation, or to their elimination.

11. New forms of microorganisms, plants, and animals will be commonplace due to advances in genetic engineering.

12. Foods for human consumption will be more diverse as a result of agricultural genetics. There will be substantially less animal protein in diets in advanced nations, compared with the present. A variety of factors will bring vegetarianism to the fore, including health, environmental, and ethical trends.

13. There will be synthetic and genetically manipulated foods to match each individual consumer's taste, nutritional needs, and medical status. Look for "extra-salty (artificial), low-cholesterol, cancer-busting french fries."

14. Farmers will use synthetic soils, designed to specification, for terrain restoration and to enhance indoor or outdoor agriculture.

15. Genetically engineered microorganisms will do many things. In particular, they will be used in the production of some commodity chemicals as well as highly complex chemicals and medicines, vaccines and drugs. They will be widely used in agriculture, mining, resource upgrading waste management, and environmental cleanup.

16. There will be routine genetic programs for enhancing animals used for food production, recreation, and even pets. In less developed countries, work animals will be improved through these techniques.

17. Remote sensing of the earth will lead to monitoring, assessment, and analysis of events and resources at and below the surface of land and sea. In many places, *in situ* sensor networks will assist in monitoring the environment. Worldwide weather reporting will be routine, detailed, and reliable.

18. Many natural disasters, such as floods, earthquakes, and landslides, will be mitigated, controlled, or prevented.

19. Per capita energy consumption in the advanced nations will be at 66 percent of per capita consumption in 1990.

20. Per capita consumption in the rest of the world will be at 160 percent of per capita consumption in 1990.

21. Resource recovery along the lines of recycling, reclamation, and remanufacturing will be routine in all advanced nations. Extraction of virgin materials through mining, logging, and drilling will be dramatically reduced, saving energy and protecting the environment.

22. Restorative agriculture (i.e., "prescription" farming) will be routine. Farmers will design crops and employ more sophisticated techniques to optimize climate, soil treatments, and plant types.

AUTOMATION AND INFOTECH

23. There will be a worldwide, broadband network of networks based on fiber optics; other techniques, such as communications satellites, cellular, and microwave will be ancillary. Throughout the advanced nations and the middle class and prosperous crust of the developing world, face-to-face, voice-to-voice, person-to-data, and data-to-data communication will be available to any place at any time from anywhere.

24. Robots and other automated machinery will be commonplace inside and outside the factory, in agriculture, building and construction, undersea activities, space, mining, and elsewhere.

25. There will be universal, on-line surveys and voting in all the advanced nations. In some jurisdictions, this will include voting in elections for local and national leaders.

26. Ubiquitous availability of computers will facilitate automated control and make continuous performance monitoring and evaluations of physical systems routine.

27. The ability to manipulate materials at the molecular or atomic level will allow manufacturers to customize materials for highly specific functions such as environmental sensing and information processing.

28. Totally automated factories will be common but not universal for a variety of reasons, including the cost and availability of technology and labor conflicts.

29. Virtual-reality technologies will be commonplace for training and recreation and will be a routine part of simulation for all kinds of physical planning and product design.

30. In text and — to a lesser extent — in voice-to-voice telecommunication, language translation will be effective for many practically significant vocabularies.

31. Expert systems, a branch of artificial intelligence, will be developed to the point where the learning of machines, systems, and devices will mimic or surpass human learning. Certain low-level learning will evolve out of situations and experiences, as it does for infants. The toaster will "know" that the person who likes white bread likes it toasted darker and the person who chooses rye likes it light.

32. The fusion of telecommunications and computation will be complete. We will use a new vocabulary of communications as *we televote, teleshop,*

telework, and *tele-everything.* We'll *e-mail, tube,* or *upload* letters to Mom. We'll go *MUDing* in cyberspace and mind our *netiquette* during virtual encounters.[1]

33. Factory-manufactured housing will be the norm in advanced nations, with prefabricated modular units making housing more flexible and more attractive, as well as more affordable.

34. In the design of many commercial products, such as homes, furnishings, vehicles, and other articles of commerce, the customer will participate directly with the specialist in that product's design.

35. New infrastructures throughout the world will be self-monitoring. Already, some bridges and coliseums have "tilt" sensors to gauge structural stress; magnetic-resonance imaging used in medical testing will also be used to noninvasively examine materials for early signs of damage so preventive maintenance can be employed.

36. Interactive vehicle–highway systems will be widespread, with tens of thousands of miles of highway either so equipped or about to be. Rather than reconstruct highways, engineers may retrofit them with the new technologies.

37. Robotic devices will be a routine part of the space program, effectively integrating with people. Besides the familiar robotic arm used on space shuttles, robots will run facilities in space operating autonomously where humans are too clumsy or too vulnerable to work effectively.

38. Applied economics will lead to a greater dependency on mathematical models embodied in computers. These models will have expanded capabilities and will routinely integrate environmental and quality-of-life factors into economic calculations. One major problem will be how to measure the economic value of information and knowledge. A Nobel prize will be granted to the economist who develops an effective theory of the economics of information.

POPULATION TRENDS

39. World population will be about 8.4 billion people.

40. Family size will be below replacement rates in most advanced nations but well above replacement rates in the less-developed world.

41. Birth control technologies will be universally accepted and widely employed, including a market for descendants of RU-486.

42. World population will divide into three tiers: at the top, World 1, made up of advanced nations and the world's middle classes living in prosperity analogous to Germany, the United States, and Japan; at the bottom, World 3, people living in destitution; and in the middle, World 2, a vast range of people living comfortably but not extravagantly in the context of their culture. We use the term *World 1, World 2,* and *World 3* for the

emerging pattern of nations, which moves us beyond the post–World War II nomenclature.

43. The population of World 1's advanced nations will be older, with a median age of 42.

44. The less-developed Worlds 2 and 3 will be substantially younger but will have made spotty but significant progress in reducing birthrates. However, the populations of these countries will not stop growing until sometime after 2025.

45. The majority of the world's population will be metropolitan, including people living in satellite cities clustered around metropolitan centers.

46. A worldwide middle class will emerge. Its growth in World 2 and to a lesser extent in World 3 will be a powerful force for political and economic stability and for some forms of democracy.

WORLDWIDE TENSIONS

47. There will be worldwide unrest reflecting internal strife, border conflicts, and irredentist movements. But the unrest will have declined substantially after peaking between 1995 and 2010.

48. Under international pressures, the United Nations will effectively take on more peace*making* to complement its historic peace*keeping* role.

49. Supranational government will become prominent and effective, though not completely, with regard to environmental issues, war, narcotics, design and location of business facilities, regulation of global business, disease prevention, workers' rights, and business practices.

50. Widespread contamination by a nuclear device will occur either accidentally or as an act of political military violence. On a scale of 1 to 10 (with Three Mile Island a 0.5 and Chernobyl a 3), this event will be a 5 or higher.

51. Increasing economic and political instabilities will deter business involvement in specific World 3 countries.

52. Despite technological advances, epidemics and mass starvation will be common occurrences in World 3 because of strained resources in some areas and politically motivated disruptions in others.

53. There will be substantial environmental degradation, especially in World 3. Governments will commit money to ease and correct the problem, but many will sacrifice long-term programs that could prevent the problem from happening in the first place.

54. There will be shifts in the pattern of world debtor and creditor countries. Japan's burst economic bubble, the ever-growing U.S. debt, and Germany's chronic unemployment problems are harbingers of things to come.

55. NIMBY ("Not In My Back Yard") will be a global-scale problem for a variety of issues, ranging from hazardous-waste disposal to refugees to prisons to commercial real-estate ventures.

56. Migration and conditions for citizenship throughout the world will be regulated under new international law.

57. Terrorism within and across international borders will continue to be a problem.

THE ELECTRONIC GLOBAL VILLAGE

58. Global environmental management issues will be institutionalized in multinational corporations as well as through the United Nations and other supranational entities.
59. A global currency will be in use.
60. English will remain the global common language in business, science, technology, and entertainment.
61. Schooling on a worldwide basis will be at a higher level than it is today. Education may approach universality at the elementary level and will become more accessible at the university level through distance education technologies.
62. In the advanced nations, lifelong learning will be effectively institutionalized in schools and businesses.
63. There will be substantial, radical changes in the U.S. government. National decisions will be influenced by electronically assisted referenda.
64. Throughout the advanced nations, people will be computer literate and computer dependent.
65. Worldwide, there will be countless virtual communities based on electronic linkages.
66. There will be a worldwide popular culture. The elements of that culture will flow in all directions from country to country. In spite of the trend toward "demassification" in both information and production, the global links of communications and trade will ensure that ideas and products will be *available* to all whether they like it or not.
67. The multinational corporation will be the world's dominant business form.
68. Economic blocs will be a prominent part of the international economy, with many products and commodities moving between these porous blocs. The principal blocs will be Europe, East Asia, and the Americas.
69. Universal monitoring of business transactions on a national and international business basis will prevail.
70. Identification cards will be universal. Smart cards will contain information such as nationality, medical history (perhaps even key data from one's genome), education and employment records, financial accounts, social security, credit status, and even religious and organizational affiliations.

PUBLIC ISSUES AND VALUES

71. Within the United States there will be a national, universal health care system.
72. In the United States, the likely collapse of the Social Security system will lead to a new form of old-age security such as one based on need-only criteria.

73. Genetic screening and counseling will be universally available and its use encouraged by many incentives and wide options for intervention.
74. There will be more recreation and leisure time for the middle class in the advanced nations.
75. The absolute cost of energy will rise, affecting the cost of transportation. Planners will reallocate terrain and physical space to make more efficient use of resources. In other words, cities will be redesigned and rezoned to improve efficiencies of energy in transportation, manufacturing, housing, [and so on].
76. There will be a rise in secular substitutes for traditional religious beliefs, practices, institutions, and rituals for a substantial portion of the population of the advanced nations and the global middle class. The New Age movement, secular humanism, and virtual communities built on electronics networking are a few harbingers.
77. Socially significant crime — [that is], the crimes that have the widest negative effects in the advanced nations — will be increasingly economic and computer-based. Examples include disruption of business, theft, money laundering, introduction of maliciously false information, and tampering with medical records, air traffic control or national-security systems.
78. Tax filing, reporting, and collecting will be computer-managed.
79. Quality, service, and reliability will be routine business criteria around the globe.
80. Customized products will dominate large parts of the manufacturing market. Manufacturers will offer customers unlimited variety in their products.
81. Economic health will be measured in a new way, including considerations of environment, quality of life, employment, and other activity and work. These new measures will become important factors in governmental planning.
82. GDP and other macroeconomic measures and accounts will include new variables such as environmental quality, accidents and disasters, and hours of true labor.
83. Sustainability will be the central concept and organizing principle in environmental management, while ecology will be its central science.

ADDITIONAL, BUT SLIGHTLY LESS PROBABLE, DEVELOPMENTS BY 2025

These next 24 developments have a somewhat lower probability than the 83 basic assumptions. If they do occur, they could have long-term, extensive startling, or disruptive effects on people and their societies.

1. Telephone communications within the United States and within Europe will be so cheap as to be effectively free.
2. Telecommunication costs will be integrated into rent or mortgage payments.

3. The greening of North Africa will begin, with megatechnologies to promote rain and build soil along the coast.

4. Antarctic icebergs will be harvested for watering the west coast of South America, Baja California, the Australian outback, Saudi Arabia, and other arid areas.

5. Going to work will be history for a large percentage of people. By 2020 or 2025, 40 percent of the workforce will be working outside the traditional office.

6. The home work-study center will be the centerpiece of the integrated, fully information-rich house and home. Mom and Dad will work there, the kids will reach out to the resources of the world, and the whole family will seek recreation, entertainment, and social contacts there.

7. Inorganic chemistry will rise to parity with organic chemistry in profit and importance in such areas as ceramics and composites.

8. Biomimetic materials and products that imitate natural biological materials will be common.

9. Micromachines the size of a typed period will be in widespread use. Nanotechnological devices 10,000 times smaller will have been developed and will be in use.

10. Radical cosmetics will leave no component of the body or mind beyond makeover. This will be accompanied by a melding of cosmetics, medicine, and surgery.

11. Ocean ranching and farming for food and energy will be widespread.

12. The asteroid watch will become a recognized institution. Among its most notable achievements will be several trial runs at altering an asteroid's path before it intersects Earth's orbit.

13. Moon mining and asteroid harvesting will be in their early stages.

14. Artificial intelligence devices will flower as aids to professionals, as adjuncts to ordinary workers, as doers of routine tasks, as checks on the functionality of software and complex systems, and as teaching and training tools.

15. Privatization of many highways, particularly beltways and parts of the interstate system, will occur. This will be tied to the evolution of an intelligent vehicle–highway system.

16. Restoration of aquifers will be a standard technology.

17. Fuel cells will be a predominant form of electromechanical energy generation.

18. Mastodons will walk the Earth again and at least 20 other extinct species will be revived.

19. Biocomputers will be in the early stage of development and applications.

20. Squaring-off of the death curve will make substantial progress in World 1 and some progress in World 2, leading to most people living to 85 years.

21. Critical experiments in life extension, to move the average lifetime of our species from 85 to 105, will begin. One hundred thousand people will be in a lifelong monitoring program. Massive numbers of other people will apply the treatments on a nonexperimental basis.

22. 120-mile-per-gallon cars will be in widespread use.
23. Hypersonic air carriers will be common.
24. Brain prostheses will be one of the practical applications of brain technology.

NOTE

1. A MUD is a "Multi-User Dungeon" or "Multi-User Dimension" — an on-line text-based form of virtual reality in which a number of people intereact in the framework of a fantasy adventure.

PART V
DILEMMAS OF NEW TECHNOLOGY I: GENETICS

Some of the most dramatic — and controversial — developments in late-twentieth-century technology have come from the life sciences. The event that captured the greatest number of headlines was undoubtedly the disclosure, in February 1997, that a Scottish scientist had succeeded in cloning a sheep (which he named Dolly after Dolly Parton) from the mammary cell of an adult ewe. The success of that experiment, marking the first time a large mammal had been cloned from an adult cell, brought an onslaught of speculation about the prospects and problems of cloning human beings.

But Dolly was only one of a series of remarkable scientific and technological developments that have cascaded out of the discovery, by James Watson and Francis Crick in the early 1950s, of the structure of DNA, the fundamental molecule of most forms of life on earth. This discovery has allowed researchers to unravel the biochemical basis of genes, those units within cells that transmit traits (e.g., eye color, height, and susceptibility to particular diseases) from one generation to the next. What sets these developments apart from most other areas of science and technology are the philosophical and religious questions they raise and their potential, ultimately, to change to course of human evolution.

In Part V of *Technology and the Future,* we move from broad, conceptual issues relating to technology and society to very specific ones in the rapidly moving area of genetics. An essay by Robert Weinberg, a distinguished molecular biologist, opens the section with a cautionary note about the potential outcomes of the Human Genome Initiative, a government-funded effort to decode the entire genetic makeup of the human organism. Weinberg, while hopeful about the prospects for preventing and treating disease and alleviating human suffering, is also deeply worried about the potential misuse of genetic knowledge for socially destructive ends.

Alta Charo, a professor of both law and medical ethics at the University of Wisconsin, raises a different set of issues in her chapter on the impacts of developments in genetics on family life. Charo examines how artificial insemination, surrogate motherhood, and other science-based modifications to traditional forms of procreation are interacting with changing social patterns (e.g., greater tolerance of homosexual lifestyles) to produce largely unprecedented patterns of family life. Finally, biomedical ethicist Leon Kass takes up the issue of whether to ban human cloning. The stakes are very high, he says; indeed, "the future of humanity hangs in the balance." Kass asserts that there are good reasons for the repugnance we feel toward the idea of cloning humans and we should heed them, rather than allowing ourselves to become slaves to unregulated technological progress.

19.   The Dark Side of the Genome

ROBERT A. WEINBERG

Among the most rapid and important scientific advances of the past two decades have been developments in molecular biology. The breaking of the genetic code and the development of new techniques to analyze genetic materials have given scientists the ability to understand the relationship between the biochemical building blocks of cells and the traits and characteristics of living organisms, including humans.

During the past several years, life scientists in several countries have begun a coordinated, systematic effort to create a complete biochemical description of the human genome (i.e., the DNA contained in the chromosomes in human cells) and to develop a map or atlas indicating which components of this genetic material determine which human traits, from susceptibility to particular disorders to eye color to mathematical or artistic ability. Already, geneticists have identified the location of genes associated with dozens of disorders, including cystic fibrosis, fragile-X syndrome (a form of mental retardation), and Huntington's disease.

These new capabilities offer the prospect of eliminating a great deal of human suffering, but they also present some serious ethical dilemmas and risks to society. Use of genetic information by insurance companies, by employers, and by government agencies could infringe on individual rights to privacy and could even make it difficult for some people to get health insurance, find employment, or find a marriage partner.

Robert A. Weinberg, one of the leading figures in molecular genetics, discusses some of these perplexing issues in his essay, "The Dark Side of the Genome." Weinberg is a professor of biology at the Massachusetts Institute of Technology and a member of the Whitehead Institute for Biomedical Research. His laboratory was among the first to recognize the existence of human oncogenes, which are responsible for converting normal cells into cancer cells. Weinberg holds a Ph.D. in biology from MIT. He is a member of the National Academy of Sciences and the recipient of a long list of honors, scientific prizes, and honorary degrees, including, in 1997, the National Medal of Science.

In the past 10 years biology has undergone a revolution that has repeatedly attracted wide attention. At first, controversy swirled over whether the genetic cloning technology that powers this revolution could create new and possibly dangerous forms of life. These fears have dissipated as thousands of investigators have found that the organisms created by gene splicing pose no threat to human health or the ecosystem around us.

A much larger stream of headlines next touted the power of genetic engineering to produce great quantities of valuable medical and agricultural products cheaply. Without doubt, over the next decades these fruits of biotechnology will enormously benefit health and economic productivity.

Largely lost amidst these stories, however, are developments that will ultimately have a far larger social impact. Recently gained abilities to analyze complex genetic information, including our own, will soon allow us to predict human traits from simple DNA tests. [In just a few years], routine tests will detect predispositions to dozens of diseases as well as indicate a wide range of normal human traits. We have only begun to confront the problems engendered by the power of genetic diagnosis.

Consider, for example, the societal problems that will likely develop from the recent isolation of the gene that in a defective form causes cystic fibrosis. Genetic counselors can now trace that version of the gene in families, thereby revealing those couples who could have children with cystic fibrosis. While providing extraordinarily useful information for cystic fibrosis carriers, this technique raises questions about the marriageability and reproductive decisions of gene carriers, and the terms under which their offspring will be able to obtain health and life insurance.

Individual successes like the isolation of the cystic fibrosis gene will soon be overshadowed by the avalanche of genetic information flowing out of research labs. The engine that will drive these advances in gene analysis is the biologists' moonshot, the Human Genome Project. (See box.) The ambitious goal of this international effort is to read out the sequence of the 3 billion bases of DNA that, strung end to end, carry the information of all the body's genes. Given a clear, easily read atlas of our genetic endowment, researchers will be able to accelerate the rate at which they discover important genes — now several dozen each year — by 10-fold and eventually maybe even 100-fold. Scientists will then be able to study how the normal versions of these genes work, and how their aberrant versions cause disease.

Some fear that by reading through the entire library of human gene sequences we will rapidly come to understand the ultimate secrets of life and the essence of our humanity. For my part, such fears are far astray of the mark. Our bodies function as complex networks of interacting components that are often influenced by our variable environment. By enumerating and studying individual components — genes, in this case — we will only begin to scratch the surface of our complexity. Nonetheless, certain genes can be especially influential in determining one or another aspect of human form and function. Herein lie the seeds of the substantial problems we will begin to encounter over the next decade.

MAPPING THE GENETIC TERRAIN

Ten to fifteen years from now — barring unforeseen technical obstacles — scientists will have described every bump in our complex genetic terrain. Yet long before this project is finished, information yielded by "mapping" this land-

DNA and Babylonian Tablets

To find every human gene, scientists will have to determine the sequence of the 3 billion characters in our DNA that together form the genetic blueprint known as the human genome. One can convey how daunting the effort will be by comparing the genome to a Babylonian library uncovered in some nineteenth-century archeological dig.

Imagine tens of thousands of clay tablets — individual genes — scattered about, each inscribed with thousands of cuneiform characters in a language with few known cognates. The library's chaos mirrors that encountered when the precisely ordered array of DNA molecules that is present in a living cell is extracted and introduced into a test tube. Imagine, too, that the library's full meaning will be understood only when most of its tablets have been deciphered.

Geneticists today have ways of laboriously sifting through heaps of "tablets" to find certain genes of special interest. Once a gene is located and retrieved, or "cloned," the sequence of its 5,000 or more bases of DNA — our cuneiform characters — can be determined.

While biologists are proud of having sequenced more than one percent of the "tablets" so far, these achievements represent only a piecemeal solution to a very large problem. Gene cloning and sequencing techniques developed in the 1970s are so time-consuming and painstaking that systematic searches for many genes have been impossible.

A better answer, in the form of the human genome project, will begin by mapping the genome — cataloguing all the Babylonian tablets. In effect, geneticists will gather and systematically shelve the scattered tablets, reconstructing their original order.

Initially, groups of tablets (DNA fragments) thought to derive from a common section (chromosomal region) of the library will be placed together on a shelf. Then geneticists will order the tablets within a group and give each a label. They will do so without any understanding of the tablets' contents.

How is this possible? Imagine that our Babylonian scribes have used the final phrases at the end of one tablet as the opening phrases of the next one. Short, redundant strings of characters would enable tablets to be shelved in the right order without any knowledge of the bulk of the text. Long, carefully ordered lists of the labels identifying individual tablets, in effect a complete library catalogue, will compose the human genome map.

Only after this work is completed can the reading of all the characters in each tablet proceed — the sequencing of the DNA bases. Great technical progress will be required before the work becomes economically viable. Sequencing a 1,000-base stretch of DNA now costs $5,000 to $10,000. And some genes are giants; the one involved in muscular dystrophy was recently found to encompass 2 million bases. The cost will have to drop by a factor of 10 through automation before sequencing can begin in earnest.

Think of the technology required to develop automated readers that could photograph 3,000-year-old tablets, analyze and read the characters with greater than 99 percent accuracy, flag ambiguous ones, and introduce everything into a computerized database. The details of the automated DNA-sequencing equipment under development differ, but the technical problems are no less challenging. — *Robert A. Weinberg* scape — breaking it into sectors of manageable size and placing them in a logical array — will make possible powerful genetic analysis techniques. These, in turn, will engender a host of ethical issues.

To understand why, it is important to know a little about the underlying biology. The human genetic landscape — our genome — consists of all the DNA information carried on the 22 pairs of chromosomes in our cells plus the X and Y chromosomes involved in determining sex. Each chromosome carries a linear molecule of DNA ranging in size from 50 million to 250 million pairs of four kinds of chemical bases. They are commonly referred to by the letters A, C, G, and T. In all, 3 billion base pairs of DNA lie on the chromosomes. Some 50,000 to 100,000 discrete segments of DNA — each several thousand or more base pairs long — constitute the genes that store our genetic information. The trick is to figure out where these genes lie, and what information each encodes.

As a first step in understanding this enormous information base, investigators have started mapping each chromosome by labeling small segments along its length. The labels used are actually built-in features of the genome. They consist of minor genetic variations called polymorphisms that occur frequently throughout human DNA sequences and distinguish one person's DNA from another's. For example, at a certain chromosomal site, one person's DNA bases may read AAGCTT while a second person's may read AAGTTT. Such polymorphisms, widely scattered throughout the genome, are readily detected using existing techniques, even without any knowledge of the genome's detailed structure.

Polymorphisms are not only important for their usefulness in marking the genome at specific places. The location of a particular gene in the human genome is usually obscure. Geneticists can track down such a gene by localizing it near one or another polymorphic marker. To do this, they ascertain the presence of markers in DNA samples collected from members of large families and even large, unrelated populations.

Researchers have already used a polymorphic marker to determine the rough location of the gene that in one variant form, or "allele," leads to Huntington's disease. This illness appears as a severe neurological deterioration in midlife. Within a large kin group studied in Venezuela, all the relatives showing the disease were found to carry a distinct polymorphic marker on a particular chromosome, while their middle-aged, disease-free relatives did not. This concordance means that the still unknown gene lies close to the polymorphic marker on that chromosome, and therefore that detection of the marker signals the presence of the gene that causes the disease. The marker will prove invaluable in helping researchers to directly identify the Huntington's gene, isolation of which offers the only real hope for understanding and treating the disease.

Genes linked to terrible diseases are not the only ones geneticists study. During the next 10 years, researchers may well make associations between polymorphic markers and normal, highly variable traits such as height, eye color, hair shape, and even foot width without knowledge of the genes that serve as blueprints for these traits. Not much further down the road, scientists may uncover links between certain markers and more complex, subtle traits, such as aspects of physical coordination, mood, and maybe even musical ability. At that point, we will confront social problems that will bedevil us for decades to come.

Imagine that investigators could predict with some accuracy certain aspects of intelligence through simple analysis of an individual's DNA. Consider the power this would give some people and the vulnerable position in which it would put others.

The magnitude of the problems of genetic diagnosis depends on one's view of how many complex human traits will be successfully associated with polymorphic markers. Some observers, such as geneticists Richard Lewontin and Jonathan Beckwith of Harvard University, believe that few such associations will be made correctly. Some people argue that traits such as perfect pitch and mathematical ability depend on the workings of dozens of genes. Yet others think that the contributions of nature and nurture can never be teased apart.

Most likely, the doubters will be correct in many cases but wrong in others. Mathematical analysis has led some geneticists to conclude that the expression of many complex traits is strongly influenced by the workings of a few genes operating amid a large number of more silent collaborators. Moreover, scientists can most easily explain rapid organismic evolution, such as humans have experienced over the last several million years, by attributing important roles to a small number of especially influential genes. According to this hypothesis, each such gene has undergone alterations over the course of evolution that have in turn resulted in profound changes in our embryological development and adult functioning.

For these reasons, I believe that a number of genetic markers will be strongly linked to certain discrete aspects of human behavior and mental functioning. Yet other traits will, as some argue, prove to be influenced by many interacting genes and the environment, and will not lend themselves to the genetic analysis soon to be at our fingertips.

What type of higher functions will be understood and predictable by genetic methods? One can only speculate. The list of possibilities — say, shyness, aggressiveness, foreign-language aptitude, chess-playing ability, heat tolerance, or sex drive — is limited only by one's imagination. Likewise, the consequences of one or another identification — and there will surely be some successes — can barely begin to be foreseen.

THE LONG REACH OF GENETIC SCREENING

From cradle to grave — even from *conception* to grave — the coming genetic diagnostic technology will have profound effects on our descendants' lives. Parents-to-be in the latter part of the 1990s will confront an ever-lengthening menu of prenatal genetic tests that will affect a variety of reproductive decisions. Terminating a pregnancy may come relatively easily to some whose offspring carry genes dooming them to crippling diseases that appear early in life, such as Tay-Sachs and cystic fibrosis. But the mutant gene leading to Huntington's disease usually permits normal life until one's 40s or 50s, typically after the trait has been passed on to half of the next generation. Will its detection in a fetus justify abortion?

As the years pass, this gray area of decision making will widen inexorably. Sooner or later, an enterprising graduate student will uncover a close association between a polymorphic marker and some benign aspect of human variability like eye color or body shape. And then genetic decision making will hinge on far more than avoiding dread disease.

Such knowledge and the tests it makes possible could lead to eugenics through elective abortion. In India, thousands of abortions are said to be performed solely on the basis of fetal sex. It would seem to be but a small step for many to use the genetic profile of a fetus to justify abortion for a myriad of other real or perceived genetic insufficiencies.

This prospect may appear remote, seemingly encumbered by complicated laboratory procedures that will limit these analyses to a privileged elite. And the revulsion built up against eugenics would seem to present a significant obstacle. But the onward march of technology will change all this. Current programs for developing new diagnostic instruments should, by the end of this decade, yield machines able to automatically detect dozens of markers in a single, small DNA sample. As genetic diagnosis becomes more automated, it will become cheap and widely available. And the responsibility for children's genetic fitness will shift from the uncontrollable hand of fate into the hands of parents. [Within a few years], the birth of a cystic fibrosis child will, in the minds of many, reflect more the negligence of parents than God's will or the whims of nature.

Still other specters loom as the coming generation matures. Twenty-five years hence, educators and guidance counselors intent on optimizing educational "efficiency" could find children's genetic profiles irresistible tools. Once correlations are developed between performance and the frequency of certain genetic sequences — and once computers can forecast the interactions of multiple genes — such analyses could be used in attempts to predict various aspects of cognitive function and general educability.

The dangers here are legion. Some will use tests that will at best provide only probabilistic predictors of performance as precise gauges of competence. And factors strongly affecting education, including personality and environment, will likely be overlooked, leading to gross misreadings of individual ability.

Only slightly less insidious could be the effects of genetic analysis on future marriages. Will courtships be determined by perceptions of the genetic fitness of prospective partners? Over the past decade, how many Jewish couples who have discovered that their children could be born with Tay-Sachs disease, and black couples with similar concerns about sickle-cell anemia, have opted to forgo marriage altogether? As we uncover genes affecting traits that fall well within the range of normal variability, will these too become the object of prenuptial examination?

Once again, such an Orwellian vision would seem to reach far beyond current realities. Yet nightmares have already occurred. Two decades ago, genetic screening among the population in central Greece for the blood disease sickle-cell anemia revealed a number of normal individuals carrying genes that predispose their offspring to the disease. Because the test results were inappropriately disclosed, these individuals became publicly identified and stigmatized, and formed an unmarriageable genetic underclass.

Along with facing new issues around marriage, young adults with unfavorable constellations of genes may be limited in their employment possibilities. Employers want to hire productive, intelligent people. Will they exploit genetic screening to decide how rapidly a prospective employee will adapt to a new job or contribute to a company's productivity?

Even more likely will be attempts to use genetic markers to predict susceptibility to dangers in the workplace. People have different tolerances to on-the-job chemical exposures, dictated by their genetic variability. There is therefore great interest in uncovering polymorphic markers that would allow companies to predict employees' susceptibility to certain chemicals encountered in the workplace.

Employers will also feel pressure to use the expanding powers of genetic diagnosis to predict lifelong disease susceptibility among workers. The staggering rise in health-insurance costs has already generated strong economic incentives for employers to improve the health of their workers by promoting smoke-free environments, routine medical screening, and healthy life-styles. Hiring only those people who pass genetic profile tests might be seen as a means to reduce health-insurance costs further.

Most employers have until now been unwilling to enter so deeply into employees' private lives. But insurance providers have shown no such reticence. For example, many have been interested in learning whether their insured carry the AIDS virus. Genetic tests predicting heart disease at an early age or susceptibility to cancer will be tempting targets for insurance companies intent on establishing allocation of risk and premiums as precisely as possible. Such logic might dictate that the risks now shared within large insurance pools should be allocated instead on the basis of individual genetic profiles.

Genetic profiles could be widely available by the year 2000, when many primary-care physicians will routinely order certain genetic tests along with the usual blood pressure reading and urinalysis. Overlooking a standard genetic test will increasingly be seen as tantamount to malpractice. And as genetic profiles are routinely entered into health records, limiting insurers' access to such data may prove difficult.

Surely legislation could limit the direct viewing of confidential genetic data by insurers, but they might circumvent even the best attempts at regulation. Imagine the health policy of 2001 that offers substantially reduced premiums to non-smokers having a desirable genetic makeup. Such incentives will drive many people to flaunt their DNA profiles. As the genetically fit flock to the low-risk, low-premium pool, those left behind will have to pay higher premiums or even forgo insurance. In time, the concept of pooling genetic risk will seem a quaint relic of a pretechnological era.

While these developments are unsettling and even frightening, they pale beside the possibility that our ever-advancing understanding of human genetics could stoke the fires of racism.

Imagine in the not-so-distant future a survey of the prevalence of certain polymorphic alleles among different ethnic and racial groups. Ten years from now, will our enterprising graduate student find a polymorphic marker correlated with acute visual perception that is unusually common among Tibetans, or another correlated with impaired mathematical ability that crops up frequently among coastal Albanians? Given the vagaries of human history and population genetics, it is more than likely that different versions of genes are unevenly distributed throughout the human species.

Will such ostensibly innocent measurements of distributions of polymorphic markers ultimately provide a scientific basis for the type of virulent racism that inflamed Europe a half-century ago? Nazi racial theories were based on a pseudo-science that today looks ludicrous. But surely some observed variations in gene frequencies will place solid scientific data in the hands of those with an openly racist agenda.

BEYOND LEGISLATION

Policies governing the use of genetic information need to be debated and put in place early in this decade, not after problems emerge. Bioethics is already a thriving cottage industry, but the problems many of its practitioners wrestle with — issues like surrogate motherhood and *in vitro* fertilization — will be dwarfed by those surrounding genetic analysis. The groups organizing the human genome project have already assembled experts to confront the ethical, legal, and social dimensions of this work. But these individuals have yet to plumb the depths of the problems.

Even if we as a society can anticipate and rein in most misuse of genetic data, we will also need to address a more insidious and ultimately far more corrosive problem of DNA profiling: the rise of an ethic of genetic determinism.

For the past century, the prevailing winds of ideology have largely driven the ebb and flow of the nature versus nurture debate. A widespread reaction against social Darwinism and Nazi racism buoyed the strong nurturist sentiments of the past half-century, but the tide is turning, pushed by the ever more frequent success of genetics. As this decade progresses, a growing proportion of the lay public will come to accept genes as the all-powerful determinants of the human condition. This uncritical embrace of genetics will not be deterred by scientists' reminders that the powers of genetic predictions are limited.

Even some experts who, through appropriate channels, will gain access to genetic profiles may overinterpret the data. DNA profiles will never be clear, fully reliable predictors of all traits. For many complex traits, such as those involved in behavior and cognition, genetics will at best provide only a probability of development. After all, many traits are governed by the interplay between genetics and the environment. Environmental variations can cause genetically similar individuals to develop in dramatically different ways. Interpreters of genetic information who overlook this fact will repeatedly and disastrously misjudge individual ability.

What a tragedy this would be. The world we thrive in was built by many people who were not shackled by their pedigree. They saw their origins as vestiges to be transcended. By and large, we Americans have viewed our roots as interesting historical relics, hardly as rigid molds that dictate all that we are and will be. What will come of a worldview that says people live and struggle to fulfill an agenda planned in detail by their genes? Such a surrender to genetic determinism may disenfranchise generations of children who might come to believe that genes, rather than spunk, ambition, and passion, must guide their life course.

A belief that each of us is ultimately responsible for our own behavior has woven our social fabric. Yet in the coming years, we will hear more and more from those who write off bad behavior to the inexorable forces of biology and who embrace a new astrology in which alleles rather than stars determine individuals' lives. It is hard to imagine how far this growing abdication of responsibility will carry us

As a biologist, I find this prospect a bitter pill. The biological revolution of the past decades has proven extraordinarily exciting and endlessly fascinating, and it will, without doubt, spawn enormous benefit. But as with most new technologies, we will pay a price unless we anticipate the human genome project's dark side. We need to craft an ethic that cherishes our human ability to transcend biology, that enshrines our spontaneity, unpredictability, and individual uniqueness. At the moment, I find myself and those around me ill equipped to respond to the challenge.

20.   And Baby Makes Three — or Four, or Five, or Six: Defining the Family after the Genetic Revolution

R. ALTA CHARO

What is a family? This fundamental unit of our social order is in flux, evolving as a result of changing patterns of human relations, changing morals, and advancing technology. Alta Charo believes that these developments are creating both the need and the opportunity to "rethink our prejudices concerning the definition of a family." In this provocative essay, Charo asks readers to consider the possibility that not just heterosexual couples, but also single persons, homosexual couples, and larger groups of adults, might serve as parents. She looks at the implications of genetic and contractual models of the family — biological parents and their offspring and adoptive parents and children, respectively. And she considers the legal and psychological aspects of such relationships as surrogate motherhood and multiple parents (involving arrangements among gay couples and friends of the opposite sex who bear their children).

Many readers will find Charo's ideas unsettling. Some may find them offensive to their religious or ethical beliefs. But all readers should find them worth considering as examples of the dilemmas that new genetic technologies create.

Alta Charo is a professor of law and medical ethics at the University of Wisconsin at Madison, where she is a member of the faculty of the UW Medical School Program in Medical Ethics and a member of the Law School faculty. She is the author of more than fifty articles, book chapters, and reports on such topics as environmental law, family planning and abortion law, and reproductive technology policy. She has been a Fulbright Lecturer in France and a Diplomacy Fellow at the U.S. Agency for International Development. Since 1996, she has been a member of the National Bioethics Advisory Commission.

After four miscarriages, Adria Blum was ecstatic when her son was born four years ago. The child's father, Barry Chersky, comforted Blum in the delivery room during the many hours of labor.

So did Adria's lover, Marilyn. So did Barry's lover, Michael Baiad. Now the four Oakland residents, all in their 40s, share custody of Ari, a rambunctious 3-year-old conceived through artificial insemination. He feels sorry for other kids because they don't all have a Mommy, a Daddy, a Marilyn and a Michael. (Tuller 1993)

The "Ten O'Clock News" in New York City used to run a public service announcement in the 1970s that read: "It's ten o'clock. Do you know where your children are?" Perhaps it is time to update the message to read: "It's the 1990s. Do you know who all your parents are?" In the 1990s, we have a marvelous opportunity to rethink our prejudices concerning the definition of a family. Our emotional attachment to a definition based on blood, our modern tendency toward a definition based on contract, and our legal definitions based on fictional recreations of the biological nuclear family are all ripe for reform and integration. The result could be an expansion in the number of adults recognized as having parental ties to a particular child, an end to unthinking opposition to homosexual or group marriage, and a flowering of classical liberal theory in which the role of government is to facilitate individual choice rather than shape it.

This chapter will review the inconsistencies in European and American legal definitions of the family. Following a description of the competing claims of gestational, genetic, and contractual relationships to preferential treatment in cases of contested parenthood, the chapter concludes that each type of relationship has been made to yield to significant nonbiological concerns. Thus, over time, biology and intention to parent have been sacrificed to the need for orderly transmission of property between generations, stability of marital units as the fundamental structure of social organization, and finally, protection of children's perceived best interests.

As it appears that social policy provides an acceptable reason to violate the integrity of parent-child relationships, this chapter argues that social policy could similarly be used to maintain that integrity. Specifically, the preference for heterosexual couples as parents is unwarranted and single persons, homosexual couples, and larger groups of adults may serve equally well as parents. Furthermore, expanding the definition of parenthood to permit all genetic, gestational, and contractual parents to be recognized simultaneously will spare the courts the task of identifying which adults to discard from the child's life. This abandonment of legal fictions — which maintain that a child has at most two parents of different gender, regardless of biological and psychological reality — is a recognition that law need not slavishly follow cramped visions of nature but can instead facilitate broader visions of justice.

THE GENETIC MODEL OF THE FAMILY

The redefinition of "family" is timely for four reasons. First, the increased frequency of divorce and stepparenting has made traditional allocations of parental rights and responsibilities unworkable in light of the day-to-day experience of children living with "stepparents." Second, the frequency of single persons and homosexual couples seeking to parent has strained the two-person, two-gender model of parenthood. Third, the advent of so-called gestational surrogacy has clouded identification of "biological" maternity, thus for the first time opening the door to an examination of just what it is about biological parenthood that entitles it to such extraordinary respect.

Finally, the Human Genome Project promises to usher in an era of genetic exploration and invention (Kevles and Hood 1992; Davis 1991; Bishop and Waldholz 1990; Wingerson 1990; Committee 1988). As with nineteenth-century advances, this knowledge may well become the basis for profound shifts in public thinking and public policy, just as Darwinian evolutionary theory became the basis of Spencerian libertarian theory and subsequent eugenic social policy (Lewontin 1991; Nelkin and Tancredi 1991; Suzuki and Knudtson 1990; Kevles 1986). With increasing understanding of genetic influences on physical and psychological phenotypical expression comes the temptation to identify genetic coding as the ultimate expression of personal identity and genetic linkages as the fundamental expression of human relationships. But such a development would be overly reductionist and lead to unfortunate public policy.

The blood ties between parent and child have almost mythological significance in every culture (Chodorow 1978). They represent both the act of procreation and the physical reflection of the parent's body in the body of the child (Sorosky, Baran, and Pannor 1984; Bluestein 1982). The importance of genetic ties is confirmed by research suggesting that many psychological attributes may also be influenced by genetic heritage (Wilson 1978), although environmental influences may swamp these effects (Lewontin, Rose and Kamin 1984). "In sum," states one commentator, "it is only natural that our sublime and complex feelings regarding this issue reflect precisely the sentiment that law should preserve as a family unit that which nature has rendered genetically similar" (Hill 1991).

* * *

However, it is easy to place too much mystical importance on genetic connections. After all, there is no statistical genetic difference between the relationship of the donor and child and the relationship between full siblings. It is the added psychological aspects of parenting that give the parental/genetic connection such an entitlement to legal recognition. Nor should the fact that one's child shares one's genes become the basis for a property rights argument in which the child is, in some sense, "owned" by the parent. Not only is this a dangerous doctrine that long led to child abuse and child labor, it fails to distinguish between owning the raw materials and owning the creation arising from them (Hill 1991; Andrews 1986a; Scott 1981). The same issue has arisen with regard to the use of a patient's spleen cell in the development of a commercially valuable cell line. . . .Thus, the progenitors of a frozen, in vitro embryo may be treated as property owners . . . in some contexts and as prospective parents in others, . . . but at the moment of birth the offspring is no longer property of any sort (Glendon 1981).

Thus the emphasis on biological formation of families may overvalue the significance of genetic linkages. Further, it marginalizes some children and adults with a significant involvement in the family. It ignores, for example, the frequent presence in nonadoptive families of children with biological ties to only one of the parents. Such children, when unrelated to the marital partner of the mother, were deemed illegitimate, severely disadvantaging them and their mothers. The biological model of the family, with this overlay of insistence upon expressing bio-logical relationships within a socially sanctioned, heterosexual marriage, resulted in the creation of a grand presumption, to wit, that all "real" families follow this model absent a formal legal intervention.

But some families had more than two parents. Some were parents by virtue of biology, a bond that cannot be broken no matter how many legal proceedings are used to push the biological parents out of the child's life. Others were parents by contract, who by virtue of marriage to the child's mother or contract with the state created a psychological, economic, and legal relationship with the child. But legal fictions were maintained, in large part due to the fear that nonexclusivity of parental status would lead to hampered decision-making among the adults and thus thwart state efforts to make parents the primary providers of services and discipline to minors.

Later developments in foster parenting and the explosion of stepparenting fol-lowed this trend. No third party could gain a permanent, legally recognized rela-tionship with a child absent an extraordinary intervention by the courts or by the permanent withdrawal of the natural parents from the child's life. These biologi-cal, or "real," parents were given an almost unbeatable presumption in their favor when it came to contested custody and parenting cases, and when supplanted by nonbiological parents, they were made to disappear in order to recreate the illu-sion of a "biological" family. Thus this Western tradition dictated that there could be only one of each type of parent, although other societies freely experimented with polygyny (Strathern 1992).

THE CONTRACTUAL MODEL OF THE FAMILY

At the same time, though, this seeming fascination with biology had a strong competitor — the need to find substitute parents when genetic linkages were missing or inconvenient. Adoption, a statutory creation not existing at common law though long taking place informally or with private legislation (Sloan 1988), is evidence of a strong social tradition that recognizes the purely social and psy-chological dimensions of parenting, even where these occur in the absence of bio-logical ties. Yet, even with adoption, adoptive parents may acquire parental status with respect to a particular child only after termination of the parental rights of the child's biological parents, particularly those of the natural mother. The "pre-sumption of biology" serves as an irrebuttable legal presumption that the birth mother of the child is its legal mother and that adoption can take place only con-sequent to a termination of the parental rights of the birth mother (Andrews 1986b; Aries 1962).

. . . In the United States, adoption began as a means for privatizing the cost of maintaining orphans. It only later became grounded in child welfare, and that welfare was generally defined as recreation of a biological-style family unit for the child to enter.

* * *

Modern adoption statutes are replete with statements that make it clear that their primary focus is the well-being of the adopted child. The requirement of many modern adoption statutes that prospective adoptive parents pass a rigorous screening process before the adoption is finalized illustrates this concern (OTA 1988). In the case of the out-of-wedlock infant given to strangers for adoption, society generally deems it in the adoptee's best interests to make the infant a full-fledged member of the adoptive family, as though the infant had been born into the adoptive family.

Furthermore, it is widely believed that an adoptee's retention of ties with the biological family can undermine the psychological aspect of this assimilation. Thus, courts have described the broad objective of adoption statutes as "giving the adopted child a 'fresh start' by treating him as the natural child of the adoptive parent," in essence a "substitution of the adoptive in place of the natural family and severance of legal ties with the child's natural family." . . .

Thus, once created by statute, adoption was designed to use law to recreate the image of a biological family unit. It required that the biological parents be permanently removed from the child's life and the adoptive parents substituted for them (Minow 1991). It was not possible for the child to be adopted without the natural parents relinquishing all parental rights and responsibilities. Under law, they became legal strangers (Dempsey 1981).

DISCARDING BIOLOGICAL RELATIONSHIPS
TO MAINTAIN BIOLOGICAL APPEARANCES

The other important purpose to be served whenever deviating from biological definitions of the family was the preservation of the heterosexual marital unit. Thus, many states passed laws that created a presumption of paternity on the part of a mother's husband. Indeed, the husband did not have to be physically present at the time of conception (Field 1988): "If a husband, not physically incapable, was within the four seas of England during the period of gestation, the court would not listen to evidence casting doubt on his paternity."

Common law went so far as to deny the biological father the opportunity to assert his own paternity of a child born to a married woman (Hill 1991), although it could be asserted against him by the mother or her husband. This generally remains true today (Hill 1991), even though forensic uses of DNA testing now enable paternity determinations to be made with great accuracy (OTA 1991).

Thus, the biological progenitor of a child does not enjoy a constitutional right to establish paternity for his own pleasure or to seek any form of legal recognition of the relationship if the mother of the child is married to another man, even where he has actively sought to establish a relationship with the child. The rule not only protects the integrity of the family but also legitimizes the child (Hill 1991). In this way, biological reality gives way to three strong public policy considerations: that a husband should not be cuckolded against his will; that an adulterer not have the opportunity to demand access to his genetic offspring; and that the appearance of a biological family unit be maintained whenever possible.

The conflicting interests here — the child's interest in having a recognized mother and father; men's interests in avoiding unwanted responsibility for nonbiological children; and men's interests in having access to biological children — are difficult to reconcile in a coherent fashion. Neither biology nor contractual relationships are the clear trump. What is clear, however, is that these interests must be sorted out within the paradigm of a two-parent, heterosexual, marital parenting unit. The solution of declaring both the husband and the progenitor as fathers is simply not available. The Uniform Parentage Act makes these policy considerations quite evident.

Thus, the genetic relationship between father and child is considered secondary to the public policy of maintaining the integrity of "traditional" marriage and of rearing children, as often as possible, within such confines. Where no such "traditional" family is available, however — for example, when the child is born to a mother who is single or part of a lesbian couple — the law does permit the biological father to assert his paternal rights, even if he clearly stated his intention, prior to conception, to have no relationship to the child. This has been the case, for example, with sperm donors. . . .

With the advent of artificial insemination by donor (AID) services, courts and legislatures faced a fresh challenge. The procedure posed squarely the problem of determining whether genetic mixing without sexual intercourse constituted an affront to the marriage. Early on, courts held that it did, likening AID to adultery, although that trend was later reversed (Andrews 1984; Wadlington 1983). Second, courts were called on to determine whether genetic parentage, by itself, would be recognized under law as equivalent to legal parentage. As in nonadulterous situations of nonmarital sexual intercourse, the answer generally was "yes." Without a husband available to substitute for the genetic father, biological linkage created legal parenthood (Wikler 1992; OTA 1988).

But when the recipient of the donor semen is married, the presumption of spousal paternity comes into play, just as it does in situations of true adultery (OTA 1988). Over half the states have passed laws specifically stating that a donor is not to be considered the legal father of a child conceived by a married woman. But if the woman is not married, she is either denied access to the service entirely, or the donor is potentially considered the legal father, despite the fact that she is resorting to AID specifically because she does not want the genetic father to have a legal status vis-à-vis the child. The hope is illusory that the magical desexualization of conception by using a syringe rather than intercourse will yield the protection of the law against unwanted intrusions by the genetic father.

THE PROBLEM OF DECEPTIVE APPEARANCES

At least with ordinary AID by married women, appearances of a typical, biologically related family can be maintained by discarding the inconvenient genetic parent. Not so with contract motherhood (more commonly known as surrogate motherhood). The wife of the genetic father, who intends to rear the child, is visibly unpregnant. Therefore, she is disfavored as compared to the biological mother (Andrews 1986b). For example, the New Jersey Supreme Court held that Mary Beth Whitehead (now Gould), the genetic and gestational mother of a child conceived with semen from Bill Stern, was still the legal mother of the child, the surrogacy contract notwithstanding. Bill Stern was the legal father, based on his biological relationship, despite the existence of Mary Beth's husband as a potential competitor for the title based on presumptions of husband paternity. And Mrs. Stern was left without any legal relationship to the child, despite the fact that she would be the child's custodial maternal figure.

This "presumption of biology" is premised on the ancient dictum *mater est quam gestatio demonstrat* (by gestation the mother is demonstrated). But ancient times had not anticipated the separation of genetic and gestational maternity into different, even commercialized, components. For most of human history, the gestational mother had to be the genetic mother. If the two are represented by different women, however, which takes precedence?

The courts have confronted this conflict only twice, both times favoring the genetic over the gestational mother (Robertson 1989; Charo 1992). In the first case, the proceeding was a "setup" to allow the egg donor to adopt the child, and in accordance with the surrogate agreement, the surrogate did not contest the ruling. In the second, the court found that the definition of a "biological" relationship is that of genetic linkage.

The reasons for favoring a genetic model of the family have already been discussed. But there are arguments to be made that where a conflict arises between genetic and gestational relationships for women, gestation should prevail. These include arguments based on prenatal and postnatal bonding; the harmful effects to the birth mother of forcibly removing the child from her care; the physical involvement of the birth mother in bringing the child to term; and the uncertainties created when no hospital and no physician can securely hand a newborn up from the birth mother's loins to her arms.

It would be simple enough, then, to state that the woman giving birth is the sole biological, and therefore legal, mother. This maintains appearances. And it would effectively protect the egg donation programs that are beginning to flourish in states such as California, where women seek to use substituted gametes in the same way that men have done since the advent of AID. Those programs require that, as with sperm donation, the female gamete donor vanish into the mists of legal fictions.

But it would appear that this is not the approach of the California courts. In a recent gestational surrogacy case, a California appellate court held that a woman giving birth may be nothing more than a glorified wet nurse, and the child's real mother is the woman whose egg was used for the conception. A woman named Crispina Calvert had usable ova but no uterus. She had one of her eggs fertilized with her husband's semen and hired a second woman, Anna Johnson, to carry the pregnancy to term. When a dispute broke out after birth, an Orange County Superior Court judge ruled that the Calverts were the "genetic, biological and natural" father and mother and entitled to retain custody (Chiang 1993).

Johnson's attorney said his client wanted only "a profound parental relationship" with the boy she gave birth to more than two years ago (Chiang 1993). Sensing that his best chance was to argue that his client was the "natural" mother, who is given preference under California law in cases of disputed custody, Johnson's attorney argued that "the term 'natural mother' means the woman who gave birth. Crispina is not the mother" (Chiang 1993).

A lawyer for the Calverts argued that state statutory guidelines for determining parentage in the context of paternity suits clearly mandate that the genetic parents be declared legal parents. "We can't deny that Anna Johnson had an important role, but does that confer a legal prescription that she is a parent?" asked the lawyer. "I think not" (Hager 1993). But Johnson's lawyer responded by arguing that "it is the relationship between the birth mother and her baby that is legally protected. It tortures the English language to say that a woman (like Mrs. Calvert) who was never pregnant and never gave birth meets the traditional definition of the term mother" (Hager 1993).

Nonetheless, the California appellate court upheld the trial court's conclusions, characterizing the woman who gave birth as merely a "foster parent" for the "natural" mother whose egg had been used. And the state supreme court, which has yet to rule, has reacted hostilely to assertions that the apparent mother, [namely], the woman giving birth, was indeed the "real" mother.

The continued viability of the "traditional" family unit, one that mimics what happens in nature, was very much on the minds of the California Supreme Court justices. Several seemed leery of the child ending up with a father and two legally recognized mothers. "Here we could have a genetic parent . . . and a gestational parent," said Justice Edward A. Panelli. "Is that the traditional family unit?" (Hager 1993). Chief Justice Malcolm M. Lucas wryly observed that it could prove awkward for a child to grow up with both a "mother" and a "genetic progenitor" (Hager 1993). And the court-appointed lawyer for the child argued: "The minor in this case can be served only by being raised in the traditional, two-parent family. To declare [Johnson] a parent would complicate the child's life — and has never been recognized under law."

This same fear of disrupting the definition of the "traditional" family unit led the New York State Bar Association's House of Delegates in February 1993 to reject a recommendation by the Special Committee on Biotechnology and the Law. The House defeated a resolution that called for expanding the definition of "parent" in the domestic relations law to include both the genetic and gestational mothers in surrogate births. Delegates, including several from the Trusts and Estates Section, were concerned that the proposal could have unexpected consequences in other fields of law. Several asked whether a child born through surrogacy would be entitled to inherit through both mothers. Limited New York precedent indicates that, unlike in California, the gestational mother would be the only woman recognized as the legal mother.

In the Johnson case, one justice seemed intent on examining the broader issues, asking whether it is possible to have two biological mothers. She also suggested during oral argument that one thing "seems to be forgotten in this tug-of-war. . . . What importance should be given to the child's best interests?" But the Calverts' attorney responded that the language of the Uniform Parentage Act, which defines a parent in terms of genetic linkages, already incorporates a child's best interests, [namely], that it is in a child's best interest to be considered the child of his or her genetic parents. The attorney did not comment, however, on the degree to which spousal paternity presumptions and adoption would therefore presumably not serve a child's best interests.

SO WHAT IS A "NATURAL" PARENT AFTER ALL?

The dilemma facing the California courts, [which] insist upon a single definition of "natural" mother but find that none will fit the needs of both egg donation programs and gestational surrogacy programs, is that they are trying to move toward a contractual model of the family without having fully abandoned the old, biological models. In fact, it is the very power of genetic relationships that is driving infertile people and the courts to find ways to make surrogacy and AID more accepted (Wagner 1990).

One of the reasons given by Bill Stern for his decision to hire a contract mother was that his family had been wiped out in the Holocaust, and he wished to have blood relations with someone, somewhere. Egg donation is sought by women who want desperately to have the experience of being pregnant and giving birth to the child whom they will raise. AID is used so that women with infertile husbands can nonetheless have children to whom they are genetically related.

However, in order to make this possible within the strait-jacketed confines of the Western, heterosexual marriage, it is necessary that we simultaneously devalue the genetic and gestational relationships of the men and women who give or sell their gametes or their capability for gestation. Those biological connections must be considered less valuable than the contract these people signed when they became donors or surrogates. But the very fact that the infertile persons or couples who sought their services did not seek adoption to begin with testifies to the enormous significance of that biological tie. And the agreement the infertile partners of these biological parents have made to raise these children as their own testifies to the parallel significance of contractual agreements to take on these children as their own.

So if we insist upon a preference for "natural" parents, perhaps the definition of "natural" mother depends not upon biology but upon psychology — the intent to take the baby home. After all, what could be more "unnatural" than a woman who denies her own child? Consider two stories from Australia. In the first, Linda K. agreed to give a child to her sister. She gestated and gave birth to a child conceived with her infertile sister's egg. As she relinquished the child to the infertile sister, she denied feeling as if she were giving up her own baby girl: "I always considered myself her aunt." By contrast, Carol C. donated eggs to her infertile sister so the sister could become pregnant and give birth to children that the sister intended to rear. Reflecting on her relationship with the resulting children, who were her genetic offspring, Carol said: "I could never regard the twins as anything but my nephews." The births in these two stories occurred in Melbourne within weeks of each other (Charo 1992).

But if the definition of the natural mother depends primarily upon the intention to take care of the resulting child, then another California court decision, in the Moschetta case, makes no sense. Cynthia and Robert Moschetta hired a woman to act as a contract mother because Mrs. Moschetta was infertile. The contract mother, Elvira Jordan, was impregnated with Mr. Moschetta's semen and relinquished the child at birth to the hiring couple. Mrs. Moschetta cared for the baby at home for seven months, until the day Mr. Moschetta walked out on the marriage, taking the baby with him. In a three-way custody battle between Mr. Moschetta, Mrs. Moschetta, and the "surrogate," the California court promptly threw out the application of the one parent who had actually taken care of the child, day in and day out, for over half a year. Mrs. Moschetta, the court explained, was not the child's natural or (yet) adoptive parent and therefore had no rights at all. An argument can be made for the moral priority of this intended mother; but for her and her husband, and their desire to have a child, there would be no infant and no need for Solomonic decisions.

The Moschetta case is reminiscent of controversies concerning foster parents where the Supreme Court has said: "No one would seriously dispute that a deeply loving and interdependent relationship between an adult and a child in his or her care may exist even in the absence of blood relationship." Nevertheless, "the usual understanding of 'family' implies biological relationships, and most decisions treating the relation between parent and child have stressed this element." "In the end," states one commentator, "the Court appeared to create a distinction based on natural law, arguing that the relationship between foster parent and child is a creation of the state, whereas the biological relationship between parent and child is grounded in a 'liberty interest in family privacy [which] has its source, and its contours . . . not in state law, but in intrinsic human rights, as they have been understood in this Nation's history and tradition. While marriage traditionally has been the most important type of relationship, ascription of paternal rights also may depend upon the type of nonmarital relationship" (Hill 1991).

SHAPING THE FAMILY TO CONFORM
TO PUBLIC POLICY NEEDS

Another possible explanation of all these seemingly inconsistent precedents is that courts are assigning parental status primarily to protect societal or child interests. Thus, the genetic father in the Michael H. case, who is both a psychological and biological father, is denied parental status because the mother's husband provides a substitute who fills important policy needs. Single women who become pregnant via intercourse or AID, regardless of the original intentions of the genetic father, are faced with court decisions declaring the donors to be the legal fathers. If these women are married, however, their husbands can substitute for the genetic father and provide the necessary camouflage. Egg donation poses no problem, as the egg donor simply vanishes in the face of the gestational mother who uses the egg to create a child for her to rear. And where competing claims are made to motherhood, based on psychological, gestational, and genetic factors, the maternal status is assigned to the woman who has two out of three characteristics. Thus, Mrs. Calvert is the "natural" mother because she is genetically linked and she was the first one who wanted the child. Carol C. may be genetically a mother, but she is not the "natural" (i.e., "legal") mother because it was her sister who wanted children and brought the twins to term.

Looked at this way, it is evident that there is nothing sacred about either genetic *or* gestational linkages or, for that matter, about psychological linkages. All are accommodated only to the extent that they are consistent with an overriding public policy in favor of placing children in homes with two parents, of different gender, and married to one another if at all possible.

This, then, opens the door to an explicit examination of which public policies are important enough to supplant our innate preference for favoring biological definitions of parenthood, and why we prefer when possible to place children in "traditional" homes, even at the expense of the interests of their genetic and gestational parents. While courts hold that primary custody should be granted to the parent who would best serve the interests of the child, these principles are not supposed to operate to remove a child from a fit parent merely to enhance the child's life chances (Ruddick 1979).

With regard to the great "gestation-versus-genetics" debate in the context of maternity, there are good policy reasons to favor a gestational definition. A majority of American courts, newspapers, and academic commentators have already adopted the term "natural" or "biological" mother to mean "genetic" mother. They write of conflicts between genetic and gestational mothers as that of "nature versus nurture," as if nine months of pregnancy were not biological, were not natural, but were some kind of extended baby-sitting job.

Perhaps it should not surprise us that so many confuse genetic links with biological links. After all, most of these judges and commentators are men whose only possible biological links are genetic. They will never have morning sickness in the afternoon or swollen ankles in the eighth month because there is a baby in their belly. They will never worry before drinking a second cup of coffee lest it affect a developing fetus.

In a woman's world, pregnancy is indisputably a biological fusing of fetal and maternal bodies, health, and well-being. In a man's world, biology begins and ends with the DNA chains that link one generation to another. This rush to impose a male definition on a uniquely female biological experience could be considered a bad feminist joke.

It might be a joke if the consequences for women were not so frightening. Names are a form of classification that shape substantive rights. When MaryBeth Whitehead, a genetic and gestational parent, was called a "surrogate" instead of a "mother," the infamous Baby M case was already half-way decided, regardless of whether a pre-conception parenting contract should be enforceable. In the words of courts and commentators, a pregnant woman may be no more than a walking womb a human incubator working on behalf of a future child. A month before the birth, one Michigan court declared that "plaintiff Mary Smith is the mother of the child to be born to defendant Jane Jones on or about July 1987." Imagine: a woman can be pregnant and already a legal stranger to the unborn child within her.

This country has seen prosecutors, hospital lawyers, and judges use court orders to stop pregnant women from smoking or to force them to undergo cae-sarean sections — all on behalf of a diffuse "societal interest" in the as-yet-unborn child. Think what could happen when it is not strangers but the "natural" and "legal" parents of an unborn child still in another's womb who are trying to ensure that the gestational mother, this "foster parent," does everything the way they would have done it. Will a pregnant woman's sense of fused biological well-being stand any chance against a legal property interest that others have in the fetus still within her body?

California's *Johnson* decision, that a gestational mother is no more than a foster parent to her own child, is almost without precedent in the world. Only Israel, bound by unique aspects of religious identity law, has adopted a genetic definition of motherhood. Every other country that has examined the problem — including the United Kingdom, Germany, Switzerland, Bulgaria, and even South Africa with its race-conscious legal structure — has concluded that the woman who gives birth is the child's mother.

It is a conclusion that is essential if women are to maintain any degree of con-trol over their own bodies during pregnancy. Anything less makes them ever more subject to the whims and coercive power of those deemed to have a supe-rior interest in the child being carried. If, as the trial court judge in the *Anna J.* case asserted, it would be "crazy making" to recognize the reality of two natural mothers, then for the sake of women's rights and bodily integrity the one who is chosen ought to be the one who has given birth. And since the lesson to be learned from the cases concerning the presumption of paternity is that social pol-icy can trump genetics, then all that is needed is a recognition that in this case a social policy favoring protection of women's physical autonomy is more important than either protecting the appearance of "traditional" family or the interests of the genetic mother.

MAKE ROOM FOR DADDY . . . AND PAPA, AND MOMMY, AND MAMA . . .

In fact, there is a better solution than choosing between competing biological mothers or between genetic and social fathers. We have already entered an era of "crazy making," where courts are reexamining the prejudice against polygamy when reviewing adoption requests by certain Mormon families and are granting visitation rights to stepparents and the homosexual partners of biological parents. Why not go further? Let us toss out legal fictions and recognize in court what has already happened in the physical world. Some children have three biological par-ents, not two. Some children have two biological mothers, not one. Acknowledg-ing that two women are biologically related to the same child, that both women are "natural" mothers, does not necessarily determine who will have superior claims to raise the child. As every divorced parent in America knows, biology alone does not dictate custody.

Hundreds of children, most in San Francisco, New York, and other urban centers, grow up with multiple parents, usually due to arrangements among gay couples and friends of the opposite sex who were involved in the conception and birth. The lovers of the biological mother and father frequently take an active role in rearing children. Private contracts attempt to spell out relative degrees of involvement. Such coparents argue that their children, far from being confused by the unusual circumstances, actually benefit from being exposed to a wider range of adult influences. These families are more significant than their numbers suggest because they challenge the foundation of laws based on the heterosexual, nuclear family model (Tuller 1993).

A year ago, a group called Prospective Queer Parents was founded, which holds brunches that some participants have affectionately dubbed "sperm-and-egg mixers" (Tuller 1993). "On the second Sunday of every month, about two dozen gay men and lesbians interested in finding coparents gather to eat, chat . . . and scope out each other's genes" (Tuller 1993). "Our family arrangement is in many ways radical and visionary, since we're a bunch of four queers," one participant said. "But in other ways, we're a very traditional family — we value longevity, and struggling through for the long haul" (Tuller 1993).

Although the logistics can be complicated, coparents generally say that their biggest troubles come from a society and a legal system that fail to acknowledge the validity of their families. Consequently, the nonbiological mothers in coparenting arrangements often have deep concerns about their role and relationship to the child. One civil rights attorney working in this area says the law should be flexible enough to recognize that some families have three parents who all have legitimate rights, warning that it is the very rigidity of the legal system that can lead some coparenting disputes to end up in court, with lesbians and gay men fighting fiercely over custody and other issues (Tuller 1993). Thus, resolution of an upcoming Vermont case concerning the opportunity of a lesbian woman to adopt a child and thereby become a second, legally recognized mother is of great importance (Liley 1993). The probate judge ruled in June 1992 that Vermont's adoption law does not allow someone who is not married to a legal, custodial parent to become a second, adoptive parent of the legal parent's children. But Vermont's adoption law, last amended in 1947, contradicts itself and could never have envisioned today's families (Liley 1993). The attorney who represents the couple cites a section from state law that allows a single person to adopt a child. She says the mother's lesbian partner meets the prerequisites. However, a separate area of the statute reads that the parental rights of a biological parent are terminated once an adoption is granted. The only exception is for stepparents, a role that the biological mother fills but cannot claim because of the prohibition on homosexual marriage.

Perhaps it is time to take a great leap in family law. We could recognize that all biological relationships — genetic and gestational — are irrevocable. The emotional and medical significance of the bonds cannot be undone by signing a contract or adoption papers. The thousands of children who have wondered about the biological parents who gave them up for adoption or the sperm donors used to conceive them already know this.

At the same time, the voluntary social responsibilities we take on when we adopt children are equally permanent and no less profound. That is why so many adopted children, though they may wonder about their biological parents, take no action to find them. Forced by society to choose among various adults, these adopted children understand that the most important parent is the one who tries to stay around.

Why not give these children a break? Once a parent enters a child's life, whether by virtue of genes, gestation, or declaration, there is an unbreakable bond of psychology and history between the two. Crispina Calvert, Anna Johnson, Elvira Jordan, Cynthia Moschetta, Linda R, Carol C., and Mary Beth Whitehead are all mothers to their children just as Robert Moschetta and Bill Stern are fathers to their children. Even for those whose parents are absent due to contract, abandonment, or involuntary events, there is a mutual tie of emotion, of wondering how the other is doing, and of moral responsibility. While courts and legislatures may see the need to determine who has a primary role in raising the child, there is no need to cut these other people out entirely. Indeed, from the child's point of view, it is simply wrong to do so.

In an age when courts have been forced to manage the untidy families created by divorce and remarriage, it is simply not enough to argue that it will be difficult to organize a regime of family law that accommodates the permanency of both contractual and biological (both genetic and gestational) ties. And having admitted already that stepparents and grandparents are indeed real family members, what legitimate obstacle remains to accepting the adults who enter family arrangements via group marriage or homosexual marriage? Surely we can be creative enough to create a new category, somewhere between custodial parent and legal stranger, that captures these relationships.

It has been said that you can never be too rich or too thin. Shall we add, perhaps, that you can never have too many parents to love you?

REFERENCES AND ADDITIONAL READING

Andrews, L 1984. '"The Stork Market The Law of the New Reproductive Technologies." *American Bar Association Journal* 70:50.

Andrews, L. 1986a. "My Body, My Property." *Hastings Center Report*16:28.

Andrews, L. 1986b. "Surrogate Motherhood: Should the Adoption Model Apply?" *Children's Legal Rights Journal* 7:13.

Aries, P. 1962. *Centuries of Childhood: A Social History of Family Life.* New York: Alfred A. Knopf.

Bishop, J. E. and Waldholz, M. 1990. *Genome: The Story of the Most Astonishing Scientific Adventure of Our Time — The Attempts to Map All the Genes in the Human Body.* New York: Simon and Schuster.

Bluestein, J. 1982. *Parents and Children: The Ethics of the Family.* Oxford: Oxford University Press.

Charo, R. A. 1992 "Surrogacy in the United States." In S. McLean, ed., *Law Reform and Human Reproduction.* Hampshire: Dartmouth Publishing.

Chiang, H. 1993 "Surrogate Mother Custody Case Argued in State High Court." *San Francisco Chronicle* (February 3), 45.

Chodorow, N. 1978. *The Reproduction of Mothering: Psychoanalysis of Gender.* Berkeley: University of California Press.

Committee on Mapping and Sequencing the Human Genome. 1988. *Mapping and Sequencing the Human Genome.* Washington, DC: National Academy Press.

Davis, J. 1991. *Mapping the Code: The Human Genome Project and the Choices of Modern Science.* New York: Wiley.

Dempsey, J. 1981. *Family and Public Policy.* Baltimore: P. H. Brookes Publishing Co.

Field, M. 1988. *Surrogate Motherhood? Surrogate Fatherhood?* Cambridge, MA: Harvard University Press.

Glendon, M. 1981. *The New Family and the New Property.* Toronto: Butterworths.

Hager, P. 1993. "Justices Cool to Orange County Surrogate Mother's Case." *Los Angeles Times* (February 3), A1, col. 5.

Hill, J. L. 1991. "What Does it Mean to be a 'Parent'? The Claims of Biology as the Basis for Parental Rights." *New York University Law Review* 66:353.

Kevles, D. J. 1986. *In the Name of Eugenics: Genetics and the Uses of Human Heredity.* Berkeley: University of California Press.

Kevles, D. J., and Hood, L., eds. 1992. *The Code of Codes: Scientific and Social Issues in the Human Genome Project.* Cambridge, MA: Harvard University Press.

Lewontin, R. C. 1991. *Biology as Ideology: The Doctrine of DNA.* New York: Harper-Collins.

Lewontin, R. C., Rose, S., and Kamin, L. 1984. *Not in Our Genes.* New York: Pantheon Books Inc.

Liley, B. 1993. "Lesbian Custody Case Goes to the Vermont Supreme Court." *Gannett News Service* (February 3).

Minow, M. 1991. "Redefining Families: Who's In and Who's Out." *Colorado Law Review* 62:269.

Nelkin, D., and Tancredi, L. 1991. *Dangerous Diagnostics: The Social Power of Biological Information.* New York: Basic Books.

Note. 1991. "Looking for a Family Resemblance: The Limits of the Functional Approach to the Legal Definition of Family." *Harvard Law Review* 104:1640.

Office of Technology Assessment of the Congress of the United States. 1988. *Infertility: Medical and Social Choices.* Washington, DC: Government Printing Office.

OTA (Office of Technology Assessment of the Congress of the United States). 1991. *Genetic Witness.* Washington, DC: Government Printing Office.

Page, E. 1984. "Parental Rights." *Journal of Applied Philosophy* 1:187.

Robertson, J. 1989. "Technology and Motherhood: Legal and Ethical Issues in Human Egg Donation." *Case Western Reserve Law Review* 39:1.

Ruddick, W. 1979. "Parents and Life Prospects." In O. O'Neill and W. Ruddick, eds., *Having Children: Philosophical and Legal Reflections on Parenthood.* Oxford: Oxford University Press.

Scott, R. 1981. *The Body as Property.* New York: Viking Press.

Sloan, I. 1988. *The Law of Adoption and Surrogate Parenting.* New York: Oceana Publications.

Sorosky, A., Pannor, R., and Baran, A. 1989. *The Adoption Triangle — Sealed or Open Records: How They Affect Adoptees, Birth Parents, and Adoptive Parents.* San Antonio: Corona Publishing Co.

Special Project. 1986. "Legal Rights and Issues Surrounding Conception, Pregnancy and Birth." *Vanderbilt Law Review* 39:597.

Spencer, G. 1993. "House of Delegates Puts Off Resolutions on AIDS Victims." *New York Law Journal* (February 1), 1.

Strathern, M. 1992. *Reproducing the Future.* Manchester: Manchester University Press.

Suzuki, D., and Knudtson, P. 1990. *Genethics: The Ethics of Engineering Life.* Cambridge, MA: Harvard University Press.

Tuller, D. 1993. "Gays and Lesbians Try Co-Parenting: Families with 2 Moms, 2 Dads." *San Francisco Chronicle* (February 4), A1.

Wadlington, W. 1983. "Artificial Conception: The Challenge for Family Law." *Virginia Law Review* 69:564.

Wagner, W. 1990. "The Contractual Reallocation of Procreative Resources and Parental Rights: The Natural Endowment Critique." *Case Western Reserve Law Review* 41:1–202.

Wikler, D. 1992. "The Family as Social Construct: Dilemmas of Kinship Determinations in Artificial Insemination." *United Nations University WIDER Institute Conference on Women, Equality, and Reproductive Technology.* Helsinki (August).

Wilson, E. 1978. *On Human Nature.* Cambridge, MA: Harvard University Press.

Wingerson, L. 1990. *Mapping Our Genes: The Genome Project and the Future of Medicine.* New York: Dutton.

21. The Wisdom of Repugnance

LEON R. KASS

The notion of cloning human beings has been a staple of science fiction at least since Aldous Huxley's Brave New World *(1932). It moved a large step closer to reality in 1997 when Ian Wilmut, a Scottish scientist, succeeded in cloning a sheep from an adult cell. While some scientists expressed skepticism about whether Wilmut had really accomplished what he claimed, a number of other experimenters have since reported success in cloning large mammals. Cloning sheep is still far removed from cloning humans, but the threshold has been crossed. Geneticists and reproductive scientists generally agree that cloning humans is possible, although they differ on how soon it could actually be accomplished. Consequently, the ethical, religious, and policy dimensions of this new technology have exploded into public discussion.*

There are profound risks in going down the road that is opened by the prospect of human cloning, believes Leon Kass. "Cloning personifies our desire fully to control the future," he writes. We are so enchanted by technology that we have lost sight of the mysteries of nature and of life. At the same time, however, many people intuitively recoil from the idea of cloning human beings, finding it repugnant. There is good reason for this, Kass argues, for it violates very basic notions of human dignity. In a concise and clearly argued essay, Kass explains the reasons for his beliefs and suggests what the government and we, as individuals, should do.

Leon Kass is one of the most respected U.S. scholars of biomedical ethics. He is the Addie Clark Harding Professor in the Committee on Social Thought and the College of the University of Chicago and the author of Toward a More Natural Science: Biology and Human Affairs *(1988) and* The Hungry Soul: Eating and the Perfecting of Our Nature *(1994). Kass is a graduate of the University of Chicago School of Medicine and also holds a Ph.D. in biochemistry from Harvard University. He has served as a surgeon for the U.S. Public Health Service and has held positions in the field of medical ethics at the National Academy of Science, St. John's College, and the Kennedy Institute of Ethics at Georgetown University.*

THE STATE OF THE ART

If we should not underestimate the significance of human cloning, neither should we exaggerate its imminence or misunderstand just what is involved. The procedure is conceptually simple. The nucleus of a mature but unfertilized egg is removed and replaced with a nucleus obtained from a specialized cell of an adult (or fetal) organism (in Dolly's case, the donor nucleus came from mammary epithelium). Since almost all the hereditary material of a cell is contained within its nucleus, the renucleated egg and the individual into which that egg develops are genetically identical to the organism that was the source of the transferred nucleus. An unlimited number of genetically identical individuals — clones — could be produced by nuclear transfer. In principle, any person, male or female, newborn or adult, could be cloned, and in any quantity. With laboratory cultivation and storage of tissues, cells outliving their sources make it possible even to clone the dead.

The technical stumbling block, overcome by Wilmut and his colleagues, was to find a means of reprogramming the state of the DNA in the donor cells, reversing its differentiated expression and restoring its full totipotency, so that it could again direct the entire process of producing a mature organism. Now that the problem has been solved, we should expect a rush to develop cloning for other animals, especially livestock, to propagate in perpetuity the champion meat or milk producers. Though exactly how soon someone will succeed in cloning a human being is anybody's guess, Wilmut's technique, almost certainly applicable to humans, makes *attempting* the feat an imminent possibility.

Yet some cautions are in order and some possible misconceptions need correcting. For a start, cloning is not Xeroxing. As has been reassuringly reiterated, the clone of Mel Gibson, though his genetic double, would enter the world hairless, toothless, and peeing in his diapers, just like any other human infant. Moreover, the success rate, at least at first, will probably not be very high: the British transferred 277 adult nuclei into enucleated sheep eggs and implanted twenty-nine clonal embryos, but they achieved the birth of only one live lamb clone. For that reason, among others, it is unlikely that, at least for now, the practice would be very popular, and there is no immediate worry of mass-scale production of multicopies. The need of repeated surgery to obtain eggs and, more crucially, of numerous borrowed wombs for implantation will surely limit use, as will the expense; besides, almost everyone who is able will doubtless prefer nature's sexier way of conceiving.

Still, for the tens of thousands of people already sustaining over 200 assisted-reproduction clinics in the United States and already availing themselves of in vitro fertilization, intracytoplasmic sperm injection, and other techniques of assisted reproduction, cloning would be an option with virtually no added fuss (especially when the success rate improves). Should commercial interests develop in "nucleus-banking," as they have in sperm-banking; should famous athletes or other celebrities decide to market their DNA the way they now market their autographs and just about everything else; should techniques of embryo and germline genetic testing and manipulation arrive as anticipated, increasing the use of laboratory assistance to obtain "better" babies — should all this come to pass, then cloning, if it is permitted, could become more than a marginal practice simply on the basis of free reproductive choice, even without any social encouragement to upgrade the gene pool or to replicate superior types. Moreover, if laboratory research on human cloning proceeds, even without any intention to produce cloned humans, the existence of cloned human embryos in the laboratory, created to begin with only for research purposes, would surely pave the way for later baby making implantations.

In anticipation of human cloning, apologists and proponents have already made clear possible uses of the perfected technology, ranging from the sentimental and compassionate to the grandiose. They include: providing a child for an infertile couple; "replacing" a beloved spouse or child who is dying or has died; avoiding the risk of genetic disease; permitting reproduction for homosexual men and lesbians who want nothing sexual to do with the opposite sex; securing a genetically identical source of organs or tissues perfectly suitable for transplantation; getting a child with a genotype of one's own choosing, not excluding oneself; replicating individuals of great genius, talent, or beauty — having a child who really could "be like Mike"; and creating large sets of genetically identical humans suitable for research on, for instance, the question of nature versus nurture, or for special missions in peace and war (not excluding espionage), in which using identical humans would be an advantage. Most people who envision the cloning of human beings, of course, want none of those scenarios. That they cannot say why is not surprising. What is surprising, and welcome, is that, in our cynical age, they are saying anything at all.

THE WISDOM OF REPUGNANCE

Offensive, grotesque, revolting, repugnant, and *repulsive* — those are the words most commonly heard regarding the prospect of human cloning. Such reactions come both from the man or woman in the street and from the intellectuals, from believers and atheists, from humanists and scientists. Even Dolly's creator has said he "would find it offensive" to clone a human being.

People are repelled by many aspects of human cloning. They recoil from the prospect of mass production of human beings, with large clones of look-alikes, compromised in their individuality; the idea of father–son or mother–daughter twins; the bizarre prospects of a woman's giving birth to and rearing a genetic copy of herself, her spouse, or even her deceased father or mother; the grotesqueness of conceiving a child as an exact replacement for another who has died; the utilitarian creation of embryonic genetic duplicates of oneself, to be frozen away or created when necessary, in case of need for homologous tissues or organs for transplantation; the narcissism of those who would clone themselves and the arrogance of others who think they know who deserves to be cloned or which genotype any child-to-be should be thrilled to receive; the Frankensteinian hubris to create human life and increasingly to control its destiny; man playing God. Almost no one finds any of the suggested reasons for human cloning compelling; almost everyone anticipates its possible misuses and abuses. Moreover, many people feel oppressed by the sense that there is probably nothing we can do to prevent it from happening. That makes the prospect all the more revolting.

Revulsion is not an argument; and some of yesterday's repugnances are today calmly accepted — though, one must add, not always for the better. In crucial cases, however, repugnance is the emotional expression of deep wisdom, beyond reason's power fully to articulate it. Can anyone really give an argument fully adequate to the horror that is father–daughter incest (even with consent), or having sex with animals, or mutilating a corpse, or eating human flesh, or raping or murdering another human being? Would anybody's failure to give full rational justification for his revulsion at those practices make that revulsion ethically suspect? Not at all. On the contrary, we are suspicious of those who think that they can rationalize away our horror, say, by trying to explain the enormity of incest with arguments only about the genetic risks of inbreeding.

The repugnance at human cloning belongs in that category. We are repelled by the prospect of cloning human beings not because of the strangeness or novelty of the undertaking, but because we intuit and feel, immediately and without argument, the violation of things that we rightfully hold dear. Repugnance, here as elsewhere, revolts against the excesses of human willfulness, warning us not to transgress what is unspeakably profound. Indeed, in this age in which everything is held to be permissible so long as it is freely done, in which our given human nature no longer commands respect, in which our bodies are regarded as mere instruments of our autonomous rational wills, repugnance may be the only voice left that speaks up to defend the central core of our humanity. Shallow are the souls that have forgotten how to shudder.

The goods protected by repugnance are generally overlooked by our customary ways of approaching all new biomedical technologies. The way we evaluate cloning ethically will in fact be shaped by how we characterize it descriptively, by the context into which we place it, and by the perspective from which we view it. The first task for ethics is proper description. And here is where our failure begins.

Typically, cloning is discussed in one or more of three familiar contexts, which one might call the technological, the liberal, and the meliorist. Under the first, cloning will be seen as an extension of existing techniques for assisting reproduction and determining the genetic makeup of children. Like them, cloning is to be regarded as a neutral technique, with no inherent meaning or goodness, but subject to multiple uses, some good, some bad. The morality of cloning thus depends absolutely on the goodness or badness of the motives and intentions of the cloners. As one bioethicist defender of cloning puts it, "The ethics must be judged [only] by the way the parents nurture and rear their resulting child and whether they bestow the same love and affection on a child brought into existence by a technique of assisted reproduction as they would on a child born in the usual way."

The liberal (or libertarian or liberationist) perspective sets cloning in the context of rights, freedoms, and personal empowerment. Cloning is just a new option for exercising an individual's right to reproduce or to have the kind of child that he wants. Alternatively, cloning enhances our liberation (especially women's liberation) from the confines of nature, the vagaries of chance, or the necessity for sexual mating. Indeed, it liberates women from the need for men altogether, for the process requires only eggs, nuclei, and (for the time being) uteri — plus, of course, a healthy dose of our (allegedly "masculine") manipulative science that likes to do all those things to mother nature and nature's mothers. For those who hold this outlook, the only moral restraints on cloning are adequately informed consent and the avoidance of bodily harm. If no one is cloned without her consent, and if the clonant is not physically damaged, then the liberal conditions for licit, hence moral, conduct are met. Worries that go beyond violating the will or maiming the body are dismissed as "symbolic" — which is to say, unreal.

The meliorist perspective embraces valetudinarians and also eugenicists. The latter were formerly more vocal in those discussions, but they are now generally happy to see their goals advanced under the less threatening banners of freedom and technological growth. These people see in cloning a new prospect for improving human beings — minimally, by ensuring the perpetuation of healthy individuals by avoiding the risks of genetic disease inherent in the lottery of sex, and maximally, by producing "optimum babies," preserving outstanding genetic material, and (with the help of soon-to-come techniques for precise genetic engineering) enhancing inborn human capacities on many fronts. Here the morality of cloning as a means is justified solely by the excellence of the end, that is, by the outstanding traits of individuals cloned — beauty, or brawn, or brains.

These three approaches, all quintessentially American and all perfectly fine in their places, are sorely wanting as approaches to human procreation. It is, to say the least, grossly distorting to view the wondrous mysteries of birth, renewal, and individuality, and the deep meaning of parent–child relations, largely through the lens of our reductive science and its potent technologies. Similarly, considering reproduction (and the intimate relations of family life!) primarily under the political-legal, adversarial, and individualistic notion of rights can only undermine the private yet fundamentally social, cooperative, and duty-laden character of child-bearing, child-rearing, and their bond to the covenant of marriage. Seeking to escape entirely from nature (to satisfy a natural desire or a natural right to reproduce!) is self-contradictory in theory and self-alienating in practice. For we are erotic beings only because we are embodied beings and not merely intellects and wills unfortunately imprisoned in our bodies. And, though health and fitness are clearly great goods, there is something deeply disquieting in looking on our prospective children as artful products perfectible by genetic engineering, increasingly held to our willfully imposed designs, specifications, and margins of tolerable error.

The technical, liberal, and meliorist approaches all ignore the deeper anthropological, social, and, indeed, ontological meanings of bringing forth a new life. To this more fitting and profound point of view cloning shows itself to be a major violation of our given nature as embodied, gendered, and engendering beings — and of the social relations built on this natural ground. Once this perspective is recognized, the ethical judgment on cloning can no longer be reduced to a matter of motives and intentions, rights and freedoms, benefits and harms, or even means and ends. It must be regarded primarily as a matter of meaning: Is cloning a fulfillment of human begetting and belonging? Or is cloning rather, as I contend, their pollution and perversion? To pollution and perversion the fitting response can only be horror and revulsion; and conversely, generalized horror and revulsion are prima facie evidence of foulness and violation. The burden of moral argument must fall entirely on those who want to declare the widespread repugnances of humankind to be mere timidity or superstition.

Yet repugnance need not stand naked before the bar of reason. The wisdom of our horror at human cloning can be partially articulated, even if this is finally one of those instances about which the heart has its reasons that reason cannot entirely know.

THE PROFUNDITY OF SEX

To see cloning in its proper context, we must begin not, as I did before, with laboratory technique, but with the anthropology — natural and social — of sexual reproduction.

Sexual reproduction — by which I mean the generation of new life from (exactly) two complementary elements, one female, one male, (usually) through coitus — is established (if that is the right term) not by human decision, culture, or tradition, but by nature; it is the natural way of all mammalian reproduction. By nature, each child has two complementary biological progenitors. Each child thus stems from and unites exactly two lineages. In natural generation, moreover, the precise genetic constitution of the resulting offspring is determined by a combination of nature and chance, not by human design: each human child shares the common natural human species genotype, each child is genetically (equally) kin to each (both) parent(s), yet each child is also genetically unique.

Those biological truths about our origins foretell deep truths about our identity and about our human condition altogether. Every one of us is at once equally human, equally enmeshed in a particular familial nexus of origin, and equally individuated in our trajectory from birth to death — and, if all goes well, equally capable (despite our mortality) of participating, with a complementary other, in the very same renewal of such human possibility through procreation. Though less momentous than our common humanity, our genetic individuality is not humanly trivial. It shows itself forth in our distinctive appearance, through which we are everywhere recognized; it is revealed in our "signature" marks of fingerprints and our self-recognizing immune system; it symbolizes and foreshadows exactly the unique, never-to-be-repeated character of each human life.

Human societies virtually everywhere have structured child-rearing responsibilities and systems of identity and relationship on the bases of those deep, natural facts of begetting. The mysterious yet ubiquitous "love of one's own" is everywhere culturally exploited, to make sure that children are not just produced but well cared for and to create for everyone clear ties of meaning, belonging, and obligation. But it is wrong to treat such naturally rooted social practices as mere cultural constructs (like left- or right-driving, or like burying or cremating the dead) that we can alter with little human cost. What would kinship be without its clear, natural grounding? And what would identity be without kinship? We must resist those who have begun to refer to sexual reproduction as the "traditional method of reproduction," who would have us regard as merely traditional, and by implication arbitrary, what is in truth not only natural but most certainly profound.

Asexual reproduction, which produces "single-parent" offspring, is a radical departure from the natural human way, confounding all normal understandings of father, mother, sibling, and grandparent and all moral relations tied thereto. It becomes even more of a radical departure when the resulting offspring is a clone derived not from an embryo, but from a mature adult to whom the clone would be an identical twin; and when the process occurs not by natural accident (as in natural twinning), but by deliberate human design and manipulation; and when the child's (or children's) genetic constitution is preselected by the parent(s) (or scientists). Accordingly, as we shall see, cloning is vulnerable to three kinds of concerns and objections, related to these three points: cloning threatens confusion of identity and individuality, even in small-scale cloning; cloning represents a giant step (though not the first one) toward transforming procreation into manufacture, that is, toward the increasing depersonalization of the process of generation and, increasingly, toward the "production" of human children as artifacts, products of human will and design (what others have called the problem of "commodification" of new life); and cloning — like other forms of eugenic engineering of the next generation — represents a form of despotism of the cloners over the cloned, and thus (even in benevolent cases) represents a blatant violation of the inner meaning of parent–child relations, of what it means to have a child, of what it means to say yes to our own demise and "replacement."

Before turning to those specific ethical objections, let me test my claim of the profundity of the natural way by taking up a challenge recently posed by a friend. What if the given natural human way of reproduction were asexual, and we now had to deal with a new technological innovation — artificially induced sexual dimorphism and the fusing of complementary gametes — whose inventors argued that sexual reproduction promised all sorts of advantages, including hybrid vigor and the creation of greatly increased individuality? Would one then be forced to defend natural asexuality because it was natural? Could one claim that it carried deep human meaning?

The response to that challenge broaches the ontological meaning of sexual reproduction. For it is impossible, I submit, for there to have been human life — or even higher forms of animal life — in the absence of sexuality and sexual reproduction. We find asexual reproduction only in the lowest forms of life: bacteria, algae, fungi, some lower invertebrates. Sexuality brings with it a new and enriched relationship to the world. Only sexual animals can seek and find complementary others with whom to pursue a goal that transcends their own existence. For a sexual being, the world is no longer an indifferent and largely homogeneous *otherness*, in part edible, in part dangerous. It also contains some very special and related and complementary beings, of the same kind but of opposite sex, toward whom one reaches out with special interest and intensity. In higher birds and mammals, the outward gaze keeps a lookout not only for food and predators, but also for prospective mates; the beholding of the many-splendored world is suffused with desire for union — the animal antecedent of human eros and the germ of sociality. Not by accident is the human animal both the sexiest animal — whose females do not go into heat but are receptive throughout the estrous cycle and whose males must therefore have greater sexual appetite and energy to reproduce successfully — and also the most aspiring, the most social, the most open, and the most intelligent animal.

The soul-elevating power of sexuality is, at bottom, rooted in its strange connection to mortality, which it simultaneously accepts and tries to overcome. Asexual reproduction may be seen as a continuation of the activity of self-preservation. When one organism buds or divides to become two, the original being is (doubly) preserved, and nothing dies. Sexuality, by contrast, means perishability and serves replacement; the two that come together to generate one soon will die. Sexual desire, in human beings as in animals, thus serves an end that is partly hidden from, and finally at odds with, the self-serving individual. Whether we know it or not, when we are sexually active we are voting with our genitalia for our own demise. The salmon swimming upstream to spawn and die tell the universal story: sex is bound up with death, to which it holds a partial answer in procreation.

The salmon and the other animals evince that truth blindly. Only the human being can understand what it means. As we learn so powerfully from the story of the Garden of Eden, our humanization is coincident with sexual self-consciousness, with the recognition of our sexual nakedness and all that it implies: shame at our needy incompleteness, unruly self-division, and finitude; awe before the eternal; hope in the self-transcending possibilities of children and a relationship to the divine. In the sexually self-conscious animal, sexual desire can become eros, lust can become love. Sexual desire humanly regarded is thus sublimated into erotic longing for wholeness, completion, and immortality, which drives us knowingly into the embrace and its generative fruit — as well as into all the higher human possibilities of deed, speech, and song.

Through children, a good common to both husband and wife, male and female achieve some genuine unification (beyond the mere sexual "union," which fails to do so). The two become one through sharing generous (not needy) love for that third being as good. Flesh of their flesh, the child is the parents' own commingled being externalized and given a separate and persisting existence. Unification is enhanced also by their commingled work of rearing. Providing an opening to the future beyond the grave, carrying not only our seed but also our names, our ways, and our hopes that they will surpass us in goodness and happiness, children are a testament to the possibility of transcendence. Gender duality and sexual desire, which first draw our love upward and outside of ourselves, finally provide for the partial overcoming of the confinement and limitation of perishable embodiment altogether.

Human procreation, in sum, is not simply an activity of our rational wills. It is a more complete activity precisely because it engages us bodily, erotically, and spiritually as well as rationally. There is wisdom in the mystery of nature that has joined the pleasure of sex, the inarticulate longing for union, the communication of the loving embrace, and the deep-seated and only partly articulate desire for children in the very activity by which we continue the chain of human existence and participate in the renewal of human possibility. Whether or not we know it, the severing of procreation from sex, love, and intimacy is inherently dehumanizing, no matter how good the product.

We are now ready for the more specific objections to cloning.

THE PERVERSITIES OF CLONING

First, an important if formal objection: any attempt to clone a human being would constitute an unethical experiment upon the resulting child-to-be. As the animal experiments (frog and sheep) indicate, there are grave risks of mishaps and deformities. Moreover, because of what cloning means, one cannot presume a future cloned child's consent to be a clone, even a healthy one. Thus, ethically speaking, we cannot even get to know whether or not human cloning is feasible.

I understand, of course, the philosophical difficulty of trying to compare a life with defects against nonexistence. Several bioethicists, proud of their philosophical cleverness, use that conundrum to embarrass claims that one can injure a child in its conception, precisely because it is only thanks to that complained-of conception that the child is alive to complain. But common sense tells us that we have no reason to fear such philosophisms. For we surely know that people can harm and even maim children in the very act of conceiving them, say, by paternal transmission of the AIDS virus, maternal transmission of heroin dependence, or, arguably, even by bringing them into being as bastards or with no capacity or willingness to look after them properly. And we believe that to do that intentionally, or even negligently, is inexcusable and clearly unethical.

The objection about the impossibility of presuming consent may even go beyond the obvious and sufficient point that a clonant, were he subsequently to be asked, could rightly resent having been made a clone. At issue are not just benefits and harms, but doubts about the very independence needed to give proper (even retroactive) consent, that is, not just the capacity to choose but the disposition and ability to choose freely and well. It is not at all clear to what extent a clone will fully be a moral agent. For, as we shall see, in the very fact of cloning, and especially of rearing him *as a clone*, his makers subvert the cloned child's independence, beginning with that aspect that comes from knowing that one was an unbidden surprise, a gift, to the world, rather than the designed result of someone's artful project.

Cloning creates serious issues of identity and individuality. The cloned person may experience concerns about his distinctive identity not only because he will be in genotype and appearance identical to another human being, but, in this case, because he may also be twin to the person who is his "father" or "mother" — if one can still call them that. What would be the psychic burdens of being the "child" or "parent" of your twin? The cloned individual, moreover, will be saddled with a genotype that has already lived. He will not be fully a surprise to the world. People are likely always to compare his performances in life with that of his alter ego. True, his nurture and his circumstance in life will be different; genotype is not exactly destiny. Still, one must also expect parental and other efforts to shape that new life after the original — or at least to view the child with the original version always firmly in mind. Why else did they clone from the star basketball player, mathematician, and beauty queen — or even dear old dad — in the first place?

Since the birth of Dolly, there has been a fair amount of doublespeak on the matter of genetic identity. Experts have rushed in to reassure the public that the clone would in no way be the same person or have any confusions about his identity: as previously noted, they are pleased to point out that the clone of Mel Gibson would not be Mel Gibson. Fair enough. But one is shortchanging the truth by emphasizing the additional importance of the intrauterine environment, rearing, and social setting: genotype obviously matters plenty. That, after all, is the only reason to clone, whether human beings or sheep. The odds that clones of Wilt Chamberlain will play in the NBA are, I submit, infinitely greater than they are for clones of [five-foot-tall former Secretary of Labor] Robert Reich.

Curiously, this conclusion is supported, inadvertently, by the one ethical sticking point insisted on by friends of cloning: no cloning without the donor's consent. Though an orthodox liberal objection, it is in fact quite puzzling when it comes from people (such as Ruth Macklin) who also insist that genotype is not identity or individuality and who deny that a child could reasonably complain about being made a genetic copy. If the clone of Mel Gibson would not be Mel Gibson, why should Mel Gibson have grounds to object that someone had been made his clone? We already allow researchers to use blood and tissue samples for research purposes of no benefit to their sources: my falling hair, my expectorations, my urine, and even my biopsied tissues are "not me" and not mine. Courts have held that the profit gained from uses to which scientists put my discarded tissues do not legally belong to me. Why, then, no cloning without consent — including, I assume, no cloning from the body of someone who just died? What harm is done the donor, if genotype is "not me"? Truth to tell, the only powerful justification for objecting is that genotype really does have something to do with identity, and everybody knows it. If not, on what basis could Michael Jordan object that someone cloned "him," say, from cells taken from a "lost," scraped-off piece of his skin? The insistence on donor consent unwittingly reveals the problem of identity in all cloning.

Genetic distinctiveness not only symbolizes the uniqueness of each human life and the independence of its parents that each human child rightfully attains. It can also be an important support for living a worthy and dignified life. Such arguments apply with great force to any large-scale replication of human individuals. But they are sufficient, in my view, to rebut even the first attempts to clone a human being. One must never forget that these are human beings upon whom our eugenic or merely playful fantasies are to be enacted.

Troubled psychic identity (distinctiveness), based on all-too-evident genetic identity (sameness), will be made much worse by the utter confusion of social identity and kinship ties. For, as already noted, cloning radically confounds lineage and social relations, for "offspring" as for "parents." As bioethicist James Nelson has pointed out, a female child cloned from her "mother" might develop a desire for a relationship to her "father" and might understandably seek out the father of her "mother," who is after all also her biological twin sister. Would "grandpa," who thought his paternal duties concluded, be pleased to discover that the clonant looked to him for paternal attention and support?

Social identity and social ties of relationship and responsibility are widely connected to, and supported by, biological kinship. Social taboos on incest (and adultery) everywhere serve to keep clear who is related to whom (and especially which child belongs to which parents), as well as to avoid confounding the social identity of parent-and-child (or brother-and-sister) with the social identity of lovers, spouses, and coparents. True, social identity is altered by adoption (but as a matter of the best interest of already living children: we do not deliberately produce children for adoption). True, artificial insemination and in vitro fertilization with donor sperm, or whole embryo donation, are in some way forms of "prenatal adoption" — a not altogether unproblematic practice. Even here, though, there is in each case (as in all sexual reproduction) a known male source of sperm and a known single female source of egg — a genetic father and a genetic mother — should anyone care to know (as adopted children often do) who is genetically related to whom.

In the case of cloning, however, there is but one "parent." The usually sad situation of the "single-parent child" is here deliberately planned, and with a vengeance. In the case of self-cloning, the "offspring" is, in addition, one's twin; and so the dreaded result of incest — to be parent to one's sibling — is here brought about deliberately, albeit without any act of coitus. Moreover, all other relationships will be confounded. What will *father, grandfather, aunt, cousin,* and *sister* mean? Who will bear what ties and what burdens? What sort of social identity will someone have with one whole side "father's" or "mother's" — necessarily excluded? It is no answer to say that our society, high incidence of divorce, remarriage, adoption, extramarital child-bearing, and the rest, already confounds lineage and confuses kinship and responsibility for children (and everyone else), unless one also wants to argue that this is, for children, a preferable state of affairs.

Human cloning would also represent a giant step toward turning begetting into making, procreation into manufacture (literally, something "handmade"), a process already begun with in vitro fertilization and genetic testing of embryos. With cloning, not only is the process in hand, but the total genetic blueprint of the cloned individual is selected and determined by the human artisans. To be sure, subsequent development will take place according to natural processes; and the resulting children will still be recognizably human. But we here would be taking a major step into making man himself simply another one of the man-made things. Human nature becomes merely the last part of nature to succumb to the technological project, which turns all of nature into raw material at human disposal, to be homogenized by our rationalized technique according to the subjective prejudices of the day.

How does begetting differ from making? In natural procreation, human beings come together, complementarily male and female, to give existence to another being who is formed, exactly as we were, *by what we are:* living, hence perishable, hence aspiringly erotic, human beings. In clonal reproduction, by contrast, and in the more advanced forms of manufacture to which it leads, we give existence to a being not by what we are but by what we intend and design. As with any product of our making, no matter how excellent, the artificer stands above it, not as an equal but as a superior, transcending it by his will and creative prowess. Scientists who clone animals make it perfectly clear that they are engaged in instrumental making; the animals are, from the start, designed as means to serve rational human purposes. In human cloning, scientists and prospective "parents" would be adopting the same technocratic mentality to human children: human children would be their artifacts.

Such an arrangement is profoundly dehumanizing, no matter how good the product. Mass-scale cloning of the same individual makes the point vividly; but the violation of human equality, freedom, and dignity is present even in a single planned clone. And procreation dehumanized into manufacture is further degraded by commodification, a virtually inescapable result of allowing baby-making to proceed under the banner of commerce. Genetic and reproductive biotechnology companies are already growth industries, but they will go into commercial orbit once the [federal government's] Human Genome Project nears completion. Supply will create enormous demand. Even before the capacity for human cloning arrives, established companies will have invested in the harvesting of eggs from ovaries obtained at autopsy or through ovarian surgery, practiced embryonic genetic alteration, and initiated the stockpiling of prospective donor tissues. Through the rental of surrogate-womb services and through the buying and selling of tissues and embryos, priced according to the merit of the donor, the commodification of nascent human life will be unstoppable.

Finally, and perhaps most important, the practice of human cloning by nuclear transfer — like other anticipated forms of genetic engineering of the next generation — would enshrine and aggravate a profound and mischievous misunderstanding of the meaning of having children and of the parent–child relationship. When a couple now chooses to procreate, the partners are saying yes to the emergence of new life in its novelty, saying yes not only to having a child but also, tacitly, to having whatever child the child turns out to be. In accepting our finitude and opening ourselves to our replacement, we are tacitly confessing the limits of our control. In this ubiquitous way of nature, embracing the future by procreating means precisely that we are relinquishing our grip, in the very activity of taking up our own share in what we hope will be the immortality of human life and the human species. This means that our children are not *our* children: they are not our property, not our possessions. Neither are they supposed to live our lives for us, or anyone else's life but their own. To be sure, we seek to guide them on their way, imparting to them not just life but nurturing, love, and a way of life; to be sure, they bear our hopes that they will live fine and flourishing lives, enabling us in small measure to transcend our own limitations. Still, their genetic distinctiveness and independence are the natural foreshadowing of the deep truth that they have their own and never-before-enacted life to live. They are sprung from a past, but they take an uncharted course into the future.

Much harm is already done by parents who try to live vicariously through their children. Children are sometimes compelled to fulfill the broken dreams of unhappy parents; John Doe, Jr., or John Doe III is under the burden of having to live up to his forebear's name. Still, if most parents have hopes for their children, cloning parents will have expectations. In cloning, such overbearing parents take at the start a decisive step that contradicts the entire meaning of the open and forward-looking nature of parent–child relations. The child is given a genotype that has already lived, with full expectation that the blueprint of a past life ought to be controlling of the life that is to come. Cloning is inherently despotic, for it seeks to make one's children (or someone else's children) after one's own image (or an image of one's choosing) and their future according to one's will. In some cases the despotism may be mild and benevolent. In other cases it will be mischievous and downright tyrannical. But despotism — the control of another through one's will — it inevitably will be.

MEETING SOME OBJECTIONS

The defenders of cloning, of course, are not wittingly friends of despotism. Indeed, they regard themselves mainly as friends of freedom: the freedom of individuals to reproduce, the freedom of scientists and inventors to discover and devise and to foster "progress" in genetic knowledge and technique. They want large-scale cloning only for animals, but they wish to preserve cloning as a human option for exercising our "right to reproduce" — our right to have children, and children with "desirable genes." As law professor John Robertson points out, under our "right to reproduce" we already practice early forms; of unnatural, artificial, and extramarital reproduction, and we already practice early form of eugenic choice. For that reason, he argues, cloning is no big deal.

We have here a perfect example of the logic of the slippery slope, and the slippery way in which it already works in that area. Only a few years ago, slippery-slope arguments were advanced to oppose artificial insemination and in vitro fertilization using unrelated sperm donors. Principles used to justify those practices, it was said, will be used to justify more artificial and more eugenic practices, including cloning. Not so, the defenders retorted, since we can make the necessary distinctions. And now, without even a gesture at making the necessary distinctions, the continuity of practice is held by itself to be justificatory.

The principle of reproductive freedom as currently enunciated by the proponents of cloning logically embraces the ethical acceptability of sliding down the entire rest of the slope — to producing children ectogenetically from sperm to term (should it become feasible) and to producing children whose entire genetic makeup will be the product of parental eugenic planning and choice. If reproductive freedom means the right to have a child of one's own choosing, by whatever means, it knows and accepts no limits.

But, far from being legitimated by a "right to reproduce," the emergence of techniques of assisted reproduction and genetic engineering should compel us to reconsider the meaning and limits of such a putative right. In truth, a "right to reproduce" has always been a peculiar and problematic notion. Rights generally belong to individuals, but this is a right that (before cloning) no one can exercise alone. Does the right then inhere only in couples? Only in married couples? Is it a (woman's) right to carry or deliver or a right (of one or more parents) to nurture and rear? Is it a right to have your own biological child? Is it a right only to attempt reproduction or a right also to succeed? Is it a right to acquire the baby of one's choice?

The assertion of a negative "right to reproduce" certainly makes sense when it claims protection against state interference with procreative liberty, say, through a program of compulsory sterilization. But surely it cannot be the basis of a tort claim against nature, to be made good by technology, should free efforts at natural procreation fail. Some insist that the right to reproduce embraces also the right against state interference with the free use of all technological means to obtain a child. Yet such a position cannot be sustained: for reasons having to do with the means employed, any community may rightfully prohibit surrogate pregnancy, polygamy, or the sale of babies to infertile couples without violating anyone's basic human "right to reproduce." When the exercise of a previously innocuous freedom now involves or impinges on troublesome practices that the original freedom never was intended to reach, the general presumption of liberty needs to be reconsidered.

We do indeed already practice negative eugenic selection, through genetic screening and prenatal diagnosis. Yet our practices are governed by a norm of health. We seek to prevent the birth of children who suffer from known (serious) genetic diseases. When and if gene therapy becomes possible, such diseases could then be treated, in utero or even before implantation. I have no ethical objection in principle to such a practice (though I have some practical worries), precisely because it serves the medical goal of healing existing individuals. But therapy, to be therapy, implies not only an existing "patient." It also implies a norm of health. In this respect, even germline gene "therapy," though practiced not on a human being but on egg and sperm, is less radical than cloning, which is in no way therapeutic. But once one blurs the distinction between health promotion and genetic enhancement, between so-called negative and positive eugenics, one opens the door to all future eugenic designs. "To make sure that a child will be healthy and have good chances in life": that is Robertson's principle, and, owing to its latter clause, it is an utterly elastic principle, with no boundaries. Being over eight feet tall, will likely produce some very good chances in life, and so will having the looks of Marilyn Monroe, and so will a genius-level intelligence.

Proponents want us to believe that there are legitimate uses of cloning that can be distinguished from illegitimate uses, but by their own principles no such limits can be found. (Nor could any such limits be enforced in practice.) Reproductive freedom, as they understand it, is governed solely by the subjective wishes of the parents-to-be (plus the avoidance of bodily harm to the child). The sentimentally appealing case of the childless married couple is, on those grounds, indistinguishable from the case of an individual (married or not) who would like to clone someone famous or talented, living or dead. Further, the principle here endorsed justifies not only cloning but, indeed, all future artificial attempts to create (manufacture) "perfect" babies.

A concrete example will show how, in practice no less than in principle, the so-called innocent case will merge with, or even turn into, the more troubling ones.

In practice, the eager parent-to-be will necessarily be subject to the tyranny of expertise. Consider an infertile married couple, she lacking eggs or he lacking sperm, that wants a child of their (genetic) own and proposes to clone either husband or wife. The scientist-physician (who is also coowner of the cloning company) points out the likely difficulties: A cloned child is not really their (genetic) child, but the child of only *one* of them; that imbalance may produce strains on the marriage; the child might suffer identity confusion; there is a risk of perpetuating the cause of sterility. The scientist-physician also points out the advantages of choosing a donor nucleus. Far better than a child of their own would be a child of their own choosing. Touting his own expertise in selecting healthy and talented donors, the doctor presents the couple with his latest catalog containing the pictures, the health records, and the accomplishments of his stable of cloning donors, samples of whose tissues are in his deep freeze. Why not, dearly beloved, a more perfect baby?

The "perfect baby," of course, is the project not of the infertility doctors, but of the eugenic scientists and their supporters. For them, the paramount right is not the so-called right to reproduce but what biologist Bentley Glass called, a quarter of a century ago, "the right of every child to be born with a sound physical and mental constitution, based on a sound genotype . . . the inalienable right to a sound heritage." But to secure that right and to achieve the requisite quality control over new human life, human conception and gestation will need to be brought fully into the bright light of the laboratory, beneath which the child-to-be can be fertilized, nourished, pruned, weeded, watched, inspected, prodded, pinched, cajoled, injected, tested, rated, graded, approved, stamped, wrapped, sealed, and delivered. There is no other way to produce the perfect baby.

Yet we are urged by proponents of cloning to forget about the science fiction scenarios of laboratory manufacture and multiple-copied clones and to focus only on the homely cases of infertile couples exercising their reproductive rights. But why, if the single cases are so innocent, should multiplying their performance be so off-putting? (Similarly, why do others object to people's making money from that practice if the practice itself is perfectly acceptable?) When we follow the sound ethical principle of universalizing our choice — would it be right if everyone cloned a Wilt Chamberlain (with his consent, of course)? would it be right if everyone decided to practice asexual reproduction? — we discover what is wrong with such seemingly innocent cases. The so-called science fiction cases make vivid the meaning of what looks to us, mistakenly, to be benign.

Though I recognize certain continuities between cloning and, say, in vitro fertilization, I believe that cloning differs in essential and important ways. Yet those who disagree should be reminded that the "continuity" argument cuts both ways. Sometimes we establish bad precedents and discover that they were bad only when we follow their inexorable logic to places we never meant to go. Can the defenders of cloning show us today how, on their principles, we shall be able to see producing babies ("perfect babies") entirely in the laboratory or exercising full control over their genotypes (including so-called enhancement) as ethically different, in any essential way, from present forms of assisted reproduction? Or are they willing to admit, despite their attachment to the principle of continuity, that the complete obliteration of "mother" or "father," the complete depersonalization of procreation, the complete manufacture of human beings, and the complete genetic control of one generation over the next would be ethically problematic and essentially different from current forms of assisted reproduction? If so, where and how will they draw the line, and why? I draw it at cloning, for all the reasons given.

BAN THE CLONING OF HUMANS

What, then, should we do? We should declare that human cloning is unethical in itself and dangerous in its likely consequences. In so doing, we shall have the backing of the overwhelming majority of our fellow Americans, of the human race, and (I believe) of most practicing scientists. Next, we should do all that we can to prevent the cloning of human beings. We should do that by means of an international legal ban if possible and by a unilateral national ban at a minimum. Scientists may secretly undertake to violate such a law, but they will be deterred by not being able to stand up proudly to claim the credit for their technological bravado and success. Such a ban on clonal baby-making, moreover, will not harm the progress of basic genetic science and technology. On the contrary, it will reassure the public that scientists are happy to proceed without violating the deep ethical norms and institutions of the human community.

* * *

The president's call for a moratorium on human cloning has given us an important opportunity. In a truly unprecedented way, we can strike a blow for the human control of the technological project, for wisdom, prudence, and human dignity. The prospect of human cloning, so repulsive to contemplate, is the occasion for deciding whether we shall be slaves of unregulated progress, and ultimately its artifacts, or whether we shall remain free human beings who guide our technique toward the enhancement of human dignity.

PART VI
Dilemmas of New Technology II:
The Information Age

While many of the social impacts of the new genetics are speculative and in the future, the impacts of the information technology are being felt right now. Computers, especially personal computers, are a part most people's lives in the United States at the turn of the millennium. Increasingly, moreover, having a PC means being connected to the Internet. Computers began to have to substantial effects on human work, on power and control in society, and on social and economic equity decades ago. But the Internet, which, in the space of a decade, has exploded into an entirely new medium of communication, has intensified these effects, added new ones, and accelerated the pace at which they are being felt.

In the first article in Part VI, Tom Forester and Perry Morrison survey the social problems and the range of ethical issues raised by developments in information technology — issues that face computer users as well as computer professionals. Although their analysis is several years old (which can be an eternity in the fast-moving world of information technology), the issues it covers still provide a solid introduction to information age dilemmas.

Fred Cate examines some of the most difficult questions posed by information technology, those associated with privacy. As we conduct more and more of our affairs on-line — banking, shopping, searching for information, entertaining ourselves — we provide increasing opportunities for others to learn about our habits, our interests, the state of our health, and our finances and to connect information about us from various sources into a picture that may challenge traditional notions of personal privacy.

Shoshana Zuboff, finally, reports on a major study of how information technology ("the smart machine") is shaping the working lives of men and women and the nature of work itself. Zuboff's influential writings are helping workers and managers alike to understand both the challenges and the opportunities created by computers in the workplace.

Although the three articles in this section address only a small subset of the many social, political, and economic issues raised by the information age, there is more on this subject in the book. Some rather different perspectives on information technology issues can be found in the debate between Nicholas Negroponte and Donald Norman in Part VII.

22. Computer Ethics

TOM FORESTER AND PERRY MORRISON

The technologies of computers, computer networks, and information processing figure in numerous readings throughout this book. As Forester and Morrison put it, "Computers are the core technology of our times." During the past forty-five years (and especially in the last two decades), they have become central to the functioning of our society. As we have become increasingly dependent on computers and networks, we have become more vulnerable to their malfunctions and their misuse. Examples abound. Forester and Morrison cite case after case, including hacker break-ins to military computers, software bugs causing aircraft accidents, software and hardware sabotage disruptions of telephone service, and the shutdown of four major U.S. air traffic control centers caused by a farmer cutting a fiber optic cable while burying a dead cow.

The pervasiveness of computer technology and its susceptibility to misuse and malfunction raise a great many ethical, social, and legal issues. How can the intellectual property rights of software developers be protected when copying software is easy and widely practiced? Are hackers criminals or just pranksters? Is electronic mail private, or do employers have the right to monitor their employees' communications? Are computer professionals legally or ethically responsible for the consequences of flaws in the systems they have created? These and other questions are the subject of Forester and Morrison's highly readable and provocative introduction to the increasingly important subject of computer ethics.

Until his death in late 1993, Tom Forester was a senior lecturer in the School of Computer and Information Technology at Griffith University in Queensland, Australia. He was the editor or author of seven books on social aspects of computing. Perry Morrison lectures on psychology at the National University of Singapore.

Computers are the core technology of out times. They are the new paradigm, the new "common sense." In the comparatively short space of forty years, computers have become central to the operations of industrial societies. Without computers and computer networks, much of manufacturing industry, commerce, transport and distribution, government, the military, health services, education, and research would simply grind to a halt.

Computers are certainly the most important technology to have come along this century, and the current Information Technology Revolution may in time equal or even exceed the Industrial Revolution in terms of social significance. We are still trying to understand the full implications of the computerization that has already taken place in key areas of society such as the workplace. Computers and computer-based information and communication systems will have an even greater impact on our way of life in the next millennium — now just a few years away.

Yet as society becomes more dependent on computers and computer networks, we also become more and more vulnerable to computer malfunctions (usually caused by unreliable software) and to computer misuse — that is, to the misuse of computers and computer networks by human beings. Malfunctioning computers and the misuse of computers have created a whole new range of social problems, such as computer crime, software theft, hacking, the creation of viruses, invasions of privacy, overreliance on intelligent machines, and workplace stress. In turn, each of these problems creates ethical dilemmas for computer professionals and users. Ethical theory and professional codes of ethics can help us resolve these ethical dilemmas to some extent, while computing educators have a special responsibility to try to ensure more ethical behavior among future generations of computer users.

OUR COMPUTERIZED SOCIETY

When computers hit the headlines, it usually results in bad publicity for them. When power supplies fail, phone systems go down, air traffic control systems seize up, or traffic lights go on the blink, there is nearly always a spokesperson ready to blame the problem on a luckless computer. When public utilities, credit-checking agencies, the police, tax departments, or motor vehicle license centers make hideous mistakes, they invariably blame it on computer error. When the bank or the airline cannot process our transaction, we're told that "the computer is down" or that "we're having problems with our computer." The poor old computer gets the blame on these and many other occasions, although frequently something else is at fault. Even when the problem is computer-related, the ultimate cause of failure is human error rather than machine error, because humans design the computers and write the software that tells computers what to do.

Computers have been associated with some major blunders in recent times. For instance, the infamous hole in the ozone layer remained undetected for seven years because of a program design error. No less than twenty-two U.S. servicemen died in the early 1980s in five separate crashes of the U.S. Air Force's Blackhawk helicopter as a result of radio interference with its novel, computer-based fly-by-wire system. At least four people died in North America because of computer glitches in the Therac-25 cancer radiotherapy machine, while similar disasters have been reported recently in England and Spain. During the 1991 Gulf war, software failure in the Patriot missile defense system enabled an Iraqi Scud missile to penetrate the U.S. military barracks in Dhahran, killing twenty-eight people, while the notorious trouble with the Hubble space telescope in the same year was exacerbated by a programming error that shut down the onboard computer.[1]

In fact, computers have figured one way or another in almost every famous system failure, from Three Mile Island, Chernobyl, and the Challenger space shuttle disaster, to the Air New Zealand antarctic crash and the downing of the Korean Air Lines flight 007 over Sakhalin Island, not to mention the sinking of HMS *Sheffield* in the Falklands war and the shooting down of an Iranian Airbus by the USS *Vincennes* over the Persian Gulf. A software bug lay behind the massive New York phone failure of January 1990, which shut down AT&T's phone network and New York's airports for nine hours, while a system design error helped shut down New York's phones for another four hours in September 1991 (key AT&T engineers were away at a seminar on how to cope with emergencies). A whole series of aerospace accidents such as the French, Indian, and Nepalese A320 Airbus disasters, the Bell V-22 Osprey and Northrop YF-23 crashes, and the downing of the Lauda Air Boeing 767 in Thailand has been attributed to unreliable software in computerized fly-by-wire systems. Undeterred, engineers are now developing sail-by-wire navigation systems for ships and drive-by-wire systems for our cars.[2]

Computers and computer networks are vulnerable to physical breaches such as fires, floods, earthquakes, and power cuts — including very short power spikes or voltage sags ("dirty power") that can be enough to knock out a sensitive system. A good example was the fire in the Setagaya telephone office in Tokyo in 1984 that instantly cut 3,000 data and 89,000 telephone lines and resulted in huge losses for Japanese businesses. Communication networks are also vulnerable to inadvertent human or animal intervention. For instance, increasingly popular fiber optic cables, containing thousands of phone circuits, have been devoured by hungry beavers in Missouri, foxes in outback Australia, and sharks and beam-trawling fishermen in the Pacific Ocean. In January 1991, a clumsy New Jersey repair crew sliced through a major optical fiber artery, shutting down New York's phones for a further six hours, while similar breaks have been reported from Chicago, Los Angeles, and Washington, D.C. The Federal Aviation Administration recently recorded the shutdown of four major U.S. air traffic control centers. The cause? "Fiber cable cut by farmer burying dead cow," said the official report.[3]

Computers and communication systems are also vulnerable to physical attacks by humans and to software sabotage by outside hackers and inside employees. For example, a saboteur entered telecommunications tunnels in Sydney, Australia, one day in 1987 and carefully severed twenty-four cables, knocking out 35,000 telephone lines in forty Sydney suburbs and bringing down hundreds of computers, automated teller machines (ATMs), and point of sale (POS), telex, and fax terminals with it. Some businesses were put out of action for forty-eight hours as engineers battled to restore services. Had the saboteur not been working with an out-of-date plan, the whole of Australia's telecommunications system might have been blacked out. In Chicago in 1986, a disgruntled employee at Encyclopaedia Brittanica, angry at having been laid off, merely tapped into the encyclopedia's database, and made a few alterations to the text being prepared for a new edition of the renowned work — like changing references to Jesus Christ to Allah and inserting the names of company executives in odd positions. As one executive commented, "In the computer age, this is exactly what we have nightmares about."[4]

Our growing dependency on computers has been highlighted further in recent years by such incidents as the theft in the former Soviet Union in 1990 of computer disks containing medical information on some 670,000 people exposed to radiation in the Chernobyl nuclear disaster. The disks were simply wiped and then resold by the teenaged thieves. In 1989, vital information about the infamous Alaskan oil spill was "inadvertently" destroyed at a stroke by an Exxon computer operator. In the same year, U.S. retailer Montgomery Ward allegedly discovered one of its warehouses in California that had been lost for three years because of an error in its master inventory program. Apparently, one day the trucks stopped arriving at the warehouse: nothing came in or went out. But the paychecks were issued on a different system, so for three whole years (so the story goes) the employees went to work every day, moved boxes around, and submitted timecards — without ever telling company headquarters. "It was a bit like a job with the government," said one worker after the blunder had been discovered.[5]

In Amsterdam, Holland, in 1991, the body of an old man who had died six months earlier was found in an apartment by a caretaker who had been concerned about a large pile of mail for him. The man had been something of a recluse, but because his rent, gas, and electricity bills were paid automatically by computer, he wasn't missed. His pension also had been transferred into his bank account every month, so all the relevant authorities assumed that he was still alive. Another particularly disturbing example of computer dependency came from London during the Gulf war, when computer disks containing the Allies' plans for Desert Storm disappeared, along with a laptop computer, from a parked car belonging to Wing Commander David Farquhar of the Royal Air Force Strike Command. Luckily for the Allies, the thieves did not recognize the value of the unencrypted data, which did not fall into Iraqi hands. But a court-martial for negligence and breach of security awaited Farquhar.[6]

Computers are changing our way of life in all sorts of ways. At work, we may have our performance monitored by computer and our electronic mail read by the boss. It's no good trying to delete embarrassing e-mail statements because someone probably will have a backup copy of what you wrote. This is what happened to White House adviser Colonel Oliver North and to John Poindexter, the former national security adviser to President Ronald Reagan, when they tried to cover up evidence of the Iran-Contra scandal. Poindexter allegedly sat up all night deleting 5,012 e-mail messages, while North destroyed a further 736, but unknown to Poindexter and North the messages were all preserved on backup tapes that were subsequently read by congressional investigators. And if you use a spell-checker or language-corrector in your word processing program, be sure that it doesn't land you in trouble. For example, the *Fresno Bee* newspaper in California recently had to run a correction that read: "An item in Thursday's Nation Digest about the Massachusetts budget crisis made reference to new taxes that will help 'put Massachusetts back in the African-American.' This item should have read 'put Massachusetts back in the black.'"[7]

Recent government reports have confirmed that our growing dependence on computers leaves society increasingly vulnerable to software bugs, physical accidents, and attacks on critical systems. In 1989, a report to the U.S. Congress from one of its subcommittees, written by James H. Paul and Gregory C. Simon, found that the U.S. government was wasting millions of dollars a year on software that was overdue, inadequate, unsafe, and riddled with bugs. In 1990, the Canadian auditor-general, Ken Dye, warned that most of the Canadian government's computer systems were vulnerable to physical or logical attack: "That's like running a railroad without signals or a busy airport without traffic controls," he said. In 1991, a major report by the System Security Study Committee of the U.S. National Academy of Sciences, published as *Computers at Risk,* called for improved security, safety, and reliability in computer systems. The report declared that society was becoming more vulnerable to "poor system design, accidents that disable systems, and attacks on computer systems."[8]

SOME NEW SOCIAL PROBLEMS CREATED BY COMPUTERS

Although society as a whole derives benefit from the use of computers and computer networks, computerization has created some serious problems for society that were largely unforeseen.

We classify the new social problems created by computers into seven main categories: computer crime and the problem of computer security; software theft and the question of intellectual property rights; the new phenomena of hacking and the creation of viruses; computer unreliability and the key question of software quality; data storage and the invasion of privacy; the social implications of artificial intelligence and expert systems; and the many problems associated with workplace computerization.

These new problems have proved to be costly: computer crime costs companies millions of dollars a year, while software producers lose staggering sums as a result of widespread software theft. In recent years, huge amounts of time and money have had to be devoted to repairing the damage to systems caused by the activities of malicious hackers and virus creators. Unreliable hardware and software costs society untold billions every year in terms of downtime, cost overruns, and abandoned systems, while invasions of privacy and database mix-ups have resulted in expensive lawsuits and much individual stress. Sophisticated expert systems lie unused for fear of attracting lawsuits, and workplace stress caused by inappropriate computerization costs society millions in absenteeism, sickness benefits, and reduced productivity.

Computer crime is a growing problem for companies, according to recent reports. Every new technology introduced into society creates new opportunities for crime, and information technology is no exception. A new generation of high-tech criminals is busy stealing data, doctoring data, and threatening to destroy data for monetary gain. New types of fraud made possible by computers include ATM fraud, EFT (electronic funds transfer) fraud, EDI (electronic data interchange) fraud, mobile phone fraud, cable TV fraud, and telemarketing fraud. Desktop printing (DTP) has even made desktop forgery possible. Perhaps the biggest new crime is phone fraud, which may be costing American companies as much as $2 billion a year. Most analysts think that reported computer crime is just the tip of an iceberg of underground digital deviance that sees criminals and the crime authorities competing to stay one jump ahead of each other.

Software theft or the illegal copying of software is a major problem that is costing software producers an estimated $12 billion a year. Recent cases of software piracy highlight the prevalence of software copying and the worldwide threat posed by organized software pirates. Computer users and software developers tend to have very different ethical positions on the question of copying software, while the law in most countries is confusing and out of date. There is an ongoing debate about whether copyright law or patent law provides the most appropriate protection for software. Meanwhile the legal position in the United States, for example, has been confused further by the widely varying judgments handed down by U.S. courts in recent years. The recent rash of look and feel suits launched by companies such as Lotus and Apple have muddied the waters still further. The central question facing the information technology (IT) industry is how to reward innovation without stifling creativity, but there is no obvious answer to this conundrum and no consensus as to what constitutes ethical practice.

Attacks by hackers and virus creators on computer systems have proved enormously costly to computer operators. In recent cases, hackers have broken into university computers in order to alter exam results, downloaded software worth millions, disrupted the 911 emergency phone system in the United States, stolen credit card numbers, hacked into U.S. military computers and sold the stolen data to the KGB, and blackmailed London banks into employing them as security advisers. Hackers also have planted viruses that have caused computer users untold misery in recent years. Viruses have erased files, damaged disks, and completely shut down systems. For example, the famous Internet worm, let loose by Cornell student Robert Morris in 1988, badly damaged 6,000 systems across the United States. There is ongoing debate about whether hackers can sometimes function as guardians of our civil liberties, but in most countries the response to the hacking craze has been new security measures, new laws such as Britain's Computer Misuse Act (1990), and new calls for improved network ethics. Peter J. Denning, editor-in-chief of *Communications of the ACM*, says that we must expect increasing attacks on computers by hackers and virus creators in the years ahead; Professor Lance J. Hoffman has called for all new computers to be fitted with antiviral protection as standard equipment, rather like seat belts on cars.[9]

Unreliable computers are proving to be a major headache for modern society. Computer crashes or downtime — usually caused by buggy software — are estimated to cost the United States as much as $4 billion a year, according to a recent report. When bug-ridden software has been used to control fly-by-wire aircraft, railroad signals, and ambulance dispatch systems, the cost of unreliable computers sometimes has had to be measured in terms of human lives. Computers tend to be unreliable because they are digital devices prone to total failure and because their complexity ensures that they cannot be tested thoroughly before use. Massive complexity can make computer systems completely, unmanageable and can result in huge cost overruns or budget runaways. For example, in 1988 the Bank of America had to abandon an $80 million computer system that failed to work, while in 1992 American Airlines announced a loss of over $100 million on a runaway computer project. The Wessex Regional Health Authority in England scrapped a system in 1990 that had cost $60 million, and Blue Cross & Blue Shield of Massachusetts pulled the plug in 1992 on a project that had cost a staggering $120 million. U.S. Department of Defense runaways are rumored to have easily exceeded these sums. Computer scientists are exploring a variety of ways to improve software quality, but progress with this key problem is slow.[10]

The problem of safeguarding privacy in a society where computers can store, manipulate, and transmit at a stroke vast quantities of information about individuals is proving to be intractable. In recent years, a whole series of database disasters involving mistaken identities, data mix-ups, and doctored data have indicated that we probably place too much faith in information stored on computers. People have had their driver's license and credit records altered or stolen and their lives generally made a misery by inaccurate computer records. There is growing concern about the volume and the quality of the data stored by the FBI's National Crime Information Center (NCIC), the United Kingdom's Police National Computer (PNC), and other national security agencies. (Such concerns even led to a public riot in Switzerland in 1990.) Moreover, new controversies have erupted over the privacy aspects of such practices as calling number identification (CNID) on phone networks, the monitoring of e-mail (by employers such as Nissan and Epson and, it seems, the mayor of Colorado Springs), and the phenomenon of database marketing, which involves the sale of mailing lists and other personal information to junk mailers (in 1990, Lotus and Equifax were forced to drop their Lotus Marketplace: Households, which put on disk personal information about 120 million Americans). Governments around the world are now being pushed into tightening privacy laws.[11]

The arrival of expert systems and primitive forms of artificial intelligence (AI) have generated a number of technical, legal, and ethical problems that have yet to be resolved. Technical problems have seriously slowed progress toward the Holy Grail of AI, while many are now asking whether computers could ever be trusted to make medical, legal, judicial, political, and administrative judgments. Given what we know about bugs in software, some are saying that it will never be safe to let computers run, for instance, air traffic control systems and nuclear power stations without human expert backup. Legal difficulties associated with product liability laws have meant that nobody dares use many of the expert systems that have been developed. In addition, AI critics are asking serious ethical questions, such as: Is AI a proper goal for humanity? Do we really need to replace humans in so many tasks when there is so much unemployment?[12]

Because paid employment is still central to the lives of most people and, according to the U.S. Bureau of Labor Statistics, about 46 million Americans now work with computers, workplace computerization is clearly an important issue. Indeed, it has proved to be fertile ground for controversies, debates, and choices about the quantity of work available and the quality of working life. While the 1980s did not see massive technological unemployment precisely because of the slow and messy nature of IT implementation, there is now renewed concern that computers are steadily eroding job opportunities in manufacturing and services. Moreover, concern about the impact of computers on the quality of working life has increased with the realization that managers can go in very different directions with the design and implementation of new work systems. Computers have the ability to enhance or degrade the quality of working life, depending upon the route chosen. Computer monitoring of employees has become a controversial issue, as have the alleged health hazards of computer keyboard usage, which has resulted recently in some celebrated RSI (repetitive strain injury) legal suits against employers and computer vendors.[13]

ETHICAL DILEMMAS FOR COMPUTER USERS

Each of the new social problems just outlined generates all sorts of ethical dilemmas for computer users. Some of these dilemmas — such as whether or not to copy software — are entirely new, while others are new versions of old moral issues such as right and wrong, honesty, loyalty, responsibility, confidentiality, trust, accountability, and fairness. Some of these ethical dilemmas are faced by all computer users; others are faced only by computer professionals. But many of these dilemmas constitute new gray areas for which there are few accepted rules or social conventions, let alone established legal case law.

Another way of saying that computers create new versions of old moral issues is to say that information technology transforms the context in which old ethical issues arise and adds interesting new twists to old problems.[14] These issues arise from the fact that computers are machines that control other machines and from the specific, revolutionary characteristics of IT. Thus new storage devices allow us to store massive amounts of information, but they also generate new ethical choices about access to that information and about the use or misuse of that information. Ethical issues concerning privacy, confidentiality, and security thus come to the fore. The arrival of new media such as e-mail, bulletin boards, faxes, mobile phones, and EDI has generated new ethical and legal issues concerning user identity, authenticity, the legal status of such communications, and whether or not free speech protection and/or defamation law applies to them.

IT provides powerful new capabilities such as monitoring, surveillance, data linking, and database searching. These capabilities can be utilized wisely and ethically, or they can be used to create mischief, to spy on people, and to profit from new scams. IT transforms relationships between people, depersonalizing human contact and replacing it with instant, paperless communication. This phenomenon can sometimes lead people into temptation by creating a false sense of reality and by disguising the true nature of their actions, such as breaking into a computer system. IT transforms relationships between individuals and organizations, raising new versions of issues such as accountability and responsibility. Finally, IT unreliability creates new uncertainties and a whole series of ethical choices for those who operate complex systems and those who design and build them. Computer producers and vendors too often neglect to adequately consider the eventual users of their systems, yet they should not escape responsibility for the consequences of their system design.[15]

Under the heading of computer crime and security, a number of ethical issues have been raised — despite the fact that the choice of whether or not to commit a crime should not present a moral dilemma for most people. For example, some have sought to make a distinction between crimes against other persons and so-called victimless crimes against, for example, banks, phone companies, and computer companies. While not wishing to excuse victimless crimes, some have suggested that they somehow be placed in a less serious category, especially when it comes to sentencing. Yet it is hard to accept that a company is any less a victim than an individual when it is deprived of its wealth. Because so many computer criminals appear to be first-time offenders who have fallen victim to temptation, do employers bear any responsibility for misdeeds that have occurred on their premises? And how far should employers or security agencies be allowed to go in their attempts to prevent or detect crime? (Should they be allowed to monitor e-mail or spy on people in toilets, for example?)

The ease with which computer software can be copied presents ethical dilemmas to computer users and professionals almost every day of the year. Some justify the widespread copying of software because everybody else does it or because the cost of well-known software packages is seen as too high. But copying software is a form of stealing and a blatant infringement of the developer's intellectual property rights. In the past, intellectual property such as literary works and mechanical inventions was protected by copyright and patents, but software is a new and unique hybrid. How do we protect the rights of software developers so as to ensure that innovation in the industry continues? What does the responsible computer professional do? Is all copying of software wrong, or are some kinds worse than others? How should the individual user behave when the law is unclear and when people in the industry disagree as to what constitutes ethical practice?

The new phenomena of computer hacking and the creation of computer viruses have raised many unresolved ethical questions. Is hacking merely harmless fun or is it the computer equivalent of burglary, fraud, and theft? When do high-tech high jinks become seriously criminal behavior? Because hacking almost always involves unauthorized access to other people's systems, should all hacking activity be considered unethical? What are we to make of hackers themselves? Are they well-intentioned guardians of our civil liberties and useful amateur security advisers, or are they mixed-up adolescents whose stock in trade is malicious damage and theft? Can the creation of viruses ever be justified in any circumstances? If not, what punishment should be meted out to virus creators? Finally, what should responsible individuals do if they hear of people who are hacking?

The reality of computer unreliability creates many ethical dilemmas, mainly for the computer professionals who are charged with creating and installing systems. Who is responsible when things go wrong? When a system malfunctions or completely crashes because of an error in a computer program, who is to blame — the original programmers, the system designer, the software supplier, or someone else?

More to the point, should system suppliers warn users that computer systems are prone to failure, are often too complex to be fully understood, have not been thoroughly tested before sale, and are likely to contain buggy software? Should software producers be made to provide a warranty on software? And to whom should individual computer professionals ultimately be responsible — the companies they work for, their colleagues, the customers, or the wider society?

The recurring issue of privacy confronts computer professionals and users in all sorts of contexts. First, there are general questions, such as what is privacy and how much of it are individuals entitled to, even in today's society. Does individual information stored on databases pose a threat to privacy? What right do governments and commercial organizations have to store personal information on individuals? What steps should be taken to ensure the accuracy of such information? Then there are the dilemmas faced by computer professionals and users over whether or not to use information collected for another purpose, whether to purchase personal information illicitly obtained, whether to link information in disparate databases, and so on. Practically every attempt to improve security (and sometimes even productivity) in organizations involves choices about the degree of privacy to which employees are entitled, while new controversies have arisen over the privacy aspects of e-mail and caller ID.

In a sense, the quest for artificial intelligence is one big ethical problem for the computing world because we have yet to determine whether AI is a proper goal — let alone a realistic goal — for humanity. Should computer professionals work on systems and devices that they know will make yet more humans redundant? Should we really be aiming to replace humans in more tasks? Isn't it somehow demeaning to human intelligence to put so much emphasis on making a machine version of it? Perhaps even more to the point, given what we know about computer unreliability, can we afford to trust our lives to artificially intelligent expert systems? What should be the attitude of responsible computer professionals: should they warn users of the risks involved or refuse to work on life-critical applications? Should they refuse to work on the many AI projects funded by the military? Moreover, should institutional users trust computers to make judicial, administrative, and medical judgments when human judgment has often proved to be superior?

Some might think that the workplace does not provide an obviously rich source of ethical dilemmas for computer professionals and users. Yet workplace computerization involves numerous choices for management about the type of system to be implemented, and different systems have radically different impacts on both the quantity and the quality of work. Generally speaking, computers in factories can be used to enhance the quality of working life, to improve job satisfaction, to provide more responsibility, and to upgrade or reskill the workforce; or, they can be used to get rid of as many people as possible and to turn those remaining into deskilled, degraded machine-minders, pressing buttons in a soulless, depersonalized environment. Office computerization can increase stress levels and thus health hazards if the new work process is badly designed or even if the new office furniture and equipment are badly designed. Employee monitoring often makes matters worse, while speedups and the creation of excessively repetitive tasks like keying-in data for hours can result in cases of repetitive strain injury. Computer professionals and managers have a responsibility to ensure that these outcomes are avoided.

HOW ETHICAL THEORY CAN HELP

"Ethics" has been defined as the code or set of principles by which people live. Ethics is about what is considered to be right and what is considered to be wrong. When people make ethical judgments, they are making prescriptive or normative statements about what ought to be done, not descriptive statements about what is being done.

But when people face ethical dilemmas in their everyday lives, they tend to make very different judgments about what is the right and what is the wrong thing to do. Ensuing discussions between the parties often remain unresolved because individuals find it hard to explain the reasoning behind their subjective, moral judgments. It is virtually impossible to conclude what ought to be the most appropriate behavior. Ethical theory — sometimes referred to as moral philosophy — is the study of the rules or principles that lie behind moral decisions. This theory helps provide us with a rational basis for moral judgments, enables us to classify and compare different ethical positions, and enables people to defend a particular position on a given issue. Thus the use of ethical theory can help us throw some light on the moral dilemmas faced by computer professionals and users and may even go some way toward determining how people ought to behave when using computers.[16]

Classical ethical theories are worth knowing because they provide useful background in some of the terminology, but they have limited relevance to everyday behavior in the IT industry. For example, Plato (429–347 B.C.) talked about the "good life," and much of his life was spent searching for the one good life. He also believed that an action was right or wrong in itself — a so-called objectivist (later, deontological) position. Aristotle (384–322 B.C.), on the other hand, adopted a more relativist and empiricist approach, arguing that there were many good and bad lives and that good lives were happy lives created by practicing "moderation in all things." Epicurus (341–270 B.C.) was the exact opposite, promoting hedonism, or the pursuit of pleasure, as the sole goal of life (although modern hedonists tend to forget that he also warned that too much pleasure was harmful and that the highest form of pleasure was practicing virtue and improving one's mind).

Diogenes (413–323 B.C.) was leader of the cynics, who believed that the world was fundamentally evil. The cynics were antisocial; they shunned public life and led an ascetic, privatized life — rising early, eating frugally, working hard, sleeping rough, and so on. Individual cynics found salvation in themselves and their honest life-style, not in worldly possessions. Modern cynics don't necessarily do this, but they are very distrustful of what they see as a thoroughly corrupt world. Finally, the stoics, such as Zeno (ca. 335–263 B.C.) and Epictetus (ca. 55–135 A.D.), were the essential fatalists, arguing that people should learn to accept whatever happened to them and that everything in the world occurs according to a plan that we do not understand. A true stoic believes that there is no such thing as good or evil and seeks to rise above the circumstances of everyday life, rejecting temptations, controlling emotions, and eschewing ambitions.

But probably the three most influential ethical theories of recent times — and the three of most likely relevance for our purposes — are ethical relativism (associated with Spinoza, 1632–1677), utilitarianism (J. S. Mill, 1806–1873) or consequentialism, and Kantianism (Kant, 1724–1804) or deontologism. Ethical relativism, which says that there are no universal moral norms, need not detain us for long, for it offers no guidance as to what is correct behavior. Ethical relativists merely point to the variety of behaviors in different cultures and conclude that the issue of right and wrong is all relative. Ethical relativism is a descriptive account of what is being done rather than a normative theory of what should be done. While it is true that people in different societies have different moralities, this does not prove that one morality might not be the correct one or that one might not constitute the universal moral code. Ethical relativism is not much use when trying to decide what is the right thing to do in today's world of computing.

Consequentialism and deontologism are much more relevant for our purposes. Consequentialism says simply that an action is right or wrong depending upon its consequences, such as its effects on society. Utilitarianism, as outlined by J. S. Mill and Jeremy Bentham, is one form of consequentialism. Its basic principle is that everyone should behave in such a way as to bring about the greatest happiness of the greatest number of people. Utilitarians arrive at this cardinal principle by arguing that happiness is the ultimate good because everything else in life is desired as a means of achieving happiness. Happiness is the ultimate goal of humans, and thus all actions must be evaluated on the basis of whether they increase or decrease human happiness. An action is therefore right or wrong depending upon whether it contributes to the sum total of human happiness.

By contrast, deontologism says that an action is right or wrong in itself. Deontologists stress the intrinsic character of an act and disregard motives or consequences. Thus a deontologist might say that the act of copying software is always wrong, regardless of other considerations, while a utilitarian might say that it was justified if it had a beneficial effect on society as a whole. Deontologists appear to be on particularly strong ground when they state, for example, that killing is wrong no matter what the circumstances, but they are on weaker ground when they say that lying is always wrong. Utilitarians would say that lying can be justified in certain circumstances, as in the case of white lies. On the other hand, utilitarians can find themselves in the position of defending actions that are morally wrong (like lying) or condoning actions that penalize the few in order to benefit the many (such as exploiting labor in a third world manufacturing plant). Consequentialists tend to look at the overall impact on society, whereas deontologists tend to focus on individuals and their rights. Kantians, in particular, argue strongly that people should always be treated as ends and never merely as means.

The distinction between consequentialists and deontologists is quite useful when we consider the ethical issues confronting computer professionals and users.

ETHICS AND THE COMPUTER PROFESSIONAL

Because computing is a relatively new field, the emerging computer profession has had neither the time nor the organizational capability to establish a binding set of moral rules or ethics. Older professions, like medicine and the law, have had centuries to formulate their codes of ethics and professional conduct. And there is another problem, too: the practice of computing, unlike the practice of medicine or the law, goes on outside the profession — this is an open field, with unfenced boundaries.

Computing, with its subdisciplines like software engineering, has not yet emerged as a full-fledged profession. Classic professions involve mental work, a high level of skill, and a lengthy period of training, and they perform some vital service to society — just like computing. But more than that, the classic profession is highly organized, with a central body that admits members only when they have achieved a certain level of skill. Although members have a considerable degree of autonomy, they are expected to exercise their professional judgment within the framework of a set of ethical principles laid down by the profession's central organization. Transgressors can be disciplined or even thrown out of the profession altogether. Some see the development of professions as a sign of a well-ordered, mature society, whereas critics have seen them as little more than self-serving protection rackets (the British author and playwright George Bernard Shaw once described all professions as "a conspiracy against the people").

So what sort of profession is computing? Members of the fledgling computer profession do not yet have the social status of doctors or lawyers. Instead, their status has been likened to that of engineers, who work mostly as employees rather than in their own right, who have esoteric knowledge but quite limited autonomy, and who often work in teams or on small segments of large projects rather than alone. Worryingly, they are often distant from the effects of their work. Yet despite the lower social status of computer professionals, the widespread use of information technology for storing all sorts of vital information puts considerable power into their hands, from the humble operator to the top systems developer. This power has not been sought specifically but arises from the nature of the technology. Computer professionals often find themselves in positions of power over employers, clients, coprofessionals, and the wider public, and this power can be abused easily by those without scruples or those who easily fall victim to temptation.[17]

Computer professionals face all sorts of ethical dilemmas in their everyday work life. First, although they have obligations to their employers, to the customers, to their coprofessionals, and to the general public, these obligations often come into conflict and need to be resolved one way or another. For example, what should be the response of a systems analyst whose employer insists on selling an overengineered, expensive system to gullible customers? Go along with the scam, or tell the customers that they are being duped? Second, almost every day the computer professional is confronted with issues of responsibility, intellectual property, and privacy. Who should take the blame when a system malfunctions or crashes? What attitude should professionals take when someone's intellectual property rights are clearly being infringed? How should they balance the need for greater system security with the right of individuals to privacy?

In an effort to help computer professionals cope with these kinds of conflicts, professional organizations such as the ACM (Association for Computing Machinery), the IEEE (Institute of Electrical and Electronics Engineers), the British Computer Society (BCS), and IFIP (International Federation for Information Processing) have been formulating and revising codes of ethics and professional conduct applicable to the IT industry. One problem with these codes is that they often have consisted mainly of motherhood statements like "I will avoid harm to others" and "I will always be honest and trustworthy." These proclamations could just as easily apply to any profession or walk of life and say nothing of specific relevance to computing. However, the new ACM code is much improved in this respect in that it talks about specific IT industry responsibilities. A more serious criticism is that these codes contain little in the way of sanctions by which their laudable aims could be enforced. A number of critics have pointed out that these codes have never been used and their language never interpreted. Furthermore, the codes usually have talked purely in terms of individuals being at fault and not whole organizations (although this, too, is addressed to some extent in the new IFIP and ACM codes).[18]

An even more fundamental difficulty with all such codes of ethics is that they don't necessarily do much to make people behave more ethically. The pressure, financial or otherwise, to conform with unethical industry practices is often too great. Thus, in a classic critique of professional ethics, John Ladd argued that attempts to develop professional codes of ethics are not only marked by intellectual and moral confusion (such as describing a code of conduct as ethics), they are also likely to fail. Codes of conduct, he says, are widely disregarded by members of professions. Worthy and inspirational though such codes may be, he says that their existence leads to complacency and to self-congratulation — and maybe even to the cover-up of unethical conduct. "Look, we have a code of ethics," professionals might say, "so everything we do must be ethical." The real objectives of such codes, Ladd says, are to enhance the image of the profession in the outside world and to protect the monopoly of the profession. In other words, they are a bit of window dressing designed to improve the status and the income of members.[19]

Another debate has arisen over suggestions that computer professionals be licensed or certified. Under this proposal, a programmer would have to obtain a certificate of competence before being allowed to work on major projects — especially those involving life-critical systems — and perhaps every computer user would have to obtain a kind of driver's license before being allowed onto the computer networks. Certification of software developers might help reduce the number of software project runaways. But there would be endless difficulties involved in measuring programming competence, and these problems could perhaps lead to religious wars in the profession![20] Moreover, there is a danger that certification could create a closed shop or craft guild that might exclude talented and innovative newcomers. On the other hand, it seems likely that some sort of certification safeguards will have to be introduced in the future to cover high-risk systems.

THE RESPONSIBILITY OF COMPUTING EDUCATORS

Recent well-publicized incidents of hacking, virus creation, computer-based fraud, and invasions of privacy have increased the pressure on computing educators to help instill a greater sense of responsibility in today's students. The world of computing has been portrayed in the media as a kind of electronic frontier society where a "shoot from the hip" mentality prevails. It is widely believed that there is far too much computerized anarchy and mayhem.

We believe that computing educators need to do three things. They must encourage tomorrow's computer professionals to behave in a more ethical, responsible manner for the long-term good of the IT industry. They also need to help make students aware of the social problems caused by computers and the social context in which computerization occurs. And they need to sensitize students to the kinds of moral dilemmas they will face in their everyday lives as computer professionals. Many of today's computer science undergraduates will go on to create systems that will have major impacts on people, organizations, and society in general. If those systems are to be successful economically and socially, graduates will need to know the lessons from the computerization story so far, the ethical and social issues involved, and the range of choices available to computer professionals.

NOTES

1. Sources for the ozone hole: *The New York Times*, Science section, 29 July 1986, page C1; the Blackhawk crashed: B. Cooper and D. Newkirk, *Risks to the Public in Computers and Related Systems*, on Internet, compiled by Peter G. Neumann, November 1987; Therac-25 and other radiation therapy cases: Jonathan Jacky, "Programmed for Disaster — Software Errors Imperil Lives," in *The Sciences*, September–October, 1989; Jonathan Jacky, "Risks in Medical Electronics," *Communications of the ACM*, vol. 33, no. 12, December 1990, page 138; "Patients Die after Radiation Mix-Up," *The Guardian*, London, 23 February 1991; John Arlidge, "Hospital Admits Errors in Treating Cancer Patients," *The Independent*, London, 7 February 1992; Patriot missile: *New York Times*, 21 May 1991, and *Patriot Missile Defense: Software Problem Led to System Failure at Dhahran, Saudi Arabia*, U.S. General Accounting Office, February 1992; Hubble trouble: *Software Engineering Notes*, vol. 17, no. 1, January 1992, page 3.
2. AT&T phone outages, January 1990 and September 1991: *Software Engineering Notes*, vol. 15, no. 2, April 1990, and vol. 16, no. 4, October 1991, pages 6–7; *Time*, 30 September 1991; *Fortune*, 13 January 1992; A320 crashes: "Airbus Safety Claim 'Cannot Be Proved,'" *New Scientist*, 7 September 1991, page 16, and successive reports in *Software Engineering Notes*, esp. vol. 13, 14, and 15; Osprey crashes: *Flight International*, 18–24 September 1991; *New Scientist*, 15 August 1792; YF-23 and other fly-by-wire glitches: *Software Engineering Notes*, vol. 16, no. 3, July 1991, pages 21–22; Lauda crash: various reports in *Software Engineering Notes*, vols. 16 and 17.

3. "The 'Dirty Power' Clogging Industry's Pipeline," *Business Week*, 8 April 1991; Naruko Taknashi et al., "The Anchilles Heel of the Information Society: Socioeconomic Impacts of the Telecommunications Cable Fire in the Setagaya Telephone Office, Tokyo," *Technological Forecasting and Social Change*, vol. 34, no. 1, 1988, pages 27–52; Beavers and dead cows: AP report in *Software Engineering Notes*, vol. 17, no. 1, January 1992; Foxes: *The Riverine Grazier*, Hay, New South Wales, Australia, 10 April 1991; Trawlers: *The Australian*, 16 April 1991; New Jersey and others: *Software Engineering Notes*, vol. 16, no. 2, April 1991, page 4, and vol. 16, no. 3, July 1991, pages 16–17.

4. "Saboteur Tries to Blank Out Oz," *The Australian*, 23 November 1987, page 1; "Laid-Off Worker Sabotages Encyclopaedia," *San Jose Mercury News*, 5 September 1986.

5. "Thieves Destroy Data on Chernobyl Victims," *New Scientist*, 22 September 1990; "Exxon Man Destroys Oil Spill Documents," UPI report in *The Australian*, 4 July 1989; "'Losing' a Warehouse," *Software Engineering Notes*, vol. 16, no. 3, July 1991, page 7.

6. "Inhabitant of Amsterdam Lies Dead in Apartment for Half a Year," *Software Engineering Notes*, vol. 16, no. 2, April 1991, page 11; "Defence of the Data," *New Scientist*, 19 January 1991, and "Theft of Computer Puts Allies' Plan at Risk," report from *The Times* (London) in *The Australian*, 14 March 1991.

7. "Poindexter Deleted 5,000 Computer Notes," Reuters and AP reports in *The Weekend Australian*, 17–18 March 1990; "Terminally Dumb Substitutions," *Software Engineering Notes*, vol. 15, no. 5, October 1990, page 4.

8. James H. Paul and Gregory C. Simon, *Bugs in the Program: Problems in Federal Government Computer Software Development and Regulation* (Subcommittee on Investigations and Oversight of the House Committee on Science, Space and Technology, U.S. Government Printing Office, Washington, DC, September 1989); Shawn McCarthy, "Dye Fears Computer Sabotage," *Toronto Star*, 31 October 1990; *Computers at Risk: Safe Computing in the Information Age* (National Academy Press 1991).

9. Peter J. Denning (ed.), *Computers, under Attack: Intruders, Worms, and Viruses* (ACM Press/Addison-Wesley, Reading, MA, 1990), page iii; Lance J. Hoffman (ed.), *Rogue Programs: Viruses, Worms, and Trojan Horses* (Van Nostrand Reinhold, New York, 1990), page 1.

10. Reports in *Business Week*, 7 November 1988, 3 April 1989, 15 June 1992, and 27 July 1992; *The Australian*, 4 August 1992.

11. Peter G. Neumann, "What's in a Name?" *Communications of the ACM*, vol. 35, no. 1, January 1992, page 186; *Software Engineering Notes*, vol. 14, no. 5, July 1989, page 11; vol. 16, no. 3, July 1991, pages 3–4; and vol. 17, no. 1, January 1992, pages 12–13; *Business Week*, 18 June 1990, 18 May 1991, and 8 June 1992; Marc Rotenberg, "Protecting Privacy," *Communications of the ACM*, vol. 35, no. 4, page 164; *The New York Times*, 4 May 1990, page A12; *The Los Angeles Times*, 8 January 1991; *Computing Australia*, 20 August 1990; Langdon Winner, "A Victory for Computer Populism," *Technology Review*, May-June 1991, page 66.

12. "Expert Systems Fail to Flourish," *The Australian*, 22 May 1990; Harvey P. Newquist III, "Experts at Retail," *Datamation* 1 April 1990, pages 53–56; Dianne Berry and Anna Hart (ed.), *Expert Systems: Human Issues* (MIT Press, Cambridge, MA, 1990); Roger Penrose, *The Emperor's New Mind* (Oxford University Press, New York, 1989).

13. Reports in *Business Week*, 19 August 1991, 15 June 1992, 13 July 1992; *Fortune*, 4 November 1991, 24 February 1992, 24 August 1992; Barbara Goldoftas, "Hands That Hurt: Repetitive Motion Injuries on the Job," *Technology Review*, January 1991, pages 43–50.

14. Deborah C. Johnson, *Computer Ethics* (Prentice-Hall, Englewood Cliffs, NJ, 1985), page 3; John Ladd, "Computers and Moral Responsibility: A Framework for an Ethical Analysis," in Carol C. Gould (ed.), *The Information Web: Ethical and Social Implications of Computer Networking* (Westview Press, Boulder, CO, 1989), pages 218–20.

15. Peter G. Neumann, "Computers, Ethics and Values," *Communications of the ACM*, vol. 34, no. 7, July 1991, page 106; Leslie S. Chalmers, "A Question of Ethics," *Journal of Accounting and EDP*, vol. 5, no. 2, Summer 1989, pages 50–53.

16. See Deborah C. Johnson, op. cit., 1985, chapter 1; and M. David Ermann, Mary B. Williams, and Claudio Gutierrez (eds.) *Computers, Ethics and Society* (Oxford University Press, New York, 1990), part 1.

17. Deborah C. Johnson, op. cit., 1985, chapter 2; Deborah C. Johnson and John W. Snapper (eds.), *Ethical Issues in the Use of Computers* (Wadsworth, Belmont, CA, 1985), part 1; Donn B. Parker, Susan Swope, and Bruce N. Baker (eds.), *Ethical Conflicts in Information and Computer Science, Technology, and Business* (QED, Wellesley, MA, 1990), parts 2, 4, 5, and 6.

18. Donn B. Parker et al., op. cit., 1990, page 5; Charles Dunlop and Rob Kling (eds.), *Computerization and Controversy: Value Conflicts and Social Choices* (Academic Press, San Diego, CA, 1991), pages 656–657; D. Dianne Martin and David H. Martin, "Professional Codes of Conduct and Computer Ethics Education," *Social Science Computer Review,* vol. 8, no. 1, Spring 1990, pages 96–108.

19. John Ladd, "The Quest for a Code of Professional Ethics: An Intellectual and Moral Confusion," in Deborah C. Johnson and John W. Snapper (eds.), op. cit., 1985, page 813.

20. Peter G. Neumann, "Certifying Professionals," *Communications of the ACM,* vol. 34, no. 2, February 1991, page 130.

23. Electronic Privacy in the Twenty-First Century

FRED H. CATE

What information about one's self should one be required to reveal to others? What information should one be permitted to keep private? The new technologies of computer networking and databases have made the collection of information about ourselves and the integration of information from many sources much faster and more efficient than it was in the past. At the same time, the value of such information has been increasing.

When we shop at our local Safeway (or many other supermarkets) and use a frequent shopper's card to get discounts on various products, we leave an electronic trail in Safeway's computers. The company's database can track the products we buy and how often we buy them. Similarly, through banking, driving a car, using a credit card, receiving medical care and insurance, collecting frequent flyer miles from an airline, ordering books on the Internet, working, paying taxes, renting videos, and enrolling in educational programs we make available data about ourselves, our likes and dislikes, the state of our health, our habits, our financial condition, and a host of other aspects of our lives.

Who should be given access to this information? Should the firms and organizations that collect it be allowed to sell it or to connect information about individuals from several sources into a comprehensive picture? Do we have a legal or constitutional right to privacy, to be protected from those who would want to know the details of our lives?

The issue of privacy protection is one of the most important and widely discussed aspects of the information age. It has also been the subject of a great deal of hype. In this chapter, Fred Cate, an attorney specializing in information law, cuts through much of the hype, examining the issues in a thoughtful, deliberate manner and suggesting principles on which policy for protecting information privacy should be based. The chapter is excerpted from Privacy in the Information Age, *a book Cate wrote under the auspices of the Brookings Institution in Washington, D.C., where he directs the* Electronic Information Privacy and Commerce Study. *Cate is also senior counsel for Ice Miller Donadio & Ryan, a law firm in Bloomington, Indiana, and Louis F. Niezer Faculty Fellow at Indiana University School of Law in Bloomington. He is well known as a speaker and writer on electronic privacy in the popular press. From 1994 to 1996, he chaired the Annenberg Washington Program's project on global information privacy.*

Privacy is a necessary element of quality life in modern society. Some protection for identifiable personal information about individuals and institutions is an essential part of privacy, as both European and U.S. law recognize. As information technologies spread and reliance on them increases, as the volume of data generated and recorded skyrockets, and as the cost of processing those data declines, the perceived need to protect information privacy is growing. This is particularly true as an increasing number of significant activities, such as banking, filing tax returns, and obtaining medical information, are shifted from the physical world to the virtual world. The proliferation of electronic information, and data about our use of these electronic services, seems certain to raise the stakes that society places on protecting information privacy.

THE PRIVACY BALANCE

As important as the values served by information privacy are today, and are likely to be in the future, none is absolute. Privacy values vary dramatically and often conflict with one another. More important, privacy is only one of the elements essential to modern life. Privacy is necessary and useful, but it is not sufficient. It is therefore only one tool, which must be used in coordination with other tools, to achieve the ends we desire, such as self-fulfillment and self-determination, societal productivity, and higher quality of life. As a result, individuals and institutions as a whole share an interest in identifying and facilitating those means — including privacy — that are necessary to achieve desired ends. What is needed is a balance, of which privacy is a part.

An important part of that balance is recognizing that protecting privacy imposes real costs. It facilitates the dissemination of false and misleading information, increases the cost of providing products and services, and interferes with meaningful evaluation of students and employees. Privacy conflicts with other important values within the society, such as society's interest in free expression, preventing and punishing crime, protection of private property, and the efficient operation of government. Privacy even conflicts with what may seem to be more mundane interests such as the desire for instant credit, better targeted mass mailings, lower insurance rates, faster service when ordering merchandise by telephone, qualified employees, or special recognition for frequent travelers. All of these and countless other benefits come at the expense of some privacy. The same features of information technologies and markets that raise the stakes of not protecting personal privacy also raise the risks of overprotecting it.

Privacy values are therefore constantly in tension with themselves and with other values. That tension is inescapable. Balancing those diverse, competing values is inherently contextual and, within each specific context, that balance will reflect a weighing of competing interests, such as cost, convenience, and quality and variety of services. Another important part of the context in which information privacy issues must be addressed are the other concerns raised by digital information, including enforcing intellectual property rights, protecting free expression, facilitating the economic stability of information networks, harmonizing divergent regulatory schemes, resolving the role of on-line anonymity, and ensuring the security of electronic transactions. No protection for information privacy is workable or desirable if it fails to take into account the variety and importance of contextual factors and the existence of competing values and concerns.

PRINCIPLES FOR PRIVACY PROTECTION

The contextuality of information privacy does not mean that it is impossible to identify fundamental principles of privacy protection. On the contrary, the importance of context and the competition of values heightens the importance of articulating basic principles to help guide the resolution of privacy issues. At the same time, these features mandate that those principles, and the ways in which they are implemented, clearly take into account the contextual issues affecting privacy's protection. This [article] proposes four sets of principles drawn from the European and U.S. experience.

Primacy of Individual Responsibility and Nongovernmental Action

The most important protection for information privacy is individual responsibility and action. This can take many forms. It certainly requires an awareness of the privacy implications of individual activities, particularly on the Internet or other networks. For many novice computer users, or people unacquainted with privacy issues, developing this awareness may require education. One must learn about the often invisible actions of software and hardware by reading instruction manuals and help screens, finding resources about privacy in print or on the Internet, and perusing the fine print in credit and other consumer transactions. A consortium of privacy advocates and software companies has announced the development of a service to make privacy self-help easier on the Internet. It is launching eTRUST, a program that will rate Internet sites according to how well they protect individual privacy. Internet sites that provide sufficient protection for individual privacy — including not collecting personal information, not disseminating information to third parties, and not using information for secondary purposes — will earn the right to display the eTRUST logo.[1]

Individual privacy action often requires the use of a technological or other form of self-help, such as an anonymous remailer or encryption software. Protecting passwords for computer accounts and restricting access to equipment are often necessary steps to take to ensure privacy protection. Other steps include refusing to provide unnecessary personal information to product and service suppliers, one of the most effective means of protecting one's privacy. Individuals may need to restructure an activity to enhance privacy protection, perhaps by changing companies or paying with cash rather than check or credit card.

Individual responsibility always requires ascertaining why data are being collected and how the collector intends to control the use, dissemination, and retention of personal information. This knowledge is exceptionally important in the context of commercial services, as many companies now promote their privacy policies for competitive purposes. If one credit card company, for example, does not offer adequate protection for personal information, others almost certainly will. If enough consumers demand better privacy protection and back up that demand, if necessary, by withdrawing their patronage, companies are certain to respond. In fact, when competitive markets exist, consumer inquiries about, and response to, corporate privacy policies are an excellent measure of how much that society really values privacy.

Public protest also has proved an effective restraint on planned corporate data processing activities. In 1991 Lotus Development Corporation and Equifax abandoned plans to sell Households, a CD-ROM database containing names, addresses, and marketing information on 120 million consumers, after they received 30,000 calls and letters from individuals asking to be removed from the database.[2] Ironically, cancellation of Households led Lotus to abandon Lotus Marketplace, a similar CD-ROM database with information on 7 million U.S. businesses.[3] Eight months later, Equifax, one of the largest credit bureaus in the United States, decided to stop selling consumer names and addresses to direct marketing firms altogether, a business that had earned the company $11 million the previous year.[4]

More recently, Lexis-Nexis, operator of one of the largest legal and general information databases in the world, has revamped plans for P-Track, a service that provides personal information, including maiden names and aliases, about "virtually every individual in America" to anyone willing to pay a search fee of eighty-five to one hundred dollars.[5] In response to a storm of protest, Lexis-Nexis has decided against providing social security numbers and is honoring the requests of anyone who wishes to be deleted from the database. The situation highlights not only the effectiveness of protests but also the potential for the very technologies that facilitate the collection and disclosure of personal information to be used to protect privacy. Word about the planned service was widely circulated by e-mail on the Internet, and many of the protests to the company have been delivered the same way.[6] Moreover, the public outcry over the planned activities by Lotus and Lexis-Nexis demonstrates the significant role of the media in informing consumers and facilitating a popular response.

Direct contact with companies may not only alert them to the value of privacy to their customers but also achieve direct, immediate results, as happens, for example, when the company receives a letter from a consumer who demands to be removed from a mailing list. Industry organizations, such as the Direct Marketing Association, also provide important rights that help to address information privacy issues more broadly. For example, the DMA operates the Mail Preference Service and the Telephone Preference Service. With a single request to each it is possible to be removed from most DMA-member company mailing and telephone solicitation lists. However, although the Mail Preference Service has been available since 1971, the DMA reports that the service is used by approximately 2 percent of the U.S. adult population.[7] This number suggests that concern over direct mail solicitations is not that great or that the public is unaware of, or not taking the initiative to use, this free service. A proposed use of data can hardly be considered unfairly invasive of personal privacy if the user gives data subjects a meaningful opportunity to object to the use. One has little ground for complaint if one fails to take advantage of those opportunities.

Individuals, rather than waiting for the government to take action, must accept the responsibility to know and insist on legal rights. For example, in the United States, any citizen may demand from the government a copy of all information, other than that within one of the Freedom of Information Act's nine enumerated exemptions, that the government possesses about her.[8] Taking advantage of this right is an effective step toward discovering and correcting inaccurate or misleading information. Similarly, every person has a legal right to the information about her held by a credit reporting agency.[9] If she has been denied credit or other benefits on the basis of a credit report, there is no charge for the access.[10] Taking advantage of that opportunity, reviewing the data carefully, and disputing incorrect or outdated information are vital ways to protect one's information privacy.

Some privacy rights exist in private agreements. The Bankcard Holders of America Association urges consumers to "just say no" to allowing merchants to record information such as a driver's license or telephone number on credit card slips.[11] Merchants are prohibited from requiring this information by their agreement with Visa and Mastercard. Similarly, some merchants require credit card information as a way of guaranteeing a check, but Visa and Mastercard prohibit this practice too.[12] These restrictions help protect individuals' privacy, and they highlight the importance of learning about, and insisting upon, consumers' rights wherever found. And there are situations [in the following discussion] in which recourse to a government agency or to the courts is appropriate.[13]

Individual responsibility, of course, applies to information users as well as to those wishing to protect their privacy. Individuals and institutions collecting, storing, using, and disseminating identifiable personal information should recognize the competitive potential of rational, articulated policies to protect personal privacy. Besides the potential for attracting customers, such policies may also serve as effective housecleaning tools, reducing information that is inaccurate or out-of-date. Such information has little value and may diminish the value of other information held by the user. Information privacy policies that include limits on data collection and retention, and procedures of updating information, serve the interests of data users as well as data subjects. Those policies and practices may also forestall government regulation and avoid costly litigation.

Often, industry associations, such as the Information Industry Association and the Interactive Services Association, have adopted guidelines and principles that may serve as models for individual policies or standards against which those policies may be judged.[14] The Direct Marketing Association offers an interactive tool for developing effective notices to consumers about the collection and use of data. These documents establish important norms of data protection of which both data subjects and users should be aware, and which may serve as a basis for negotiations between consumers and service providers. Corporate compliance with these standards and other privacy standards may constitute an important accolade in competitive markets, much like the Good Housekeeping Seal of Approval, while inattention to them might be a source of public embarrassment and competitive disadvantage in the eyes of consumers who are concerned about protecting their privacy. Moreover, industry associations can often be approached to help persuade member organizations to adopt and adhere to industry norms for privacy protection. The DMA, for example, has begun issuing quarterly reports on members who are being disciplined for violating DMA codes of conduct.

Steven Bibas, Scott Shorr, and others have written about a contractual approach to information privacy, in which privacy would be protected according to an explicit agreement between the data subject and the data user.[15] This is the practical outgrowth of both information supplier and user exercising individual responsibility for information privacy. Information contracts allow targeted privacy protection for those consumers who are concerned about it. They are especially effective in the absence of consensus about privacy, and they may be preferable to uniform privacy protection because they are more sensitive to the specific context and to individual preferences. Like price mechanisms in general, this approach to privacy "takes into account individual values, needs, and trade-offs, allocating resources to their most-valued uses. . . . A contractual approach, by pricing information, would thus more efficiently allocate data than would a centrally planned solution."[16] Privacy protection based on mutual consent is not possible in all situations, for example, when the data subject and the data processor have no direct contact, but when applicable, this approach is an excellent example of the benefits of individual action to protect privacy.

Individual responsibility is not a panacea. Commissioner David Flaherty, Paul M. Schwartz and Joel R. Reidenberg, Colin Bennett, and many other privacy scholars have noted flaws in the U.S. self-regulation, self-help model of privacy protection. Many of the criticisms center on what is perceived as the intrinsic conflict that occurs when data users promulgate their own data protection codes of conduct; the lack of public disclosure of, and scrutiny over, corporate privacy policies; the unwillingness of companies and industry organizations to take privacy protection seriously; and the failure of many of these groups to act consistently with their public pronouncements on privacy or to live up to the promises they make.[17] These observations are pertinent to the direct marketing industry in the United States, while they are less relevant, and becoming even less so, in industries such as consumer banking and credit, which have increasingly adopted and publicized their privacy policies as a competitive strategy.

Some of the critiques are misplaced, because they judge self-help efforts against normative standards that are found nowhere else in U.S. legal or commercial culture. As desirable as some privacy advocates believe European standards of data protection to be, they are not the appropriate tests of U.S. organizational behavior. And many of the criticisms fail to reflect significant recent successes of the self-regulatory, self-help model. Nonetheless, the failures of the past highlight the importance of making individual responsibility work better by ensuring that consumers become more aware of their own privacy and the options they have for protecting it. They signal the significance of new technological and market developments that increase the potential for exercising individual responsibility for privacy. Past shortcomings also focus attention on the importance of collective action by data subjects, rather than just by data users. And they suggest the contours of legal rights necessary to help facilitate and supplement individual measures to protect personal privacy.

The Role of National Law

Individual and collective nongovernmental action is critical to protecting information privacy; there can be no effective protection of information privacy without it. However, private action alone is likely to be insufficient to protect information privacy adequately. Particularly when the absence of competition interferes with the development of market mechanisms for protecting privacy, citizens will need to have recourse to legal protection for certain basic privacy rights. This will help guarantee the availability of sufficient, reliable information on the proposed use of the data to make individual action meaningful, and protect privacy in situations in which consent and other forms of self-help are unworkable or inapplicable.

The specific content of privacy laws is a matter of considerable disagreement among nations, information users and subjects, and privacy scholars. My recommendations for the essential components of privacy protection are set forth below. As important as the specific rights protected by those laws are, however, the clarity, consistency, precision, and intelligibility of that protection and the laws that afford it are equally significant. The interests of information suppliers and users are best served by laws that are consistent, deliberate, and specific. This can be accomplished through a single, omnibus privacy law, supplemented as necessary by specific legal measures, or through a series of sectoral privacy statutes, each of which addresses an industrial sector or specific type of information. In either case, the laws that protect privacy should result in consistent protection for similar privacy interests in similar situations.

In the United States, existing privacy protection is a cacophony of constitutional rights, narrow sectoral statutes, state legislation, federal regulations, and common law torts. This undesirable situation results in ineffective, incomplete, inconsistent, and inefficient privacy protection. In its report on telecommunications-related personal information, the National Telecommunications and Information Administration stressed the inconsistency of current legal protections:

Like services do not have like privacy protection. With respect to telephony services, for example, Federal regulations grant individuals the right to ask for confidential treatment of CPNI [Customer Proprietary Network Information] but only from certain telephone companies — the Bell companies and GTE. Similarly, the notice requirements that apply to the Bell companies and GTE differ depending on the type of customer. Multi-line customers are given notice about their privacy rights; single-line customers are not. To complicate matters further, a few states provide privacy protection for intrastate service regardless of which telephone company is involved.

There is also a lack of intraservice uniformity for video carriage. The privacy provisions of the Cable Act do not apply to DBS [direct broadcast satellite] and wireless cable operations. . . .

In addition, there is lack of *inter*service uniformity because like-types of information are not treated in like-ways, across different communications services.[18]

The inconsistency in protection for CPNI and other information largely results from two factors: the absence of uniform, rational principles undergirding information privacy protection in the United States, and the diversity of laws, agencies, industries, and issues involved in information privacy. Much statutory privacy protection in the United States is a by-product of some other legislative effort, most often regulating an industry such as telephone service, banking, or cable television. Privacy protection is an afterthought or a secondary purpose. A statutory approach that provides a basic level of privacy protection, either across the board or at least across a given industry or type of information, would yield more rational and consistent protection.

The need for consistency also argues for increased federal attention to privacy and a corresponding preemption of some state activity in the area. Although some privacy rights are amenable to local regulation, information privacy, especially when it involves information technologies — telephone service, broadcast and cable television, and the Internet — and institutions with geographically far-flung activities — national banking, insurance, and credit reporting companies — ought to be the subject of national, or even multinational, attention. This is one of the great strengths of the European Union data protection directive: it establishes detailed, across-the-board privacy protection applicable throughout the fifteen European member states.[19] Individual nations may adopt additional protections or may implement the directive in various ways consistent with its terms, but the directive establishes a uniform base of protection.

Clarity is also an essential feature of effective privacy protection. Clarity requires specificity as well as care in the drafting of statutes. Privacy legislation may do more harm than good if its rights and obligations cannot be readily understood by information users and suppliers. Moreover, to the extent that measures designed to protect information privacy run the risk of conflicting with other legally protected rights, precise drafting may help avoid constitutional infirmity.

What to protect and how much to protect it are at the heart of the current debate over information privacy. The EU directive provides very high protection, with a necessarily high degree of resulting intrusion into the activities and expression of individuals and institutions. That level of protection is unworkable and undesirable in the U.S. context. However, U.S. citizens and institutions would benefit from a more definitive set of information privacy protections. Dozens of organizations and scholars have recommended what components should constitute basic privacy protection. Many of those recommendations embrace the breadth of the EU directive, while shying away from its legal force. The effect is often to propose very little concrete protection for a wide variety of rights. Other proposals have sought to replicate the directive in U.S. law, resulting in recommendations that are unlikely to pass constitutional scrutiny, contrary to many other widely shared values in American society, and politically unworkable.

The specific content of privacy laws is no more important than the consistency, rationality, and accessibility of those laws. Moreover, the concept of privacy and the principles undergirding a democratic political system and a market economy focus on the importance of individual choice. It is therefore important that privacy laws provide only the protection necessary to facilitate nongovernmental action and fill the gaps left by such arrangements, and that those laws extend protection consonant with other legally protected, popularly shared values. With those goals in mind, statutory privacy protection should include three elements. These elements would overlay existing privacy protection, such as that provided by the Fourth Amendment, which applies outside of the information privacy context.

Notice. The law should require any person collecting identifiable information about any other natural person to disclose the reason for which he is collecting the information, the extent to which he may put it to other uses, whether he will disseminate it to others, how long he will store it or on what basis he will make the determination to retain the information, whether the information must be provided, and, if so, under what compulsion. This notice requirement guarantees that the necessary information is available so that one may determine whether or not to furnish the requested data.

This notice requirement would apply only to identifiable information — information on the physical, physiological, mental, economic, cultural, political, or social identity of a living individual that directly or indirectly identifies that person. This information would include all information about living people, except for aggregate data that could not be interpreted as referring to a specific person. Such data reveal nothing about an individual and therefore pose no risk to a person's privacy. The notice requirement would be triggered only when the person identified by the information was an individual, as opposed to a company, institution, or association. Although organizations, as well as individuals, benefit from privacy, their disclosures are governed in the United States by other laws relating to publicly traded securities, corporate organization and governance, trade secrets, misappropriation, unfair competition, employment, disabilities, and many other subjects.[20] The restriction of the notice requirement to information about living people reflects the maxim in U.S. law that interests in privacy, like those in reputation, are personal and do not survive the individual.[21]

Notice should be required only to the person supplying the data (the data supplier), who may or may not be the person whom the information is about (the data subject). As a practical matter, identifiable personal information may be transferred from the data subject to the ultimate users of that information in one of two ways: the data subject may *deliberately disclose* it, either voluntarily or under some compulsion, or the activities of the data subject may *generate* personal information, of which the data subject may not even be aware. This is true irrespective of the technological context. A consumer who makes a purchase in a bookstore may deliberately disclose data, such as his credit card number or the address printed on his check. His participation in that transaction may also, unbeknownst to him, generate personal data if, for instance, the clerk writes down his name and the name of the book purchased or a bystander photographs the consumer entering or leaving the store. Similarly, a consumer who purchases a book by Internet is certain to disclose information knowingly, most likely by providing a credit card number and mailing address, and to generate additional information by logging onto the Internet and accessing the bookseller's site. In the same way, if the consumer orders the book by telephone, he deliberately discloses information (the contents of the telephone call), while the act of placing the call generates additional data (the information necessary for the telephone company to place his call and bill him for the service).

The information user may obtain the deliberately disclosed information directly from the data subject or from some intermediary, such as someone who sells customer lists. The generated information cannot be obtained directly from the data subject because he usually is not even aware of creating the data, but it can be observed directly by the user or acquired from some intermediary who observed the data. The source of the data — the data supplier — may be the data subject, the data user, or one of many intermediaries.

Notice should be required when an information user is obtaining identifiable personal information from another party — a data subject or an intermediary — but only upon the request of the data supplier. In some situations, the data supplier may not request the notice because the information it would provide is already known from the specific context of the request. For example, if one invites a friend to dinner and the friend asks the host to supply his address, the host is unlikely to seek notice. In other situations, the data supplier may not request the notice because he intends to provide the requested information irrespective of the content of the notice. In most situations, notice would be sought as a protection against future, unanticipated uses of the data. Congress or an administrative agency could modify or eliminate the requirement in situations in which the information is not necessary or in which the duty to provide the notice conflicts directly with other fundamental rights, such as the ability of the press to gather information. When applicable, however, the notice must be available prior to the information being provided the first time and, in appropriate situations (such as continuing credit transactions), at regular intervals thereafter.

Clearly, the notice is important if the information is being knowingly provided by the data subject. But what if the data are being observed or provided by an intermediary? Notice should be required, if requested, to the supplier of the information even if he is not the subject of the information. This allows the data supplier to evaluate better whether to provide the requested information, and it facilitates his explaining his own data protection standards to data subjects or other intermediary data suppliers. It also helps the data supplier to adhere to agreements concerning personal information he may have entered into with data subjects or suppliers.

Requiring notice when data may be observed, rather than solicited, is more complicated. If the data are observed in a traditionally public setting, no notice should be necessary. Our book purchaser may be photographed entering the store without his consent. This comports with widely shared U.S. societal values, reflected in U.S. constitutional, statutory, and decisional law, that one has no legal right to hide activities that take place in public. To restrict the collection and dissemination of information observed in public settings would run afoul of the First Amendment and be nonsensical. Under current law, one may restrain certain highly offensive or misleading commercial uses of publicly observed information (such as using a photograph of a celebrity to endorse a product without her consent). But there is and should be no legal power to interfere otherwise with the collection and use of those data.

If the information user is gathering the data itself from observations not generally available to the public, such as through the provision of telephone, cable, or Internet service, then notice should be required. This is especially true when the ability to collect the information results from a relationship between the information supplier and user. When a relationship exists, such as a patient visiting a physician or a customer subscribing to Internet service, notice is particularly useful and can be provided at relatively low cost. For example, notice can be given when the patient or customer first arranges for service, and, if he chooses, the patient or customer can act on that notice and seek service elsewhere, from someone who better protects privacy. If the information user is gathering data generated by the data subject's actions in a private setting in which the user has no legal authority to be, then his actions already are likely to violate existing European and U.S. laws prohibiting wiretapping, eavesdropping, theft, and trespass. Because these activities are already against the law, the question of notice is moot, although notice might still be required as a further disincentive to those activities.

In sum, notice should therefore be required, upon request, if the information user is asking the data subject or any other data supplier to disclose identifiable personal information. Notice should also be required when the data user is observing data being generated by the data subject, and the data user is in the position to make those observations because of some existing relationship with the data subject. Notice is not required to collect information being generated by the data subject when the activities generating those data take place in a traditionally public setting. "Traditionally public setting" is defined as a physical or virtual space in which an information user may observe the activities of a data subject not because of any special relationship or service being provided to the data subject, but rather on an equal basis with any other member of the public. Activities that occur in a physical or virtual space that can be accessed only through permission of the data subject, or a physical invasion or theft of property, are never public.

An Internet service provider, through which subscribers obtain access to the Internet, would be required to meet the notice requirement, upon request, regarding its treatment and use of identifiable personal subscriber data. However, an Internet user who collects data on the electronic addresses of other Internet users who access specific World Wide Web pages would have no obligation to disclose his activities to those users.

As a practical matter, the notice requirement will be carried out by most companies through routine disclosures, printed on the back of application forms or account statements or included on World Wide Web pages. The burden of notice is therefore presumed to be light, although it may nonetheless discourage the gathering of gratuitous data. The requirement will facilitate more informed decision making by consumers, as well as attention to data processing activities by data users. It also creates a chain of custody and knowledge. A data supplier seeking to comply with its own privacy policies or with legal constraints, such as the EU directive's prohibition on transferring data to countries lacking an "adequate level of protection," would have ready access to information about how its data will be used and what protections will guard against its misuse.[22]

Consent. The law should provide an opportunity for data suppliers to consent to, or withhold consent for, the information processing activities outlined in the notice. Historically, the requirement for obtaining consent can take many forms and have many ramifications. As a general matter, unless an information collector wishes to provide opportunities for a more detailed response, the law would merely require that the data supplier be given an a opportunity to give (to "opt in") or deny (to "opt out") consent to all of the data processing activities proposed by a single user. In a situation in which notice was not required, neither would the opportunity to consent be necessary.

The failure to consent can result in the denial of service. Although this may have the immediate effect of denying access to a product or service, in the longer term it is likely to compel data processors to conform their activities to widely accepted norms to avoid decreasing their potential market. Individuals seeking greater protection than that provided by the norm may seek to obtain it through the self-help measures outlined [here], but they cannot impose the additional protection, and the cost associated with it, on society as a whole.

There is no requirement that consent be explicit: information users may, after providing the required notice, specify that a failure to object (opt out) within a reasonable period of time will constitute consent. This provision should be clear and specific, but it is adequate in all contexts except those in which registering an objection is impossible, impractical, or unduly expensive or burdensome in relation to the transaction generating the data. In those limited situations, affirmative consent (opting in) may be necessary. For example, if notice was not provided to the data supplier, or if it failed to contain an address or other way of contacting the party to whom the objection must be given, or if it specified only a telephone number that was always busy, opting out would not be a viable option. The data supplier would therefore have to obtain explicit consent for subsequent use of the data. Similarly, even a procedure for opting out that required the data supplier to bear the cost of calling a long-distance telephone might be unduly burdensome if the data resulted from a routine, face-to-face transaction. As these examples suggest, the effect of these provisions is to encourage data users to provide clear, straightforward notice, with a meaningful, convenient opportunity to object, so that a court does not subsequently find that the notice was inadequate or the opportunity to object impractical or unduly burdensome, and therefore prohibit the use of the data without first obtaining explicit consent. In addition, new consent would always be necessary whenever a change in conditions rendered the notice under which consent was obtained inaccurate.

Many commentators have forcefully suggested that subsequent disclosure or use of "sensitive" information such as medical information should require explicit consent. I do not agree. There is no consensus as to what constitutes "sensitive" information, and the definition appears to depend on personal preferences. For many individuals, information in their medical files is no more sensitive than their financial information, unlisted telephone numbers, or college transcripts. There should be no special requirement of explicit consent for the use of such an ill-defined category of data. Moreover, the EU directive defines "sensitive" information to include data on "racial or ethnic origin, political opinions, religious beliefs, [and] philosophical or ethical persuasion,"[23] despite the fact that much of this type of data is either readily observable or known only if disclosed by the data subject. Why should the law accord special protection to information that can be observed by any passerby or that is voluntarily disclosed by the data subject?

The same features that may make information sensitive may also heighten the importance of its availability. For example, a criminal record may be sensitive information, but it is precisely the type of information one would want to know before hiring a house cleaner or security guard.[24] Many people may be loathe to accurately report medical information to a new employer, but the cost of failing to report or reporting inaccurately a preexisting medical condition may be very high and is ultimately borne by the employer and its other employees. The EU directive specifically includes within its definition of "sensitive" information data on "sexual life." Yet knowledge about sexually transmitted diseases is exactly what a potential sexual partner, health care provider, or anyone who will come into intimate contact with the data subject needs to have. The law should facilitate the disclosure and verification of such data.

In the regulatory framework I am proposing, a different consent requirement for sensitive information than for other information would make little sense in any event, because consent is provided by the data supplier, who in many cases will not be the data subject. Information that may be sensitive to the data subject is not likely to be viewed differently from other information by subsequent data suppliers. Requiring the explicit consent of data suppliers for the use of information that may or may not have been sensitive to the data subject merely imposes a greater burden and higher cost on the data user with no discernible benefit. Most important, however, the whole thrust of the notice and consent requirements specified above is that notice be clear and intelligible and the opportunity to withhold consent for the data processing activities covered by the notice convenient and accessible. In the light of these requirements, the distinction between "opting in" and "opting out" is simply not that significant vis-à-vis the data subject. However, allowing individuals to opt out avoids the high costs that an opt-in system would impose on data users. Such a price for so little resulting benefit is not worth paying.

Accountability. The law should hold information users accountable for the claims they make in their notices to data suppliers. Users should be liable if their representations are not substantially accurate as to why information is being collected, how it will be used, whether it will be disseminated to others, how long it will be stored and how that decision will be made, whether the information must be provided, and, if so, upon what compulsion. Liability would also exist when a data user failed to respect withholding of consent by a data supplier. Liability would attach only with respect to information that is linked to a specific living individual, as opposed to aggregate data or information about an organization or deceased person.

Liability may be established in many ways and take many forms. For reasons already outlined and further discussed below, I do not believe that government enforcement of rules concerning information is generally appropriate. The preferred remedy is civil liability, established by an aggrieved data supplier or data subject bringing a claim in federal court. The penalty could take the form of actual or statutory damages or an injunction, and should be calculated to provide a disincentive for providing inaccurate information or failing to adhere to promises made to data suppliers. There may be specific contexts, such as violations by an industry regulated by a federal agency, in which administrative review and a government-imposed fine or other sanction would be appropriate. Those situations could be identified in sectoral statutes or administrative regulations. In any case, the standard of liability should be that the information user knew or had reason to know that its notice was substantially false or misleading or that it knew or should have known that a subsequent activity exceeded the scope of the notice or the consent obtained.

These three concepts — notice, consent, and accountability — should form the basis of protection for information privacy. That protection may be implemented in many ways. In Europe, these rights — and many others — are provided in an omnibus directive that applies across the Continent. Although each nation has adopted its own legal protections consistent with the data protection directive, thereby creating the potential for some variation in implementation, even at the national level the approach is broad-based protection. The United States might choose to adopt an omnibus information privacy law providing the basic protections outlined [previously], or it could deploy those same protections through well-targeted sectoral statutes. In either case, protection must extend nationally, and therefore the statute(s) should be enacted by Congress. Moreover, the focus of these legal rights is to ensure adequate notice and a meaningful opportunity to grant or deny consent only in those situations in which nongovernmental action is unlikely to supply adequate protection for information privacy. Those rights are intended to maximize individual choice, not supplant it.

The advantages of a single law are that it facilitates more uniform protection; it avoids definitional problems in crafting sectoral statutes; it eliminates the potential for conflicting interpretations of overlapping laws; and it emerges from a process that is likely to facilitate more thoughtful and comprehensive debate. On the other hand, an omnibus law runs the risk of imposing a one-size-fits-all legislative solution on diverse issues that occur in a wide variety of distinct contexts, thereby creating too little or too much protection in specific situations. A single law may need to be supplemented with other laws designed to address specific situations or types of information or may require separate administrative agencies to craft divergent regulations for implementing that law in the sectors they regulate. The result could easily be as much inconsistency as would result from sectoral protection from the outset. Finally, broad-ranging laws are often politically controversial and difficult to move through Congress because of the many interests affected. This is why Congress only infrequently rewrites comprehensive laws, such as the Copyright Act (completely revised in 1909 and again in 1976), preferring instead to rely on specific amendments, even those that fundamentally alter the underlying law.

Sectoral privacy protection presents parallel opportunities and risks. Such laws may be crafted with the input of more of the affected parties and respond more sensitively to the needs of a particular sector. However, separate laws run the risk of conflict and overlap, or Congress may simply tire of the process of adopting such laws, resulting in long delays in obtaining broad protection or possibly never obtaining such protection at all. In the current legal environment in the United States, in which all statutory privacy protection (except that applicable to the federal government itself) is sectoral, sectoral protection is most likely. But in the long term, a single basic law, even if supplemented when necessary by specific laws, may be preferable, provided that it facilitates, rather than interferes with, the development of private mechanisms for protecting privacy and the exercise of individual choice.

* * *

CONCLUSION

The proliferation of computers, networks, electronic information services, and digital data has increased concern about privacy in Europe, in the United States, and around the world. How those concerns have been and should be addressed depends on many factors: how privacy is defined; what values privacy is perceived to serve; what values conflict or are affected by the protection of privacy; the societal, legal, and cultural setting in which the issues are raised; and the services, products, and benefits associated with the activities that impinge on personal privacy. In short, while privacy may be characterized as a fundamental human right in Europe and as an amorphous, shifting constitutional right in the United States, the protection of information privacy is always balanced with competing rights and the contours of that protection are shaped by context. As U.S. Supreme Court Justice John Harlan wrote almost thirty years ago: "Our expectations [of privacy], and the risks we assume, are in large part reflections of laws that translate into rules the customs and values of the past and present."[25]

Despite the considerable differences in their legal rights to privacy, Europe and the United State share many, but not all, basic principles undergirding information privacy. For example, both the European data protection directive and the U.S. *Privacy and the National Information Infrastructure: Principles for Providing and Using Personal Information* recognize similar obligations and responsibilities for personal information users.[26] Both the EU directive and the U.S. principles require that individuals be given notice whenever personal information about them is collected and an opportunity to grant or withhold consent for certain uses of personal information. Both extend greater protection to sensitive data.

Europe and the United States diverge most sharply on the role of the government in protecting privacy. In Europe, an important principle of information privacy is that the government oversee the data processing activities of private parties and enforce the law when necessary. The United States does not generally recognize this principle, and the nation's constitutional commitment to a government of limited powers, particularly when expression is involved, poses a substantial obstacle to the creation of a government privacy authority. This suggests the most fundamental difference between European and U.S. privacy protection: the extent to which other values restrict the government's role in protecting information privacy. European laws suggest that European citizens fear the invasive activities of private parties more than the involvement of the government; in the United States, the opposite is true.

Meaningful privacy protection in the context of the explosion in digital data and the globalization of networks, markets, and institutions requires not only national legal protections but also nongovernmental action, such as individual self-help and market-based solutions, and intergovernmental action to create a multinational framework to protect information privacy.

In the U.S. context, information subjects and users must continue to develop their own privacy protection through their separate activities, mutual agreements, market-based accommodations, group action, and adherence to voluntary codes of practice. Individual responsibility, not regulation, is the principal and most effective form of privacy protection in most settings.

The law should serve as a gap-filler, facilitating individual action in those situations in which the lack of competition has interfered with private privacy protection. In those situations, the law should only provide limited, basic privacy rights, including requiring notice of why information is being collected, the extent to which it may be put to other uses, whether it will be disseminated to others, how long it will be stored, whether the information must be provided, and, if so, under what authority; providing an opportunity to data suppliers to grant or withhold consent for the information processing activities outlined in the notice; and holding information users accountable for the claims they make in their notices and for the extent to which they respect the consent, or lack of consent, by information suppliers. The purpose of these rights is to facilitate — not interfere with — the development of private mechanisms and individual choice as a means of valuing and protecting privacy.

These rights could be contained in a single law or in a series of sectoral laws, provided that the protection afforded is consistent, deliberate, and specific. This is a particular challenge in light of the current frenzy of attention, although little action, in Washington about privacy. During its two years of work, the 104th Congress faced 980 bills — more than 12 percent of all bills introduced — that included provisions on a wide range of privacy issues. The pressure to "do something" often interferes with the research and thoughtful deliberation necessary to develop effective laws that are consistent with one another and with other important values.

The government should play a circumscribed role, limited primarily to articulating principles for information privacy; enacting laws when necessary to protect the rights outlined above; adjudicating disputes concerning such rights; facilitating discussion, education, and cooperation; and leading multinational negotiations to resolve conflicts among competing national privacy laws. The long-term goal is the promulgation of basic multinational principles on privacy protection to facilitate the activities of information users and the valuable services and products they offer, ensure consistent international privacy protection for personal information, and reduce the cost of administering and complying with inconsistent national legal regimes.

NOTES

1. "Gathering of Personal Data on Internet Triggers Advent of Privacy-Approved Sites," *Daily Economic Report* (BNA), October 10, 1996, p. A23. The eTRUST site on the World Wide Web is located at <http://www.etrust.org>.
2. Lawrence M. Fisher, "New Data Base Ended by Lotus and Equifax," *New York Times*, January 24, 1991, p. D4.
3. Ibid.
4. Shelby Gilje, "Credit Bureau Won't Sell Names," *Seattle Times*, August 9, 1991, p. D6.
5. Kathy M. Kristof, "Deluged Lexis Purging Names from Databases," *Los Angeles Times*, November 8, 1996, p. D5. The database reportedly includes current and previous addresses, birth dates, home telephone numbers, maiden names, and aliases. Initially, Lexis was also providing social security numbers. However, in response to a storm of protest, Lexis stopped displaying social security numbers but has kept them in the data files so that requesters can search the database by social security number.
6. Ibid.
7. Direct Marketing Association, *Name Removal Services* (available at <http://www.the-dma.org/home_pages/consumer/dmasahic.html#removal>.
8. 5 U.S.C. § 552 (1997).
9. 15 U.S.C. § 1681m (1997).
10. Ibid. § 1681j.
11. "BHA: Put Your Mouth Where Your Money Is," *Times-Picayune*, January 12, 1996, p. E8.
12. Ibid.
13. See "National Law."
14. See, for example, *Direct Marketing Association Guidelines for Personal Information Protection; Direct Marketing Association Guidelines for Ethical Business Practices;* Information Industry Association, *Fair Information Practices Guidelines;* and Direct Marketing Association and Interactive Services Association, *Principles for Unsolicited Marketing E-Mail.*
15. Steven A. Bibas, "A Contractual Approach to Data Privacy," *Harvard Journal of Law and Public Policy,* vol. 17 (Spring 1994), p. 591; and Scott Shorr, "Personal Information Contracts: How to Protect Privacy without Violating the First Amendment," *Cornell Law Review,* vol. 80 (September 1995), p. 1756.
16. Bibas, "A Contractual Approach," pp. 604–5.
17. See, for example, Paul M. Schwartz and Joel R. Reidenberg, *Data Privacy Law: A Study of United States Data Protection* (Charlottesville, Va.: Michie, 1996), pp. 307–48; and Joel R. Reidenberg, "Setting Standards for Fair Information Practice in the U.S. Private Sector," *Iowa Law Review,* vol. 80 (March 1995), pp. 497, 509–40.
18. U.S. Department of Commerce, National Telecommunications and Information Administration, *Privacy and the NII: Safeguarding Telecommunications-Related Personal Information* (Washington, D.C.: 1995), II-D Emphasis in original.
19. Directive 95/46/EC of the European Parliament and of the Council on the Protection of Individuals with Regard to the Processing of Personal Data and on the Free Movement of Such Data (Eur. O.J. 95/L281).

20. See Bruce W. Sanford, *Libel and Privacy*, 2d ed. (Englewood Cliffs, N.J.: Aspen Law and Business, 1996), § 11.3.10.
21. Ibid.
22. Directive 95/46/EC, art. 26(1).
23. Ibid., art. 8.
24. . . . it is precisely for this reason that federal law requires states to mandate that persons convicted of a sexual offense against a minor register with law enforcement officials upon their release from prison and at least annually for at least ten years therefore. 42 U.S.C. § 14071(a) (1996).
25. *United States* v. *White*, 401 U.S. 745, 786 (1971) (Harlan, J., dissenting).
26. President's Information Infrastructure Task Force, Information Policy Committee, Privacy Working Group, *Privacy and the National Information Infrastructure: Principles for Providing and Using Personal Information* (Washington, D.C.: 1995).

24.   In the Age of the Smart Machine

SHOSHANA ZUBOFF

*As discussed in several previous readings, developments in computers and informa-
tion technology are a driving force in virtually all areas of technological advance.
Nowhere are the impacts likely to be more profound than in the nature of work, its
organization and its management. In her widely discussed and influential book* In
the Age of the Smart Machine: The Future of Work and Power, *Shoshana
Zuboff argues that the computerized workplace is qualitatively different from its
predecessors. Traditional approaches to organizing and managing work will not
work in the new, "informated" environment. An alternative vision is needed for the
organization of the twenty-first century.*

*Changes in the workplace will affect the fundamental nature of society, as
authority relationships, class structure, individuals' control over their own fates,
and opportunities for self-fulfillment all take new shapes. The new information
technology "offers a historical opportunity to more fully develop the economic and
human potential of our work organizations," according to Zuboff. If we fail to seize
this opportunity, we run the risk of seeing the future become nothing but a "stale
reproduction of the past." Like many of the other works represented in this anthol-
ogy,* In the Age of the Smart Machine *is rich and complex, and the brief excerpt
that follows can do little but give the reader an idea of its flavor and introduce a few
of its basic ideas.*

*Shoshana Zuboff is Charles Edward Wilson Professor of Business Administra-
tion at Harvard University's Graduate School of Business Administration, where
she joined the faculty in 1981. She holds a Ph.D. in social psychology from Harvard
and an undergraduate degree from the University of Chicago. She has published
numerous articles and cases on information technology in the workplace and lectures and consults widely on this subject.*

Piney Wood, one of the nation's largest pulp mills, was in the throes of a mass
modernization effort that would place every aspect of the production process
under computer control. Six workers were crowded around a table in the snack
area outside what they called the Star Trek Suite, one of the first control rooms to
have been completely converted to microprocessor-based instrumentation. It
looked enough like a NASA control room to have earned its name.

It was almost midnight, but despite the late hour and the approach of the shift
change, each of the six workers was at once animated and thoughtful. "Knowledge and technology are changing so fast," they said, "What will happen to us?"
Their visions of the future foresaw wrenching change. They feared that today's

working assumptions could not be relied upon to carry them through, that the future would not resemble the past or the present. More frightening still was the sense of a future moving out of reach so rapidly that there was little opportunity to plan or make choices. The speed of dissolution and renovation seemed to leave no time for assurances that we were not heading toward calamity — and it would be all the more regrettable for having been something of an accident.

The discussion around the table betrayed a grudging admiration for the new technology — its power, its intelligence, and the aura of progress surrounding it. That admiration, however, bore a sense of grief. Each expression of gee-whiz-Buck-Rogers breathless wonder brought with it an aching dread conveyed in images of a future that rendered their authors obsolete. In what ways would computer technology transform their work lives? Did it promise the Big Rock Candy Mountain or a silent graveyard?

> In fifteen years there will be nothing for the worker to do. The technology will be so good it will operate itself. You will just sit there behind a desk running two or three areas of the mill yourself and get bored.

The group concluded that the worker of the future would need "an extremely flexible personality" so that he or she would not be "mentally affected" by the velocity of change. They anticipated that workers would need a great deal of education and training in order to "breed flexibility." "We find it all to be a great stress," they said, "but it won't be that way for the new, flexible people." Nor did they perceive any real choice, for most agreed that without an investment in the new technology, the company could not remain competitive. They also knew that without their additional flexibility, the technology would not fly right. "We are in a bind," one man groaned, "and there is no way out." The most they could do, it was agreed, was to avoid thinking too hard about the loss of overtime pay, the diminished probability of jobs for their sons and daughters, the fears of seeming incompetent in a strange, new milieu, or the possibility that the company might welsh on its promise not to lay off workers.

During the conversation, a woman in stained overalls had remained silent with her head bowed, apparently lost in thought. Suddenly, she raised her face to us. It was lined with decades of hard work, her brow drawn together. Her hands lay quietly on the table. They were calloused and swollen, but her deep brown eyes were luminous, youthful, and kind. She seemed frozen, chilled by her own insight, as she solemnly delivered her conclusion:

> I think the country has a problem. The managers want everything to be run by computers. But if no one has a job, no one will know how to do anything anymore. Who will pay the taxes? What kind of society will it be when people have lost their knowledge and depend on computers for everything?

Her voice trailed off as the men stared at her in dazzled silence. They slowly turned their heads to look at one another and nodded in agreement. The forecast seemed true enough. Yes, there was a problem. They looked as though they had just run a hard race, only to stop short at the edge of a cliff. As their heels skidded in the dirt, they could see nothing ahead but a steep drop downward.

Must it be so? Should the advent of the smart machine be taken as an invitation to relax the demands upon human comprehension and critical judgment? Does the massive diffusion of computer technology throughout our workplaces necessarily entail an equally dramatic loss of meaningful employment opportunities? Must the new electronic milieu engender a world in which individuals have lost control over their daily work lives? Do these visions of the future represent the price of economic success or might they signal an industrial legacy that must be overcome if intelligent technology is to yield its full value? Will the new information technology represent an opportunity for the rejuvenation of competitiveness, productive vitality, and organizational ingenuity? Which aspects of the future of working life can we predict, and which will depend upon the choices we make today?

The workers outside the Star Trek Suite knew that the so-called technological choices we face are really much more than that. Their consternation puts us on alert. There is a world to be lost and a world to be gained. Choices that appear to be merely technical will redefine our lives together at work. This means more than simply contemplating the implications or consequences of a new technology. It means that a powerful new technology, such as that represented by the computer, fundamentally reorganizes the infrastructure of our material world. It eliminates former alternatives. It creates new possibilities. It necessitates fresh choices.

The choices that we face concern the conception and distribution of knowledge in the workplace. Imagine the following scenario: Intelligence is lodged in the smart machine at the expense of the human capacity for critical judgment. Organizational members become ever more dependent, docile, and secretly cynical. As more tasks must be accomplished through the medium of information technology (I call this "computer-mediated work"), the sentient body loses its salience as a source of knowledge, resulting in profound disorientation and loss of meaning. People intensify their search for avenues of escape through drugs, apathy, or adversarial conflict, as the majority of jobs in our offices and factories become increasingly isolated, remote, routine, and perfunctory. Alternatively, imagine this scenario: Organizational leaders recognize the new forms of skill and knowledge needed to truly exploit the potential of an intelligent technology. They direct their resources toward creating a work force that can exercise critical judgment as it manages the surrounding machine systems. Work becomes more abstract as it depends upon understanding and manipulating information. This marks the beginning of new forms of mastery and provides an opportunity to imbue jobs with more comprehensive meaning. A new array of work tasks offer unprecedented opportunities for a wide range of employees to add value to products and services.

The choices that we make will shape relations of authority in the workplace. Once more, imagine: Managers struggle to retain their traditional sources of authority, which have depended in an important way upon their exclusive control of the organization's knowledge base. They use the new technology to structure organizational experience in ways that help reproduce the legitimacy of their traditional roles. Managers insist on the prerogatives of command and seek methods that protect the hierarchical distance that distinguishes them from their subordinates. Employees barred from the new forms of mastery relinquish their sense of responsibility for the organization's work and use obedience to authority as a means of expressing their resentment. Imagine an alternative: This technological transformation engenders a new approach to organizational behavior, one in which relationships are more intricate, collaborative, and bound by the mutual responsibilities of colleagues. As the new technology integrates information across time and space, managers and workers each overcome their narrow functional perspectives and create new roles that are better suited to enhancing value-adding activities in a data-rich environment. As the quality of skills at each organizational level becomes similar, hierarchical distinctions begin to blur. Authority comes to depend more upon an appropriate fit between knowledge and responsibility than upon the ranking rules of the traditional organizational pyramid.

The choices that we make will determine the techniques of administration that color the psychological ambiences and shape communicative behavior in the emerging workplace. Imagine this scenario: The new technology becomes the source of surveillance techniques that are used to ensnare organizational members or to subtly bully them into conformity. Managers employ the technology to circumvent the demanding work of face-to-face engagement, substituting instead techniques of remote management and automated administration. The new technological infrastructure becomes a battlefield of techniques, with managers inventing novel ways to enhance certainty and control while employees discover new methods of self-protection and even sabotage. Imagine the alternative: The new technological milieu becomes a resource from which are fashioned innovative methods of information sharing and social exchange. These methods in turn produce a deepened sense of collective responsibility and joint ownership, as access to ever-broader domains of information lend new objectivity to data and preempt the dictates of hierarchical authority.

[The book from which this selection is drawn] is about these alternative futures. Computer-based technologies are not neutral; they embody essential characteristics that are bound to alter the nature of work within our factories and offices, and among workers, professionals, and managers. New choices are laid open by these technologies, and these choices are being confronted in the daily lives of men and women across the landscape of modern organizations. [The] book is an effort to understand the deep structure of these choices — the historical, psychological, and organizational forces that imbue our conduct and sensibility. It is also a vision of a fruitful future, a call for action that can lead us beyond the stale reproduction of the past into an era that offers a historical opportunity to more fully develop the economic and human potential of our work organizations.

THE TWO FACES OF INTELLIGENT TECHNOLOGY

The past twenty years have seen their share of soothsayers ready to predict with conviction one extreme or another of the alternative futures I have presented.

From the unmanned factory to the automated cockpit, visions of the future hail information technology as the final answer to "the labor question," the ultimate opportunity to rid ourselves of the thorny problems associated with training and managing a competent and committed work force. These very same technologies, have been applauded as the hallmark of a second industrial revolution, in which the classic conflicts of knowledge and power associated with an earlier age will be synthesized in an array of organizational innovations and new procedures for the production of goods and services, all characterized by an unprecedented degree of labor harmony and widespread participation in management process.[1] Why the paradox? How can the very same technologies be interpreted in these different ways? Is this evidence that the technology is indeed neutral, a blank screen upon which managers project their biases and encounter only their own limitations? Alternatively, might it tell us something else about the interior structure of information technology?

Throughout history, humans have designed mechanisms to reproduce and extend the capacity of the human body as an instrument of work. The industrial age has carried this principle to a dramatic new level of sophistication with machines that can substitute for and amplify the abilities of the human body. Because machines are mute, and because they are precise and repetitive, they can be controlled according to a set of rational principles in a way that human bodies cannot.

There is no doubt that information technology can provide substitutes for the human body that reach an even greater degree of certainty and precision. When a task is automated by a computer, it must first be broken down to its smallest components. Whether the activity involves spraying paint on an automobile or performing in a clerical transaction, it is the information contained in this analysis that translates human agency into a computer program. The resulting software can be used to automatically guide equipment, as in the case of a robot, or to execute an information transaction, as in the case of an automated teller machine.

A computer program makes it possible to rationalize activities more comprehensively than if they had been undertaken by a human being. Programmability means, for example, that a robot will respond with unwavering precision because the instructions that guide it are themselves unvarying, or that office transactions will be uniform because the instructions that guide them have been standardized. Events and processes can be rationalized to the extent that human agency can be analyzed and translated into a computer program.

What is it then, that distinguishes information technology from earlier generations of machine technology? As information technology is used to reproduce, extend and improve upon the process of substituting machines for human agency, it simultaneously accomplishes something quite different. The devices that automate by translating information into action also register data about those automated activities, thus generating new streams of information. For example, computer-based, numerically controlled machine tools or microprocessor-based sensing devices not only apply programmed instructions to equipment but also convert the current state of equipment, product, or process into data. Scanner devices in supermarkets automate the checkout process and simultaneously generate data that can be used for inventory control, warehousing, scheduling of deliveries, and market analysis. The same systems that make it possible to auto-mate office transactions also create a vast overview of an organization's opera-tions, with many levels of data coordinated and accessible for a variety of analytical efforts.

Thus, information technology, even when it is applied to automatically repro-duce a finite activity, is not mute. It not only imposes information (in the form of programmed instructions) but also produces information. The action of a machine is entirely invested in its object, the product. Information technology, on the other hand, introduces an additional dimension of reflexivity: it makes its contribution to the product, but it also reflects back on its activities and on the system of activities to which it is related. Information technology not only pro-duces action but also produces a voice that symbolically renders events, objects, and processes so that they become visible, knowable, and shareable in a new way.

Viewed from this interior perspective, information technology is characterized by a fundamental duality that has not yet been fully appreciated. On the one hand, the technology can be applied to automating operations according to a logic that hardly differs from that of the nineteenth-century machine system — replace the human body with a technology that enables the same processes to be performed with more continuity and control. On the other, the same technology simultaneously generates information about the underlying productive and administrative processes through which an organization accomplishes its work. It provides a deeper level of transparency to activities that had been either partially or completely opaque. In this way information technology supersedes the tradi-tional logic of automation. The word that I have coined to describe this unique capacity is *informate*. Activities, events, and objects are translated into and made visible by information when a technology *informates* as well as *automates*.

The information power of intelligent technology can be seen in the manufac-turing environment when microprocessor-based devices such as robots, program-mable logic controllers, or sensors are used to translate the three-dimensional production process into digitized data. These data are then made available within a two-dimensional space, typically on the screen of a video display terminal or on a computer printout, in the form of electronic symbols, numbers, letters, and graphics. These data constitute a quality of information that did not exist before. The programmable controller not only tells the machine what to do — imposing information that guides operating equipment — but also tells what the machine has done — translating the production process and making it visible.

In the office environment, the combination of on-line transaction systems, information systems, and communications systems creates a vast information presence that now includes data formerly stored in people's heads, in face-to-face conversations, in metal file drawers, and on widely dispersed pieces of paper. The same technology that processes documents more rapidly, and with less interven-tion, than a mechanical typewriter or pen and ink can be used to display those documents in a communications network. As more of the underlying transac-tional and communicative processes of an organization become automated, they too become available as items in a growing organizational data base.

In its capacity as an automating technology, information technology has a vast potential to displace the human presence. Its implications as an informating technology, on the other hand, are not well understood. The distinction between *automate* and *informate* provides one way to understand how this technology represents both continuities and discontinuities with the traditions of industrial history. As long as the technology is treated narrowly in its automating function, it perpetuates the logic of the industrial machine, which, over the course of this century, has made it possible to rationalize work while decreasing the dependence on human skills. However, when the technology also informates the processes to which it is applied, it increases the explicit information content of tasks and sets into motion a series of dynamics that will ultimately reconfigure the nature of work and the social relationships that organize productive activity.

Because this duality of intelligent technology has not been clearly recognized, the consequences of the technology's informating capacity are often regarded as unintended. Its effects are not planned, and the potential that it lays open remains relatively unexploited. Because the informating process is poorly defined, it often evades the conventional categories of description that are used to gauge the effects of industrial technology.

These dual capacities of information technology are not opposites; they are hierarchically integrated. Informating derives from and builds upon automation. Automation is a necessary but not sufficient condition for informating. It is quite possible to proceed with automation without reference to how it will contribute to the technology's informating potential. When this occurs, informating is experienced as an unintended consequence of automation. This is one point at which choices are laid open. Managers can choose to exploit the emergent informating capacity and explore the organizational innovations required to sustain and develop it. Alternatively, they can choose to ignore or suppress the informating process. In contrast, it is possible to consider informating objectives at the start of an automation process. When this occurs, the choices that are made with respect to how and what to automate are guided by criteria that reflect developmental goals associated with using the technology's unique informating power.

Information technology is frequently hailed as "revolutionary." What are the implications of this term? *Revolution* means a pervasive, marked, radical change, but *revolution* also refers to a movement around a fixed course that returns to the starting point. Each sense of the word has relevance for the central problem of this [study]. The informating capacity of the new computer-based technologies brings about radical change as it alters the intrinsic character of work — the way millions of people experience daily life on the job. It also poses fundamentally new choices for our organizational futures, and the ways in which labor and management respond to these new choices will finally determine whether our era becomes a time for radical change or a return to the familiar patterns and pitfalls of the traditional workplace. An emphasis on the informating capacity of intelligent technology can provide a point of origin for new conceptions of work and power. A more restricted emphasis on its automating capacity can provide the occasion for that second kind of revolution — a return to the familiar grounds of industrial society with divergent interests battling for control, augmented by an array of new material resources with which to attack and defend.

The questions that we face today are finally about leadership. Will there be leaders who are able to recognize the historical moment and the choices it presents? Will they find ways to create the organizational conditions in which new visions, new concepts, and a new language of workplace relations can emerge? Will they be able to create organizational innovations that can exploit the unique capacities of the new technology and thus mobilize their organization's productive potential to meet the heightened rigors of global competition? Will there be leaders who understand the crucial role that human beings from each organizational stratum can play in adding value to the production of goods and services? If not, we will be stranded in a new world with old solutions. We will suffer through the unintended consequences of change, because we have failed to understand this technology and how it differs from what came before. By neglecting the unique informating capacity of advanced computer-based technology and ignoring the need for a new vision of work and organization, we will have forfeited the dramatic business benefits it can provide. Instead, we will find ways to absorb the dysfunctions, putting out brush fires and patching wounds in a slow-burning bewilderment.

NOTE

1. See, for example, Michael Piore and Charles F Sabel, *The Second Industrial Divide: Possibilities for Prosperity* (New York: Basic Books, 1984).

PART VII
DEBATING TECHNOLOGY:
TURN-OF-THE-MILLENNIUM STYLE

It is hard to think of a better way of characterizing the diference between the state of thought on technology and society in the late 1960s and the late 1990s than the contrast between the debate between Mesthene and McDermott in Part II and the debate between Nicholas Negroponte and Donald Norman in Part VII.

Some might argue that the comparison is not really a fair one, that there are better contemporary parallels to the 1960s-style ideological dispute between Mesthene and McDermott than the two writers represented in this section, both of whom are technophiles. In one sense, this is undoubtedly true. There are still lively arguments between those who see technology as humanity's salvation and those who see it as tool with which those in power maintain their control over the rest of the population. But such debates today seem much further removed from the daily reality of most people than the Mesthene–McDermott debate did in its day.

This is not to say that arguments over the beneficial or harmful impacts of technology or of specific technologies are not relevant today. They are as important as ever — as many of the selections in the first six sections of this book demonstrate. The point is that if one must choose a dispute over technology in this time and place, the Negroponte–Norman debate seems representative of the current *zeitgeist* in the same way that Mesthene and McDermott reflect the spirit of the United States in the 1960s.

Negroponte, founder of MIT's famed Media Lab, describes how the ability to digitize information — to transform words, sounds, and still and moving pictures into "bits" — is making fundamental changes in the organization of knowledge, in the economy, and ultimately in society. Norman, a former executive with Apple Computer and Hewlett-Packard Corporation who now has his own consulting firm, believes that Negroponte has things backwards in his emphasis on "being digital." "We are analog beings trapped in a digital world," he writes. We create technologies that must be treated on their own terms instead of designing things that are suited to ourselves, and this is the source of most of the problems we have with computers and other technologies.

Each of these writers makes a fascinating and persuasive case. Moreover, in many important respects, *both* are correct. Certainly, both deserve our careful attention.

25.   Being Digital

NICHOLAS NEGROPONTE

One doesn't have to turn many pages in Nicholas Negroponte's book, Being Digital, from which this chapter is excerpted, to see where he's coming from. The book is dedicated to his wife, Elaine, "who has put up with my being digital for exactly 11111 years." Those of us who are more accustomed to thinking in base ten numbers might need a few moments to figure out, that 11111 is the equivalent in binary of 31 in conventional base ten notation. Binary digits (i.e., bits) are, of course, what digital computers, whose circuits consist of elements that exist in only two states (off and on, or 0 and 1), use to process information. And Negroponte believes that "bits," 'the DNA of information,' are rapidly replacing atoms as the basic commodity of human interaction." In other words, everything can be seen as a form of information, and information can be expressed in bits.

Using this as a point of departure, Negroponte explores the revolution in information technology, which he sees as taking computers out of their boxes and putting them into virtually everything we use in daily life. The implications of this "digitization" are enormous, merging the technologies of computers and television, changing the meaning of "mass communication," making copyright law obsolete, undermining the economics of telecommunications, and creating opportunities for new products and services barely imagined today (except perhaps by Negroponte and his colleagues). This chapter offers a sampling of Negroponte's insights and approach.

Nicholas Negroponte's name is virtually synonymous with that of the Massachusetts Institute of Technology's Media Laboratory, which he founded in Cambridge, Massachusetts, in 1985. The Media Lab conducts advanced research into such information technologies as digital television, holographic imaging, computer music and vision, artificial intelligence, and education-related technologies. Negroponte, who studied at MIT, joined the faculty there in 1966 and is today professor of media technology. He is regarded as one of the most creative and original thinkers on information technology and the future, is a prolific writer and speaker, and publishes a regular column in Wired *magazine.*

I think of myself as an extremist when it comes to predicting and initiating change. Nonetheless, when it comes to technological and regulatory changes, as well as new services, things are moving faster than even I can believe — there is obviously no speed limit on the electronic highway. It's like driving on the autobahn at 160 kph. Just as I realize the speed I'm going, *zzzwoom*, a Mercedes passes, then another, and another. Yikes, they must be driving at 120 mph. Such is life in the fast lane of the infobahn.

Although the rate of change is faster than ever, innovation is paced less by scientific breakthroughs like the transistor, microprocessor, or optical fiber and more by new applications like mobile computing, global networks, and multimedia. This is partly because of the phenomenal costs associated with the fabrication facilities for modern chips, for which new applications are sorely needed to consume all that computing power and memory, and also because, in many areas of hardware, we are coming close to physical limits.

It takes about a billionth of a second for light to travel one foot, which is something not likely to change. As we make computer chips smaller and smaller, their speed can increase a little. But in order to make a big difference in overall computer power, it will be necessary to design new solutions, for example, with many machines running at the same time. The big changes in computers and telecommunications now emanate from the applications, from basic human needs rather than from basic material sciences. This observation has not gone unnoticed by Wall Street.

Bob Lucky, a highly acclaimed author and engineer and the vice president for applied research at Bellcore (formerly the exclusive research arm of the seven Baby Bells), noted recently that he no longer keeps up to date technically by reading scholarly publications; instead he reads the *Wall Street Journal.* One of the best ways to focus on the future of the "bit" industry is to set the tripod of one's telescope on the entrepreneurial, business, and regulatory landscape of the United States, with one leg each in the New York, American, and NASDAQ exchanges.

When QVC and Viacom battled for Paramount, analysts proclaimed the winner to be the loser. Paramount's financial performance did decline after the courtship started, but remains, nonetheless, a beautiful catch for Viacom because now it owns a wider variety of bits. Both Sumner Redstone and Barry Diller know that if your company makes only one kind of bit, you are not in very good shape for the future. The Paramount story was about bits, not egos.

The valuation of a bit is determined in large part by its ability to be used over and over again. In this regard, a Mickey Mouse bit is probably worth a lot more than a Forrest Gump bit; Mickey's bits even come in lollipops (consumable atoms). More interestingly, Disney's guaranteed audience is refueled at a rate that exceeds 12,500 births each hour. In 1994 the market value of Disney was $2 billion greater than that of Bell Atlantic, in spite of Bell Atlantic's sales being 50 percent greater and profits being double.

TRANSPORTING BITS

Transporting bits is an even worse business to be in than that of the airlines with their fare wars. The telecommunications business is regulated to such a degree that NYNEX must put telephone booths in the darkest corners of Brooklyn (where they last all of forty-eight hours), while its unregulated competitors will only put their telephone booths on Fifth and Park Avenues and in airline club lounges.

Worse, the entire economic model of pricing in telecommunications is about to fall apart. Today's tariffs are determined per minute, per mile, or per bit, all three of which are rapidly becoming bogus measures. The system is being ruptured by the wild extremes of time (a microsecond to a day), distance (a few feet to fifty thousand miles), and numbers of bits (1 to 20 billion). In days when those differences were not so extreme, the old model worked well enough. When you used a 9,600-bps modem, you paid 75 percent less for connect time than you did with your 2,400-bps modem. Who cared?

But now the spread is huge, and we do care. Time is an example. Ignoring the transmission speed and the number of bits, am I to believe that I will be paying the same price to see a two-hour movie as I will be paying to have thirty different four-minute conversations? If I can deliver a fax at 1.2 million bps, am I really going to pay $\frac{1}{125}$ the cost of what I pay today? If I can piggyback 16,000 bps voice on an ADSL[1] movie channel, am I really going to pay five cents for a two-hour conversation? If my mother-in-law returns home from the hospital with a remotely monitored pacemaker that needs an open line to the hospital to monitor a half-dozen randomly spaced bits each hour, should those bits be tariffed the same way as the 12 billion bits in *Gone with the Wind?* Try figuring out that business model!

We have to evolve a more intelligent scheme. It may not use time, distance, or bits as the controlling variable and basis for tariff. Maybe bandwidth should be free, and we buy movies, long-distance health monitoring, and documents because of their value, not the channel's. It would be unconscionable to think of buying toys based on the number of atoms in them. It is time to understand what the bits and atoms mean.

If the management of a telecommunications company limits its long-term strategy to carrying bits, it will not be acting in its shareholders' best interest. Owning the bits or rights to the bits, or adding significant value to the bits, must be a part of the equation. Otherwise, there will be no place to add revenue, and telephone companies will be stuck with a service fast becoming a commodity, the price of which will go down further and further because of competition and increased bandwidth.

When I was growing up, everyone hated the telephone company (as an adult I would put insurance companies at the top of the list). Any cunning 1950s child would have a scheme or a scam, and it was considered almost sporting to rip off the telephone company. Today, cable companies have assumed this honor, because many have provided poor service while raising their rates. Worse, the cable companies are not "common carriers"; they control what goes down their lines.

The cable industry has enjoyed many of the benefits of an unregulated monopoly, originally intended to be little more than a patchwork of community services. As cable franchises started to fuse and become national networks, people took notice of the fact that these companies indeed controlled both the telecommunications channel and the content. Unlike the telephone company, they were not obliged to provide a right-of-way except for very local and communal purposes.

Regulating the telephone industry is based on a simple principle: everybody is allowed to use it. But it is not clear what happens in a broadband system if it is more like today's cable companies than a telephone network. Congress is nervous about the fairhandedness with which a channel owner will welcome a content owner, given a choice. Also, if you own both content and channel, can you maintain your neutrality?

To put it another way, if AT&T and Disney merge, will the new company make it less expensive for children to access Mickey Mouse than Bugs Bunny?

In the fall of 1993, when Bell Atlantic agreed to buy cable giant Tele-Communications Inc. for $21.4 billion, pundits of the *information superhighway* took it as a signal that the digital age had truly begun. The digital ribbon had been cut.

However, the merger flew in the face of regulatory logic and common sense. Telephony and cable had positioned themselves as archrivals, regulation precluded most joint ownership, and loops and stars were thought to mix like oil and vinegar. Just the sheer level of investment dropped jaws.

Four months later, when the Bell Atlantic/TCI discussions collapsed, the pendulum overcompensated, and new jargon emerged about "roadkill" and "construction delays" on the information superhighway. The digital age had suddenly been postponed again, TCI's stock dropped more than 30 percent, and other associated companies took a spill as well. The champagne had to go back into the bottle.

But from my point of view, this was not an important casualty. In fact, the Bell Atlantic and TCI agreement was one of the least interesting corporate mergers. It was as if two plumbing-supply houses, marketing two distinctly different pipe sizes, had decided to combine their inventory. It was really not about the deep-rooted combination of channel and content, blending bit manufacturing with bit distribution. Disney and Hollywood king Michael Ovitz each teaming up in 1994 with three regional telephone companies — now that's more interesting.

Consumer electronics companies have tried to do this with entertainment companies. In principle, the idea is very powerful, but so far has had little synergy because of cultural differences of all kinds. When Sony bought CBS Records and then Columbia Pictures, Americans cried foul. Like the sale of Rockefeller Center, these purchases raised the issue of symbolic and real foreign control of a national cultural asset. When Matsushita bought MCA a while later, people were even more startled, because MCA's chairman, Lew Wasserman, was considered by many to be the most American chief executive. I remember visiting MCA headquarters after the first oil crisis and seeing stickers on the elevator buttons (a message from Lew) that said, "Walk up one and down two, for your health and your country." These purchases bring up deep cultural divides, not just between Japanese and American thought but between engineering and the arts. So far they have not worked, but I suspect they will.

CULTURE CONVERGENCE

There is a perceived polarity (however artificial) between technology and the humanities, between science and art, between right brain and left. The burgeoning field of multimedia is likely to be one of those disciplines, like architecture, that bridges the gap.

Television was invented through purely technological imperatives. When pioneers like Philo Farnsworth and Vladimir Zworykin looked at postage-stamp-size electronic images in 1929, they were driven to perfect the technology purely on the basis of its own merit. While Zworykin had some naive ideas about the use of television in the early days, he was sadly disappointed in his later years.

Former MIT president Jerome Wiesner tells a story about Zworykin's visiting him one Saturday at the White House when Wiesner was [John F. Kennedy's] science advisor (and close friend). He asked Zworykin if he had ever met the president. As Zworykin had not, Wiesner took him across the hall to meet JFK Wiesner introduced his visitor to the president as "the man who got you elected." Startled, JFK asked, "How is that?" Wiesner explained, "This is the man who invented television." JFK replied how that was a terrific and important thing to have done. Zworykin wryly commented, "Have you seen television recently?"

Technological imperatives — and only those imperatives — drove the development of television. Then it was handed off to a body of creative talent, with different values, from a different intellectual subculture.

Photography, on the other hand, was invented by photographers. The people who perfected photographic technology did so for expressive purposes, fine-tuning their techniques to meet the needs of their art, just as authors invented romance novels, essays, and comic books to fit their ideas.

Personal computers have moved computer science away from the purely technical imperative and are now evolving more like photography. Computing is no longer the exclusive realm of military, government, and big business. It is being channeled directly into the hands of very creative individuals at all levels of society, becoming the means for creative expression in both its use and development. The means and messages of multimedia will become a blend of technical and artistic achievement. Consumer products will be the driving force.

The electronic-games business ($15 billion worldwide) is an example. These games represent a business that is larger than the American motion-picture industry and growing much faster as well. Games companies are driving display technology so hard that virtual reality will become a "reality" at very low cost, whereas NASA was able to use it with only marginal success at a cost of more than $200,000. On November 15, 1994, Nintendo announced a $199 virtual reality game called "Virtual Boy."

Consider [1995's] fastest Intel processor, which runs at 100 million instructions per second (MIPS). Compare that to Sony, which just introduced a $200 "Playstation" with a 1,000 MIPS [processor] for the games market. What is going on? The answer is simple: our thirst for new kinds of entertainment is seemingly unquenchable, and the new, real-time 3-D content, which the games industry is banking on, needs that kind of processing and those new displays. The application is the imperative.

PULLING VERSUS PUSHING

Many of the big media companies like Viacom, News Corporation, and the publisher of this book add most of their value to information and entertainment content in one way: distribution. As I said earlier, the distribution of atoms is far more complex than of bits and requires the force of an enormous company. Moving bits, by contrast, is far simpler and, in principle, precludes the need for these giant corporations. Almost.

It was through the *New York Times* that I came to know and enjoy the writing of the computer and communications business reporter John Markoff. Without, the *New York Times*, I would never have known of his work. However, now that I do, it would be far easier for me to have an automatic method to collect any new story Markoff writes and drop it into my personalized newspaper or suggested-reading file. I would probably be willing to pay Markoff the proverbial "two cents" for each of his stories.

If one two-hundredth of the 1995 Internet population were to subscribe to this idea and John were to write a hundred stories a year (he actually writes between one-hundred-twenty and one-hundred-forty), he would earn $1,000,000 per year, which I am prepared to guess is more than the *New York Times* pays him. If you think one two-hundredth is too big a proportion, then wait a short while. The numbers really do work. Once somebody is established, the added value of a distributor is less and less in a digital world.

The distribution and movement of bits must also include filtering and selection processes. The media company is, among other things, a talent scout, and its distribution channel provides a test bed for public opinion. But after a certain point, the author may not need this forum. In the digital age, Michael Crichton could surely make far more money selling his next books direct. Sorry, Knopf.

Being digital will change the nature of mass media from a process of pushing bits at people to one of allowing people (or their computers) to pull at them. This is a radical change, because our entire concept of media is one of successive layers of filtering, which reduce information and entertainment to a collection of "top stories" or "best-sellers" to be thrown at different "audiences." As media companies go more and more toward narrowcasting, like the magazine business, they are still pushing bits at a special-interest group, like car fanatics, Alpine skiers, or wine enthusiasts. I recently encountered the idea of a niche magazine for insomniacs, which cleverly would advertise on late-night television, when the rates are low.

The information industry will become more of a boutique business. Its marketplace is the global information highway. The customers will be people and their computer agents. Is the digital marketplace real? Yes, but only if the interface between people and their computers improves to the point where talking to your computer is as easy as talking to another human being.

* * *

AN AGE OF OPTIMISM

I am optimistic by nature. However, every technology or gift of science has a dark side. Being digital is no exception.

The next decade will see cases of intellectual-property abuse and invasion of our privacy. We will experience digital vandalism, software piracy, and data thievery. Worst of all, we will witness the loss of many jobs to wholly automated systems, which will soon change the white-collar workplace to the same degree that it has already transformed the factory floor. The notion of lifetime employment at one job has already started to disappear.

The radical transformation of the nature of our job markets, as we work less with atoms and more with bits, will happen at just about the same time the 2 billion–strong labor force of India and China starts to come on-line (literally). A self-employed software designer in Peoria will be competing with his or her counterpart in Pohang. A digital typographer in Madrid will do the same with one in Madras. American companies are already outsourcing hardware development and software production to Russia and India, not to find cheap manual labor but to secure a highly skilled intellectual force seemingly prepared to work harder, faster, and in a more disciplined fashion than those in our own country.

As the business world globalizes and the Internet grows, we will start to see a seamless digital workplace. Long before political harmony and long before the GATT talks can reach agreement on the tariff and trade of atoms (the right to sell Evian water in California), bits will be borderless, stored and manipulated with absolutely no respect to geopolitical boundaries. In fact, time zones will probably play a bigger role in our digital future than trade zones. I can imagine some software projects that literally move around the world from east to west on a twenty-four-hour cycle, from person to person or from group to group, one working as the other sleeps. Microsoft will need to add London and Tokyo offices for software development in order to produce on three shifts.

As we move more toward such a digital world, an entire sector of the population will be or feel disenfranchised. When a fifty-year-old steelworker loses his job, unlike his twenty-five-year-old son he may have no digital resilience at all. When a modern-day secretary loses his job, at least he may be conversant with the digital world and have transferrable skills.

Bits are not edible; in that sense they cannot stop hunger. Computers are not moral; they cannot resolve complex issues like the rights to life and to death. But being digital, nevertheless, does give much cause for optimism. Like a force of nature, the digital age cannot be denied or stopped. It has four very powerful qualities that will result in its ultimate triumph: decentralizing, globalizing, harmonizing, and empowering.

The decentralizing effect of being digital can be felt no more strongly than in commerce and in the computer industry itself. The so-called management information systems (MIS) czar, who used to reign over a glass-enclosed and air-conditioned mausoleum, is an emperor with no clothes, almost extinct. Those who survive are usually doing so because they outrank anybody able to fire them and the company's board of directors is out of touch or asleep or both.

Thinking Machines Corporation, a great and imaginative supercomputer company started by electrical engineering genius Danny Hillis, disappeared after ten years. In that short space of time it introduced the world to massively parallel computer architectures. Its demise did not occur because of mismanagement or sloppy engineering of their so-called Connection Machine. It vanished because parallelism could be decentralized; the very same kind of massively parallel architectures have suddenly become possible by threading together low-cost, mass-produced personal computers.

While this was not good news for Thinking Machines, it is an important message to all of us, both literally and metaphorically. It means the enterprise of the future can meet its computer needs in a new and scalable way by populating its organization with personal computers that, when needed, can work in unison to crunch on computationally intensive problems. Computers will literally work both for individuals and for groups. I see the same decentralized mind-set growing in our society, driven by young citizenry in the digital world. The traditional centralist view of life will become a thing of the past.

The nation-state itself is subject to tremendous change and globalization. Governments fifty years from now will be both larger and smaller. Europe finds itself dividing itself into smaller ethnic entities while trying to unite economically. The forces of nationalism make it too easy to be cynical and dismiss any broad-stroke attempt at world unification. But in the digital world, previously impossible solutions become viable.

Today, when 20 percent of the world consumes 80 percent of its resources, when a quarter of us have an acceptable standard of living and three-quarters don't, how can this divide possibly come together? While the politicians struggle with the baggage of history, a new generation is emerging from the digital landscape free of many of the old prejudices. These kids are released from the limitation of geographic proximity as the sole basis of friendship, collaboration, play, and neighborhood. Digital technology can be a natural force drawing people into greater world harmony.

The harmonizing effect of being digital is already apparent as previously partitioned disciplines and enterprises find themselves collaborating, not competing. A previously missing common language emerges, allowing people to understand across boundaries. Kids at school today experience the opportunity to look at the same thing from many perspectives. A computer program, for example, can be seen simultaneously as a set of computer instructions or as concrete poetry formed by the indentations in the text of the program. What kids learn very quickly is that to know a program is to know it from many perspectives, not just one.

But more than anything, my optimism comes from the empowering nature of being digital. The access, the mobility, and the ability to effect change are what will make the future so different from the present. The information superhighway may be mostly hype today, but it is an understatement about tomorrow. It will exist beyond people's wildest predictions. As children appropriate a global information resource, and as they discover that only adults need learner's permits, we are bound to find new hope and dignity in places where very little existed before.

My optimism is not fueled by an anticipated invention or discovery. Finding a cure for cancer and AIDS, finding an acceptable way to control population, or inventing a machine that can breathe our air and drink our oceans and excrete unpolluted forms of each are dreams that may or may not come about. Being digital is different. We are not waiting on any invention. It is here. It is now. It is almost genetic in its nature, in that each generation will become more digital than the preceding one.

The control bits of that digital future are more than ever before in the hands of the young. Nothing could make me happier.

NOTE

1. "Asymmetric Digital Subscriber Line," a technology that permits high-speed access to the Internet over regular telephone lines. As of mid-1999, available only in certain areas.

26.   Being Analog

DONALD A. NORMAN

What would computer technology be like if it were made to conform to human needs instead of forcing humans to conform to its requirements? Donald Norman is a technological critic and designer concerned with human–machine interaction. His book, The Invisible Computer, *from which this chapter is drawn, is, in the words of one review, "a wake-up call for today's technologists . . . [to] reorient their thinking away from the technically possible and towards the human being." It explains (in the words of its subtitle), "why good products can fail, the personal computer is so complex, and information appliances are the solution."*

Norman compares the nature of humans with that of the machines we have built for ourselves and sees a "horrible mismatch." The digital signals that computers use are abstractions of real signals encoded for the convenience of the machines. Digitized music on a CD is an example. Humans are analog devices that are imprecise, tolerate ambiguity, and respond to continuous variations in signals, more like a phonograph needle responds to the wiggles and changing depth on a vinyl LP record. Recognizing these differences is the key to creating technologies that serve us rather than those that force us to adapt to their ways. Think about Nicholas Negroponte dedicating his book (in Chapter 25) to his wife of "11111" years: This is how a computer sees "31." Which numbering system do you prefer to think in?

Like Negroponte, but with a much different style and approach, Donald Norman is a guru of the information age who can provoke us into seeing familiar things in new ways. Norman is principal of the Nielsen Norman Group, an executive consulting firm concerned with human-centered design, which he cofounded in 1998. He is also a professor emeritus at the University of California, San Diego, where he taught for many years and founded and chaired the Department of Cognitive Science. During his career, he has held positions at Apple Computer and Hewlett-Packard. Norman holds a B.S. in electrical engineering from the Massachusetts Institute of Technology, as well as an M.S. (in electrical engineering) and Ph.D. (in mathematical psychology) from the University of Pennsylvania. Among his many books are The Design of Everyday Things *(1990) and* Things That Make Us Smart *(1993).*

We are analog beings trapped in a digital world, and the worst part is, we did it to ourselves.

We humans are biological animals. We have evolved over millions of years to function well in the environment, to survive. We are analog devices following biological modes of operation. We are compliant, flexible, tolerant. Yet we have constructed a world of machines that requires us to be rigid, fixed, intolerant. We have devised a technology that requires considerable care and attention, that demands to be treated on its own terms, not ours. We live in a technology-centered world where the technology is not appropriate for people. No wonder we have such difficulties.

Here we are, wandering about the world, bumping into things, forgetful of details, with a poor sense of time, a poor memory for facts and figures, unable to focus attention on a topic for more than a short duration, reasoning by example rather than by logic, and drawing upon our admittedly deficient memories of prior experience. When viewed this way, we seem rather pitiful. No wonder we have constructed a set of artificial devices that are very much not in our own image. We have constructed a world of machinery in which accuracy and precision matter. Time matters. Names, dates, facts, and figures matter. Accurate memory matters. Details matter.

All the things we are bad at matter, all the things we are good at are ignored. Bizarre.

MAKING SENSE OF THE WORLD

People excel at perception, at creativity, at the ability to go beyond the information given, making sense of otherwise chaotic events. We often have to interpret events far beyond the information available, and our ability to do this efficiently and effortlessly, usually without even being aware that we are doing so, greatly adds to our ability to function. This ability to put together a sensible, coherent image of the world in the face of limited evidence allows us to anticipate and predict events, the better to cope with an ambiguous, ever-changing world.

Here's a simple test of your memory:

How many animals of each type did Moses take on the ark?

What's the answer? How many animals? Two? Be careful: What about an amoeba, a sexless, single-celled animal that reproduces by dividing itself into two cells? Did he need to take two of these?

Answer: None. No animals at all. Moses didn't take any animals onto the ark. It was Noah.

Some of you were fooled. Why? Because people often hear what is intended, not what is said. In normal language, people ask real questions that have real answers and real meaning. It is only psychology professors and jokesters who ask trick questions. If you spotted the trick, it is because you were unnaturally suspicious or alert. We don't need such alertness in normal human interaction. Those of you who were fooled responded normally: That is how we are meant to be.

Your mind interpreted the question meaningfully, making sense of the information. It may have confused "Moses" with "Noah," but it was aided by the fact that those names have a lot of similarity: both are short, with two syllables. Both are biblical, from the Old Testament. In normal circumstances, the confusion would be beneficial, for it is the sort of error that a speaker might make, and it is useful when a listener can go beyond superficial errors.

Note that the ability to be insensitive to simple speech errors does not mean that people are readily fooled. Thus, you would not have been fooled had I asked:

How many animals of each type did Clinton take on the ark?

The name Clinton is not sufficiently close to the target: it requires a biblical name to fool you.[1] From a practical point of view, although a speaker might say "Moses" when "Noah" was intended, it is far less likely that someone would mistakenly say a nonbiblical name such as "Clinton." The automatic inaccurate interpretation of the original question is intelligent and sensible. The fact that the first question can fool people is a testament to our powers, not an indictment of them. Once again, in normal life, such corrections are beneficial. Normal life does not deliberately try to fool us. Take note of this example, for it is fundamental to understanding people and, more important, to understanding why computers are so different from people, why people and today's technology are such a bad match.

Why do accuracy and precision matter? In our natural world, they don't. We are approximate beings; we get at the meanings of things, and for this, the details don't much matter. Accurate times and dates matter only because we have created a culture in which these things are important. Accurate and precise measurements matter because the machines and procedures we have created are rigid, inflexible, and fixed in their ways, so if a measurement is off by some tiny fraction, the result can be a failure to operate. Worse yet, it can cause a tragic accident.

People are compliant: We adapt ourselves to the situation. We are flexible enough to allow our bodies and our actions to fit the circumstances. Animals don't require precise measurements and high accuracy to function. Machines do.

The same story is true of time, of facts and figures, and of accurate memory. These matter only because the mechanical, industrialized society created by people doesn't match people. In part, this is because we don't know how to do any better. Can we build machines that are as compliant and flexible as people? Not today. Biology doesn't build; it grows, it evolves. It constructs life out of flexible parts, parts that are self-repairable. We don't know how to do this with our machines. We build information devices only out of binary logic, with its insistence upon logic and precision. We invented the artificial mathematics of logic the better to enhance our own thought processes.

The dilemma facing us is the horrible mismatch between the requirements of these human-built machines and human capabilities. Machines are mechanical, we are biological. Machines are rigid and require great precision and accuracy of control. We are compliant. We tolerate and produce huge amounts of ambiguity and uncertainty, very little precision and accuracy. The latest inventions of humankind are those of the digital technology of information processing and communication, yet we ourselves are analog devices. Analog and biological.

An analog device is one in which the representation of information corresponds to its physical structure. In an analog recording the stored signal varies in value precisely in the same way as sound energy varies in time. A phonograph recording is analog; it works by recreating the variations in sound energy by wiggles and changes of depth in the groove. In a tape recording, the strength of the magnetic field on the tape varies in analogous fashion to the sound energy variations. These are analog signals.

Digital signals are entirely different. Here, what is recorded is an abstraction of the real signals. Digital encoding was invented mainly to get rid of noise. In the beginning, electrical circuits were all analog. But electrical circuits are noisy, meaning they are susceptible to unwanted voltage variations. The noise gets in the way, mostly because the circuits are unable to distinguish between the stuff that matters and the stuff that doesn't.

Enter the digital world. Instead of using a signal that is analogous to the physical event, the event is transformed into a series of numbers that describes the original. In high-quality recording of music, the sound energy is sampled over 40,000 times each second, transformed into numbers that represent the energy value at the time each sample was made. The numbers are usually represented in the form of binary digits rather than the familiar decimal ones, which means that any digit can have only one of two states, 0 or 1, rather than the ten possible states of a decimal digit. When there are only two states to be distinguished between, the operation is far simpler and less subject to error than when it has to determine a precise value, as is required with an analog signal. Binary signals are relatively insensitive to noise.

As you can imagine, to record and play back a digital representation of sound waves requires a lot of processing. It is necessary to transform the sound into numbers, store the numerical digits, and then retrieve and restore them back to sound energy. Such rapid transformation wasn't possible at an affordable price until recently, which is why the emphasis on digital signals seems new. It is only recently that the technology was capable of high-quality digital encoding of audio and television signals, although the concept is old.

There are a number of common misconceptions about digital and analog signals. One is that *analog* means continuous, whereas *digital* means discrete. Although this is often the case, it is not the basis for the distinction. Think *analog* as meaning *analogous*: analogous to the real world. If the real world event is discrete, so too will be the analog one. If the physical process is continuous, then so too will be the analog one. Digital, however, is always discrete: one of a limited number of values, usually one of two, but occasionally one of three, four, or ten.

A widespread misconception is that digital is somehow good, analog bad. This just isn't so. Yes, digital is good for our contemporary machines, but analog might be better for future machines. And analog is certainly far better for people. Why? Mainly because of the impact of noise.

We have evolved to match the world. If you want to understand how human perception works, it helps to start off by understanding how the world of light and sound works, because the eyes and ears have evolved to fit the nature of these physical signals. What this means is that we interact best with systems that are either part of the real world or analogous to them — analog signals.

Analog signals behave in ways human beings can understand. A slight error or noise transforms the signals in known ways, ways the body has evolved to interpret and cope with. If there is some noise in a conventional television signal, encoded in analogical form, we see some noise on the screen. Usually we can tolerate the resulting image, at least as long as we can make sense of it. Small amounts of noise have slight impact. People are analog, able to extract meanings despite noise and error. As long as the meanings are unchanged, the details of the signals do not matter. They are not noticed, they are not remembered.

In a digital signal, the representation is so arbitrary that a simple error can have unexpected consequences. Digital encodings use compression technologies that eliminate redundancy. Digital television signals are compressed to save space and bandwidth, the most common scheme being the algorithms devised by the Motion Picture Expert Group (MPEG). If any information is lost, it takes a while before the system resends enough information to allow recovery. MPEG encoding breaks up the picture into rectangular regions. Noise can make it impossible for the system to reconstruct an entire region. As a result, when the image is noisy, whole regions of the screen break up and distort in ways the human brain cannot reconstruct, and it takes a few seconds until the picture reforms itself.

The real problem with being digital is that it implies a kind of slavery to accuracy, a requirement that is most unlike the natural workings of the person. It is perfectly proper and reasonable for machines to use digital encodings for their internal workings. Machines do better with digital encoding. The problem comes about in the form of interaction between people and machines. People do best with signals and information that fit the way they perceive and think, which means analogous to the real world. Machines do best with signals and information that are suited for the way they function, which means digital, rigid, precise. So when the two have to meet, which side should dominate? In the past, it has been the machine that dominates. In the future, it should be the person. . . .

HUMANS VERSUS COMPUTERS

The ever-increasing complexity of everyday life brings with it both great opportunities and major challenges.[2] One of the challenges, that the brain does not work at all like a computer, also provides us with an opportunity: the possibility of new modes of interaction that allow us to take advantage of the complementary talents of humans and machines.

The modern era of information technology has been with us but a short time. Computers are less than a century old. The technology has been constructed deliberately to produce mechanical systems that operate reliably, algorithmically, and consistently. They are based upon mathematics, or more precisely, arithmetic in the case of the first computing devices and logic in the case of the more modern devices.

Contrast this with the human brain. Human beings are the result of millions of years of evolution, where the guiding principle was survival of the species, not efficient, algorithmic computation. Robustness in the face of unexpected circumstances plays a major role in the evolutionary process. Human intelligence has coevolved with social interaction, cooperation, rivalry, and communication. Interestingly enough, the ability to deceive seems to have been one driving force. Only the most intelligent of animals is able to employ a sophisticated level of intentional, purposeful deception. Only the most sophisticated animal is capable of seeing through the deceit. Sure, nature also practices deception through camouflage and mimicry, but this isn't willful and intentional. Primates are the most skilled at intentional, willful deception, and the most sophisticated primate — the human — is the most sophisticated deceiver of all.

Note that some deception is essential for the smooth pursuit of social interaction: the "white lie" smoothes over many otherwise discomforting social clashes. It is not always best to tell the truth when people ask how we like their appearance, or their presentation, or the gift they have just given us. One could argue that computers won't be truly intelligent or social until they, too, are able to deceive.

We humans have learned to control the environment. We are the masters of artifacts. Physical artifacts make us stronger, faster, and more comfortable. Cognitive artifacts make us smarter. Among cognitive artifacts are the invention of writing and other notational systems, such as those used in mathematics, dance, and musical transcription. The result of these inventions is that our knowledge is now cumulative; each generation grows upon the heritage left behind by previous generations. This is the good news. The bad news is that the amount to be learned about the history, culture, and techniques of modern life increases with time. It now takes several decades to become a truly well educated citizen. How much time will be required in fifty years? In one hundred years?

The biological nature of human computation, coupled with the evolutionary process by which the brain has emerged, leads to a very different style of computation from the precise, logic-driven systems that characterize current computers. The differences are dramatic. Computers are constructed from a large number of fast, simple devices, each following binary logic and working reliably and consistently. Errors in the operation of any of the underlying components are not tolerated, and they are avoided either by careful design to minimize failure rates or through error-correcting coding in critical areas. The remarkable power of the computer is a result of the high speed of relatively simple computing devices.

Biological computation is performed by a very large number of slow, complex devices — neurons — each doing considerable computation and operating through electrochemical interactions. The power of the computation is a result of the highly parallel nature of the computation and the complex computations done by each of the billions of neural cells. Moreover, the cells are bathed in fluids whose chemistry can change rapidly, providing a means for rapid dispersion of hormones and other signals to the entire system, chemicals that are site-specific. Think of it as a packet-switching deployment of chemical agents. The result is that the computational basis is dynamic, capable of rapid, fundamental change.

Affect, emotion, and mood all play a powerful — and as yet poorly understood — role in human cognition. Certainly all of us have experienced the tension when logic dictates one course of action but mood or emotion another. More often than not, we follow mood or emotion.

Whatever the mode of computation — and the full story is not yet known — it is certainly not binary logic. Each individual biological element is neither reliable nor consistent. Errors are frequent — cells continually die — and reliability is maintained through massive redundancy as well as through the inherently error-tolerant nature of the computational process and, for that matter, the relatively high error-tolerance of the resulting behavior.

These last points cannot be overemphasized. The body, the brain, and human social interaction have all coevolved to tolerate large variations in performance under a wide-ranging set of environmental conditions. It is a remarkably error-tolerant and forgiving system. It uses both electrical and chemical systems of communication and processing. Conscious and subconscious processing probably use different computational mechanisms, and the role of emotions and affect is not yet understood.

Human language serves as a good example of the evolution of a robust, redundant, and relatively noise-insensitive means of social communication. Errors are corrected so effortlessly that often neither party is aware of the error or the correction. Communication relies heavily upon a shared knowledge base, intentions, and goals; people with different cultural backgrounds often clash, even though they speak the same language. The result is a marvelously complex structure for social interaction and communication. Children learn language without conscious effort, yet the complexities of human language still defy complete scientific understanding.

Biological versus Technological Evolution

We humans have evolved to fit the natural environment. At the same time we have learned to modify and change the environment. This process, in which we've changed to fit the world while simultaneously changing the world, leads to further evolutionary change. Until recently, this coevolution proceeded at a human pace. We developed language and tools. We discovered how to control fire and construct simple tools. The tools became more complex as simple tools became machines. The process was slow, the better to fit the new ways with the old, the new methods with human capabilities.

Biological evolution of humankind proceeds too slowly to be visible, but there is a kind of technological and environmental evolution that proceeds rapidly. We evolve our human-made artifacts to fit our abilities. This evolution is similar to, yet different from, the biological kind. For one thing, it has a history: It is Lamarckian, in that lessons learned in one generation can be propagated to future ones. Nonetheless, it is an evolutionary process, because it tends to be unguided except by rules of survival. Each new generation is but a small modification of the previous one.

A good illustration of how an evolutionary process shapes our human-invented artifacts is sports. Sports require an exquisite mix of the doable and the difficult. Make a game too easy and it loses its appeal. Make it too difficult and it is unplayable. The range from too easy to too difficult is huge, and fortunately so. One of our traits is the ability to learn, to develop skills far beyond that which the unpracticed person can do. Thus, some games, such as tic-tac-toe, which seem difficult when first encountered, are so readily mastered that they soon become boring. A successful game is one that has a wide range of complexity, playable by beginners and experts alike, although not necessarily at the same time. Successful games include soccer, rugby, tennis, basketball, baseball, football, chess, go, checkers, poker, and bridge. These are multidimensional, rich, and multifaceted. As a result, the beginner can enjoy part of their charm while the expert can exploit all the multiple dimensions.

Games work well when they do not use too much technology. The reason is simple: Games are suited to human reaction times, size, and strength. Add too much technology to the mix, and you soon move the game beyond the reach of human abilities. This is aptly illustrated in war, the deadly dueling exercises in which the armies of the world pit themselves one against the other. But here, the technologies are deliberately exploited to exceed human capability, so much so that it can take ten years of training to master a modern jet fighter plane, and even then the human pilot is rendered temporarily unconscious during violent maneuvers. These are games not fit for people.

Alas, the slow, graceful coevolution of people and environment, and of the tools, artifacts, and games that we have designed, no longer holds. Each generation benefits from the one before, and the accumulated knowledge leads to more rapid change. We benefit greatly from this cumulative buildup of knowledge, but the price we pay is that each succeeding generation has more and more to learn. The result is that the past acts both as a wonderful starting point, propelling us forward on the shoulders of giants, and as a massive anchor, compelling us to spend more and more time at school, learning the accumulated wisdom of the ages, to the point that one's motivation and energy may be depleted before the studies are over.

The Ever-Increasing Pace of Change

Once upon a time it was possible for people to learn a great deal about their culture. After all, things changed slowly, at a human pace. As they grew up, children learned about what had happened before, and from then on, they could keep up with the rate of change. The technology changed slowly. Moreover, it was mechanical, which meant it was visible. Children could explore it. Teenagers could disassemble it. Young adults could hope to improve it.

Once upon a time technological evolution proceeded at a human pace. Crafts and sports evolved over a lifetime. Even though the results could be complex, the reason behind the complexity could usually be seen, examined, and talked about.

The technology could be lived with and experienced. As a result, it could be learned.

Today, this is no longer possible. The slow, evolutionary pace of life is no longer up to the scale and pace of technological change. The accumulation of knowledge is enormous, increasing with every passing year. Once upon a time, a few years of schooling — or even informal learning — were efficient. Today, formal schooling is required, and the demands upon it continually increase. The number of different topics that must be mastered, from history and language to science and technology to practical knowledge and skills, is ever-increasing. Once a grade-school education would suffice for most people. Then high school was required, then college, postgraduate education, and even further education after that. Today, no amount of education is sufficient.

Scientists no longer are able to keep up with advances even within their own field, let alone in all of science. As a result, we are in the age of specialization, where it is all one person can do to keep up with the pace in some restricted domain of endeavor. But with nothing but specialists, how can we bridge the gaps?

The new technologies can no longer be learned on their own. Today, technology tends to be electronic, which means that its operation is invisible, for it takes place inside of semiconductor circuits through the transfer of voltages, currents and electromagnetic fields, all of which are invisible to the eye. A single computer chip may have 10 million components, and chips with 100 million components are in the planning stage. Who could learn such things by disassembly, even were disassembly possible? So, too, with computer programs; a program with hundreds of thousands of lines of instructions is commonplace, and some have millions of lines.

Worse, the new technology can often be arbitrary, inconsistent, overly complex, and irrelevant. It is all up to the whim of the designer. In the past, physical structures posed their own, natural constraints upon the design and the resulting complexity. But with information technologies, the result can be as simple or complex as the designer wills it to be, and far too few designers have sufficient appreciation for the requirements of the people who must use their designs.

Even when a designer is considerate of the users of the technology, there may be no natural relationship between one set of designs and another. In the physical world, the natural constraints of physical objects meant that similar tools worked in similar ways. Not so in the world of information: Very similar tools may work in completely different — perhaps even contradictory — ways.

TREATING PEOPLE LIKE MACHINES

What an exciting time the turn of the century must have been! The period from the late 1800s through the early 1900s was one of rapid change, in many ways paralleling the changes that are taking place now. In a relatively short period of time, the world went through rapid, almost miraculous technological invention, forever changing the lives of its citizens, society, business, and government. In this period, the incandescent light was developed and electric power plants sprung up across the nation. Electric motors were developed to power factories. The telegraph spanned the American continent and the world, followed by the telephone. With the phonograph, for the first time in history voices, songs, and sounds could be preserved and replayed at will. At the same time, mechanical devices were increasing in power. The railroad was rapidly expanding its coverage. Steam-powered ships traveled the oceans. The automobile was invented, first as expensive, hand-made machines, starting with Daimler and Benz in Europe. Henry Ford developed the first assembly line for the mass-production of relatively inexpensive automobiles. The first airplane was flown and within a few decades would carry mail, passengers, and bombs. Photography was common and motion pictures were on the way. Radio was soon to come, allowing signals to be sent all across the world without the need for wire. It was a remarkable period of change.

It is difficult today to imagine life without these products of technology. At night the only lighting was through flames: candles, fireplaces, oil and kerosene lamps, and in some places, gas. Letters were the primary means of communication, and although mail delivery within a large city was rapid and efficient, with delivery offered more than once each day, delivery across distances could take days or even weeks. Travel was difficult, and many people never ventured more than 30 miles from their homes during their entire lives. But in what to a historian is a relatively short period, the world changed dramatically in ways that affected everyone — not just the rich and upper class, but all levels of society.

Light, travel, entertainment: All changed through human inventions. Work did too, although not always in beneficial ways. The factory already existed, but the new technologies and processes brought forth new requirements, along with opportunities for exploitation. The electric motor allowed a more efficient means of running factories. But as usual, the largest impact was social and organizational: the advent of time-and-motion studies, of "scientific management," and of the assembly line. These developments analyzed human work patterns into a series of small actions. The belief was that if each action could be standardized, each organized into "the one best way,"[3] then automated factories could reap the benefits of even greater efficiency and productivity. The consequence was dehumanization of the worker. Now the worker was considered to be just another machine in the factory, analyzed like one, treated like one, and asked not to think on the job, for thinking slowed down the action.

The era of mass production and the assembly line resulted in part from the efficiencies of the "disassembly line" developed by the meat-packing factories. The tools of scientific management took into account the physical properties of the human body but overlooked the mental and psychological ones. The result was to cram ever more motions into the working day, treating the factory worker as a cog in a machine, deliberately depriving work of its meaning, all in the name of efficiency. These beliefs have stuck with us, and although today we do not go to quite the extremes advocated by the early practitioners of scientific management, the die was cast for the mind-set of ever-increasing efficiency, ever-increasing productivity from the workforce. The principle of improved efficiency is hard to disagree with. The question is, at what price?[4]

The work of Frederick Taylor, some people believe, has had a larger impact upon the lives of people in this century than that of anyone else. He thought there was "the one best way" of doing things. His book, *The Principles of Scientific Management,* published in 1911, guided factory development and workforce habits throughout the world, from those in the United States to Stalin's attempt to devise an efficient communist workplace in the newly formed Soviet Union.[5] He is primarily responsible for our notions of efficiency and of the work practices followed in industry around the world, and even for the sense of guilt we sometimes feel when we have been "goofing off" instead of attending to business.

Taylor's "scientific management" was a detailed, careful study of jobs, breaking down each task into its basic components. Once you knew the components, you could devise the most efficient way of doing things, devise procedures that enhanced performance and increased the efficiency of workers. If Taylor's methods were followed properly, management could raise workers' pay while increasing company profit. In fact, Taylor's methods required management to raise the pay, for money was used as the incentive to get workers to follow the procedures. According to Taylor, everybody would win: The workers would get more money, the management more production and more profit. Sounds wonderful, doesn't it? The only problem was that workers hated it.

Taylor, you see, thought of people as simple machines. Once management found the best way to do things, it should have its workers do it that way, hour after hour, day after day. Efficiency permitted no deviation. Thought was eliminated. According to Taylor, the sort of people who could shovel dirt, do simple cutting, lathing, and drilling, those who perform the lowest-level tasks, were not capable of thought. He regarded them as "brute laborers." Furthermore, if thought was called for, there must be some lack of clarity in the procedures or the process, which signaled that the procedures were wrong. The problem with thinking, explained Taylor, was not only that most workers were incapable of it, but that it slowed the work down. That's certainly true: Why, if we never had to think, just imagine how much faster we could work. In order to eliminate the need for thought, Taylor stated that it was necessary to reduce all work to the routine:[6] That is, all work except for people like him who didn't have to keep fixed hours, who didn't have to follow procedures, who were paid hundreds of times greater wages than the so-called brutes, and who were allowed, even encouraged, to think.

Taylor thought that the world was neat and tidy. If only everyone would do things according to procedure, everything would run smoothly, producing a clean, harmonious world. Taylor may have thought he understood machines, but he certainly didn't understand people. In fact, he didn't really understand the complexity of machines or of work. And he certainly didn't understand the complexity of the world.

The World Is Not Neat and Tidy

Not only don't things always work as planned, but the notion of "plan" itself is suspect. Organizations spend a lot of time planning, but although the act of planning is useful, the plans themselves are often obsolete even before their final printing.

There are many reasons for this. Those philosophically inclined can talk about the fundamental nature of quantum uncertainty, of the fundamental statistical nature of matter. Alternatively, one can talk of complexity theory and chaos theory, where tiny perturbations can have major, unexpected results. I prefer to think of the difficulties as consequences of the complex interactions that take place among the trillions of events and objects in the world, so many interactions that even if science were advanced enough to understand each individual one there are simply too many combinations and variations possible ever to have worked out all possibilities. All of these views are compatible with one another.

Consider these examples of complex situations in which things habitually go wrong:

- A repair crew disconnects a pump from service in a nuclear power plant, carefully placing tags on the controls so that the operators will know the particular unit is temporarily out of service.[7] Later, as the operators attempt to deal with an unrelated problem, they initially diagnose it in an erroneous, albeit reasonable, way. Eventually, the problem becomes so serious that the entire plant is destroyed in the worst accident in the history of American nuclear power. Among the factors hindering the correct diagnosis of the situation is that the tags so carefully placed to indicate the out-of-service unit hang in front of another set of indicators, blocking them from view. Could this have been predicted beforehand? Maybe. But it wasn't.

- A hospital x-ray technician enters a dosage for an x-ray machine, then corrects the setting after realizing the machine is in the wrong mode.[8] The machine's computer program, however, wasn't designed to handle a rapidly made correction, so it did not properly register the new value. Instead, it delivered a massive overdose to the patient. Sometime later, the patient died as a result. The accident goes undiagnosed, because as far as anyone can determine, the machine had performed correctly. Moreover, the effect of overdosage doesn't show up immediately, so when the symptoms are reported, they are not correlated with the incident, or for that matter, with the machine. When the machine's performance first comes under suspicion, the company who manufactured it explains in detail why such an accident is impossible. The situation repeats itself in several different hospitals, killing a number of patients before a sufficient pattern emerges, so that the problem can be recognized and the design of the machine fixed. Could this have been predicted beforehand? Maybe. But it wasn't.

- The French air-traffic controllers seem to be forever complaining, frequently calling strikes and protests. American air-traffic controllers aren't all that happy either. And guess what the most effective method is? Insisting on following procedures: On normal days, if the workers follow the procedures precisely, work slows up, and in the case of air-traffic control, airline traffic around the entire world is affected. The procedures must be violated to allow the traffic to flow smoothly. Of course, if there is an accident and the workers are found not to have followed procedures, they are blamed and punished.

- The United States Navy has a formal, rigid hierarchy of command and control, with two classes of workers — enlisted crew and officers — and a rigid layer of formal rank and assignment. There are extensive procedures for all tasks. Yet in their work habits, especially in critical operations, rank seems to be ignored and crew members frequently question the actions. Sometimes they even debate the appropriate action to be taken. The crew, moreover, is always changing. There are always new people who have not learned the ship's procedures, and even the veterans often don't have more than two or three years' experience with the ship; the Navy has a policy of rotating assignment. Sounds horrible, doesn't it? Isn't the military supposed to be the model of order and structure? But wait. Look at the outcome: The crew functions safely and expertly in dangerous, high-stress conditions. What is happening here?

These examples illustrate several points. The world is extremely complex, too complex to keep track of, let alone predict. In retrospect, looking back after an accident, the problem seems obvious. There are usually a few simple actions that, had they been taken, would have prevented the accident, precursor events that, had they been perceived and interpreted properly, would have provided sufficient warning. Sure, but this is hindsight after we know how things turned out.

Remember, life is complex. Lots of stuff is always happening, most of which is irrelevant to the task at hand. We all know that it is important to ignore the irrelevant and attend to the relevant. But how does one know which is which?

We humans are a complex mixture of motives and mechanisms. We are sense-making creatures, always trying to understand and give explanations for the things we encounter. We are social animals, seeking company, working well in small groups. Sometimes this is for emotional support, sometimes for assistance, sometimes for selfish reasons, so we have someone to feel superior to, to show off to, to tell our problems to. We are narcissistic and hedonistic, but also altruistic. We are lots of things, sometimes competing, conflicting things. And we are also animals, with complex biological drives that strongly affect behavior: emotional drives, sexual drives, hunger drives. Strong fears, strong desires, strong phobias, and strong attractions.

Making Sense of the World

If an airplane crashes on the border between the United States and Canada, killing half the passengers, in which country should the survivors be buried?

People try to make sense of the world. We assume that information is sensible, and we do the best we can with what we receive. This is a virtue. It makes us successful communicators, efficient and robust in going about our daily activities. It also means we can readily be tricked. It wasn't Moses who brought the animals aboard the ark, it was Noah. It isn't the survivors who should be buried, it is the casualties.

It's a good thing we are built this way: This compliance saves us whenever the world goes awry. By making sense of the environment, by making sense of the events we encounter, we know what to attend to, what to ignore. Human attention is the limiting factor, a well-known truism of psychology and of critical importance today. Human sensory systems are bombarded with far more information than can be processed in depth; some selection has to be made. Just how this is done has been the target of prolonged investigation by numerous cognitive scientists who have studied people's behavior when overloaded with information, by neuroscientists who have tried to follow the biological processing of sensory signals, and by a host of other investigators. I was one of them: I spent almost ten years of my research career studying the mechanisms of human attention.

One useful tool to deepen our understanding of the cognitive process of attention comes from the notion of a "conceptual model." . . . A conceptual model is, to put it simply, a story that makes sense of a situation.

I sit at my desk with a large number of sounds impinging upon me. It is an easy matter to classify the sounds. What is all that noise outside? A family must be riding bicycles and the parents are yelling to their children. And the neighbor's dogs are barking at them, which is why my dogs started barking. Do I really know this? No. I didn't even bother to look out the window. My mind subconsciously, automatically created the story, creating a comprehensive explanation for the noises, even as I concentrated upon the computer screen.

How do I know what really happened? I don't. I listened to the sounds and created an explanation, one that was logical, heavily dependent upon past experience with those sound patterns. It is most likely correct, but I don't really know.

Note that the explanation also told me which sounds went together. I associated the barking dogs with the family of bicyclists. Maybe the dogs were barking at something else. Maybe. How do I know they were on bicycles? I don't, but it is a common activity near my home, which means it is reasonably likely. The point is not that I might be wrong, the point is that this is normal human behavior. Moreover, it is human behavior that stands us in good stead. I am quite confident that my original interpretations were correct, confident enough that I won't bother to check. I could be wrong.

A good conceptual model of events allows us to classify them into ones that are relevant, and ones that are not, dramatically simplifying life. We attend to the relevant and only monitor the irrelevant. Mind you, this monitoring and classification are completely subconscious. The conscious mind is usually unaware of the process. Indeed, the whole point is to reserve the conscious mind for the critical events of the task being attended to by suppressing most of the other irrelevant events.

On the whole, human consciousness avoids paying attention to the routine. Conscious processing attends to the nonroutine, to discrepancies and novelties, to things that go wrong. As a result, we are sensitive to changes in the environment, remarkably insensitive to the commonplace, the routine.

Most of the time people do brilliantly. People are very good at predicting things. Experts are particularly good at this because of their rich experience. When a particular set of events occurs, they know exactly what will follow.

But what happens when the unexpected happens? Do we go blindly down the path of the most likely interpretation? In fact, this is the recommended strategy and will usually lead to a correct diagnosis. Most of the time we can then find a solution. You seldom hear about those instances. Headlines appear when things go wrong, not when they go right.

Look back at the incidents I described earlier. Consider the role played by conceptual models in the nuclear power incident, the famous Three Mile Island event that destroyed the power-generating unit and caused such a public loss in confidence in nuclear power that no American plant has been built since. The operators' conceptual model of the events led them to misdiagnose the situation, leading to a major calamity. But the misdiagnosis was a perfectly reasonable one. As a result, they concentrated on items they thought relevant to their diagnosis and missed other cues, which they thought were just part of the normal background noise. The tags that blocked the view would not normally have been important.

In the hospital x-ray situation, the real error was in the design of the software system, but even here, the programmer erred in not thinking through all of the myriad possible sequences of operation, something not easy to do. There are better ways of developing software that would have made it more likely to have caught these problems before the system was released to hospitals, but even then, there are no guarantees.[9] As for the hospital personnel who failed to understand the relationship, well, they too were doing the best they could to interpret the events and to get through their crowded, hectic days. They interpreted things according to normal events, which was wrong only because this one was abnormal.

Do we punish people for failure to follow procedures? This is what Frederick Taylor would have recommended. After all, management determines the one best way to do things, writes a detailed procedure to be followed in every situation, and expects workers to follow it. That's how we get maximum efficiency. But how is it possible to write a procedure for absolutely every possible situation, especially in a world filled with unexpected events? Answer: It's impossible.

Procedures and rule books dominate industry. The rule books take up huge amounts of shelf space. In some industries, it is impossible for any individual to know all the rules. The situation is made even worse by legislatures that can't resist adding new rules. Was there a major calamity? Pass a law prohibiting some behavior, or requiring some other behavior. Of course, the law strikes at the factor easiest to blame, whereas in most complex situations, multiple factors interact and no single one is fully responsible. Nonetheless, new rules are written, controlling sense and reasonableness in the conduct of business.

Do we need procedures? Of course. But procedures must be designed with care and attention to the social, human side of the operation. The best procedures will mandate outcomes, not methods. Methods change; it is the outcomes we care about. Remember the striking air-traffic controllers who brought things to a halt following procedures? The same condition exists in most industries. If the procedures are followed exactly, work slows to an unacceptable level. In order to perform properly it is necessary to violate the procedures. Workers get fired for lack of efficiency, which means they are subtly, unofficially encouraged to violate the procedures — unless something goes wrong, in which case they can be fired for failure to follow the procedures.

Now look at the Navy. The constant critiques and arguments are not what they seem to be. The apparent chaos is a carefully honed system, tested and evolved over generations, that maximizes safety and efficiency in the face of numerous mistakes, novel circumstances, and a wide range of skills and knowledge among the crew. Having everyone participate and question the actions serves several roles simultaneously. The very ambiguity; the continual questioning and debate keep everyone in touch with the activity, thereby providing redundant checks on the actions. This adds to the safety, for now it is likely for errors to get detected before they have caused problems. The newer crew members have a lot to learn, and the public discussions among the other crew serve as valuable training exercises, not in some abstract fashion, but in situations where it really matters. And by not punishing people when they speak out, question, or even bring the operations to a halt, they encourage continual learning and performance enhancement. It makes for an effective, well-tuned team.

New crew members don't have the experience of older ones. This means they are not efficient, don't always know what to do, and perform slowly. They need a lot of guidance. The system automatically provides this constant supervision and coaching, allowing people to learn on the job. At the same time, because the minds of the new crew members are not yet locked into the routines, their questioning can sometimes reveal errors. Their fresh approach challenges the official mind-set, asking whether the generally accepted explanation of events is correct. This is the best way to avoid errors of misdiagnosis.

The continual challenge to authority goes against conventional wisdom and is certainly a violation of the traditional hierarchical management style. But it is so important to safety that the aviation industry now has special training in crew management, where the junior officers in the cockpit are encouraged to question the actions of the captain. In turn, the captain, who used to be thought of as the person in command, with full authority and never to be questioned, is now trained to encourage crew members to question every act. The end result may look less disciplined, but it is far safer.

The navy's way of working is sensible. Accidents are minimized. Despite the fact that the navy is undertaking dangerous operations under periods of fast pace and high stress, there are remarkably few mishaps. If the navy would follow formal procedures and a strict hierarchy of rank, the result would very likely be an increase in the accident rate.[10] Other industries would do well to copy this behavior. Fred Taylor would turn over in his grave (efficiently, without any wasted motion).

Human Error

Machines, including computers, don't err, in the sense that they are fully deterministic, always returning the same value for the same inputs and operations.

Someday we may have stochastic or quantum computation, but even then we will expect them to follow precise laws of operation. When computers do err, it is either because a part has failed or because of human error, either in design specification, programming, or faulty construction. People are not fully deterministic; ask a person to repeat an operation, and the repetition is subject to numerous variations.

People do err, but primarily because they are asked to perform unnatural acts: to do detailed arithmetic calculations, to remember details of some lengthy sequence or statement, or to perform precise repetitions of actions, all the result of the artificial nature of invented artifacts. They err when attempting to alter habitual behavior, forgetting to mail a letter on the way to work or stop at the store on the way home. Slips of the tongue are common, although often the intended meaning is still conveyed sufficiently well that the errors are not even noticed by either speaker or listener. People leave jackets on airplanes and babies on buses. They lock themselves out of home and car. People are expert at making errors.

Human error matters primarily because we followed a technology-centered approach in which it matters. A human-centered approach would make the technology robust, compliant, and flexible. The technology should conform to the people, not people to the technology.

Human languages provide an excellent example of how systems can be tailored for human capabilities, providing a rich structure for communication and social interaction while being extremely tolerant of error. Language is so natural to learn that it is done without any formal instruction: only severe brain impairment can eliminate the capability of learning language. Note that "natural" does not mean "easy"; it takes ten to fifteen years to master one's native language. Second language learning can be excruciatingly difficult.

Natural language, unlike programming language, is flexible, ambiguous, and heavily dependent on shared understanding, a shared knowledge base, and shared cultural experiences. Errors in speech are seldom important: Utterances can be interrupted, restarted, even contradicted, with little difficulty in understanding. The system makes natural language communication extremely robust.

Today, when faced with human error, the traditional response is to blame the human and institute a new training procedure: blame and train. But when the vast majority of industrial accidents is attributed to human error, it indicates that something is wrong with the system, not the people. Consider how we would approach a system failure caused by a noisy environment: We wouldn't blame the noise, we would instead design a system that was robust in the face of noise.

This is exactly the approach that should be taken in response to human error: redesign the system to fit the people who must use it. This means avoiding the incompatibilities between human and machine that generate error, making it so that errors can be rapidly detected and corrected, and being tolerant of error. To blame and train does not solve the problem.

HUMANS AND COMPUTERS AS COMPLEMENTARY SYSTEMS

Because humans and computers are such different kinds of systems, it should be possible to develop a strategy for complementary interaction. Alas, today's approaches are wrong. One major theme is to make computers more like humans. This is the original dream behind classic artificial intelligence: to simulate human intelligence. Another theme is to make people more like computers. This is how technology is designed today; the designers determine the needs of the technology and then ask people to conform to those needs. The result is an ever-increasing difficulty in learning the technology, and an ever-increasing error rate. It is no wonder that society exhibits an ever-increasing frustration with technology.

Consider the following attributes of humans and machines presented from today's machine-centered point of view:[11]

The Machine-Centered View

People	Machines
Vague	Precise
Disorganized	Orderly
Distractible	Undistractible
Emotional	Unemotional
Illogical	Logical

Note how the humans lose: All the attributes associated to people are negative, all the ones associated with machines are positive. But now consider attributes of humans and machines presented from a human-centered point of view:

The Human-Centered View

People	Machines
Creative	Unoriginal
Compliant	Rigid
Attentive to change	Insensitive to change
Resourceful	Unimaginative

Now note how machines lose: all the attributes associated with people are positive, all the ones associated with machines are negative.

The basic point is that the two different viewpoints are complementary. People excel at qualitative considerations, machines at quantitative ones. As a result, for people, decisions are flexible because they follow qualitative as well as quantitative assessment, modified by special circumstances and context. For the machine, decisions are consistent, based upon quantitative evaluation of numerically spec-ified, context-free variable. Which is to be preferred? Neither: We need both.

It's good that computers don't work like the brain. The reason I like my elec-tronic calculator is that it is accurate; it doesn't make errors. If it were like my brain, it wouldn't always get the right answer. This very difference is what makes the device so valuable. I think about the problems and the method of attack. It does the dull, dreary details of arithmetic — or in more advanced machines, of algebraic manipulation and integration. Together, we are a more powerful team than either of us alone.

The same principle applies to all our machines; we should capitalize on the dif-ference, for together we complement one another. This is useful, however, only if the machine adapts itself to human requirements. Alas, most of today's machines, especially the computer, force people to use them on their terms, terms that are antithetical to the way people work and think. The result is frustration, an increase in the rate of error (usually blamed on the user — human error — instead of on faulty design), and a general turning away from technology.

Will the interactions between people and machines be done correctly in the future? Might schools of computer science start teaching the human-centered approach that is necessary to reverse the trend? I don't see why not.

NOTES

1. T. A. Erickson and M. E. Mattson, "From Words to Meaning: A Semantic Illusion," *Journal of Verbal Learning and Verbal Behavior* 20 (1981): 540–552: The paper that started the quest for understanding why people have trouble discovering the problem with the ques-tion, "How many animals of each kind did Moses take on the ark?"

   Reder and Kusbit followed up on the work and present numerous other examples of sentences that show this effect. L. M. Reder and G. W, Kusbit, "Locus of the Moses Illu-sion: Imperfect Encoding, Retrieval, or Match?" *Journal of Memory and Language* 30 (1991): 385–406.

2. This section modified from D. A. Norman, "Why It's Good That Computers Don't Work Like the Brain." In *Beyond Calculation: The Next Fifty Years of Computing*, ed. P. J. Denning and R. M. Metcalfe (New York: Copernicus: Springer-Verlag, 1997).

3. R. Kanigel, *The One Best Way: Frederick Winslow Taylor and the Enigma of Efficiency* (New York: Viking, 1997).

4. For an excellent, in-depth analysis of the price paid in the name of efficiency, see J. Rifkin, *The End of Work: The Decline of the Global Labor Force and the Dawn of the Post-Market Era* (New York: G. P. Putnam's Sons, 1995).

5. F. W. Taylor, *The Principles of Scientific Management* (New York: Harper & Brothers, 1911). (See note 6.)

6. Taylor's work is described well in three books. First, there is Taylor's major work, cited in note 5. Second, there Is the masterful and critical biography of Taylor, one that illustrates the paradox between what Taylor professed and how he himself lived and acted: Kanigel, *The One Best Way*. Finally, there is Rabinbach's masterful treatment of the impact of changing views of human behavior, the rise of the scientific method (even when it wasn't very scientific), and the Impact of Taylor not only on modern work, but on political ideolo-gies as well, especially Marxism and Fascism: A. Rabinbach, *The Human Motor: Energy, Fatigue, and the Origins of Modernity* (New York: Basic Books, 1990). Also see "Taylorismus + Fordismus = Amerikanismus," chapter 6 of T. P. Hughes, *American Genesis: A Century of Invention and Technological Enthusiasm, 1870–1970* (New York: Viking, 1989).

7. This is an oversimplified account of some of the many factors of the Three-Mile Island nuclear power accident. See J. G. Kemeny et al., *Report of the President's Commission on the Accident at Three Mile Island* (New York: Pergamon, 1979); E. Rubenstein, "The Accident That Shouldn't Have Happened," *IEEE Spectrum* 16, no. 11 (November 1979): 33–42.

8. See Appendix A, "Medical Devices: The Therac-25 Story," in N. G. Leveson, *Safeware: System Safety and Computers* (Reading, MA: Addison-Wesley, 1995). This book also includes nice appendices on the Therac-25 story (X-ray overdosage), the Bhopal chemical disaster, the Apollo 13 incident, DC-10s, and the NASA *Challenger* and the various nuclear power industry problems, including Three Mile Island and Chernobyl.

9. See H. G. Leveson, *Safeware: System Safety and Computers* (Reading, MA: Addison-Wesley, 1995). For a scary discussion of the failures of system design, see P. Neumann, *Computer-Related Risks* (Reading, MA: Addison-Wesley, 1995).

10. See Hutchins's analysis of crew training and error management in ship navigation: E. Hutchins, *Cognition in the Wild* (Cambridge, MA: MIT Press, 1995). See also T. R. La Porte and P. M. Consolini, "Working in Practice but Not in Theory: Theoretical Challenges of High-Reliability Organizations," *Journal of Public Administration Research and Theory,* 1991, 19–47.

   These issues are well treated by Robert Pool In both his book and the excerpt in the journal *Technology Review:* R. Pool, *Beyond Engineering: How Society Shapes Technology* (New York: Oxford University Press, 1997). R. Pool, "When Failure Is Not an Option" *Technology Review* 100, no. 5 (1997): 38–45. (Also see <http://web.mit.edu/techreview/>.)

11. This chart and the following chart of the human-centered view come from D. A. Norman, *Things That Make Us Smart* (Reading, MA: Addison-Wesley, 1993).

PART VIII
CODA

The last article in *Technology and the Future* is included here for fun. But it is fun with a purpose. Novelist Douglas Coupland challenges us to pack for a trip to the end of the twenty-second century. Is it possible to imagine what the world will be like nearly two hundred years from now? If not, can one at least choose the right things to bring, in order to provide for a range of possible futures? Coupland's suggestions are generally light-hearted and meant to amuse, but the thoughts behind them are serious. Many instructors assign students to make their own packing lists before reading this chapter. Comparing your list with Coupland's and with those of other students can be both entertaining and enlightening. You are invited to post yours to the "packing list" page that can be found on the *Technology and the Future* Web site <http://www.ateich.com/future8/htm>.

27. Packing Tips for Your Trip (to the Year 2195)

DOUGLAS COUPLAND

What would you take with you on a trip to the future? Food? Money? A gun? How would you prove to the people you encountered there that you were a visitor from the late twentieth century and not simply a lunatic? What would you bring back to show your friends (and the rest of the world)?

Douglas Coupland has some original and amusing answers to these questions. His list may give you food for thought — and it may make you think twice before stepping into any time machines you happen to come across.

Coupland is the author of four novels — Generation X, Shampoo Planet, Microserfs, *and* Girlfriend in a Coma *— as well as two collections of short stories. He has also written for* Wired *magazine, where this piece appeared (under the pseudonym Sandra Noguchi) in a special issue on the future published in October 1995.*

Congratulations! You've just won a two-week, round-trip ticket to exactly where you are right now — but in the year 2195. So pack quickly! Your only packing restrictions:

- You can't bring anything of a size that United Airlines wouldn't allow you to take along.
- You have to bring one object that *proves* you're from the year 1995.

ISSUES TO CONSIDER BEFORE FETCHING THE SAMSONITE

Life Support

In accepting your ticket, you also accept that the world might not be biologically inhabitable in 2195. Do you bring a radiation suit? A Geiger detector! Bottled water? Freeze-dried camping meals? (*Yuck!*) Topographical maps? What does the U.S. Army pack when it wants to enter zones of possible profound uninhabitability? Is Tang called for?

- camping meals
- geological survey maps of your neighborhood
- Evian
- Tang

The Future May Well Be an Ugly Dump

Whenever people get misty-eyed about traveling backward in time, they usually assume their journey will be "vaccinated." That is to say, they want a return ticket, pox and polio vaccinations, contact lenses, appendix removal, membership in the ruling elite of the time they wish to visit, vitamins, etc. To reverse this situation, how might this sensibility work if a person were to travel *forward* in time? Is the future a Third World country? What hygiene essentials will a traveler require?

- antibiotics and tetanus booster
- toilet paper
- Halazone tablets to purify water

Arms, Armor, and Ammo

Imagine that you live in George Washington's time — and you visit 1995. You might bring a blunderbuss and look awfully silly walking around your neighborhood. Would you even *need* a blunderbuss or any other weapon in 2195? It's your decision.

- handgun and bullets
- Swiss Army knife
- Mace

Prove That You're from 200 Years Ago

As far as I know, you could *already* be from 200 years ago. Assuming people 200 years from now still speak your language, they'll probably look at you and say, "*Get out of my face, loser,*" before you get a chance to elaborate. Therefore, you want to bring along something that has no conceivable chance of existing 200 years from now:

- a Komodo dragon or some other animal on the cusp of extinction (but what if factories make pandas and spotted owls in 2195?)
- a box of Pop-Tarts with 1995 packaging, plus expiration dates
- CDs, this week's favorites

(Question: How will these people know that you're not really from the *future* and are tricking them into thinking you're from the past? It can get dodgy here.)

Money? What's *Money?*

Gold, platinum, or thorium may well be valueless in 2195. What artifacts from now might you bring if you had to trade in order to get, say, *food?* Remember, chances are that the things of value in the future are the things you could have had no way of knowing would be valuable: an autograph from Button Gwinnett; IBM stock; fertilized passenger pigeon eggs. Future citizens might also end up ransacking you for semi-random items — like Monty Hall of *Let's Make A Deal* offering you U.S. $500 for every paper clip you've got. Some packing ideas:

- comic books
- fruit juices
- celebrity autographs
- Franklin Mint Star Trek dinner plates
- drugs or mood-altering pharmaceuticals
- baseball cards or stamps
- samples of your own blood or reproductive cells
- California chardonnay
- Freon

(Tip: Do you know any *information* right now that might be useful to people in 2195? What could somebody from 1795 tell you right now that might even be interesting, let alone valuable?)

We Come in Peace

Future humans may well be prepared to be nice to you . . . *assuming you bear a friendly enough gift as a gesture.* Would a letter from the president do? Partridge Family cassettes with a battery-loaded boom box? Perhaps simply being unarmed would be gesture enough.

- Partridge Family cassettes and child's boom box

Your Friends Will Want to See Pictures

What sort of camera will you bring? What sort of devices for trapping liquids, solids, and artifacts from the year 2195?

- Olympus Stylus camera and lots of film

The Future Might Well Suck beyond All Belief

If this is the case, perhaps you'll want to crawl into a hidden nook somewhere (surely you can find *one* safe location) and sedate yourself for 14 days until you return to 1995. In this case you might need these:

- syringe and large supply of barbiturates
- sleeping bag
- animal repellent
- Deep Woods Off!
- whatever minimal food and water might stretch over 14 days (Jenny Craig meals?)

Happy packing, future traveler. Hope to see you two weeks from now, and hope you have many tales to tell. Will Ronald Reagan be president again? Will fresh water be a form of currency? And how many United Airlines points will it take for a first-class return trip to the moon? Only *you* can tell. Bon voyage.

Wendell Berry. "Why I Am Not Going to Buy a Computer." From *What Are People For?: Essays* by Wendell Berry. Copyright © 1990 by Wendell Berry. Reprinted by permission of North Point Press, a division of Farrar, Straus & Giroux, Inc.

Samuel C. Florman, "Technology and the Tragic View." From *Blaming Technology: The Irrational Search for Scapegoats* by Samuel C. Florman. Copyright © 1981 by Samuel C. Florman. Reprinted with permission from Bedford/St. Martin's.

Emmanuel G. Mesthene, "The Role of Technology in Society." From *Technology and Culture* 10:4 (1969). Reprinted by permission of the author and The University of Chicago Press.

John McDermott, "Technology: The Opiate of the Masses." From *The New York Review of Books*, July 31, 1969. Copyright © 1969 by John McDermott. Reprinted by permission of the author.

E. F. Schumacher, "Buddhist Economics." From *Small is Beautiful: Economics As If People Mattered*. Copyright © 1973 by E. F. Schumacher. Reprinted by permission of HarperCollins Publishers, Inc., and Blond & Briggs, London WC1N 3HZ, England.

Paul Goodman, "Can Technology Be Humane?" From *The New Reformation: Notes of a Neolithic Conservation*. Copyright © 1969 by Paul Goodman. By permission of Sally Goodman.

Richard Sclove, "Technological Politics As If Democracy Really Mattered." From *Technology for the Common Good*, ed. Michael Shuman and Julia Sweig, "Technological Politics As If Democracy Really Mattered: Choices Confronting Progressives" by Richard Sclove. Copyright © 1993 by Richard Sclove. Reprinted by permission of the author.

Timothy L. Jenkins and Khafra K. Om-Ra-Seti. Reprint selection (Chapter 1, "From GateKeepers to GateCrashers") from *Black Futurists in the Information Age: Vision of a Twenty-first Century Technological Renaissance*. Copyright © 1997 by Khafra K. Om-Ra-Seti and Timothy L. Jenkins. Reprinted by permission of KMT Publications, San Francisco and Unlimited Visions, Washington, DC.

Judy Wajcman, "Feminist Perspectives on Technology," originally titled "Feminist Critiques of Science and Technology." From *Feminism Confronts Technology* by Judy Wajcman (University Park: Pennsylvania State University Press, 1991), pp. 1–25. Copyright © July Wajcman 1991. Reproduced by permission of the publisher.

Langdon Winner, "Do Artifacts Have Politics?" Reprinted by permission of *Daedalus*, Journal of the American Academy of Arts and Sciences, from the issue entitled, "Modern Technology: Problem or Opportunity?" Vol. 109 (Winter 1980): pp. 121–136. Copyright © 1980 by the American Academy of Arts and Sciences.

Herman Kahn and Anthony J. Wiener. *The Next Thirty-Three Years: A Framework for Speculation*. Reprinted by permission of *Daedalus*, Journal of the American Academy of Arts and Sciences, from the issue entitled, "Toward the Year 2000: Work in Progress," Vol. 96, (Summer 1967): pp. 705–732. Copyright © 1967 by the American Academy of Arts and Sciences.

Herb Brody, "Great Expectations: Why Technology Predictions Go Awry." From *Technology Review* (July 1991). Copyright © 1991. Reprinted with permission from *Technology Review*.

Paul Ceruzzi, "An Unforeseen Revolution: Computers and Expectations, 1935–1985." From *Imagining Tomorrow: History, Technology and the American Future*, edited by Joseph J. Corn (Cambridge, MA: MIT Press, 1986). Reprinted by permission.

Joseph F. Coates, John B. Mahaffie, and Andy Hines. "107 Assumptions About the Future." Excerpt from *2025 Scenarios of U.S. and Global Society Reshaped by Science and Technology*. (Greensboro, NC: Oakhill Press, 1997), pp. 4–13. Copyright © 1996 Coates and Jarratt, Inc.

Robert A. Weinberg, "The Dark Side of the Genome," From *Technology Review* (April 1991). Copyright © 1991. Reprinted with permission of *Technology Review*.

R. Alta Charo, "And Baby Makes Three — Or Four, or Five, or Six: Defining the Family After the Genetic Revolution." From *The Genetic Frontier: Ethics, Law, and Policy* by Mark S. Frankel and Albert Teich (Washington, DC: AAAS, 1994, pp. 25–44. Copyright © 1994 American Association for the Advancement of Science.

Leon R. Kass. "The Wisdom of Repugnance." From *The Ethics of Human Cloning* by Leon R. Kass and James Q. Wilson (Washington, DC: AEI Press, 1998), pp. 3–59. Copyright © 1998 The American Enterprise Institute for Public Policy Research.

Tom Forrester and Perry Morrison, "Computer Ethics." From *Computer Ethics: Cautionary Tales and Ethical Dilemmas in Computing*, 2nd ed. (Cambridge, MA: The MIT Press, 1993), pp. 1–22. Reprinted by permission of MIT Press.

Fred H. Cate. "Electric Privacy in the Twenty-first Century." From *Privacy in the Information Age* (Washington, DC: Brookings Institution Press, 1997), pp.101–132. Copyright © 1997 by the Brookings Institution.

Shoshana Zoboff, "In the Age of the Smart Machine." From *In the Age of the Smart Machine*, pp. 3–12. Copyright © 1988 by Basic Books, Inc. Reprinted by permission of Basic Books, a division of HarperCollins Publishers, Inc.

Nicholas Negroponte. "Being Digital." Excerpts from *Being Digital* by Nicholas Negroponte. Copyright © 1995 by Nicholas Negroponte. Reprinted by permission of Alfred A. Knopf Inc.

Donald A. Norman, "Being Analog." Chapter 7 from *The Invisible Computer: Why Good Products Can Fail*. (Cambridge, MA: MIT Press, 1998), pp. 135–161. Copyright © 1998 Donald A. Norman. Reprinted by permission of Massachusetts Institute of Technology.

Sandra Noguchi [Douglas Coupland], "Packing Tips for Your Trip (to the Year 2195)." From *Wired Scenarios*, special issue, October 1995. Reprinted by permission of the author.